ISBN 978-1-331-56374-7
PIBN 10206408

English
Français
Deutsche
Italiano
Español
Português

www.forgottenbooks.com

Mythology Photography **Fiction**
Fishing Christianity **Art** Cooking
Essays Buddhism Freemasonry
Medicine **Biology** Music **Ancient**
Egypt Evolution Carpentry Physics
Dance Geology **Mathematics** Fitness
Shakespeare **Folklore** Yoga Marketing
Confidence Immortality Biographies
Poetry **Psychology** Witchcraft
Electronics Chemistry History **Law**
Accounting **Philosophy** Anthropology
Alchemy Drama Quantum Mechanics
Atheism Sexual Health **Ancient History**
Entrepreneurship Languages Sport
Paleontology Needlework Islam
Metaphysics Investment Archaeology
Parenting Statistics Criminology
Motivational

OF

VILLIAM WILBERFORC

BY HIS SON

SAMUEL WILBERFORCE, D.D.

LORD BISHOP OF OXFORD

REVISED AND CONDENSED FROM THE ORIGINAL EDITION

Happy is the state
In which ye, father, here do dwell at ease,
Leading a life so free and fortunate
From all the tempests of these worldly seas

Spenser

LONDON

JOHN MURRAY, ALBEMARLE STREET

1868

5406
Phi. Ld.
April 20, 1868

PREFACE.

THE 'LIFE OF WILBERFORCE' was published in the year 1838, in five volumes; to which were afterwards added, in 1840, two volumes of 'Correspondence.' The sale within a few years of 7,500 copies bore testimony to the interest which it excited. It has been for some years out of print. The time seems, therefore, to have come for preparing a wholly revised edition of the work. Such is this volume: partly re-written; corrected in some important points where blemishes had been detected; with some additions from the volumes of correspondence and other sources; whilst it has been so condensed as, without omitting anything essential to the narrative, to be compressed into a single volume. This has been effected mainly by a careful excision of all repetitions; especially of those connected with that inner life of personal religion which, after the great change which passed upon him, was the mainspring of all Mr. Wilberforce's exertions for others. It has seemed enough to show distinctly, and that more than once, these interior works of the great machine, without perpetually returning to their exhibition.

The history of the long struggle with which the name of William Wilberforce is identified, and which ended first in the abolition of the Slave Trade, and at last in the abolition of Slavery in the colonies of Great Britain, is traced in these pages more plainly than in the original volumes in which the narrative was in some measure overlaid with details; whilst, upon a full weighing of the matter, all attempts to fix the different degrees of merit which belonged to the several labourers in this great cause have been omitted as unnecessary and invidious. To have shared at all in such a work ennobles any name; and though filial devotion may excuse such an attempt, it seems strange to the idea of such a life, and at variance with the character it exhibits, to enter in any degree whatever on such a contention.

A volume which at all worthily records the life of such a Christian philanthropist may well aspire to take an enduring place in English literature; whilst the biography of William Wilberforce, from his close intimacy with the greatest of his contemporaries, from his intimate relations with William Pitt, and from his habit early formed, and continued to the end, of recording in a journal his view of the events which were passing before his eyes, and his estimate of the actors, in them, besides its being a record of himself, becomes a running commentary upon the history of the eventful days in which his lot was cast. It is now given to the world in the belief that there are many to whom the former volumes are unattainable, who will rejoice to possess such a biography of William Wilberforce.

CUDDESDEN PALACE:
    Feb. 1, 1868.

CONTENTS.

CHAPTER I.

1759–1783.

CHAPTER II.

FIRST ELECTION FOR YORKSHIRE.

1783, 1784.

CHAPTER III.

APRIL 1784 TO APRIL 1786.

CHAPTER IV.

APRIL 1786 TO SEPTEMBER 1787.

CHAPTER V.

SEPTEMBER 1787 TO DECEMBER 1788.

CHAPTER VI.

DECEMBER 1788 TO JULY 1790.

CHAPTER VII.

JULY 1790 TO DECEMBER 1791.

CHAPTER VIII.

DECEMBER 1791 TO DECEMBER 1792.

CONTENTS.

CHAPTER XIII.

JANUARY 1801 TO DECEMBER 1802.

CHAPTER XIV.

JANUARY 1803 TO MAY 1804.

CHAPTER XV.

MAY 1804 TO FEBRUARY 1806.

ERRATA.

THE

LIFE OF WILBERFORCE.

———◆———

CHAPTER I.

Birth — Parentage — Education — Hull election — Wilberforce comes to London—Goostree's—Cured of gambling—Houses at Wimbledon and Rayrigg—Intimacy with Pitt—Lord Camden—Independents—Foreign tour—Rheims—Fontainebleau—Letter to Bankes.

1759-1783.

WILLIAM WILBERFORCE, only son of Robert Wilberforce and his wife Elizabeth, daughter of Thomas Bird, Esq., of Barton, Oxon, was born at Hull upon the feast of St. Bartholomew, August 24, A.D. 1759. He was the third of four children, of whom one sister only arrived at maturity.

His ancestors had long been settled in the county of York. In the reign of the second Henry, Ilgerus de Wilberfoss served in the Scottish wars under Philip de Kyme, with a daughter of whose powerful house he had intermarried. The township of Wilberfoss, eight miles east of York, gave him a mansion and a name.

At Wilberfoss the family was fixed through many generations, until, after a gradual decline in wealth and numbers, it disappeared from the place about a century ago.—'Note, that all these,' says Robert Glover, Somerset herald, after enumerating sixteen descents, 'did successively occupy the Soake of Cotton, which containeth six villages, &c.'[1] About the middle of the sixteenth century, the son of William Wilberfoss of Wilberfoss, by his second marriage, settled in the neighbouring town of Beverley.

[1] Herald's Vis. A.D. 1584.

B

William Wilberfoss was mayor of Beverley at the opening
of the great rebellion; and the same office was twice filled at
Hull, in the succeeding century, by a great-grandson William
Wilberfoss, or, as he finally fixed its spelling, Wilberforce;
who continued in the Baltic trade, though, besides his patri-
monial fortune, he inherited a considerable landed property
from his mother, an heiress of the Davye family.   Robert,
the younger of his two children, father of William Wilberforce, was a partner in the house at Hull; and here was spent
the early childhood of his distinguished son.

Of the early years of William Wilberforce little is recorded.
His frame from infancy was feeble, his stature small, his
eyes weak. . . . It was one amongst the many expressions of
his gratitude in after-life, 'that I was not born in less civilised
times, when it would have been thought impossible to rear
so delicate a child.'   But with these bodily infirmities were
united a vigorous mind, and a temper eminently affectionate.
An unusual thoughtfulness for others marked his youngest
childhood.   At seven years old he was sent to the grammar
school of Hull.   'Even then his elocution was so remarkable,'
says Isaac Milner,[2] 'that we used to set him upon a table,
and make him read aloud as an example to the other boys.'
Thus he spent two years, going daily from his father's house
to school with his 'satchel on his shoulder,' and occasionally
visiting his grandfather at Ferribly, a pleasant village seven
miles distant, on the Humber.   The death of his father in the
summer of 1768 transferred him to the care of his uncle
William Wilberforce, at Wimbledon and in St. James's Place,
whence he attended a school at Putney, where, he says, 'they
taught everything and nothing.'[3]

He remained two years at this school, spending his holidays at his uncle's house, and is described at this time as 'a
fine sharp lad,' whose activity and spirit made up in boyish
sports for some deficiency of strength.   Here he was subjected to a new and powerful influence.   His aunt was a
great admirer of Whitefield's preaching, and mixed much
with the early Methodists.   The lively affections of his heart,

[2] Isaac Milner, afterwards Dean of Carlisle.
[3] Conversational Mem.

warmed by the kindness of his friends, readily assumed their tone ; and one at least who then met him remarked in him a rare and pleasing character of piety in his twelfth year.[4]

The rumour of his incipient methodism caused great alarm at Hull, and it was at once determined that his mother, an excellent, able, and highly-cultivated woman, of the Archbishop Tillotson school, should repair to London, and remove him from the dangerous influence. He returned with her to Yorkshire. ' I deeply felt,' he says, 'the parting, for I loved them as parents: indeed, I was almost heart-broken at the separation.' At twelve years old he returned to his mother's house, where it became the object of his friends to charm away that serious spirit which had taken possession of his youthful bosom.

The habits of society in Hull favoured their design. ' It was then as gay a place as could be found out of London. The theatre, balls, great suppers, and card-parties were the delight of the principal families in the town. This mode of life was at first distressing to me, but by degrees I acquired a relish for it, and became as thoughtless as the rest. I was everywhere invited and caressed. The religious impressions which I had gained at Wimbledon continued for a considerable time after my return to Hull, but my friends spared no pains to stifle them. I might almost say, that no pious parent ever laboured more to impress a beloved child with sentiments of piety, than they did to give me a taste for the world and its diversions.'[5] He was placed, soon after his return to Hull, with the Rev. K. Basket, master of the endowed grammar school of Pocklington, and formerly Fellow of St. John's College, Cambridge, a man of easy and polished manners, and an elegant scholar. Here he led a life of idleness and pleasure. His talents for general society with his rare skill in singing rendered him everywhere an acceptable guest, and his time was wasted in a round of visits to the neighbouring gentry. Already, however, he gave proofs of an active mind, and one remarkable anticipation of his future course is yet remembered. ' His abomination of

---

[4] Private Journal of J. Russell, Esq.   [5] MS. Mem.

the slave trade,' writes a surviving school-fellow,[6] ' he evinced when he was not more than fourteen years of age.' 'He greatly excelled all the other boys in his compositions, though he seldom began them till the eleventh hour.' For his own amusement he committed English poetry to memory, and he went up to the University 'a very fair scholar.'

After such a life he entered St. John's College, Cambridge, October 1776, at the age of seventeen years. And here he was at once exposed to new temptations. Left, by the death of his grandfather and uncle, the master of an independent fortune under his mother's sole guardianship, ' I was introduced,' he says, 'on the very first night of my arrival, to as licentious a set of men as can well be conceived. They drank hard, and their conversation was even worse than their lives. I lived amongst them for some time, though I never relished their society,—often indeed I was horror-struck at their conduct,—and after the first year I shook off in great measure my connection with them.' For the last two years he spent at Cambridge he was the centre of a higher circle. Amiable, animated, and hospitable, he was a universal favourite. ' There was no one,' says the Rev. T. Gisborne, ' at all like him for powers of entertainment. Always fond of repartee and discussion, he seemed entirely free from conceit and vanity.' He had already commenced the system of frank and simple hospitality, which marked his after life. ' There was always a great Yorkshire pie in his rooms, and all were welcome to partake of it. My rooms and his were back to back, and often when I was raking out my fire at ten o'clock, I heard his melodious voice calling aloud to me to come and sit with him before I went to bed. It was a dangerous thing to do, for his amusing conversation was sure to keep me up so late, that I was behind-hand the next morning.' He lived much at this time amongst the Fellows of the college. ' But those,' he says, ' with whom I was intimate, did not act towards me the part of Christians, or even of honest men. Their object seemed to be, to make and keep me idle. If ever I appeared studious, they would say to me, " Why in the world should a man of your fortune

[6] Rev. T. T. Walmsley, D.D.

trouble himself with fagging?" I was a good classic, and acquitted myself well in the college examinations; but mathematics, which my mind greatly needed, I almost entirely neglected, and was told that I was too clever to require them. Whilst my companions were reading hard and attending lectures, card-parties and idle amusements consumed my time. The tutors would often say within my hearing, that "*they* were mere saps, but that I did all by talent." This was poison to a mind constituted like mine.' Yet though, in after life, 'he could not look back without unfeigned remorse' on those wasted years, it was no neglect of opportunities of moral and intellectual profit, no vicious practice or abandoned principles he had to deplore.[7] 'I certainly did not then think and act as I do now,' he declared long afterwards; 'but I was far from what the world calls licentious.'

Diligently did he strive in after-years to supply the omissions of his youth; but to the end of life he ceased not to deplore a certain want of mental regularity, which he traced to the neglect of early discipline, and he subsequently remonstrated with the tutor to whose charge he had been confided, on the guilt of suffering those, of whom he was in some sort the guardian, to inflict upon themselves so irreparable an injury.

Before he quitted college, Mr. Wilberforce had resolved to enter upon public life. The house which his grandfather had founded at Hull had been managed for him during his minority by his cousin, Abel Smith. But his ample fortune, and a taste for more liberal pursuits, gave a different direction to his thoughts. He declined business, and as a speedy dissolution was expected, commenced a canvass for the representation of his native town in Parliament. This he continued in London, where about three hundred Hull freemen resided in the vicinity of the river: these he entertained at suppers in the different public-houses of Wapping, and, by his addresses to them, first gained confidence in public

---

[7] Lord Clarendon, his friend at college and through life, thus describes his conduct:—'He had never in the smallest degree a dissolute character.'

speaking. During this year he resided in lodgings in the Adelphi, and constantly frequented the gallery of the House of Commons. Here he often met Mr. Pitt, then serving a like apprenticeship to public business. They had formed at Cambridge a slight acquaintance, which now ripened into intimacy. As the summer advanced, he returned to Hull, and, on September 11, was engaged in all the bustle of a sharply contested election. Against him were arrayed the interest of Lord Rockingham, the most powerful nobleman in the county; that of Sir George Savile, its wealthy and respected representative, himself a frequent resident at Hull; and that of Government, always strong at a seaport. To these he could oppose nothing but the personal influence and independent character of a young man of twenty. Yet such was the hold he possessed on the affections of his townsmen, that, at the close of the poll, he numbered singly as many votes as his opponents had received together. The numbers were—

Lord Robert Manners	673
David Hartley	453
William Wilberforce	1,126

This election cost him between 8,000*l.* and 9,000*l.* The more matured judgment of Mr. Wilberforce condemned the custom to which he here conformed; and rather than so enter Parliament, with his later principles, he has declared that he would have remained always a private man. His great success threw no small lustre on his entry into public life; and he was welcomed upon his return to London into every circle. He was at once elected a member of all the leading clubs. 'When I went up to Cambridge,' he has said, speaking of the risks to which he was then exposed, 'I was scarcely acquainted with a single person above the rank of a country gentleman; and now I was at once immersed in politics and fashion.' 'The very first time I went to Boodle's I won twenty-five guineas of the Duke of Norfolk. I belonged at this time to five clubs—Miles and Evans's, Brookes's, Boodle's, White's, Goostree's. The first time I was at Brookes's, scarcely knowing any one, I joined from mere shyness in play at the faro table, where George

Selwyn kept bank. A friend who knew my inexperience, and regarded me as a victim decked out for sacrifice, called to me " What, Wilberforce, is that you ? " Selwyn quite resented the interference, and turning to him said, in his most expressive tone, "Oh, sir, don't interrupt Mr. Wilberforce ; he could not be better employed." Nothing could be more luxurious than the style of these clubs. Fox, Sheridan, Fitzpatrick, and all your leading men, frequented them, and associated upon the easiest terms ; you chatted, played at cards, or gambled, as you pleased.' Though he visited occasionally these various clubs, his usual resort was with a choicer and more intimate society, about twenty-five in number,[8] who met at ' Goostree's.' They were for the most part young men who had passed together through the university, and whom the general election of 1780 had brought at the same time into public life. Pitt was an habitual frequenter of this club, supping there every night during the winter of 1780–81. Here their intimacy greatly increased. Though less formed for general popularity than Fox, Pitt, when free from shyness and amongst his intimate companions, was the very soul of merriment and conversation. 'He was the wittiest man I ever knew, and, what was quite peculiar to himself, had at all times his wit under entire control. Others appeared struck by the unwonted association of brilliant images ; but every possible combination of ideas seemed always present to his mind, and he could at once produce whatever he desired. I was one of those who met to spend an evening in memory of Shakspeare, at the Boar's Head, East Cheap. Many professed wits were present, but Pitt was the most amusing of the party, and the readiest and most apt in the required allusions. He entered with the same energy into

[8] The club, named from the owner of the house where they met, consisted of Mr. Pratt (afterwards Marquis of Camden), Lords Euston, Chatham, Graham, Duncannon, Althorpe, Apsley, G. Cavendish, and C. Lennox, Mr. Eliot (elder brother of Lord St. Germains), St. Andrew (afterwards Lord) St. John, Bridgeman (afterwards Lord Bradford), Morris Robinson (afterwards Lord Rokeby), R. Smith (afterwards Lord Carrington), W. Grenville (afterwards Lord Grenville), Pepper Arden (afterwards Lord Alvanley), Mr. Edwards (afterwards Sir Gerard Noel), Mr. Marsham, Mr. Pitt, Mr. Wilberforce, Mr. Bankes, Mr. Thomas Steele, General Smith, and, after a time, Mr. Windham.

all our different amusements; we played a good deal at Goostree's; and I well remember the intense earnestness which he displayed when joining in those games of chance. He perceived their increasing fascination, and soon after suddenly abandoned them for ever.'[9]

It was by this vice that he was himself most nearly ensnared. A brief diary of this period records more than once the loss of 100*l.* at the faro table. He was weaned from it in a characteristic manner. 'We can have no play to-night,' complained some of the party at the club, 'for St. Andrew is not here to keep bank.' 'Wilberforce,' said Mr. Bankes (who never joined himself), 'if you will keep it I will give you a guinea.' The playful challenge was accepted, but as the game grew deep, he rose the winner of 600*l.*, from several who could ill afford the loss, and by the pain this gave him was cured of a taste which seemed but too likely to become predominant.

At the same time he attended closely to the House of Commons. From the first he was an independent man: he had entered parliament as the opponent of the war with America, and of Lord North's administration; yet to this ministry he gave his first vote, opposing the re-election of Sir Fletcher Norton,[1] as Speaker of the House of Commons.

In January, 1781, he was joined by Mr. Pitt, who having contested Cambridge University without success at the general election, now sat for Appleby, and took his place amongst the opposition which, under Lords Rockingham and Shelburne, were now in two confederate bands, attacking the ministry of Lord North. Their friendship soon grew warm; yet not even to friendship with Pitt would he sacrifice his independence. 'I well remember,' he said long afterwards, 'the pain I felt in being obliged to vote against Pitt, the second time he spoke in parliament[2] against Lord North's

---

[9] Con. Mem.

[1] 'When they were all talking of Sir Fletcher's health requiring his retirement, Rigby came into the House, and said with his ordinary bluntness, "Don't tell me about health; he has flown in the king's face, and we won't have him." '—*Con. Mem.*

[2] 'The division was far from affording any cause of triumph to the young orator, since Lord North carried his negative by ninety-eight votes against forty-two.'—Lord Stanhope's *Life of Pitt,* i. 59.

proposal to appoint commissioners of public accounts.' Yet though attentive to public business, he did not hasten to join in the debates. 'Attend to business,' he said in later life to a friend [3] entering the House of Commons, 'and do not seek occasions of display; if you have a turn for speaking, the proper time will come. Let speaking take care of itself. I never go out of the way to speak, but make myself acquainted with business, and then if the debate passes my door I step out and join it.'

Upon April 31 he wrote to a constituent, 'Sir George Savile gave notice yesterday, that on Tuesday next he should move that the Delegates' [4] Petition be taken into consideration. The papers would inform you by what a trick it was laid upon the table. The petitioners were said to be private freeholders; and as such were gravely read over the names Christ. Wyvill, C. Fox, R. Fitzpatrick, &c. They will, I doubt not, proceed artfully, but let them once but put in their noses in their delegate capacity, and they will be hunted out as they deserve; and I will accompany the hounds in full cry with my Lord Advocate [Dundas] at their head— and a fine leader of a pack he is.'

His first speech was upon May 17, 1781, in a debate upon the laws of revenue, when, having presented a petition from the town of Hull, he forcibly attacked them as oppressive and unjust. He gives the sketch of the session in a letter[5]:—

London, June 9, 1781.

' I agree with you in thinking the Lord Advocate the first speaker on the ministerial side in the House of Commons, and there is a manliness in his character which prevents his running away from the question; he grants all his adversaries' premises, and fights them upon their own ground. The only India affairs we have yet had before us relate to Lord North's claim on the Company of 600,000*l.*, and it is not in the power even of the Lord Advocate to put a good face on that transaction.'

' The papers will have informed you how Mr. William

[3] Sir Thomas Dyke Acland, Bart.
[4] From the Deputies of Associated Counties.—Wyvill's *Pol. Papers*, I. 332.   [5] To B. B. Thompson, Esq., Hull.

Pitt, second son of the late Lord Chatham, has distinguished himself; he comes out as his father did, a ready-made orator, and I doubt not but that I shall one day or other see him the first man in the country. His famous speech, however, delivered the other night, did not convince me, and I staid in with the old fat fellow;[6] by the way, he grows every day fatter.'

It was a misfortune that his landed property in York-shire contained no country mansion; for the home occu-pations of a country gentleman would have been a useful discipline for his mind; as it was, he was left at liberty, when released from parliamentary attendance, to choose his place of residence. His passion for the beauties of scenery and the retirement of the country was unusually strong, and for seven years he rented a house at Rayrigg, on the banks of Windermere. Hither he retired with a goodly assortment of books, ' classics, statutes at large, and history,' as soon as the recess commenced, both in this and the succeeding sum-mer. His studious attentions were however frustrated by the attractions of society. ' St. Andrew St. John was with me for months together during this summer; occasionally, too, my mother and my sister, and different college friends, joined our party. Boating, riding, and continual parties at my own house and Sir Michael le Fleming's, fully occu-pied my time until I returned to London in the following autumn.'[7]

He took more part this session in general business; and assisted in the general onslaught on Lord North's policy as to the war with America, which, after several close divisions, led, on March 20, to the resignation of Lord North and the forma-tion of the Rockingham administration. A speech on Feb-ruary 22, 1782, against Lord North's administration, was so greatly praised, that the new administration tried to win his support. ' In 1782,' he says, ' I first knew Fox well. . . he giving us dinners twice or thrice . . . very pleasant and un-affected.'[8] He was the guest of Lord Rockingham, and ' was invited to attend at Tommy Townshend's during the formation of the ministry; and I can remember when the

---

[6] Lord North.   [7] MS. Mem.   [8] Ib.

jealousy between the Rockingham and Shelburne parties was first betrayed by Fox's awkward manner, when he let out that the King had been seen by no one but Lord Shelburne.'[9]

This feeble and ill-cemented administration was broken up after a few months by the death of Lord Rockingham. In spite of the efforts of Fox, Lord Shelburne was placed by the King at the head of the new ministry, and he at once offered Pitt the seat in the cabinet without which he had already declared that he would never take office. Though Pitt's accession to its ranks did not lead Mr. Wilberforce to pledge himself absolutely to government, yet he assumed a more forward position amongst the general supporters of his friend. They were now united in the closest intimacy. In the course of this spring, they set off for Brighton, to spend the Easter holidays together ; and being driven thence on the very night of their arrival, by the inclemency of the weather, proceeded to Bath for the rest of the vacation. 'We fixed our quarters at the York House, and as Pitt was then upon the western circuit, he entertained the barristers, Jekyll amongst the rest. We had, too, abundance of corporation dinners and jollity.'[1] The early possession of his fortune increased their intimacy, as he was the only member of their set who owned a villa within reach of London. The house of his late uncle at Wimbledon, with some trifling alteration, gave him the command of eight or nine bed-rooms ; and here Pitt, to whom it was a luxury to sleep in country air, took up not unfrequently his residence : their easy familiarity permitting him to ride down late at night and occupy his rooms, even though the master of the house was kept in town. In one spring Pitt resided there four months, and thither he repaired when, in April, 1783, he resigned his official residence to the Coalition ministry.

'Eliot, Arden, and I,' writes Pitt one afternoon, 'will be with you before curfew, and expect an early meal of peas and strawberries. Bankes, I suppose, will not sleep out of Duke Street, but he has not yet appeared in the House of Commons, half-past four.'

[9] MS. Mem.   [1] Ib.

On December 11, 1782, Lord Shelburne's ministry met the House of Commons, but it adjourned after some sharp skirmishes over the Christmas holidays. On its reassembling, an address, declaring the assent of Parliament to the peace concluded with America, France, and Spain, which was the great measure of the new government, was to be the trial of strength. Lord Shelburne's ministry, weak and divided within itself, had to stand the joint assaults of Lord North and Fox. Mr. Wilberforce's diary contains many notices which illustrate that stormy season.

'Saturday, February 15, 1783. Dined Tommy Townshend's. Pitt asked me at night to second the address. Bed at twelve, and sleep disturbed at the thought of a full House of Commons.—16th. Walked after church till almost four. Dined at home, then called at Pitt's. Went to hear the address read at Tommy Townshend's.—17th. Walked down morning to House to get Milner into gallery. Seconded the address. Lost the motion by sixteen. Did not leave House till about eight in the morning, and bed about nine.'

The notorious coalition between Fox and Lord North was only just cemented, and when he came down to the House to second the address he inquired of Mr. Bankes, 'Are the intentions of Lord North and Fox sufficiently known to be condemned?' 'Yes,' was the reply, 'and the more strongly the better.' In his speech accordingly he inveighed against that scandalous intrigue, with a vehemence and force which never forsook him in all his subsequent assaults on party spirit.

'Friday, 21st. Tommy Townshend's. Debate on Lord John's motions (which condemned the recent treaty). Beat by seventeen. Spoke. Pitt spoke most capitally for two hours and three-quarters. Home immediately after the House, and bed a little after four.'

This speech he has elsewhere noted as an instance of those amazing powers of mind, which bodily infirmity seemed never to obscure in Mr. Pitt. 'Pitt's famous speech on second day's debate—first day's not so good. Spoke three hours, till four in the morning. Stomach disordered, and actually holding Solomon's porch[2] door open with one hand,

[2] Portico behind the old House of Commons.

while vomiting during Fox's speech to whom he was to reply.[3] This second defeat sealed the fate of Lord Shelburne's ministry, and on the 23rd he resigned the seals of office. Though compelled to accept the resignation, the King was most unwilling to receive the Opposition into power; and with the full assent of the retiring minister offered Mr. Pitt the place of first minister.'

'24th. Dined Pitt's—heard of the very surprising propositions.—25th. Ministry still undecided.—28th. Ministers still unappointed. T. Townshend called, and in vain persuaded Pitt to take it.—29th. Church—Lindsey's—the chariot to Wimbledon. Pitt, &c. to dinner and sleep. Nothing settled.—March 3. This evening, or on Sunday evening, the King sent for Lord North, having previously seen Lord Guildford, and they parted on bad terms; Rex refusing to take Charles Fox, and North to give him up.—5th. King saw North a second time. Both continue stout.—12th. This day Lord North was commissioned, being sent for by the King, to desire the Duke of Portland to form a Ministry.—20th. Dined upstairs, Bankes, Pepper Arden, &c., then home. Read. Bed early. The matter said by Lord G. Cavendish and Lord Duncannon to be completely off, by Fox and North not being able to agree about Stormont.—21st. Dined Pitt's. Fox's friends gave up the point of Lord Stormont; and Coke did not make his motion, understanding arrangement likely. Staid at Pitt's till late.—Sunday, 23rd. All day at Wimbledon. — 24th. Dined Pitt's. All off between the Coalition and the King, owing to the one demanding a complete list, the other refusing it.' The coolness of Mr. Pitt's judgment and the noble character of his ambition were remarkably displayed in the mode in which, throughout these weeks, he dealt with the highest prize in political life, which was almost forced on his acceptance. At length, under the immediate threat of an address in the House of Commons, the Coalition ministry adjusted their differences.—'31st. Pitt resigned to-day. Dined Pitt's.—April 3. Wimbledon, where Pitt, &c., dined and slept. Evening walk—bed a little past two.—4th. Delicious day—lounged morning at Wimbledon

[3] MS. Mem.

with friends *foining* at night, and running about the garden for an hour or two.'

Little was it known, by those who saw him only in his public course, that the stiffness of Mr. Pitt's ordinary manner could thus at times unbend, and wanton in these exuberant bursts of natural vivacity. The sports of the rigid Scipio and meditative Lælius in their ungirded hours were equalled by the 'foinings' of the garden at Wimbledon, where Pitt's overflowing spirits carried him to every height of jest. 'We found one morning the fruits of Pitt's earlier rising in the careful sowing of the garden beds with the fragments of a dress hat, in which Ryder had overnight come down from the opera.' It was in this varied and familiar intercourse that their mutual affection was matured; an affection which Mr. Wilberforce retained through life in spite of difference in politics and on yet more important subjects, and the remembrance of which would often cast a momentary sadness over the habitual cheerfulness of his aged countenance.

'Sunday, May 18. To Wimbledon with Pitt and Eliot, at their persuasion.—26th. House. Spoke. Dined at Lord Advocate's—Mr. and Mrs. Johnstone, Thurlow, Pepper, Pitt: after the rest went, we sat till six in the morning.—Monday, June 30th. House. Ranelagh, Mrs. Long there with Lord George Gordon.—Sunday, July 6. Wimbledon. Persuaded Pitt and Pepper to church. — 11th. Fine hot day, went on water with Pitt and Eliot fishing; came back, dined, walked evening. Eliot went home, Pitt staid.'

This was the most critical period of his course. He had entered in his earliest manhood upon the dissipated scenes of fashionable life, with a large fortune and most acceptable manners. His ready wit, his conversation continually sparkling with polished raillery and courteous repartee, his chastened liveliness, his generous and kindly feelings—all secured him that hazardous applause with which society rewards those who are at once its ornaments and its victims. His rare accomplishment in singing tended to increase his danger. 'Wilberforce, we must have you again; the Prince says he will come at any time to hear you sing,' was the incense offered to him after his first meeting with the Prince of Wales, in 1782, at the luxurious soirées of Devonshire House.

He was also an admirable mimic, and until reclaimed by the kind severity of the old Lord Camden, would often set the table in a roar by his perfect imitation of Lord North. His affection for Lord Camden was an intimation at this very time of the higher texture of his mind. Often would he steal away from the merriment and light amusements of the gayer circle, to gather wisdom from the weighty words and chosen anecdotes in which the veteran Chancellor abounded. His affection was warmly returned by Lord Camden, who loved the intelligent earnestness with which he sought for knowledge. 'Lord Camden noticed me particularly,' he said,[4] 'and treated me with great kindness. Amongst other things, he cured me of the dangerous art of mimicry. When invited by my friends to witness my powers of imitation, he at once refused, saying slightingly for me to hear it, "It is but a vulgar accomplishment." "Yes, but it is not imitating the mere manner; Wilberforce says the very thing Lord North would say." "Oh," was his reply, "every one does that."' This friendly intercourse was long continued. 'How many subjects of politics and religion,' writes the old lord, with a pressing invitation to Camden Place, in 1787, 'might we not have settled by this time, in the long evenings.'

But if he escaped the seductions of frivolity and fashion, he was in equal danger from the severer temptations of ambition. With talents of the highest order, and eloquence surpassed by few, he entered upon public life possessed of the best personal connections, in his intimate friendship with Mr. Pitt. Disinterested, generous, lively, fond of society, by which he was equally beloved, and overflowing with affection towards his numerous friends, he was indeed little tempted by the low and mercenary spirit of worldly policy. But ambition has baits for men of every temper; and how far he was then safe from its fascinations, may be learned from the conduct of his brother 'Independents.' They were a club of about forty members of the House of Commons,

[4] Con. Mem.

most of them opponents of the Coalition Ministry, whose principle of union was a resolution to take neither place, pension, nor peerage. Yet in a few years so far was the fierceness of their 'independence' abated, that he and Mr. Bankes alone of all the party retained their early simplicity of station. He himself was the only county member who was not raised to the peerage. He too would no doubt have been entangled in the toils of party, and have failed of those great triumphs he afterwards achieved,[5] but for the entrance into his soul of higher principles. His later journals abound in expressions of thankfulness that he did not at this time enter on official life, and waste his days amidst the trappings of greatness.

The close of the session, July 16, set him at liberty. After visiting the St. Johns at Tunbridge Wells, he spent the month of August in Yorkshire, and repaired early in September to the seat of Mr. Bankes in Dorsetshire, to meet Mr. Pitt and Mr. Eliot, with whom he had engaged to pay a visit to the Continent. 'I am of opinion,' writes Pitt, 'that the air of Rheims is exactly the thing for you. I hope to find it equally sovereign for toothaches and swelled faces, which have persecuted me ever since I have been here, as if it was the middle of a session. We shall agree excellently as invalids, and particularly in making the robust Eliot fag for us and ride bodkin, and letting him enjoy all the other privileges of health' (Aug. 30, 1785).

On September 11, the three friends met at Canterbury, and on the following day embarking at Dover, in spite of a heavy sea, crossed to Calais. Thence they proceeded straight to Rheims, to find, as Mr. Pitt expressed it, 'some charitable persons who will let us practise our French upon them,'[6] before they went to Paris. Each had trusted to the other to obtain the needful introductions; and when at last the omission was discovered they had only time to write to Mr. Robert Smith for letters. He had no better resource than to obtain from Peter Thellusson an introduction to the correspondent

---

[5] 'After all,' said one of the most famous and successful of modern politicians in 1833, 'which of *us* shall ever do what he has done?'
[6] Life of Pitt, i. 131.

of his house. With these credentials they arrived at Rheims, then under that episcopal government which had lasted from the time of Clovis, and to which may be traced, according to Guizot, the origin of European civilisation. At the time of their arrival the Archbishop (Périgord) was absent, and the ordinary routine of government devolved upon Mons. de Lageard, as secretary to the conseil d'état. Their first adventures are thus related in a letter to Mr. Bankes. 'From Calais we made directly for Rheims, and the day after our arrival dressed ourselves unusually well, and proceeded to the house of a Mons. Coustier to present, with not a little awe, our only letters of recommendation. It was with some surprise that we found Mons. Coustier behind a counter distributing figs and raisins. I had heard that it was very usual for gentlemen on the Continent to practise some handicraft trade or other for their amusement, and therefore for my own part I concluded that his taste was in the fig way, and that he was only playing at grocer for his diversion; and viewing the matter in this light, I could not help admiring the excellence of his imitation ; but we soon found that Mons. Coustier was a " véritable épicier," and not a very eminent one. He was very fair and candid, however, and acknowledged to us that he was not acquainted with any of the gentry of the place, and therefore could not introduce us to them. We returned to our inn, and after spending nine or ten days without making any great progress in the French language, which could not indeed be expected from us, as we spoke to no human being but each other and our Irish courier, we began to entertain serious thoughts of leaving the place in despair. By way of a parting effort we waited on our épicier, and prevailed on him to put on a bag and sword and carry us to the intendant of. the police, whom he supplied with groceries. This scheme succeeded admirably. The intendant was extremely civil to us, and introduced us to the archbishop, who gave us two very good and pleasant dinners and would have had us stay a week with him. (N.B. Archbishops in England are not like archevêques in France ; these last are jolly fellows of about forty years of age, who play at billiards, &c. like other people.)

'We soon got acquainted with as many of the inhabitants
as we could wish, especially an Abbé de Lageard, a fellow
of infinite humour, and of such extraordinary humanity, that
to prevent our time hanging heavy on our hands he would
sometimes make us visits of five or six hours at a stretch.
Our last week passed very pleasantly, and for myself I was
really very sorry when the day arrived for our setting off for
Paris.'

The Abbé de Lageard (since Mons. de Cherval) has furnished some recollections of this visit. 'One morning, when
the intendant of police brought me his daily report, he informed me, there are three Englishmen here of a very suspi-
cious character. They are in a wretched lodging, they have
no attendance, yet their courier says, they are "grand seig-
neurs," and that one of them is the son of the great Chatham;
but it is impossible. They must be "des intrigants." I had
been in England, and knew that the younger sons of your
noble families are not always wealthy, and I said to Mons.
du Chatel, who wished to visit them officially and investi-
gate their character, "Let us be in no hurry; it may be,
perhaps, as they represent; I will inquire about them myself."
I went to their lodgings the same evening, and got their
names from the courier, and true enough they were said to
be Mr. W. Pitt, Mr. Wilberforce, and Mr. Eliot, all three
members of the British Parliament, and one of them lately a
leading member of the government. The next morning I
visited them, and as I was at once satisfied by their appearance, I asked whether I could be of any use to them, and
offered whatever the town of Rheims could afford for their
amusement. Amongst other things, Mr. Pitt complained,
" Here we are in the middle of Champagne, and we cannot
get any tolerable wine." "Dine with me to-morrow," I replied, "and you shall have the best wine the country can
afford." They came and dined with me, and instead of
moving directly after dinner, as we do in France, we sat
talking for five or six hours.'

The Abbé de Lageard, a man of family and fortune, was
one of those whom the revolution stripped of everything but
their faith and loyalty; and when residing as an emigrant in

England, he received from Mr. Wilberforce a willing and ample return of his present hospitality. Nothing could exceed his kindness to them ; for a fortnight he was their constant attendant; he made them acquainted with the noblesse who resided in the neighbourhood of Rheims ; he gave them permission to sport over the domain of the Archbishop; and, upon his return, introduced them to a familiar footing at the palace. In their many conversations with the Abbé, Mr. Pitt was the chief speaker. Although no master of the French vocabulary, his ear, quick for every sound but music, caught readily the intonations of the language ; and he soon spoke it with considerable accuracy. He inquired carefully into the political institutions of the French; and the Abbé has stored up his concluding sentence . . . 'Monsieur, vous n'avez point de liberté politique, mais pour la liberté civile, vous en avez plus que vous ne croyez.'

As he expressed in the strongest terms his admiration for the system which prevailed at home, the Abbé was led to ask him, since all human things were perishable, in what part the British constitution might be first expected to decay? Pitt, a parliamentary reformer, and speaking within three years of the time when the House of Commons had agreed to Mr. Dunning's motion, that the influence of the Crown had increased, was increasing, and ought to be diminished, after musing for a moment, answered, 'The part of our constitution which will first perish is the prerogative of the King, and the authority of the House of Peers.' 'I am greatly surprised,' said the Abbé, 'that a country so moral as England can submit to be governed by a man so wanting in private character as Fox; it seems to show you to be less moral than you appear.' 'C'est que vous n'avez pas été sous la baguette du magicien,' was Pitt's reply; 'but the remark,' he continued, 'is just.'

Through the Abbé's kindness they mixed familiarly with different ranks, and saw much of the interior of French society. 'October 3. Dined at Vallery — La Marechale d'Etrées, &c.' A following entertainment at the house of a wealthy wine merchant of Rheims is described as 'a sad party — drunken prior — sang — seventy-three [years old].'

The story of their early embarrassments at Rheims' preceded them to Fontainebleau, where, by special invitation,
they soon joined the gala festivities of the court, and Mr.
Pitt was often rallied by the Queen, who asked whether he
had lately heard from his friend the épicier.

The diary of this period gives a brief notice of each day's
proceedings.

'October 16. At eleven, went with ambassador. In-
troduced to King, Queen, Monsieur, Madame, Compte
and Comptesse d'Artois, and two aunts. Dined Mons. de
Castries's, minister of the marine department. Saw there
Vicomte de Noailles, pleasant fellow, and Marquis de la
Fayette, Chaillière, Castries's son and his wife. Marmontel
there. After dinner went to Vergennes', and then to
Madame Polignac's to visit the Queen; she chatted easily.
Supped at Count Donson's. Round table : all English
but Donson, Noailles, Dupont. Queen came after supper.
Cards, trictrac, and backgammon, which Artois, Lauzun, and
Chartres played extremely well. Home at one.—17th. Morning—Pitt stag hunting. Eliot and I in chaise to see King.
Clumsy, strange figure in immense boots. Dined home—
then play. Then home, and supped Castries's, at small
table very rudely.[7] Afterwards to Polignac's to the Queen,
who came there after supper — billiards. Home, where
lounged till almost three o'clock.—18th. The boar hunting.
After dinner called Vergennes'. Supped Seguier's. Afterwards Lamballe's, where the Queen. Great assembly—billiards.—19th. Returned to Paris. Dined Walpole's. Then
home.—20th. Dined Marquis de la Fayette's, pleasing enthusiastical man : his wife a sweet woman. Dr. Franklin,
Mr. Page, Crillon's aide-du-camp, young Franklin, Noailles,
Madame Boufflers there.'

Mr. Wilberforce received with interest the hearty greetings
which Dr. Franklin tendered to a rising member of the
English Parliament, who had opposed the war with America.
But what most attracted his attention was the singular

[7] The English then at Fontainebleau made a considerable party, and
instead of mingling with their hosts, they assembled at a separate table,
headed by their ambassador (the Duke of Manchester), to discuss English politics in their own language.

position occupied by La Fayette, who seemed, in the very presence of the monarch, to be the representative of the democracy. His establishment was formed upon the English model; and, amidst the gaiety and ease of Fontainebleau, he assumed an air of republican austerity. When the fine ladies of the court attempted to drag him to the card table, he shrugged his shoulders, with an affected contempt for the customs and amusements of the old regime. Meanwhile the deference which this champion of a new state of things received, above all from the ladies of the court, intimated clearly the disturbance of the social atmosphere, and presaged the coming tempest.

A special messenger recalling Mr. Pitt to London, cut short their further observations; and, after a six weeks' absence, Mr. Wilberforce returned to England, October 24, 'better pleased with his own country than before he left it.' He thus reports to Mr. Bankes his foreign operations in a letter, part of which has been already given[8]:—At Fontainebleau we dined and supped with ministers, and every night we spent with the Queen, who is a monarch of most engaging manners and appearance. The King is so strange a being (of the hog kind), that it is worth going a hundred miles for a sight of him, especially a boar hunting. They all, men and women, crowded round Pitt in shoals; and he behaved with great spirit, though he was sometimes a little bored when they talked to him about the parliamentary reform. They are certainly, we have every reason to say, a most obliging people; and we all returned charmed with our reception.'

[8] London, October 28, 1783.

CHAPTER II.

FIRST ELECTION FOR YORKSHIRE.

*State of parties in the autumn of 1783—Diary—Meeting at York against
the Coalition—Dissolution of Parliament—Yorkshire election—Wilberforce suddenly proposed to represent the county—Elected for Hull—
Nomination for the county—Elected member—Letter from Pitt—Effect
of this election on the country.*

1783–1784.

November, 1783, was a season of great political excitement.
'Returned,' he says,[1] 'to England in November, and secret
plottings. The King groaning under the ministry which
had been imposed upon him. Difference about provision
for Prince of Wales, when ministry gave up the measure
rather than their places.—Afterwards Fox's India Bill, which
thrown out—Lord Temple's fracas and long interregnum—
at length Pitt prime minister.' The failure of the India
Bill, which, by the patronage it created, would have made
the Coalition almost independent of the Crown — an attempt styled by Fox himself as 'vigorous and hazardous'[2]
—destroyed the government. It died indeed slowly, and
almost amidst the throes of anarchy; but from the first the
end was inevitable. Then came that memorable season,
when one man swayed absolutely the destinies of a people;
when Pitt, undismayed by threats and unincensed by pro-
vocations, upheld with a strong hand and a bold heart the
prerogatives of the Crown and the liberties of the subject.
Throughout this period Mr. Wilberforce shared constantly in
the private counsels and parliamentary labours of his friend.
The part he took in these debates attracted more notice
than any of his previous speeches; and the Opposition papers
of the day defy Mr. Pitt 'in spite of the assistance he receives
from the eloquence of Mr. Wilberforce.'

[1] MS. Mem.   [2] Lord Stanhope's *Life of Pitt*, vol. i. p. 139.

Here are some extracts from his diary :—

'Nov. 1. Wimbledon.   Pitt and Eliot came in at four— dined and slept.—2nd. Pitt staid all day.—3rd. They left me—alone—read.—8th. Sat. Eliot and Pitt came to dinner; and all night.—9th. Pepper and John Villiers came, and staid all night. Pitt and Eliot left after dinner.—11th. Begun hard at Reports.—13th. House—Reports. Supped Edwards's— Ramsay, negroes.—17th. Pitt went to Cambridge to meet Euston. Went to Surrey nomination meeting.—18th. House —Fox's India Motion. Express from Euston that the Duke would not let him stand. Debate about Pitt. Determined he should not stand.[3]—20th. House—spirited debate about putting off India Bill.—24th. Night, Pitt's India people.— 27th. Great day in the House. Sat till past four in the morning.—30th. Dined Lord Chatham's—meeting. Dec. 1. House—late night. Home about five, immediately after de- bate. Fox spoke wonderfully.—2nd. Catch-club—Sandwich —then opera. Mrs. Crewe there. Supped Lord George's. Lord John there—Mrs. Crewe—Duchess of Portland— converts. Mrs. Crewe made the party [promise] to ad- journ to Downing Street next night.—3rd. Supped Duchess of Portland's, Downing Street. Charles Fox came in— whispering over chair. Heavy evening.—6th. Dined Hamil- ton's—opera. Supped Burlington House—Mrs. Crewe— Duchess of Portland—Mrs. Sheridan sang old English songs angelically—promised her our votes.— 16th. House—reso- lutions relative to King's interference. Home late.—19th. Pitt, Lord Temple, Thurlow, accepted.—20th. Morning Pitt's.—21st. Pitt's—supped Lord Chatham's.—22nd. Lord Temple resigned. No dissolution declared. Drove about for Pitt. "So your friend Mr. Pitt means to come in," said Mrs. Crewe;[4] "well, he may do what he likes during the holidays, but it will only be a mince-pie administration, depend on it." This was a day of deep anxiety to the young premier. Lord Temple's unexplained resignation was fol- lowed by Mr. Erskine carrying, without a division, a hostile address against a dissolution or prorogation of Parliament

[3] Mr. Mansfield (solicitor-general) was re-elected.
[4] MS. Mem.

in the House of Commons. It is interesting to have a near view of this great man at such a moment.—' 23rd. Morning Pitt's. Dined Sir C. Middleton's. Pitt nobly firm. Evening Pitt's. Cabinet formed. We had a great meeting that night of all Pitt's friends in Downing Street. As Pratt, Tom Steele, and I were going up to it in a hackney coach from the House of Commons, " Pitt must take care," I said, " whom he makes Secretary of the Treasury ; it is rather a roguish office." " Mind what you say," answered Steele, " for I am Secretary of the Treasury." At Pitt's we had a long discussion ; and I remember well the great penetration showed by Lord Mahon. "What am I to do," said Pitt, " if they stop the supplies." " They will not stop them," said Mahon ; " it is the very thing which they will not venture to do."— 24th. House—spoke very well.'

' January 1, 1784. After breakfast to Cambridge—Combination room. Townshend asked me if Pitt would stand.[5]— 20th. House—coalition talked of. Dined Independents'— opera—and supped Goostree's.'

The Country party hoped at this time to secure an union between Fox and Pitt, who, though repeatedly outvoted, maintained his ground against diminishing majorities.

' 23rd. House—Pitt's Bill—up at three.—'February 10. White's. Wanted, but in vain, old North to come in.—22nd. Dined G. Hardinge's. Mrs. Siddons sung charmingly.— 25th. They put off the House by a trick. Address carried up.' This address, carried by Mr. Fox with a majority of twenty-one, besought the King to form an united and efficient administration.—26th. Dined at Lord Chatham's to settle about the 25.—28th. Pitt returned from city. Affray —he got safe into White's. Called there—and bed about three o'clock.' This was a remarkable instance of the violence of the times. Mr. Pitt had received that morning, at his brother's house in Berkeley Square, the freedom of the City, and had dined afterwards, amidst loud demonstrations of good will, in the hall of the Grocers' Company. It was on

[5] At the ensuing general election, Mr. Pitt and Lord Euston were returned for the *U*niversity of Cambridge in the place of Messrs. Townshend and Mansfield.

his return at night that the opposite party, irritated by the display of his rising popularity, ranged their forces round their club at Brookes's, and mobbed the carriage of the minister.

'March 1. Spoke'—on an address moved by Fox for the dismissal of ministers—'at night to Dundas's.—4th. Dined D'Adhemar's—French ambassador.—6th. Pitt bolted in.—7th. Sunday—morning, church. Dined Lord Salisbury's.—Then with Dundas to Mr. Seaton's to sup with Mrs. Siddons.—12th. House till eleven—Parliamentary Reform.—17th. Came to town. Dined Lord Bulkeley's. Then Pitt's, where supped.'

All this time the struggle between Mr. Pitt and his opponents was fiercely maintained; but there had been no lack of symptoms as to its final issue. The feeling outside the House was plainly with Pitt, and it was gradually telling on the divisions in Parliament. At length, upon the 8th of March, when the Opposition made their last great attempt, Mr. Fox succeeded in carrying through his manifesto by only 191 to 190.

'How anxiously,' he has said of this important crisis, 'we watched the events of each succeeding day, counting every vote, in the earnest hope that Pitt might make a successful stand against the Coalition.'

But the time was now come, when he could render more essential service to his friend. The rising feeling of the country in support of Mr. Pitt, had been already shown in the many urgent addresses presented to the King. But Yorkshire had not as yet declared itself; and the supporters of the Coalition, calculating upon the influence of their vast possessions in the county, looked eagerly for its declaration in their favour. 'Great head,' say the papers [6] of the day, 'is making in Yorkshire against the address to be proposed there on the 28th; the Fitzwilliams and Cavendishes are all gone down, and are busy in their canvass. Their success in Yorkshire is now the sheet-anchor of the Coalition. An address from that populous and extensive county would prove a death-blow to their future hopes. Their agents and emissaries, therefore, are driving about from place to place,

[6] Public Advertiser, March 18 and 19.

day and night. Some of their ablest hands are employed
in this important service. As some principals of their party
have so great an interest in the county, a failure there would
entirely blow up their cause; and, besides, the example of
Yorkshire could not fail to determine other counties, which
have not yet addressed.' To this overbearing influence there
was a strong spirit of opposition in the county. The West
Riding clothiers were all Tories, and ready to rise in support
of the throne. The Yorkshire Association declared against
the Coalition. It had been formed in 1779, from the gentry
of moderate fortunes and the more substantial yeomen,
under the pressure of those burdens which resulted from
the war with America, with the view of obtaining, first an
economical, and then a parliamentary, reform. But in the
various changes which soon afterwards perplexed the political
world, its first object was almost forgotten; and its most
important character was the front of opposition, which it
now maintained against that powerful aristocracy, which had
long ruled the county with absolute dominion. To the
general hostility to the Coalition, Yorkshire therefore added
a peculiar element of opposition. In contending with the
great Whig lords, she fought the battle of her own freedom,
as well as of political right. The sturdy yeomen of the north
gathered round the Association, and formed a union of all
the middle classes against the great barons of the county.
The castle-yard at York was to be their Runnymede, and
the address their Magna Charta. .

Yet so undisputed hitherto had been the rule against
which they were about to rise, that, in spite of this state of
feeling, Mr. Wilberforce declared, three days before the
county meeting, ' I hope we may be able to get up an opposition in Yorkshire, though I doubt whether it be possible.'
He had determined upon making the attempt, and though
the poet Mason, then a canon residentiary at York, was well
nigh his sole acquaintance beyond his own corner of the
county, he hastened into Yorkshire to head the party. On
the 22nd of March he reached York. ' Dressed,' says his
diary, ' and went and supped at York Tavern. Lord Fauconberg, Wyvill, and I, helped to draw up an address—Mason,

&c.—24th. Up early—at York Tavern—and walking all day. Numbers came to York.—25th. Cold, hailing day. Castle-yard meeting from ten till half-past four. Messenger came to me there.'

'In those days,' he has said,[7] 'they kept up a vast deal of state, and the great men all drove up in their coaches and six. An immense body of the freeholders was present. It was a wonderful meeting for order and fair hearing.' An address to the King condemning the Coalition Ministry was proposed by Mr. Buck, recorder of Leeds, and supported by Mr. H. Duncombe, Mr. Baynes, Mr. Milnes, Mr. Stanhope, and Lord Fauconberg. On the other side appeared the late Duke of Norfolk (then Lord Surrey), Lord Carlisle, Lord John Cavendish, Lord Fitzwilliam, and many other men of rank and influence. When the proposers of the address had spoken, and the Whig lords had been heard in answer, the day was far advanced, and the listeners were growing weary of the contest. At this time Mr. Wilberforce mounted the table, from which, under a great wooden canopy before the high sheriff's chair, the various speakers had addressed the meeting. The weather was so bad 'that it seemed,' says an eye-witness, 'as if his slight frame would be unable to make head against its violence.' The castle-yard, too, was so crowded, that men of the greatest physical powers had been scarcely audible. Yet such was the magic of his voice and the grace of his expression, that by his very first sentence he arrested, and for above an hour he continued to enchain, the attention of the surrounding multitude. 'I saw,' said Boswell,[8] describing the meeting to Dundas, 'what seemed a mere shrimp mount upon the table; but, as I listened, he grew, and grew, until the shrimp became a whale.' 'It is impossible,' says one who heard him, 'though at the distance of so many years, to forget his speech, or the effect which it produced. He arraigned with the utmost vigour the Coalition ministry, and the India Bill which they had proposed—a measure which he described as "the off-

---

[7] MS. Mem.

[8] 'I rejoice in the happy prospect of things with you,' writes Mr. Dundas from Edinburgh to Mr. Wilberforce, March 30. 'Boswell has just been with me, and gives me an account of your feats at York.'

spring of that unnatural conjunction, marked with the features of both its parents, bearing token to the violence of the one, and the corruption of the other."' He was distinctly heard to the utmost limits of the crowd, and interrupted only by an express from Mr. Pitt, which enabled him with the greatest possible effect to announce to the assembled county, that, by dissolving Parliament, the King had at that very moment appealed to the decision of the nation.

Here is Pitt's letter:—

' Dear Wilberforce,—Parliament will be prorogued to-day, and dissolved to-morrow. The latter operation has been in some danger of delay by a curious manœuvre, that of stealing the great seal last night from the Chancellor's ; but we shall have a new one ready in time.

' I send you a copy of the speech which will be made in two hours from the throne. You may speak of it in the *past* tense, instead of the *future.*

' A letter accompanies this from Lord Mahon to Wyvill, which you will be so good as to give him. I am told Sir Robert Hildyard is the right candidate for the county. You must take care to keep all our friends together, and to *tear the enemy to pieces.*

' I set out this evening for Cambridge, where I expect, notwithstanding your boding, to find every thing favourable. I am sure, however, of a retreat at Bath.[9]

' Our prospect as to elections improves every hour.'

' At the commencement of the meeting,' he has said, ' the two parties opposed to Mr. Fox were themselves divided, and I was able to unite them. ' The honest independent freeholders of that great county,' says the " Public Advertiser," ' looked the Duke of Devonshire, Lord John Cavendish, the Earls of Carlisle and Fitzwilliam, in the face ; and against that mighty aristocracy voted a loyal address to their Sovereign.'

The great ability which he had thus displayed before the county, produced a most unexpected result. The immense expense of contesting its representation had reduced Yorkshire to the condition of a nomination borough in the

[9] Downing Street, Wednesday, March 24, half-past twelve.

hands of the Whig nobility. 'Hitherto,' said its popular representative, Sir George Savile, when in 1780 he was supported by the Yorkshire Association, before which his colleague had given place to Mr. Henry Duncombe, 'hitherto I have been elected in Lord Rockingham's dining-room —now I am returned by my constituents.' 'To get up an opposition' at the approaching election, had been one end of Mr. Wilberforce's presence. And he himself, warned doubtless by that internal consciousness of power, by which great men are prepared for high attempts, had already secretly presaged the actual issue.

[1] 'I had formed the project of standing for the county. To any one besides myself I was aware that it must appear so mad a scheme, that I never mentioned it to Mr. Pitt, or any of my political connections. It was undoubtedly a bold idea, but I was then very ambitious.[2] I carefully prepared myself for the debate which was soon to follow in the face of the whole county; and both at the public meeting, and in the subsequent discussions, it was this idea which regulated the line, as well as animated the spirit, of my exertions. My being elected for that great county appears to me, upon the retrospect, so utterly improbable, that I cannot but ascribe it to a providential intimation, that the idea of my obtaining that high honour suggested itself to my mind.'

'Great as our majority may be at the county meeting,' writes Mr. Wyvill,[3] 'what friend have we to propose who could hazard the expense of a contest, or what probability is there that any candidate would be supported by a subscription.' Sir Christopher Sykes had been the only person announced in the county papers as a possible candidate. But events were advancing to a different issue. Whilst he was yet speaking in the castle-yard, the admiration of the freeholders burst forth in the shout, 'We'll have this man for our county member;' and his conduct in the succeeding meet-

[1] MS. Mem.
[2] 'Notables in my life. My being raised to my present situation just before I became acquainted with the truth, and one year and a half before I in any degree experienced its power. This, humanly speaking, would not have taken place afterwards.'—*Journal,* September 4, 1796.
[3] Letter to Rev. W. Mason, Feb. 28, 1784.

ings suggested the same idea to independent men of greater influence.

'The meeting in the castle-yard was followed by a great public dinner of our side, at the York Tavern. In the evening, I made up a quarrel which had broken out between associators and non-associators, Whigs and Tories. Whigs, Lord Effingham, &c.; Tories, West Riding clothiers. This confirmed the disposition to propose me for the county, an idea which had begun to be buzzed about at dinner, amongst all ranks.'[4] 'Mr. Wilberforce,' wrote one of the company to Lord Hawke, 'has gained the hearts and admiration of all that heard him speak; and when we broke up at the York Tavern, at twelve o'clock on Thursday night, there was a sudden and spontaneous cry of "Wilberforce and Liberty!" which was his first nomination for the county.'

'26th. Meeting at York Tavern. Message from Bluitt's, about supporting any one, if we would support Foljambe —our answer. Stanhope, Fauconberg, &c. mentioned me. Sir Robert Hildyard spoke—I speechified again—and they agreed that all should separately sound their neighbours, and come with the result to the county meeting about a week afterwards, so putting off the determination concerning me till the nomination.'[5]

'27th. Canvassed the York voters, and got them all for Galway and Milnes. People not pleased at my not canvassing.—28th. Hull. Morning busy—made some calls.—29th. Began canvass, which continued till night. Hartley drawn into the town.—30th. Canvass all day.—31st. Morning—election went on well. At three, poll interrupted—Hartley desired in vain by friends to give up.'

'April 1. Hartley declined—election went on. Snowballs, &c. thrown at me in the chair.'[6] This slight expression of resentment was aimed at his intended resignation of his seat, if elected for the county. 'But when,' says an eye-witness, 'the procession reached his mother's house, he sprung from the chair, and presenting himself with surprising quick-

---

[4] MS. Mem.　　　　　　　　　　　[5] Diary.
[6] At the close of the poll the numbers stood—W. Wilberforce, 807; S. Thornton, 751; D. Hartley, 357.

ness at a projecting window—it was that of the nursery in
which his childhood had been passed — he addressed the
populace with such complete effect, that he was able afterwards to decide the election of his successor.'

The same evening he was on his road to York.

' 7th. At night went to Market Weighton, twenty-one miles
—crowds—orgies in Beverley.—8th. Up early—to York—
nomination day.'

He found a welcome greeting upon reaching York; and
was immediately proposed with Mr. Duncombe, in opposition to Mr. Weddell and Mr. Foljambe, both men of large
fortune and great connections, and one [7] the former member,
and heir to the influence of Sir George Savile.

The brunt of opposition was of course directed against
the new candidate, whom Lord Mulgrave recommended to
the freeholders as 'approved already by a large part of the
county, the bosom friend of the present minister, and second
only to him in eloquence, unexampled at their years.' 'It
was a great meeting for the nomination, in a long room between the courts; the speakers mounted on a table, and
haranguing thence: I replying to lawyer Hill of Tadcaster.'[8]
This speech, in a vein of cutting sarcasm, of which in after-
life he would never allow himself the use, ' I well remember,
says one who heard it, ' for the hearty mirth which its powers
of ridicule excited.' The show of hands was, by a 'vast
majority,' in favour of himself and Mr. Duncombe; and the
reports made upon the day of nomination, as the result of
local canvassing, gave them a return of promises,[9] as three
or four to one. To meet the anticipated charge of such a
contest, a subscription was immediately commenced, to
which the candidates in vain requested leave to add 2,000*l.*
a-piece. Of the sum thus contributed (18,670*l.*), about one-

---

[7] Mr. Wilberforce would often mention with peculiar pleasure the
generous feeling with which, at a subsequent election, Mr. Foljambe
came to York, as one of his supporters.

[8] MS. Mem.

[9] An exact revision of the county, by which the names, residences,
and possessions of every freeholder were ascertained, showed that whilst
there were doubtful, or against them, 2,510 votes, no less than 11,173
were promised to the two independent candidates.

fourth proved sufficient to defray the whole expense of the election.

From the hall of nomination the candidates passed to another public dinner at the York Tavern; and on the following morning set out to spend in a hasty personal canvass the four days which preceded the election. Their road by Doncaster led them through a hostile neighbourhood. 'We passed many great houses that morning, but not one did we see that was friendly to us. "This looks very ill," was my remark to Duncombe.' But with night their tide of popularity set in.

'April 3. To Rotherham — drawn into town — public dinner. At night to Sheffield—vast support—meeting at Cutlers' Hall.—4th. Off to Barnsley. Honest Edmunds of Worsborough, in sight of Lord Fitzwilliam's, but a warm friend. Then to Wakefield, where slept.—5th. Canvassed. Then off to Halifax. Drawn into town. One hundred people dined with us. Speechified at the other house after dinner—warm friends. After dinner (drunken postboy) to Bradford. Drawn into town—vast support. Then on to Leeds, and bed.—6th. Wonderful cloth halls—kindly received. At York Tavern—Lord John Cavendish and Sir W. Milner beat. At eight o'clock a message from Bluitt's, saying Foljambe and Weddell decline. Wrote number of letters. — 7th. Up early — breakfasted tavern — rode frisky horse to castle—elected—chaired—dined York Tavern. Spencer Stanhope spoke to me.'

Many were the greetings which poured in upon him, and not the least affectionate was this with which Mr. Pitt closed a series of daily letters :[1]

'I can never enough congratulate you on such glorious success. I am going to dine at Wimbledon to-day, to mix my joy with Mrs. Dixon's, who has all the trophies of victory, such as handbills, ballads, &c., to adorn your kitchen, and your boy. I hope you will have a worthy successor in the person of Spencer Stanhope. I have seen Manners, who has no thought of standing, and will write to his friends in favour of Stanhope. I hope his accomplishments cannot

[1] Downing Street, April 8, 1784.

fail to conciliate the previous confidence necessary for your sanction.

' P.S. Westminster goes on well, in spite of the Duchess of Devonshire, and the other *women of the people*, but when the poll will close is uncertain.'

' Everything,' he hears from Pepper Arden, ' goes on well, both at Cambridge and the world in general, as to elections. Pitt, thank God ! keeps his health and spirits amidst a series of fatigues which would make me mad.'[2]

Thus was accomplished this great triumph of independent principles. Its effect upon the struggle then at issue was most important. ' Numbers of members have confessed to me,' writes Mr. Duncombe,[3] ' that they owed their success in their own counties to the example set by ours.' By it, and nearly two hundred other victories over the adherents of the Coalition party, Mr. Pitt became as strong in the House of Commons, as he had before been in the affections of the people.

CHAPTER III.

APRIL 1784 TO APRIL 1786.

Takes his seat for Yorkshire—Travels to Nice with Isaac Milner—His stay there—Return to London—Session of Parliament—Parliamentary Reform—Return to the Continent—Genoa—Geneva—Spa—Gradual change in his principles.

MAY 14. Mr. Wilberforce took his seat as member for the county of York. He possessed already enough to intoxicate his mind. whilst prospects of gratified ambition seemed to open without limit before him. He attended constantly through the first session of the new Parliament, and swelled the triumphant majorities, which secured the supremacy of his friend. Upon the prorogation of Parliament, he went down into the north, and presenting himself at York as ' the joy' of the races, spent his twenty-fifth birthday at the top wave and highest flow of those amusements, which had swallowed up

---

[2] March 31.   [3] To W. Wilberforce, Esq., 1789.

D

so large a portion of his youth.   Yet at this very time the
providence of God was guiding him into that path which
issued in his altered character.

After a hasty visit to Westmoreland, and 'looking again
on all the old scenes with vast pleasure,'[1] he started for the
Continent upon October 20.   One carriage was occupied by
Isaac Milner and himself, whilst in another followed his
mother, sister, and two female relatives.   Crossing France
to Lyons they embarked upon the Rhone ; dropped down
it to Avignon, and then by Marseilles and Toulon reached
Nice on the 30th of November.

Here they were soon settled 'in a house separated from
the Mediterranean only by a grove of orange trees,' and
found themselves surrounded by many of the higher ranks
of their own countrymen.   'Duke of Gloucester, Lady
Rivers, and G. Pitt, Sir I. Wroughton, Bosanquet, Duchess
of Ancaster and Lady Charlotte, &c., here—the commandant
Comte de St. André, and the Comte de Revel, and Chevalier de Revel, extremely obliging to the English.'[2]   'The
natives were in general a wretched set—several of them,
however, poor noblesse.   There were nightly card parties at
the different houses, and a great deal of gambling.   The
most respectable person amongst them was the Chevalier de
Revel : he spoke English well, and was a great favourite of
Frederic North's, who was then at Nice in a very nervous state,
and giving entire credit to the animal magnetizers.   The chief
operator, M. Taulay, tried his skill on Milner and myself,
but neither of us felt anything, owing, perhaps, to our incre-
dulity.   North, on the contrary, would fall down upon entering a room in which they practised on him ; and he even
maintained to me, that they could affect the frame though
in another room, or at a distance, and you were ignorant of
their proceedings.'[3]   'Staid here till Feb. 3[4]—dined frequently in the open air during the last three weeks—rode
out with Milner,—dined early, and to bed.   Out at assemblies and balls frequently.   Gave dinners often.'

In all these scenes he was constantly accompanied by

---

[1] Diary, September 19.   [2] Diary.
[3] MS. Mem.   [4] Diary.

Milner, whose vivacity and sense, in union with most un-
polished manners, continually amused his friends. 'Pretty
boy, pretty boy,' uttered in the broadest Yorkshire dialect,
whilst he stroked familiarly his head, was the mode in which
he first addressed the young Prince William of Gloucester.
'Though Milner's religious principles were now, on his record, in theory, those of his later life, yet they had at this
time little practical effect upon his conduct. He was free
from every taint of vice, but not more attentive than others
to religion.[5] Though a clergyman, he never thought of
reading prayers during their whole stay at Nice. He appeared in all respects like an ordinary man of the world,
mixing, like myself, in all companies, and joining, as readily
as others, in the prevalent Sunday parties. Indeed, when I
engaged him as a companion in my tour, I knew not that
he had any deeper principles. The first time I discovered
it, was at the public table at Scarborough. The conversation turned on Mr. Stillingfleet;[6] and I spoke of him as a
good man, but one who carried things too far. "Not a bit
too far," said Milner; and to this opinion he adhered, when
we renewed the conversation in the evening on the sands.
This declaration greatly surprised me ; and it was agreed that
at some future time we would talk the matter over. Had I
known at first what his opinions were, it would have decided
me against making him the offer; so true is it that a gracious
hand leads us in ways that we know not, and blesses us not
only without, but even against, our plans and inclinations.'[7]
The imperfect recollection which he now retained of what he
had seen and felt, when beneath his uncle's roof at Wimbledon, inclined him to condemn, as Methodism, all serious
attention to religion; and this tendency had doubtless been
increased by his attendance at Mr. Lindsey's meeting, which
he frequented, 'not from any preference for his peculiar
doctrines, for in this, except on some great festivals, his
preaching differed little from that which was then common amongst the London clergy, but because he seemed
more earnest and practical than others.'[8] Milner, on the

[5] MS. Mem. [6] Rev. I. Stillingfleet, rector of Hotham.
[7] MS. Mem. [8] Con. Mem.

D 2

contrary, though little governed by religion, respected it in others ; and whenever his lively companion treated it with raillery, would seriously combat his objections, adding, ' I am no match for you, Wilberforce, in this running fire, but if you really wish to discuss these subjects seriously, I will gladly enter on them with you.'   No great impression could be expected on another from reasonings which had so little influence on himself; and their discussions appear to have been merely speculative up to the period of their quitting Nice in the winter of 1784-5.   Just before this journey, Mr. Wilberforce took up casually Doddridge's ' Rise and Progress of Religion,' which Mr. Unwin, Cowper's correspondent, had given to the mother of one amongst his fellow-travellers, and casting his eye over it hastily, asked Milner what was its character.   ' It is one of the best books ever written,' was his answer; ' let us take it with us and read it on our journey.'   He easily consented, and they read it carefully together, with thus much effect, that he determined at some future season to examine the Scriptures for himself, and see if things were stated there in the same manner.   In this journey he was alone with Milner, and the strong friendship was matured, which lasted to the end of life, between the rough coarse philosopher and the genial and accomplished statesman.

Leaving his family at Nice, he returned to support Mr Pitt's intended motion for parliamentary reform. ' It is,' wrote Mr. Robert Smith, ' a specific proposition to increase the county members, with a plan for diminishing the number of the rotten boroughs.   Pitt declares that he will exert his influence to the uttermost in this measure.   Wyvill is in town, and all the reformers are stirring.'   From Pitt he had already heard the details of his plan; and had been entreated to secure support for it in his own county.· ' Your suggestions to *your party* (which, I believe, is not less numerous in proportion in Yorkshire than in the House of Commons) may be of great use. . . . Your taking some steps may be very material.   Adieu; I must conclude, having no time for foining.'[9] Late in January, he heard again from Mr. Pitt, that a day

[9] Dec. 24, 1784.

was fixed for the discussion of the motion, and he set out at
once to give it his support. The journey across France at
that season of the year was not then accomplished without
some risks. Leaving summer behind them at Nice, they
travelled from Antibes, through eighteen days of snow.
Once upon the hills of Burgundy, as they climbed a frozen
road, the weight of their carriage overpowered the horses,
and it was just running over a frightful precipice, when
Milner, who was walking behind, perceived the danger, and
by a sudden effort of his great strength of muscle arrested
its descent. 'Took up my quarters at Pitt's.—24th. Balloted
into Penryn committee—Pitt's maid burnt my letters'[1]—a
dangerous mistake for the young representative of Yorkshire.
—' March 3. Sawbridge's motion to discontinue the scrutiny
carried by thirty-nine, and Opposition in high spirits—sat
late—did not vote.—10th. Dined Camelford's—" Pitt does
not make friends," and yet, at this period, he sometimes at
least endeavoured to do so.'—' Pitt,' their common friend
Eliot wrote to him just before his return to England, 'has
found time to be very civil and attentive to your favourite,
the Countess of Salisbury (Sally Salisbury). He dined there
about five weeks ago, and, what is almost ridiculous, went to
her twelfth-night ball, very much to the edification of the
butchers and bakers of Hertford and St. Alban's. Steele
showed him about with great propriety, and they became
" sworn brothers to" several "leash of drawers."' — Mr.
Pitt's motion for Reform was fixed for March 23, when,
says Mr. Wilberforce's diary, ' Pitt's Reform put off for want
of a ballot.' They were now closely engaged in perfecting
its details.—' At Pitt's all day—it goes on well—sat up late
chatting with Pitt—his good hopes of the country, and noble,
patriotic heart.—To town—Pitt's—House—Parliamentary
Reform—terribly disappointed and beat.'[2]

During the remainder of the session he attended constantly in his place, and took part in the debates. He lived
too in a constant round of amusement, dining twice or three
times a week with Mr. Pitt—joining in the festivities in
which Dundas delighted at Wimbledon and Richmond; whilst

[1] Diary.   [2] Ib. April 18.

' sitting up all night singing—shirked Duchess of Gordon, at Almack's—danced till five in the morning,' are fair samples of his life. Yet already, amongst these lighter memorials, there appears from time to time a new tone of deeper feeling. ' At the levee, and then dined at Pitt's—sort of cabinet din-·ner—was often thinking that pompous T. and elegant C. would soon appear in the same row with the poor fellow who waited behind their chairs.' But these thoughts exerted as yet no apparent influence upon his conduct.

The session which had been expected to terminate in May was not concluded at the end of June, and before he could leave town on his return to Provence the increasing heat of summer had emptied Nice. He met his mother therefore at Genoa, and on the 11th of July set out thence for Switzerland. They travelled as in their former journey, and Mr. Wilberforce and Milner began to read together the Greek Testament, and to examine carefully the doctrines which it taught. From Genoa they went by Turin to Geneva, travelled through Switzerland, and reached Spa upon September 8th.

His discussions with Isaac Milner were continued throughout this journey, until, ' by degrees,[3] I imbibed his sentiments, though they long remained merely as opinions assented to by my understanding, but not influencing my heart. At length I began to be impressed with a sense of their importance. Milner, though full of levity on all other subjects, never spoke on this but with the utmost seriousness, and all he said tended to increase my attention to religion.' In this state of feeling he arrived at Spa, and spent almost six weeks in that ' curious assemblage from all parts of Europe.' ' I hear of you,' writes Pitt, ' at Spa, where you have free choice at once of all nations in a small compass; at least, a collection of what your friend calls excellent specimens, and which must resemble a little the forest in our own garden of "les peuples végétaux surpris de croitre ensemble." The produce of our revenue is glorious, and I am half mad with a project which will give our supplies the effect almost of magic in the reduction of debt. I hope you will profit

---

[3] MS. Mem.

by the waters. I have been here about three weeks in the en
joyment of exercise and leisure, and eating and drinking things
which to me, from their antiquity, were nearly forgotten, and
for that very reason have the charm of novelty.'[4]

Here he found many of his English friends; and though
on some few points he now controverted their opinions, yet
in general he joined freely in their ordinary pleasures. 'Mrs.
Crewe,' he says, ' cannot believe that I can think it wrong
to go to the play. Surprised at hearing that halting on
the Sunday was my wish, and not my mother's.' Yet
though his outward appearance gave little evidence of their
existence, deeper feelings were at work beneath. [5] 'Often,'
he records, 'while in the full enjoyment of all that this
world could bestow, my conscience told me that, in the true
sense of the word, I was not a Christian. I laughed, I sang,
I was apparently gay and happy, but the thought would
steal across me, " What madness is all this; to continue
easy in a state in which a sudden call out of the world would
consign me to everlasting misery, and that when eternal
happiness is within my grasp !" For I had received into my
understanding the great truths of the gospel. At length such
thoughts as these completely occupied my mind, and I began
to pray earnestly.' 'Began three or four days ago,' he says,
[6] Oct. 25, ' to get up very early. In the solitude and self-
conversation of the morning had thoughts which I trust will
come to something.' ' As soon as I reflected seriously upon
these subjects, the deep guilt and black ingratitude of my
past life forced itself upon me in the strongest colours, and
I condemned myself for having wasted my precious time,
and opportunities, and talents.' Thus he returned home,
already another man in his inner being, yet manifesting out-
wardly so little of the hidden struggle, ' that it was not,' says
one of his companions, ' until many months after our return,
that I learned what had been passing in his mind.'

Upon the 10th of November he reached Wimbledon, and
was much alone, and the more he reflected, the deeper became his new impressions.

---

[4] Brighthelmstone, Sept. 30, 1785.
[5] Mem. of Conversation, and MS. Mem.   [6] Diary.

Whilst this struggle was at its height, he commenced a private journal, with the view of making himself 'humble and watchful.' [7]

'Nov. 24th. Heard the Bible read two hours,—Pascal one hour and a quarter—meditation one hour and a quarter—business the same. Pitt called, and commended Butler's Analogy—resolved to write to him, and discover to him what I am occupied about.'

He wrote accordingly to Mr. Pitt, opening fully the grounds on which he acted, and the bearing of his new principles upon his public conduct—' I told him that though I should ever feel a strong affection for him, and had every reason to believe that I should be in general able to support him, yet that I could no more be so much a party-man as I had been before.' [8] On the 2nd of December ' I got,' he says, ' Pitt's answer—much affected by it—to see him in the morning.' [9] ' It was full of kindness—nothing I had told him, he said, could affect our friendship; that he wished me always to act as I thought right. I had said that I thought when we met we had better not discuss the topics of my letter. " Why not discuss them ? " was his answer; " let me come to Wimbledon to-morrow, to talk them over with you." He thought that I was out of spirits, and that company and conversation would be the best way of dissipating my impressions.' [1] Mr. Pitt came the next morning as he had proposed, and found his friend not unprepared for the discussion. ' I had prayed,' he says, [2] ' to God, I hope, with some sincerity, not to lead me into disputing for my own exaltation, but for His glory. Conversed with Pitt near two hours, and opened myself completely to him. I admitted that as far as I could conform to the world, with a perfect regard to my duty to God, myself, and my fellow-creatures, I was bound to do it; that no inward feelings ought to be taken as demonstrations of the Spirit being in any man, but only the change of disposition and conduct. He tried to reason me out of my convictions, but soon found himself unable to combat their correctness, if Christianity were true. The fact is, he was so absorbed

[7] Journal, Nov. 21.   [8] Con. Mem.
          [9] Diary.   [1] Ib.   [2] Journal.

in politics, that he had never given himself time for due reflection on religion. But, amongst other things, he declared to me, that Bishop Butler's work raised in his mind more doubts than it had answered.' [3]

His relations with Pitt were altogether peculiar. The reserve which clogged even long private intercourse with all his other friends, except his brother-in-law, Eliot, melted away under the fascinations of Wilberforce's society. Whilst, therefore, he often withheld from the rest who stood the closest to him the inner workings of his mind, he habitually opened all his heart to Eliot and Wilberforce. This strong affection survived all the jars of public life, and the strain of a widening diversity of religious views. Pitt's resistance to the influence which, as to these high interests, he might have exerted on him, he always traced to the cold shadow of Bishop Pretyman. It was in the confidence of this affection that Wilberforce, though he had at first shrunk from doing so, now explained himself to Pitt, clinging with the affectionateness of his own nature to his early friend, and longing to draw him into sympathy with his own new-found convictions.

Though he now felt more than ever the need of like-minded associates, he could scarcely bring himself to form such new connections. On the 2nd of December, however, he wrote to Mr. Newton :—

' I wish to have some serious conversation with you, and will take the liberty of calling on you for that purpose, in half-an-hour ; when, if you cannot receive me, you will have the goodness to let me have a letter put into my hands at the door, naming a time and place for our meeting, the earlier the more agreeable to me. I have had ten thousand doubts within myself, whether or not I should discover myself to you ; but every argument against doing it has its foundation in pride. I am sure you will hold yourself bound to let no one living know of this application, or of my visit, till I release you from the obligation.'

This letter he took with him, upon Sunday, Dec. 4th, into the city, and ' delivered it ' himself ' to old Newton at his

[3] Con. Mem.

church.' The following Wednesday was named for an interview; and then, says he,[4] 'after walking about the square once or twice before I could persuade myself, I called upon old Newton—was much affected in conversing with him—something very pleasing and unaffected in him. He told me he always had entertained hopes and confidence that God would some time bring me to Him—that he had heard from J. Thornton we had declined Sunday visits abroad—on the whole he encouraged me—though got nothing new from him, as how could I, except a good hint, that he never found it answer to dispute. When I came away I found my mind in a calm, tranquil state, more humbled, and looking more devoutly up to God.'

Great had been the old man's thankfulness at welcoming such a neophyte. ' The joy,' he writes some years after, ' that I felt, and the hopes I conceived, when you called on me in the vestry of St. Mary's, I shall never forget.'[5] It was a happy choice which sent him to so calm an adviser. There were many then who would have tried to turn him from the public life which was his true vocation. Newton, though a man of no genius, had in his stormy experience of life matured a calm judgment, and he urged now upon the young statesman that he should not hastily form new connections, nor widely separate himself from his former friends. This very day, accordingly, he says, ' as I promised, I went to Pitt's.'

' 7th. At Holwood—up early and prayed—then to the St. Johns' at Beckenham. In chaise opened myself to ——, who had felt much four years ago when very ill. He says that H. took off his then religious feelings—but what did he give him in the room of them?'

A letter[6] from his 'most devoted kinsman,' J. Thornton, gives a good picture of his state at this time. 'You may easier conceive than I can express the satisfaction I had from a few minutes' converse with Mr. Newton yesterday afternoon. As in nature, so in grace, what comes very quickly forward, rarely abides long : I am aware of your difficulties, which call for great prudence and caution. You cannot be

[4] Journal, Dec. 6.   [5] Sept. 1788.   [6] Clapham, Dec. 24.

too wary in forming connections. The fewer new friends, .
the better. I shall at any time be glad to see you here, and
can quarter you, and let you be as retired as possible, and
hope we shall never be on a footing of ceremony.'

'January 11th.' He says, 'To town and Woolnooth—
after church, brought Mr. Newton down in chaise—dined
and slept at Wimbledon—composure and happiness of a true
Christian. 12th. Newton staid—T. A. surprised us together
on the common in the evening. Expect to hear myself now
universally given out to be a Methodist: may God grant it
may be said with truth.'

He assured his mother, who had been alarmed by such a
rumour, that she need not fear his meaning to shut himself
up either in his closet in town, or in his hermitage in the
country. 'This would merit no better name than desertion;
and if I were thus to fly from the post where Providence
has placed me, I know not how I could look for the blessing
of God upon my retirement; and without this heavenly assistance, either in the world or in solitude, our own endeavours
will be equally ineffectual.'[7]

This is not the heated tone of enthusiasm, but the sober
reality of a reasonable faith. It was to a gradual work that
he looked forward.

'Watch and pray,' he wrote earnestly to his sister;[8] 'read
the word of God, imploring that true wisdom which may
enable you to comprehend and fix it in your heart, that it
may gradually produce its effect under the operation of the
Holy Spirit, in renewing the mind and purifying the conduct.
This it will do more and more the longer we live under its
influence: and it is to the honour of religion, that those who
when they first began to run the Christian course, were in
extremes — enthusiastical perhaps, or rigidly severe — will
often by degrees lose their several imperfections: . . . . like
some of our Westmoreland evenings, when though in the
course of the day the skies have been obscured by clouds
and vapours, yet towards its close the sun beams forth with
unsullied lustre, and descends below the horizon in the full
display of all his glories: shall I pursue the metaphor, just

[7] Feb. 19.   [8] May 21.

to suggest, that this is the earnest of a joyful rising, which will not be disappointed? By the power of habit which God has been graciously pleased to bestow upon us, our work will every day become easier, if we accustom ourselves to cast our care on him, and labour in a persuasion of his co-operation. The true Christian will desire to have constant communion with his Saviour. The eastern nations had their talismans, which were to advertise them of every danger, and guard them from every mischief. Be the love of Christ our talisman.'

He who thus sought for peace, could not fail to find it. Upon Good Friday, April 14, he for the first time communicated; and upon the following Easter Sunday enters in his journal: 'At Stock with the Unwins—day delightful, out almost all of it—communicated—very happy.'

'It is more than a month,' he writes to his sister,[9] 'since I slept out of town, and I feel all that Milton attributes to the man who has been

> 'long in populous cities pent,
> Where houses thick and sewers annoy the air.'

I scarce recollect to have spent so pleasant a day as that which is now nearly over. My heart opens involuntarily to Unwin and his wife; I fancy I have been with them every day since we first became acquainted at Nottingham, and expand to them with all the confidence of a twelve years' intimacy. The day has been delightful. I was out before six, and made the fields my oratory, the sun shining as bright and as warm as at Midsummer. I think my own devotions become more fervent when offered in this way amidst the general chorus, with which all nature seems on such a morning to be swelling the song of praise and thanksgiving. Surely this sabbath, of all others, calls forth these feelings in a supreme degree; a frame of united love and triumph well becomes it, and holy confidence and unrestrained affection.'

The sky was brightening over him into clear sunshine. 'By degrees,' he said in the calm retrospect of a peaceful age, 'the promises and offers of the gospel produced in me

---

[9] Stock, April 16, 1786.

something of a settled peace of conscience. I devoted myself for whatever might be the term of my future life, to the service of my God and Saviour, and with many infirmities and deficiencies, through his help, I continue until this day.'

CHAPTER IV.

APRIL 1786 TO SEPTEMBER 1787.

Registry Bill—Gives up his villa at Wimbledon—Journal—Intercourse with his family and friends—Employment of time—Visit to Bath— Returns to London, February, 1787—State of religion—Resolves to attempt its revival—Society for the Reformation of Manners—He visits the bishops and establishes the association.

IN the spring of 1786, Mr. Wilberforce returned an altered man to the House of Commons. There were indeed no external symptoms to announce the change which had passed over him. 'Though I had told Pitt,' he says, 'that I could not promise him unqualified support, I was surprised to find how generally we agreed.' Yet many silent intimations now bespoke the presence of higher motives than a mere desire of personal distinction. In this very session he was diligently occupied with two important measures. Hopeless, after Mr. Pitt's failure, of at present carrying any general measure of parliamentary reform, he applied himself to introduce some practical improvements into the representation of the people. The plan which he proposed was aimed directly at purifying county elections, by providing a general registration of the freeholders, and holding the poll in various places at the same time.

He had at first proposed to limit his attempt to Yorkshire, which chiefly needed such a change; but at the request of Lord Mahon, its mover, who during this session succeeded to a seat in the Upper House, he undertook the conduct of a general measure to the same effect : ' Fought through Lord Stanhope's bill,' he says, May 15th. In the House of

Lords it was afterwards defeated, 'by a coalition of the King's friends and the Whig aristocracy.'[1]

In the latter part of the session Mr. Wilberforce, who delighted in escaping for a single night from London, 'began to sleep constantly at Wimbledon;' yet thinking it an unfavourable 'situation for his servants,' a needless increase of his personal expenses, and a cause of some loss of time, he determined to forego in future the luxury of such a villa. The influence of his new principles was rapidly pervading all his conduct.

'To endeavour from this moment,' he says, June 21st, 'to amend my plan for time. I hope to live more than heretofore to God's glory and my fellow-creatures' good, and to keep my heart more diligently. Books to be read—Locke's Essay—Marshall's Logic—Indian Reports. To keep a proposition book with an index—a friend's book' (*i.e.* memoranda to render his intercourse with them more useful according to their characters and circumstances)—'a commonplace book, serious and profane—a Christian-duty paper. To try this plan for a fortnight, and then make alterations in it as I shall see fit. To animate myself to a strict observance of my rules by thinking of what Christ did and suffered for us; and that this life will soon be over, when a sabbath will remain for the people of God.'

With the close of the session 'I got·off at last from town,' says the diary. 'July 6th. Slept at Pepper's,[2] Highgate; and Friday at Grantham; thence through Hull to Scarborough.' Here he joined his mother and sister, and with them the following week arrived at Wilford, the seat of his cousin, Mr. Samuel Smith. His first care was to recommend his new opinions by greater kindness in domestic life. Rumours of his altered habits had preceded his arrival, and his mother was prepared to mourn over eccentric manners and enthusiastic principles. All that she observed was greater kindness and evenness of temper. 'It may tend,' he had written down before he joined her as his rule, 'to remove prejudices of. . . . if I am more kind and affectionate

---

[1] Wyvill's Parliamentary Papers, vol. iv. p. 542.
[2] Pepper Arden's.

than ever — consult her more — show respect for her judg
ment, and manifest rather humility in myself than dissatisfaction concerning others.' His habitual cheerfulness, and the
patient forbearance of a temper naturally quick, could not
escape her notice; and a friend who had shared in her
suspicions, remarked shrewdly, when they parted company
at Scarborough, 'If this is madness, I hope that he will
bite us all.' At Wilford he remained almost two months,
diligently employing the quiet time afforded him by its retirement. The entrance of God's word into his heart gave
light to his intellectual as well as to his moral nature.
A keen remembrance of wasted time, and a sense of his
deficiency in the power of steady application, led him to
set about the task of self-education. Various and accurate
were now his studies, but the book which he studied most
carefully, and by which, above all others, his mental faculties were ripened, was the Holy Scripture. This he read
and weighed and pondered over, studying its connection
and details, and mastering, especially in their own tongue,
the apostolical epistles. This was his chief occupation at
Wilford. It was now his daily care to instruct his understanding and discipline his heart. It was no easy path upon
which he had set out, and his progress was the fruit of unremitting toil and watchfulness. 'To form,' he writes, ' my
plan as carefully as I can. Think how to serve those in the
house — in the village — your constituents. Look to God
through Christ. . . . . How does my experience convince
me that true religion is communion with God. Frequent
aspirations. To call in at some houses in the village.
To endeavour to keep my mind in a calm, humble frame—
not too much vivacity. To put my prayers into words
to prevent wandering. Consider always before you take
up any book what is your peculiar object in reading it,
and keep that in view. To trust less to my own resolutions, and more to Christ.'[3]

'Above all, let me watch and pray with unremitting fervency.
When tempted, recollect that Christ, who was also tempted,
sympathises with thy weakness, and that he stands ready

[3] Journal, Aug. 4.

to support thee, if thou wilt sincerely call on him for help.'[4]

'I have often meditated,' he wrote upon October 20, 'from the king's highway,' to Lord Muncaster, 'and still more fre- quently longed for, an excursion into your wondrous country; but have not been able to gratify my wishes, and am now bound for the south. . . . I have been for a few days at Leeds, consulting Mr. Hey. . . . He thinks I have suffered by living too low; and advises that I should try the Bath water, and this I shall possibly do before the meeting of Parliament, though my motions are somewhat uncertain, for they will partly depend on the state in which I find poor Eliot and Pitt. I well know how feelingly you have sympa- thised with them.[5] I don't believe there ever existed between brother and sister a more affectionate attachment than between Pitt and Lady Harriet. Public business, however, will be an assistance to him in getting over the shock, by necessarily calling him from his own melancholy reflections; but I fear it will go hard with Eliot, whose natural temper is ill-calculated for bearing up against such a stroke. If either of them should be in such a state as that I should think my company would be of material service, I shall dedicate my- self to this employment.

'O my dear Muncaster, how can we go on as if present things were to last for ever, when so often reminded by acci- dents like these, "that the fashion of this world passes away!"'

He was soon fixed at Bath, watching his own heart as carefully amongst its crowded scenes, as he had done in the domestic privacy of Wilford. 'Walk charitably,' he writes down as his law; 'wherever you are be on your guard, remembering that your conduct and conversation may have some effect on the minds of those with whom you are, in rendering them more or less inclined to the reception of Christian principles, and the practice of a Christian life. Be ready with subjects for conversation, and for private thought.'[6]

Early in the following year he was again in London,

---

[4] Journal, Oct. 8.
[5] Lady Harriet Eliot, second daughter of the first Lord Chatham, died Sept. 25, 1786.   [6] Journal.

attending in his place in Parliament, and holding his own amidst those keen encounters in which, according to Lord Monboddo's description, ' Pitt spoke, Fox barked, and Lord North screamed and groaned'—adding that he ' could have had no conception of such a man as Pitt living in modern times: he really spoke as Demosthenes and Cicero wrote : he spoke in periods and in language in which no other man could either speak or write.'[7]   His chief exertions in the House this session were efficient speeches in behalf of Mr. Pitt's treaties with France[8] and Portugal ;[9] and upon the impeachment of Mr. Warren Hastings.[1]   But his thoughts were principally occupied through this spring in concerting measures for a public effort at reforming manners.   The utter irreligion which so soon afterwards produced in France its deadly fruits of bloodshed and horror, had to no slight degree spread amongst ourselves.   He had been roused out of the prevalent lethargy, and when he looked around him on society, he saw how universal was the evil from which he had himself escaped.   Nor could he wonder that the gay and busy world were almost ignorant of Christianity, amidst the lukewarmness and apathy which possessed the very watchmen of the faith.   The deadly leaven of Hoadley's latitudinarian views had spread to an alarming extent amongst the clergy ; and whilst numbers confessedly agreed with his Socinian tenets, few were sufficiently honest to resign with Mr. Lindsey[2] the endowments of the Church.   The zealous spirit which had begun to spread during the reign of Anne,[3] had been benumbed by this evil influence.   No efforts were now made to disseminate in foreign lands the gospel of Christ.   At home a vast population was springing up in our metropolis, and around our manufactories, but there was no thought of providing for them church accommodation or spiritual oversight.   Non-residence without scruple was spreading through the Church ; and all the cords of moral obligation were relaxed as the spirit of religion slumbered.

---

[7] Letter from Hawkins Brown to W. W., June, 1787.

[8] Feb. 6.   [9] Feb. 15.   [1] Feb. 7.

[2] The Rev. Theophilus Lindsey had resigned the living of Catterick in 1773.   Sup. p. 76.

[3] Vide Nelson's *Address to Persons of Quality.*

Against this universal apathy John Wesley had recently arisen with a giant's strength. But his mission was chiefly to the poor, and his measures, even from the first, tended to foster a sectarian spirit. There was needed some reformer of the nation's morals, who should raise his voice in the high places of the land; and do within the Church, and near the throne, what Wesley had accomplished in the meeting-house, and amongst the multitude. To this high and self-denying office God put it into the heart of his servant to aspire. 'God,' he says, 'has set before me as my object the reformation of [my country's] manners.'[4] Having once accepted this commission, he devoted all his powers to its fulfilment, and for years kept it steadily in view in all his undertakings. His first attempt was to form, on the model of one which, in 1692, had done good service, a Society for the Reformation of Manners, to resist the spread of open immorality, 'an object worthy of the labours of a whole life.'[5] In this zealous spirit he undertook the work. He endeavoured to infuse amongst his numerous friends a determination to resist the growing vices of the times. 'The most effectual way,' he tells one of them,[6] 'to prevent crime, is by endeavouring to repress that general spirit of licentiousness, which is the parent of every species of vice.'

With this view he obtained the issue of a Royal Proclamation against vice and immorality, and then suggested the formation of his proposed association to carry it into effect.

'It would give you no little pleasure,' he tells Mr. Hey,[7] 'could you hear how warmly the Archbishop of Canterbury expresses himself: and he assures me that one still greater, to whom he has opened the subject in form, is deeply impressed with the necessity of opposing the torrent of profaneness which every day makes more rapid advances.'

His first object was to prevail upon the bishops to become members of the association; and for this he trusted much to the effect of personal intercourse with them.

Upon the 21st of June therefore, he set off from London and visited in succession the prelates of Worcester, Hereford,

<hr />

[4] Journal.   [5] June 12.   [6] Mr. Wyvill.
[7] London, May 29, 1789.

Norwich, Lincoln, York, and Lichfield,[8] and gained many to his scheme. He called too upon many influential laymen. At Norwich he lingered a whole day in the hope of seeing Windham, and was followed after his departure by a friendly letter.

'I have seldom felt more vexed,' writes Mr. Windham, 'than I do at this instant, at hearing that you have left Norwich about half-an-hour. Among other losses I am to regret that of not being made acquainted with your plan, in which I may venture almost to promise beforehand that I shall be happy to concur.'

In his various applications he was no stranger to refusals. —'So you wish,' said a nobleman whose house he visited, 'to be a reformer of men's morals. Look then, and see there what is the end of such reformers,' pointing as he spoke to a picture of the crucifixion—no likely argument to daunt a follower of the Cross. Yet though sometimes opposed, upon the whole his plan succeeded. One, at least, amongst his earlier associates joined him heartily, and long discharged the somewhat irksome service of a regular com- mittee-man. Affliction had opened the heart of Mr. Eliot to the healing power of true religion, and the regard which had long subsisted between them ripened into the full blessing of Christian friendship. 'I am glad,' he writes,[9] 'you have found so much success in your plan. I am not only willing but desirous of joining myself to it. Lord North's name is sufficient to obviate one difficulty I had respecting it ; and for the other, every day decreases it. I have every day less fear of my temper of mind being thought a transitory effect of grief: I feel myself every day looking upon my condition here with more steadiness and resignation, and to a future life with more earnestness and desire. God bless you, and make you happy here, as well as hereafter ; you have not re- quired a visitation of providence to turn you to your God.'

The society was soon in active and useful operation. The Duke of Montagu opened his house for its reception, and

[8] He had designed to visit Chester, but a favourable answer from the bishop (Porteus) met him on the road.
[9] Aug. 29.

presided over its meetings—a post which was filled after his death by the Lord (Chancellor) Bathurst, who was followed by Bishop Porteus: and before its dissolution it had obtained many valuable acts of Parliament, and greatly checked the spread of blasphemous and indecent publications.

CHAPTER V.

SEPTEMBER 1787 TO DECEMBER 1788.

Retirement at Bath—Causes which led him to the Abolition of the Slave Trade—Pitt's advice—Slave Trade Committee formed—Negociation on the subject with France—His habits in London—Burke—Pitt's interest in the abolition — Evidence before privy council — Wilberforce dangerously ill, and compelled to postpone his motion to the next year—Middle-Passage Bill—Cambridge—Westmoreland—King's illness.

THE autumn of this year was spent by Mr. Wilberforce at Bath. 'I find here,' writes Hannah More, 'a great many friends; but those with whom I have chiefly passed my time are Mr. Wilberforce's family. That young gentleman's character is one of the most extraordinary I ever knew for talents, virtue, and piety. It is difficult not to grow wiser and better every time one converses with him.' He was now seriously preparing for the great work of his life, the abolition of the Slave Trade. This was one fruit of his religious change. The miseries of Africa had long ago attracted his attention. Even in his boyhood he had written on the subject for the daily journals. 'It is,' he has said in conversation, 'indicative of the providential impulses by which we are led into particular lines of conduct, that, as early as the year 1780, I had been strongly interested for the West Indian slaves, and I expressed my hope, that I should redress the wrongs of those wretched beings.' In November, 1783, he records a conversation concerning the condition of the negroes with Mr. Ramsay, who was then publishing the work from which sprung the long and bitter controversy which first brought the question forward. Through the years 1784 and 1785, Mr.

Ramsay fought alone in this holy cause, nor did he quit the strife until he sunk under its virulence in the summer of 1789.

William Wilberforce was endowed with many natural qualifications for the conduct of such a cause. His glowing and persuasive eloquence, his high political influence, combined with unusual independence, marked him out for a leader in such a work. Yet at this time he wanted that one requisite without which all the rest would have proved insufficient. Personal ambition and generous impulses would have shrunk from the greatness of the undertaking, or wearied in the protracted struggle, and these had been till now the main springs of his conduct. ' The first years that I was in Parliament,' he has said, ' I did nothing to any good purpose ; my own distinction was my object.' But now he acted upon new principles ; he regarded his powers of mind, his eloquence in speech, his influence with Mr. Pitt, his general popularity, as talents lent to him by God, for the due use of which he must render an account. Now, therefore, his previous imaginative interest in the condition of the West Indian slaves led to practical exertion. 'God,'—he says, in undertaking what became at once a sacred charge,—' God has set before me two great objects, the suppression of the slave trade and the reformation of manners.[1] In this spirit he approached the strife, and let it never be forgotten, that it was a belief in God's call which armed him for his championship of the liberty of the oppressed.

It was with no inconsiderate haste that he undertook the cause. ' It was the condition of the West Indian slaves which first drew my attention, and it was in the course of my inquiry that I was led to Africa and the abolition.'[2] These inquiries he was busily pursuing amongst the African merchants throughout the year 1786. ' I found them,' he says,[3] ' at this time ready to give me information freely, the trade not having yet become the subject of alarming discussion. I got also together at my house from time to time persons who knew anything about the matter. Several of us met at breakfast at Sir C. Middleton's : also at Mr. Bennet

---

[1] Journal, Sunday, Oct. 28, 1787.
[2] Letter to James Stephen, Esq., Jan. 15, 1817.   [3] MS. Mem.

Langton's, and at my own house.' 'When I had acquired so much information, I began to talk the matter over with Pitt and Grenville. Pitt recommended me to undertake its conduct, as a subject suited to my character and talents. At length, I well remember, after a conversation in the open air at the root of an old tree at Holwood just above the steep descent into the vale of Keston, I resolved to give notice on a fit occasion in the House of Commons of my intention to bring the subject forward.' The 'old tree' has been identified by the careful scrutiny of his kinsman the Earl of Stanhope, who with pious zeal has placed beside it a solid stone seat, with an appropriate inscription, that the memory of such a discourse between two such men might be literally graven upon the rock. In the spring of 1787, Mr. Clarkson, who had published a Prize Essay upon the subject in the preceding year, was in London, and was introduced to Mr. Wilberforce ; but though they frequently conversed upon the subject, Mr. Wilberforce never divulged his own determination, until he avowed it at Mr. Bennet Langton's table, in answer to a question from his host.

Important consequences followed this avowal. A growing interest in the question had already arisen simultaneously in many different places. Several humane men had been for months communicating upon the subject, who now determined upon immediate action, and formed themselves into a committee to raise the funds and collect the information necessary for procuring the abolition of the trade. Their first meeting was held upon May 22, 1787, when Granville Sharpe was elected chairman of the twelve who met together, most of whom were London merchants, and all but two Quakers. This body soon increased and grew into a valuable ally of Mr. Wilberforce. His name was not at first enrolled amongst their number, because his independent exertions promised to be more effectual; but from the first he directed their endeavours.[4] They had amongst them patient, resolute men, who had solemnly devoted themselves to this cause, and whom nothing would turn aside from it. Chief amongst them stood Thomas Clarkson,

[4] Vide MS. transactions of the Abolition Society.

whose name is imperishably connected with this holy cause.
By their means evidence upon the subject was obtained in
Liverpool and Bristol; contributions were raised to defray
the general expenses of the cause, and they became a central body, from which emanated many similar societies in
the chief provincial towns. 'At this place,' writes a correspondent from Manchester, 'large subscriptions have been
raised for the slave business, and, "te duce, Teucro," we are
warm and strenuous.'[5]   Their great work, and that in
which this year they actively engaged, was to rouse the
slumbering indignation of the country against the cruelty of
the traffic. And here was felt the exceeding importance
of their leader's character. In the year 1780, the slave trade
had attracted Mr. Burke's attention, and he had even proceeded to sketch out a code of regulations which provided
for its immediate mitigation and ultimate suppression. But
after mature consideration he had abandoned the attempt,
from the conviction that the strength of the West Indian
body would defeat the utmost efforts of his powerful party,
and cover them with ruinous unpopularity. Nor could any
mere political alliance have been ever more likely to succeed.
The powerful interests with which the battle must be fought
could be resisted only by the general moral feeling of the
nation. There was then no example upon record of any
such achievement, and in entering upon the struggle it was
of the utmost moment that its leader should be one who
could combine, and so render irresistible, the scattered sympathies of all the religious classes. Granville Sharpe, the
chairman of the London committee, did not fail to point out
this advantage. 'Mr. W.,' he writes, 'is to introduce the
business to the House. His position as member for the
largest county, the great influence of his personal connections, added to an amiable and unblemished character,
secure every advantage to the cause.' Its first supporters,
accordingly, were not found amongst the partisans of political commotion, but amongst the educated and religious
classes. 'Many of the clergy,' writes Granville Sharpe, 'are

[5] Letter from T. B. Bayley, Esq., to W. Wilberforce, Esq., Dec. 15,
1787.

firm and cordial friends to the undertaking:' and soon after
he rejoices 'in their continual support.'

In this early stage of deliberation, the importance of procuring the concurrence of our foreign neighbours was evident
to Mr. Wilberforce; and from the friendly relations which
at this time subsisted with the court of Versailles, he hoped
that France might be induced to unite with England in this
work. To promote this union, he proposed to Mr. (afterwards Lord) Grenville to go with him to Paris in the December of 1787:—

'I would have answered'[6] (is the reply to his proposal)
'your letter yesterday, but that I waited for an opportunity
of speaking to Pitt upon the subject. I have seen him to-
day, and talked with him upon it, and he entirely agrees with
me in the opinion that no advantage could be derived from
a journey to Paris, for the purpose.'

It was therefore laid aside, and he was established in
Palace Yard for the season. Though the alteration in his
principles had led him to devote to higher objects the time
which had of old been wasted in the frivolities of fashionable life, yet he by no means withdrew from intercourse
with society. He began at this time a habit which he long
maintained, of calling upon his different friends, on those
evenings in which he was not occupied by the House of
Commons business, and thus reserved his mornings for
severer occupations. His relations with Mr. Pitt were as
intimate as ever. 'They were,' says one who often witnessed
their familiar intercourse, 'exactly like brothers.'—'Dined
at Pitt's,' says the diary of this date. 'Called in at Pitt's at
seven, for a short time; and staid supper—Apsley, Pitt, and
I.' 'Pitt, Bearcroft, Graham, &c. &c., dined with me.'
'Pitt's before House—dined.' 'After House to Pitt's—supped.' 'Jan. 29. Burke, Sir G. Elliot, St. Andrew St. John
dined with me. First not in spirits.' To these entertainments given once each session to Mr. Burke he has often
referred with satisfaction. 'Parr ill-naturedly endeavoured
to revive a difference which had existed between Burke and
myself in 1787. It was during the period of his violent

[6] Whitehall, Dec. 18, 1787.

attacks on Pitt.   He had delivered a most intemperate in-
vective against the French Navigation Treaty; a measure
which was particularly welcome to many of my Yorkshire
constituents.   In reply to him I said, " We can make allowance for the hon. gentleman, because we remember him in
better days."   The sarcasm, though not unkindly meant, and
called for, as Pitt declared in the debate, by Burke's outrageous violence, yet so exactly described the truth, that it
greatly nettled him.   But it soon passed over, and I had
peculiar pleasure in his dinners with me, as an evidence of
our perfect harmony.   He was a great man—I never could
understand how he grew to be at one time so entirely
neglected.   In part undoubtedly it was, that, like Mackintosh afterwards, he was above his audience.   He had come
late into Parliament, and had had time to lay in vast stores of
knowledge.   The field from which he drew his illustrations
was magnificent.   Like the fabled object of the fairy's
favours, whenever he opened his mouth, pearls and diamonds
dropped from him.'

Mr. Wilberforce's general intercourse with society was now
made subservient to the interests of the Abolition cause.
' Mr. Hartley, African, &c., breakfasted with me.'—' Dined
Braithwaite's—Sir P. Gibbs—Archedeckne—James Grenville
— Slave Trade — Archedeckne warm.'—' Collins, Ramsay,
Edwards, Gordons, supped—Slave Trade discussed '— are
amongst his daily entries.   He had given notice in the House
of Commons of his intended motion on the subject for February 22, and the prospect of immediate success had not
as yet been clouded over.   'The cause of our poor Africans,'
he writes on January 25, to Mr. Wyvill, 'goes on most prosperously.   I trust there is little reason to doubt of the motion
for the Abolition being carried in Parliament.   But it is highly
desirable that the public voice should be exerted in our support as loudly and as universally as possible.   Many places
and some counties have already determined on petitions to
Parliament, and I should be sorry that our little kingdom
should be backward.'

' It would delight you to hear Pitt talk on this question.'
Long and frequent were his conferences with Mr. Pitt upon

the conduct of the case.   Entries like the following now
occur frequently in his diary :—' Unwell, and so did not dine
at Pitt's, but met Ramsay there in the evening and discussed;' and again, 'Called at Pitt's at night — he firm
about African trade, though we begin to perceive more difficulties in the way than we had hoped there would be.'
How fully Pitt entered into the details of the question may
be seen in the following characteristic letter :—

' In thinking over the difficulty respecting the African
business, it has occurred to me to be very material to ascertain whether a large proportion of the slaves now annually
imported into the West Indies may not be for the purpose
of bringing each year new lands into cultivation.   I believe
this has been a good deal the case, particularly in Dominica,
St. Vincent's, and Grenada.   You will see immediately the
use of this proposition, if it can be made out.

' If you could contrive to come here to-night or to-morrow,
I would stay another day quietly in the country, and should
like extremely to have a full prose on all this business.   Remember you owe me at least a week.'[7]

With such interest and care had Mr. Pitt already entered
upon this subject, yet such was his constitutional reserve,
that to Mr. Clarkson, when admitted to a personal interview
on Mr. W.'s introduction, a month after this time, he appeared so ignorant of the facts and dead to the merits of the
case, that his visitor recorded, ' In this interview I had
given birth in the minister to an interest in our cause.'

Mr. Pitt's heartiness in the cause has been often questioned.
It is true that his government, as a body, were not in its favour.
' This,' says Mr. Wilberforce, ' has afforded to his enemies a
plausible, though certainly no just, ground for doubting his
sincerity.   What shall, and what shall not be, a government
question, is not an arbitrary arrangement dependent on the
part of the minister—it turns upon the question, Is the sta-
bility of the ministry at stake?   In the instance, therefore,
of my motion, as on Pitt's own motion for the improvement
of the Poor Laws, every one was perfectly at liberty to vote
as he saw fit.   It was in no sense a party question.'

[7] Holwood, Tuesday, Jan. 29.

It had now become clear that the trade had struck its roots so deep into the commercial interests of the country, that it would not fall before a single blow.   A great body of facts must be collected on which to base the attack.   To procure this evidence Mr. Pitt consented that the Privy Council should examine, as a board of trade, into our commerce with Africa.

The first witnesses before the Privy Council were those deputed by the African merchants.   They undertook to establish not only the necessity, but the absolute humanity, of the trade.

At this important moment, it seemed but too probable that Mr. Wilberforce would be withdrawn for ever from the conduct of the cause.   It was in spite of the hinderances of a delicate constitution that all his labours were performed ; but in the course of this spring his health appeared entirely to fail, from an absolute decay of the digestive organs.   On the last day of January he says in his diary, after many previous records of indifferent health, ' Very unwell, so did not dine at Pitt's, but met Ramsay there in the evening and discussed.   Did not go to House.'   This attack passed off after a few days, but within three weeks he experienced a relapse. Feb. 22nd, he records : ' Feverishness very troublesome— all last night no sleep—constant thirst and heat.—23rd. Called at Pitcairne's—worse—never stirred out after this morning until March 1, when Milner came, having put off his lectures, &c., to see how I was going on.—March 3. Head utterly unfit for business all this time.   All my friends very kind, and Muncaster anxiety itself.—4th.   At P.'s request went to Clapham, but returned next day.—5th. I thank God I mend—get out an airing middle of the day when fine.' On the 8th his complaint returned with increased violence.

' March 27.   Friends forced me to call in Warren with Pitcairne.   Muncaster and Montagu most tenderly assiduous in watching me during the course of my illness, and the rest of my friends universally kind.'

His disorder had assumed the character of an entire decay of all the vital functions.   A consultation of the chief physicians of the day ended in the declaration to his family,

' That he had not stamina to last a fortnight.' Judging the case to be beyond the skill of the masters of human art, they decently dismissed their patient to the Bath waters. He complied with their desire, but soberly forecasting the doubtful issue of his sickness, first saw Pitt, and obtained from him a promise that he would charge himself with the interests of the Abolition cause. Satisfied with this pledge he set out for Bath, which he reached upon April 5, in a state of extreme exhaustion.

Upon this promise Mr. Pitt at once acted so far as to superintend, with the help of Bishop Porteus, the Privy Council inquiries which were now in progress. Meanwhile the session of Parliament was advancing, and the country adherents of the Abolition, who had sent no less than one hundred petitions to the House of Commons, began to grow impatient of delay. Some of them even wrote to suggest the propriety of immediate action under another leader. The London committee restrained their eagerness by suggesting to them the evil of any alteration in its conduct; adding that, ' if Mr. Wilberforce was at last unable to resume his post, they should leave to him the selection of his substitute.' At the same time (April 11) they wrote to Mr. Wilberforce for his directions as to their conduct ' in this emergency.' This communication reached him when reduced to such a state that he could not read any letter upon business. His friends, therefore, judging for him that the proper time was come, wrote in his name to Mr. Pitt,[8] and committed the cause to him. Upon this call Mr. Pitt immediately acted. Upon April 22, Mr. Granville Sharpe reported to the committee that he had been sent for by the minister, and officially informed of the pledge which he had given to his friend. Upon May 9, accordingly, Mr. Pitt moved a resolution binding the House to consider the Slave Trade early in the following session. In the debate, Mr. Fox said he had ' almost made up his mind to immediate abolition,' Mr. Burke was its declared advocate, and twelve members avowed themselves its earnest supporters.

[8] The letter was written by Mrs. Wilberforce, Miss Bird, and Mr. Hawkins Brown.

The representatives of slave-trading Liverpool were alone found bold enough to intimate dissent; yet even then were heard whispers of that commercial ruin which was soon afterwards predicted in so confident a tone. The danger of such discussions was prophetically announced, and 'Mr. Wilberforce for negro' affirmed to be already in the island of Grenada the secret watchword of servile insurrection. All the friends of Abolition were warm in lamenting Mr. Wilberforce's illness, and his consequent absence. 'It is better,' said Mr. Fox, 'that the cause should be in his hands than in mine; from him I honestly believe that it will come with more weight, more authority, and more probability of success.' One important measure of practical relief was carried during this session. 'Some of our principal supporters,' says Mr. Wilberforce, 'one of whom was the venerable Sir W. Dolben, were led by curiosity to inspect with their own eyes the actual state of a slave ship then fitting out in the river Thames. They came back to the House of Commons with a description which produced one universal feeling of pity, shame, and indignation. In particular they found, in contradiction of the confident assertion that self-interest would secure kind treatment to these wretched victims of avarice, that they were crowded into a space so miserably small, as exceedingly to aggravate their sufferings, and cause, from the spread of infectious sickness, a prodigious mortality. At once it was resolved, that such enormities should not exist unchecked even for another session; and a bill, limiting the number of slaves, and providing some precautions against their sufferings, was proposed and carried by a large majority.'

This bill was introduced upon May 1. The slave merchants opposed it fiercely. But though they used every manœuvre known in House of Commons' tactics, they were defeated by a large majority, and on June 10 the bill was carried to the House of Lords. There it met with more dangerous opposition. The Lord Chancellor Thurlow exhausted in assailing it all that fertility of objection and hardihood in assertion which marked his rugged character; and the name of Rodney may be found amongst its most vehement opposers. It passed the Upper House by a decided though reduced majority, and received the royal assent upon July 11.

Mr. Wilberforce watched the contest patiently at a distance. Contrary to all expectation he was visibly gaining strength at Bath. His returning health was in great measure the effect of a sparing use of opium, a medicine which even Dr. Pitcairne's authority could scarcely make him use. As a stimulant he never knew its effect, nor in twenty years did he increase the dose. ' If I take,' he would often say, 'but a single glass of wine, I can feel its effect; but I never know, by my feelings, when I have taken my medicine.' Its intermission was at once followed by the recurrence of disorder.

On May 5 he left Bath for Cambridge, performing the journey leisurely, sometimes upon horseback, and sometimes in his carriage with his own horses. 'May 7. Through Aylesbury to Dunstable. Mounted on horseback for the first time these I know not how many months.'

Upon May 8 he reached Cambridge, and after dining with Isaac Milner proceeded to St. John's College, where he was hospitably received by Dr. Chevalier at the Lodge. Upon June 7 he reviews the month which he had spent at the University. 'Lived more regularly and quietly than I had done for a long time. Chiefly with Milner in the evenings. Dined commonly in Hall—Bishop of Llandaff dined twice. In health mended. Quartered at the Lodge, where very comfortable. I always passed my Sundays pleasantly.'

Still he says of College society, 'They were not what I had expected; they had neither the solidity of judgment possessed by ordinary men of business, nor the refined feelings and elevated principles which become a studious and sequestered life.

Leaving Cambridge he set out for Westmoreland. Reached Kendal on June 17, and after a short tour amongst the lakes, was settled in the house he had for some years rented at Rayrigg.

One of his objects in this visit to the lakes was to enjoy, amidst his favourite scenes, the society of Pitt, who 'pro-

mised to steal down for a few days.' This excursion, which
had been planned and interrupted in the former year, was
this summer also prevented by the pressure of public business ; but his house was thronged, the whole summer
through, with a succession of other guests. 'July 3. Passing
through Bowness see Duchess of Gordon's carriage, and she
and Lady Charlotte at the window before we could finish
dinner. Their tapping at our low window announced that
they had discovered our retreat, and would take no denial.
I went to them and told the Duchess, I cannot see you here ;
I have with me my old mother, who being too infirm to make
new acquaintances, is no more in your way than you are in
hers.[9] Milner and I went and supped with them at Low
Wood. — 4th. Morning—Duchess of Gordon—walked to
Rydale. Curious conversation respecting Dundas.' The
Duchess sought to heal, through Mr. Wilberforce's influence
with Mr. Pitt, a misunderstanding with Mr. Dundas, through
whom 'the rays of regal bounty' then shone in the north.
'She pressed us to go with her to Keswick, but I expect
Lord Camden, who accordingly (Saturday, the 5th) comes
to dinner.—Sunday, 6th. Camden off early.—7th. Balgonies
came.—10th. Muncaster came. He a most warm-hearted
and affectionate creature.—22nd. Bishop Llandaff dined and
slept.—24th. Bishop off about twelve.—31st. Scott, Law,
and other lawyers came. August 4th. Duncombe and Mason
came. Lionized Waterheard, Ulswater, &c.'[1]

This constant stream of company continued until his
leaving Westmoreland about the middle of September. His
friends delighted in sharing with him the day's excursions
and the evening's converse, prolonged often with unflagging
gaiety till midnight. 'Here I am,' says Mr. Canning in a
letter of September 4, 1814, 'on Winandermere lake, not
far from the inn at Bowness, where in old time, I am told,
you used to read aloud all night, to the great disturbance
of the then landlady and her family.' As his character had
risen, his delight in the beauties of nature had increased.
'I never enjoyed the country more than during this visit,
when in the early morning I used to row out alone, and

[9] Con. Mem.   [1] Diary.

find an oratory under one of the woody islands in the middle of the lake.'

With all these interruptions of society he let slip no opportunity of doing good. The Duchess of Gordon hears from the chance mouth of ' a poor man ' at Windermere, that he ' does a vast of good.'[2] Still his experience of that summer led him to resolve to sacrifice this favourite residence, and he gave up the house, when his lease determined, in the following spring.

Throughout this time, he directed the operations of the London Committee for procuring the Abolition of the Slave Trade ; and seized every opening to advance the cause. It was of great moment to gain as much support as possible in the following session ; and to secure the influence of Lord Lonsdale (the exact number of whose subject votes is recorded in his homely soubriquet of the Premier's Cat-o'-nine-tails) was of the first importance. With a view to this, he resolved to visit Lowther Castle before he quitted Westmoreland.   ' I cannot but too well remember,' playfully wrote Lord Muncaster two years afterwards, 'the stolen expedition when you crept over the hills to plead the cause of freedom before the hardened despot of the north.' ' Resolved,' says the diary of September 11, ' to go to Lord Lonsdale's (Slave Trade business)—Sir J. Graham, Garforth, Saul, Fielding, Jno. Lowther, and two or three more—we all commend— the terrace—John Lord Lonsdale.' The success of this embassy he has not recorded ; but it brought at least before him, in ' the despot of the north,' surrounded by his dependent senators, a singular and now extinguished phase of social life.

After paying Hull a short visit, he set off for Bath. ' Saturday, October 4. Arrived late at Burford, where I spent the Sunday, October 5. A Sunday spent in solitude spreads and extends its fragrance ; may I long find the good effects of this.' There had been a time when a lonely day affected him very differently. ' I scarce ever felt,' he has said, ' such wretchedness as during those days which I spent by myself at Rayrigg, in 1784. My eyes were so bad that I

[2] Letter of Duchess of Gordon, Nov. 17, 1788.

could not read; the rain would not let me leave the house, and I had not a creature with whom to converse: I stood resting my forehead on the chimney-piece in a state of weariness not to be described.' But now he had learned to 'commune with his own heart and to be still;' he had drunk into that 'free spirit,' by which alone such self-converse can be happily maintained.

He reached Bath on the 6th, where he hears from Pitt: 'Pretyman has sent me your letter mentioning the curate you have found for New Holland. I will take care of the business.'[3] And again, (December 8): 'The scheme of Botany Bay is approaching fast to its execution. The particular part of it about which you inquire, has been for some time arranged, to the entire satisfaction of your poor curate.' 'To you,' writes Newton, 'as the instrument, we owe the pleasing prospect of an opening for the propagation of the gospel in the southern hemisphere. Who can tell what important consequences may depend on Mr. Johnson going to New Holland.'[4]

'October 27,' says his diary, 'left Bath for London on my way to York to attend the jubilee.—28th. Arrived in town, and dined at Pitt's.—30th. Went to Holwood—Pitt and Grenville—discussed Slave Trade.'

'November 3. On to Dick Milnes'—where dined and slept—she a pleasing woman, had long thought of slaves.— 4th. On to York—dined Morritt's—Duncombe—Mason— Burgh.—5th. Jubilee day—dined tavern—and ball at night, our enemy grandees there.—11th. To Lichfield, where first heard a confused account of the King's illness. On to Birmingham, where stopped all day for intelligence.—Off next afternoon.—Wednesday, to Worcester.—Thursday, to Petty France—heard all along that the King dying.—Friday, 14th, to Bath—found letters—obliged to go to town to Parliament, which cannot be prorogued on account of King's illness.' This took a favourable turn. 'The accounts,' wrote Mr. Steele from Downing Street, 'of this day are prodigiously favourable. . . . The King slept a good deal in the course of yesterday, and was much more composed and calm

---

[3] Holwood, Oct. 14, 1788.	[4] Nov. 1786.

F

when he was awake.   The physicians do not hesitate to say
that there is a visible alteration for the better, and his recovery seems to be now much more probable than 'anybody
ventured to suppose it to be some days ago.   It is very
desirable that you should be in town on Thursday.'

He obeyed the call.—December 4. Parliament met, and
adjourned to Monday, December 8, when physicians' committee appointed.   Never were Pitt's great qualities more
severely tested than at this crisis of the King's illness.   Fox
had been summoned from abroad in eager haste.   The power
for which he had so long struggled seemed just within his
reach.   The Prince acted altogether at his bidding, and too
many were found ready to worship the rising sun.   Pitt's
resolution was unshaken.   He would give the Regent the
power needful for the temporary discharge of the royal
functions, and no more ; that if the King recovered, he
might find no hindrance created to his natural resumption
of his sovereignty.   These restrictions on the Regent's power
were bitterly resented by the Prince and his partisans.   In the
strife Mr. Wilberforce stood resolutely by his friend, sharing
all his counsels and warmly supporting his measures, embarrassed as they were by Fox's open violence, by the un-
disguised hostility of the heir-apparent, the secret wiles of
Lord Loughborough, and the deep treachery of Thurlow,
'whose conduct,' wrote Mr. Wilberforce to Lord Muncaster,
'if ever it be made public, must cover him with confusion.'[5]

'December 9 and 10.   Attended committee and made our
report.   11th. Precedent committee, and reported.'

Posterity has abundantly ratified his judgment on Pitt's
conduct, formed at the moment, and thus expressed in a
letter to Mr. Wyvill :—

'My friend,' he says, 'is every day matter of fresh and
growing admiration.   I wish you were as constantly as I am
witness to that simple and earnest regard for the public welfare, by which he is so uniformly actuated ; great as I know
is your attachment to him, you would love him more and
more.'

[5] Nov. 7, 1789.

CHAPTER VI.

DECEMBER 1788 TO JULY 1790.

Serious resolutions—Increased diligence—Wilberforce prepares to move for the Abolition—Pitt's co-operation—Mr. Stephen—Retirement at Teston—Motion lost—Visit to H. More—Cheddar—Schools commenced—Buxton —Country visits— Return to town — Life in Palace Yard during the session of Parliament— Test Act — Examinations before Slave Trade committee—Crowther—General election.

THE year 1788 closed with the death of that aunt under whose roof had been passed so large a portion of his early years. 'Wednesday, December 23. Called at Blackheath —saw my aunt—whispered that she was comfortable. Oh that I may die the death of the righteous! Returned to Montagu's, and there all day—M. took me to task for peculiarities—saying grace, &c. 25th, Christmas-day. Church at Eltham—and sudden opportunity of receiving the sacrament —serious conversation in the evening.

'Friday, 26th. Called at Blackheath, and saw my aunt for the last time—she sensible—too weak to talk, but expressed her inward satisfaction and composure. Oh may God enable me to have as firm grounds of confidence in those awful moments! Came on to town and dined at Pitt's.

'Saturday, 27th. My aunt died at ten o'clock.'

The first entries of the new year are marked by the impressions of this scene. ' Received the sacrament. Thought over my future plan of conduct and resolutions.'

To those who knew the clear serenity of his later life, it may be matter of surprise to hear that his earlier sky was overcast by storms. It may encourage others to know that this peace was the result of previous conflicts. For though at this time most strictly temperate, and inclined in the judgment of his fellows to abstemiousness rather than to excess, he was himself sensible of many struggles before his body was brought under that 'sober government' which renders it the meetest instrument of the renewed spirit. His diary affords many instances of these contentions with himself, upon which he entered not without some indignation[1] at discovering their necessity, such as, 'M. and I made an agreement to pay a guinea forfeit when we broke our rules, and not to tell particulars to each other.' Thus he entered upon the year 1789.

'Jan. 1. Eliot breakfasted with me, and I went with him to the Lock—received the sacrament. Dined at home. Thought over future plan of conduct. Called at Pitt's. Last night the Speaker put off the House by a note in Warren's handwriting, after he had sent word he had passed a good night — we suspect a trick. — Jan. 2. Cornwall the speaker died, after a very short illness, this morning. We had laughed at his indisposition the day before, deeming it political, and thinking him "*be-Warrened.*" How much more likely for life was he than I ! — 5th. House—chose Grenville speaker, Sir Gilbert Elliot being opposed, 215 to 144. —6th. Committee named for examining physicians.—7th. Committee morning—sat till half-past five. Dined Pitt's : then friends at home till late.—8th. Committee till after five. Dined at home—Scott, Muncaster, &c. : then committee till past one. Pitt and Dundas till three.—9th and 10th. Committee as before.—Sunday, 11th. Dreadfully severe weather all this time. Dined at Addington's—serious talk with him. —15th. A charming morning. Yesterday the frost broke up. The river had been frozen over below the bridge—booths. Would not go to Dundas's with Pitt because a large party, and I thought I might infringe my rules and be kept up late —and next day a great day in the House; so resolved to dine at home with Muncaster for the sake of reading the Report together immediately after dinner.—17th. Pitt's, where staid too late ; but could not well get away—discussing with Dundas and Rose the Household business.—18th. Sunday. Called at Pitt's and advised him to reconsider the Household

---

[1] 'Itaque freni gutturis temperatâ relaxione et constrictione tenendi sunt. Et quis est, Domine, qui non rapiatur aliquando extra metam necessitatis ? Quisquis est magnus est. Magnificet nomen tuum— Ego autem non sum quia peccator homo sum.' *S Aug. Confess.* lib. x. c. 31.

business.   Church.   Then obliged to disturb my head with politics.   Called on Pitt—he gone out, and the conference over.—19th. Spoke—Household restrictions. Agreeably disappointed in the division, and general impression.   Muncaster, Montagu, Scott, Villiers, Bayham, home with me.'

' I was rejoiced,' writes Sir H. Hill on the following day, 'to hear you speak in so animated a manner in your reply to Mr. Fox.   The unreasonable conduct of Opposition in the late resolutions outdoes *if possible* all their former effrontery.   They would make two kings, instead of a regent and a king.'

' 21st. At dinner, and all night, till very late—Pitt, Mulgrave, Ryder, &c.—25th, Sunday.   Heard Mr. Woodd—with Eliot.   Blessed be God, who hath appointed these solemn returns of the day of rest.'

Beside the ordinary occupations of society and the House of Commons, he was now engrossed by his great object. ' House,' he says on Jan. 26, ' till near six—slave business all the evening, with only biscuit and wine and water.—28th. Slave business, Hawkins Brown's.—31st. Slave business— Mr. Stephen breakfasted.' He was just returned from a long residence in the West Indies.   There his generous spirit had burned indignantly within him at the misery he daily witnessed; and throughout an eleven years' residence in those colonies, he maintained the resolution, which a dread of the debasing influence of the system had at first suggested, and would never be the owner of a slave.   During this visit to England, and by letter from St. Kitt's until he came forward amongst the ablest advocates for Abolition, he communicated freely with Mr. Wilberforce.   Official intercourse between them soon ripened into personal attachment, which, cemented afterwards by a family alliance, grew in strength until Mr. Stephen's death at Bath, almost in the presence of his friend, a few months before his own decease.   'Animus vero non illum deserens, sed respectans, in ea profecto loca discessit quo illi ipsi cernebat esse veniendum.'

One or two extracts from his diary will shew his life :—

' February 9. Went to Pitt's to talk on Slave Trade. King much better — thank God. — 10th. Dined at Pitt's

before the House.—14th. Opposition sadly embarrassed whether to accept or not.   Sixty-eight major-generals — four
field-marshals—vacant.   Bishoprics—justice in eyre, &c.
Dined Pitt's and sat with him.   Morning at Kew.   Willis's
—much talk—King greatly better.—15th. Sunday.   Morning Lock—Scott—Eliot much affected.   Much affected all
day with a sense of heavenly things. Westminster Abbey in
the afternoon.   Once more I thank God for the intervention of the Sabbath.—17th. Morning Eliot—Slave business.
King declared by report to be *convalescent*.   Pitt doubtful
what to do.   Called Lord Camden's and Pitt's—evening
kept late.—20th. Lords had stopped the Regency Bill the
night before, and Thurlow with the King for two hours this
morning.—23rd. Prince of Wales and Duke of York saw
the King for the first time—King bore it well.   Tom Willis
about Pitt's going to see the King betimes.   Sent to Pitt
to be early. — 24th. I called on John Wesley—a fine old fellow.—25th. Pitt showed me the King's excellent letter—long
conversation, in which he inquired after everybody.   Milner
at Kew—he comes in and gives me the extraordinary account—all surprise and astonishment.   Bulletin, " Free from
complaint."   Walked to the Observatory and back.   There
Milner saw him, and at night in the circle.—26th. Slave committee breakfasted with me.   House—business went off, no
questions asked.—March 1, Sunday. Eliot breakfasted and
Lock — Scott — Called Lord Chatham's about politics (a
work of real necessity).   Strongly and deeply affected by an
examination of myself.   The world is my snare.   I require
more solitude than I have had of late.   Early hours night
and morning.   Abstinence as far as health will permit.   Regulations of employment for particular times.   Prayer three
times a day at least, and begin with serious reading or contemplation.   Self-denial in little things.   Slave Trade my main
business now.'[2]

' Slave business,' accordingly, is now the daily entry in his
diary, interrupted grudgingly even by the ' gentle compulsion with which on the 3rd Montagu forced me to dine with
him—Pitt and Mrs. Montagu.'

[2] Diary.

'Went on the 17th, with Pitt, Eliot, and Addington, to Holwood,' where he has a serious discussion with Pitt.

At length, on the 23rd, he 'noticed a day for Slave motion,'
and withdrew into the country 'for the next fortnight, to
prepare for Slave discussion.'

'Went on Friday,' he says on his return to Teston,[3] 'to
meet Pitt at Holwood. Would not go to London to the
thanksgiving-day that I might apply close to business. Pitt
very earnest about the Slave Trade. Returned on Saturday
to Teston. The report to be presented to-day.'—'I staid at
Teston attending to my Slave business. Thursday the 5th,
to Holwood—Pitt's with Burgh to do business together.
Friday, Pitt went to town about dissenters. Resolved to
stay, my mind not being made up, and needing time to settle
it, and my main business requiring all my moments. Saturday, Pitt came again and Eliot.'

The time which he was thus employing had not been
wasted by his opponents. Meeting followed meeting; resolutions, newspapers, and pamphlets daily assailed the public
with clamours of injury and threats of ruin: not merely
colonial prosperity, but the commercial existence of the
nation, it was boldly asserted, were at hazard; and it was
evident that the timidity and selfishness of interest were
growing into a powerful opposition. In the midst of this
rising storm a pleasant letter from Mr. Gisborne playfully
advised him:—'I have been as busy in town as a member
of Parliament preparing himself to maintain the Abolition
of the Slave Trade, and no doubt much more usefully employed. I shall expect to read in the newspapers of your
being carbonadoed by West Indian planters, barbecued by
African merchants, and eaten by Guinea captains; but do
not be daunted, for—I will write your epitaph.'

At length on May 12 the question came before the House.
'Monday, May 11,' says his diary, 'went to Montagu's
with Burgh ; where also Ramsay and John Clarkson. Came
to town, sadly unfit for work, but was enabled to make my
motion so as to give satisfaction—three hours and a half—I
had not prepared my language, or even gone over all my

---

[3] Diary.

matter, but being well acquainted with the whole subject I got on. My breast sore, but *de ceteris* pretty well. How ought I to labour, if it pleases God to make me able to impress people with a persuasion that I am serious, and to incline them to agree with me !'

The speech with which he opened the debate argued forcibly the whole question. Its effect both upon his friends and their opponents warrants the declaration of Mr. Burke, when warmed by its present influence, ' that the House, the nation, and Europe, were under great and serious obligations to the hon. gentleman for having brought forward the subject in a manner the most masterly, impressive, and eloquent. The principles,' he said, ' were so well laid down, and supported with so much force and order, that it equalled anything he had heard in modern times, and was not perhaps to be surpassed in the remains of Grecian eloquence.'

Mr. Pitt and Mr. Fox were no less loud in their eulogies; and the following character of the speech from a witness of a different order is an interesting testimony to its effect. Bishop Porteus writes on May 13 to the Rev. W. Mason: ' It is with heart-felt satisfaction I acquaint you that Mr. Wilberforce yesterday opened the important subject of the Slave Trade in the House of Commons, in one of the ablest and most eloquent speeches that was ever heard in that or any other place. He was supported in the noblest manner by Mr. Pitt, Mr. Burke, and Mr. Fox. It was a glorious night for this country.' ' I congratulate you,' writes Mr. Gisborne, ' not merely on account of your speech, but of the effect which it seems to have produced, and of the manner in which it was supported by others, even by the inconsistent and incomprehensible Burke.'

Mr. Wilberforce recorded, in twelve resolutions, the case of Abolition on the Journals of the House. On May 21, after a debate of unusual warmth, the planters succeeded in deferring the decision of the House until counsel had been heard and evidence tendered at the bar. The first witness was summoned on the following Tuesday, and the examinations lasted until June 23 ; when the lateness of the season postponed to another session the decision of the question.

Throughout this period his personal attendance in Parliament was incessant, and ' House—Slave Trade—extremely exhausted,' is no unfrequent entry amongst his private memoranda. Nor did he confine his attention to Parliamentary exertion. His house in Palace Yard was open to all the supporters of Abolition; and 'friends to supper,' or ' dined before House,' is almost daily in his diary. He was always on the watch to turn to good account the resources of his personal influence. He persuaded Dr. Peckard, the original advocate of the cause at Cambridge, to mount again in its behalf the pulpit of St. Mary's, and enticed a reluctant witness through the resistless influence of the Duchess of Gordon. With her, and with all the leaders of the fashionable world, his wit and the charms of his society made him an universal favourite; and his private memoranda contain not unfrequently curious records of the stream of life then flowing past him. Here are some instances:

' June 3. Breakfasted with the Bishop of London, and had some serious talk with him. Miss More there. Returned to Clapham—writing letters.—4th. King's birthday. Dined Pitt's; great party.—5th. To town to meet sub-committee at my house—afterwards Grenville's appointment to secretary of stateship declared—chair vacant.—8th. General meeting of the Society for Reforming Manners. House—unfit for work, which prevented my speaking, and showing my friendship for Addington. Addington chosen 215 to 143.—July 16. Went to town and dined at Lord Camden's, who very chatty and good-humoured. Exceeded rules, and will forfeit to M.

' Dined with 1 ;[4] he very chatty and pleasant. Abused 2 for his duplicity and mystery. Said 3 had said to him occasionally he had wished them, *i.e.* 2 and 4, to agree; for that both necessary to him, one in the Lords, the other in the

---

[4] A sheet of ' Private Table Talk,' dated July 16, 1789, found among Mr. W.'s papers. The numbers seem to indicate

1 Lord Camden.	6 Lord Bute.	11 ——
2 Lord Thurlow.	7 ——	12 Prince of Wales.
3 The King.	8 ——	13 Duke of York.
4 Mr. Pitt.	9 ——	14 Duke of Cl⁻
5 Mr. Dundas.	10 ——	

Commons. 2 will never do anything to oblige 1, because he is a friend of 4. 1 himself, though he speaks of 4 with evident affection, seems rather to complain of his being too much under the influence of any one who is about him, particularly of 5, who prefers his countrymen whenever he can. 1 is sure that 6 got money by the Peace of Paris. He can account for his sinking near 300,000*l.* in land and houses; and his paternal estate in the island which bears his name was not above 1,500 a-year, and he is a life-tenant only of Wortley, which may be 8,000*l.* or 10,000*l.* 1 does not believe 6 has any the least connection with 3 now, whatever he may have had. 1 believes 7 got money by the last peace. 3 has told 1 that he dislikes 8 for having deserted 9. 2 is giving constant dinners to the judges, to gain them over to his party. 10 was applied to by 11, a wretched sort of dependent of 12, to know if he would lend money on the joint bond of 12, 13, 14, to receive double the sum lent, whenever 3 should die, and either 12, 13, or 14 come into the inheritance. The sum intended to be raised is 200,000*l.*' ' 'Tis only a hollow truce, not a peace, that is made between 2 and 4. They can have no confidence in each other.'[5]

' 17th. Obliged to dine with S., to meet Duchess of Gordon—Chatham and P. Arden. He notes at this time that one of his fellow-labourers in the Abolition cause was sinking under his burden. The Rev. James Ramsay, who, by his work upon the treatment of the West Indian negroes, commenced in the year 1784 that public controversy which was closed only by the abolition of the trade, had been once stationed in the island of St. Kitt's, and was now vicar of Teston, in Kent. Forewarned by Bishop Porteus to expect a merciless revenge, he calmly engaged in the holy strife. He was soon assailed with every species of malignant accusation. ' I have long,' he wrote to Mr. Wilberforce in 1787, ' been considered as a marked man, of whom it was lawful to suggest anything disadvantageous, however false; to whom it was good manners to say anything disagreeable, however insulting.' His wounded spirit at length bowed before the storm; and the malignant calumnies heaped upon him in the

[5] Jan. 16, 1790.

debate of May 21, evidently hastened his deliverance from a world of cruelty and falsehood. The hatred which had embittered a shortened life, triumphed without disguise over his grave. ' His chief traducer,' writes Mr. Stephen, ' announced the decease of the public enemy to his natural son in this island, in these terms: " Ramsay is dead—I have killed him." '—' Heard that poor Ramsay died yesterday, at ten o'clock. A smile on his face now,' is the entry, July 21, of Mr. Wilberforce's Journal.

On the 27th he set off for Bath, and thence visited Mrs. H. More, who had now retired from the flattery and bustle of the literary world to Cowslip Green.

' Thursday, Aug. 20. At Cowslip Green all day.—21st. After breakfast to Cheddar. Intended to read, dine, &c., amongst the rocks, but could not get rid of the people; so determined to go back again. The rocks very fine. Had some talk with the people, and gave them something— grateful beyond measure—wretchedly poor and deficient in spiritual help.—I hope to amend their state.' It was this visit to Cheddar, thus simply related in Mr. Wilberforce's diary, which gave rise to Mrs. More's great exertions for her neglected neighbours. The vicar of Cheddar at that time was non-resident, and his curate, who lived nine miles off at Wells, visited the parish on Sundays only. The spiritual destitution of such a parish, seen with his own eyes, greatly affected Mr. Wilberforce. The effects which followed from his visit are thus recorded in an unpublished journal of Mrs. Martha More :

' In the month of August, 1789, providence directed Mr. Wilberforce and his sister to spend a few days at Cowslip Green. We recommended Mr. W. not to quit the country till he had spent a day in surveying the cliffs of Cheddar. He was prevailed on and went. When he returned, with the eagerness of vanity (having recommended the pleasure) I inquired how he liked the cliffs? He replied, they were fine, but the poverty and distress of the people was dreadful. This was all that passed. He retired to his apartment and dismissed even his reader. I said to his sister and mine, I feared Mr. W. was not well. The cold chicken and wine put into the carriage for his dinner were returned untouched. Mr. W. appeared at supper, seemingly refreshed with a higher feast than we had sent with him. The servant at his desire was dismissed, when immediately he began, "Miss Hannah More, something must be done for Cheddar." He then proceeded to a particular account of his day, of the inquiries he had made respecting the poor ; there was no resident minister, no manufactory, nor did there appear any dawn of comfort, either temporal or spiritual. The method or possibility of assisting them was discussed till a late hour; it was at length decided in a few words, by Mr. W.'s exclaiming, "If you will be at the trouble, I will be at the expense." Something, commonly called an impulse, crossed my heart, that told me it was God's work, and it would do. Mr. Wilberforce and his sister left us in a day or two afterwards. We turned many schemes in our head, every possible way; at length those measures were adopted which led to the foundation of different schools.'

With a many sidedness of character, which led superficial observers to doubt the steadiness of his exertions, he never abandoned such a cause as this, and from Buxton he writes to Mrs. Hannah More :—

'A letter from Cowslip Green brings with it in some sort the portraiture of its own scenery, and greatly mends the prospect to one shut up amidst bleak, rugged hills, and barren, unprotected valleys. But it is not on this account only that yours is acceptable, but as it excites various other pleasing and refreshing images, which having once found a place in my mind will continue there, I trust, during the remainder of my life. May they be of still longer duration, and the benefits and the comforts of our friendship be experienced by both of us when time shall be no more. Now to business.

'Your plan is a very good one. As for the expense, the best proof you can give me that you believe me hearty in the cause is to call on me for money without reserve. I shall take the liberty of enclosing a draft for 40*l.*; but this is only meant for beginning with.

'Now for the mission . . . indeed, I fear with you nothing

can be done in the regular way. But these poor people must
not, therefore, be suffered to continue in their present lamentable state of darkness. You know you told me they never
saw the sun but one day in the year, and even the moon appeared but once a week for an hour or two. The gravita-
tion to Wells was too strong to be resisted. My advice
then, is, send for a comet—Whiston had them at command,
and John Wesley is not unprovided. Take care, however,
that eccentricity is not his only recommendation, and, if possible, see and converse with the man before he is determined on.'

With the Wesley family Mr. Wilberforce had formed a
personal acquaintance through Mrs. More at R. Henderson's.
'When I came into the room, Charles Wesley rose from the
table, around which a numerous party sat at tea, and coming
forwards to me, gave me solemnly his blessing. I was scarcely
ever more affected. Such was the effect of his manner and appearance, that it altogether overset me, and I burst into tears,
unable to restrain myself.' He ever retained his reverence
for this good man, and hearing after his death that his widow
needed aid, he writes: ' The widow of Charles Wesley ought,
if health required it, to feed on ortolans.'[6] These were not
mere words—he made her a yearly allowance till her death
in 1822. In recommending one of ' Wesley's comets,' Mr.
Wilberforce, though ever brotherly with men of piety of all
denominations, had no intention of encouraging dissent ;
for John Wesley was no dissenter from the Church of England, nor were any of his preachers suffered during his life-
time to administer the sacraments of the Church ; and Mr.
Wilberforce was a conscientious, though very far from being
a high churchman. In this very year he dissuaded a relation,
who complained that in her place of residence she could
find no religious instruction in the church, from attending at
the meeting-house. ' Its individual benefits,' he wrote in
answer to her letter of inquiry, ' are no compensation for
the general evils of dissent.'

The moral desolation which he found in Cheddar was a
striking illustration of his common maxim, that the ' dissenters

[6] Letter to T. Babington, August, 1792.

could do nothing if it were not for the Established Church;' for the absence of a resident clergyman had brought the village into a state of general ignorance. 'I have taken measures,' he wrote again to Mrs. More upon October 2, 'to send a competent supply of the books which you desired. Your labours can only be equalled by Spenser's lady knights, and they seem to be much of the same kind too, I mean, you have all sorts of monsters to cope withal.' The 'monsters' were all subdued by this intrepid lady knight, supported by her generous champion (the 'Red Cross Knight' was his familiar name with Mrs. Montagu), without the eccentric succour of 'a comet.' 'Your accounts,' he writes somewhat later, 'have afforded me the utmost pleasure, and I persuade myself that they will be as comfortable next year. I trust you will speak freely when the money is exhausted—indeed, I conceive it must be all spent already—not to do so would be to give way either to pride or to false delicacy.'

His purse was always open to every good work. 'I wish to know,' he tells Mr. Hey, 'in what state are the funds of your West Riding Charity[7] for catching the colts running wild on Halifax Moor, and cutting their manes and tails, and sending them to college. If a contributor would be acceptable, I would most cheerfully give something towards an institution I so highly approve, but my name must not be mentioned.'

Devotional entries record the opening of another year.— 'January 1, 1790. Lock—Scott—with Henry Thornton—"These forty years in the wilderness"—received the sacrâment. Most deeply impressed with serious things.'

Though his health would have justified repose, this year was one of incessant occupation. 'Business first and grand,' says his plan, 'for this winter—1. Slave Trade. 2. General preparation for parliamentary business. 3. General topics. 4. Historical and political, &c. axioms. 5. Ferguson's History and Society, Shakspeare, Cowper, Adam Smith (Swift, Pope, Addison, Johnson, &c. for relaxation), English History, Barrow, South, &c. 6. Finances. 7. Reformation Society and its plans—Sunday-travelling Bill—wine licenses, &c.'

[7] The Elland Society.

His intercourse with general society, 'from which I dare not more withdraw,' and into which he endeavoured to carry his high principles of action, occupied much time. His great cause alone furnished matter for unremitting toil. But, besides this, he applied himself with diligence to all the important questions which were brought forward in Parliament; and was most assiduous in his attention to the private business of the great county which he represented. 'When you appear on this stage,' writes Mr. James Grenville, 'you must always expect to be scrambled for. The landowner, the manufacturer, the canal man, the turnpike man, and the iron man will each have a pull in his turn.'

His house was continually open to an influx of men of all conditions. Pitt and his other parliamentary friends might be found there at 'dinner before the House.' So constant was their resort, that the violence of party spirit once put forward the charge, that he received a pension for entertaining the partisans of the minister. Once every week the 'Slave Committee' dined with him; whilst Clarkson, Dickson, and others, whom Mr. Pitt jocosely called his 'white negroes,' were his constant inmates, and were employed in classing, revising, and abridging evidence under his own eye. 'I cannot invite you here,' he writes to a friend who was about to visit London for advice, 'for, during the sitting of Parliament, my house is a mere hotel.' His breakfast-table was thronged by those who came to him on business, or with whom, for any of his many plans of usefulness, he wished to become personally acquainted. He took a lively interest in the Elland Society; and, besides subscribing to its funds 100*l.* per annum (under four anonymous entries), he invited to his house the young men who were being educated there, that he might be able to distribute them in proper situations. His life brought him into contact with all varieties of character. His anteroom was thronged from an early hour; its first occupants being generally invited to his breakfast-table, and its later tenants only quitting it when he himself went out on business. Like every other room in his house it was well stored with books, which had gradually been changed from the smaller volumes, with which it was originally furnished, for cumbrous folios, 'which could not be carried off by accident in the pocket of a coat.' The group which it presented to the eye of an observer was often most amusing, and provoked the wit of Mrs. H. More to liken it to 'Noah's ark, full of beasts clean and unclean.' On one chair sat a Yorkshire constituent, manufacturing or agricultural; on another a petitioner for charity, or a House of Commons client; on another a Wesleyan preacher; while, side by side with an African, a foreign missionary, or a Haytian professor, not seldom waited some man of rank who sought a private interview, and whose name had accidentally escaped announcement. To these mornings succeeded commonly an afternoon of business, and an evening in the House of Commons.

He was much occupied in the early part of this session by the fresh application made by the Dissenters for the repeal of the Test and Corporation Acts. Though he was by no means a High Churchman, and though he disliked the peculiar form of a sacramental test, yet he deemed some restriction so needful, that he had opposed and voted against his friend Mr. Beaufoy, in 1787, as to the repeal of these enactments. In the spring of 1789 he would not leave Holwood to vote upon the question, 'his mind not being made up.' Since that time he had maturely weighed the subject, and his reluctance 'to oppose the repeal of these laws had been overcome by his conviction of their present necessity;' and soon after he calls on Mr. Hey, to rejoice with him at the memorable majority—294 to 105—against the Dissenters' application.

But the main business of this spring was the conduct of the Abolition cause. He had opened the campaign by a motion made upon the 14th, and carried after much opposition upon January 27, for referring to a special committee the further examination of witnesses. This became now his daily work, and, with the help of the late William Smith, he conducted personally all the examinations. Here he reaped the fruit of his deep acquaintance with the whole subject, as well as of those habits of self-government which he had been at such pains to form. Nothing but his accurate knowledge of details could have prevented his being duped by the mis-

representation of too many of the witnesses; whilst the
angry discussions in which he was continually involved
rendered a practised temper no less needful than a sagacious judgment.

This was a period of no ordinary labour to the leader in
the struggle.   In a letter, written forty-two years later,[8] he
reminds W. Smith of these early labours : ' You cannot, any
more than myself, have forgotten the weeks after weeks, or
rather months after months, in which our chief, though not
most cherished companions, were that keen, sour S———,
that ponderous, coarse, Jack Fuller-like F———; a very gra-
phical epithet if you remember the man.'   His house too,
throughout this time, was continually full.   The evening
hours were devoted to consultations on the common cause;
and to keep so many different agents in harmonious exertion
required no little management.   A few extracts from his
diary will illustrate these employments :—

' March 18.   Dined at home—William Smith tête-à-tête
(partly religious); then Clarkson came, and Muncaster, and
looked over evidence. — 20th.   Clarkson and Eliot dined
(Slave business), then Hunter and Sansom came from the
city; a different set of ideas in their minds, and in those in
our friends.—22nd.   Dined at home—Smith, Clarkson, and
Dickson.   Slave business till eleven at night.—25th.   Committee as usual.—27th.   Town from Clapham to committee
as usual.   Dined Bishop of Salisbury's—Miss More, Sir J.
Bankes, Mrs. Garrick, &c.   We talked of Captain Bligh's
affair, and Sir Joshua (like myself) was not surprised at it.
Otaheite Calypso's island.—April 4th. Easter Sunday. Sent to
Christian to go to Lock, hoping, in his present state of mind,
having lately heard of his brother's conduct, an impression
might, by God's blessing, be made upon him.—5th. Up $6\frac{3}{4}$—
bed 12.   Hard at work on Slave Trade evidence all day
with " white negroes," two Clarksons and Dickson.'

On the afternoon of this day he set off to spend a single
day at Holwood.   ' 7th. Walked about after breakfast with
Pitt and Grenville — wood with bills.   We sallied forth

[8] From Brighstone, Isle of Wight, May 5, 1832.

armed with billhooks, cutting new walks from one large tree to another, through the thickets of the Holwood copses.'

The witnesses in favour of the trade had now been heard, but those on the other side were not admitted without a new struggle. ' 20th. Saw Pitt in bed, and talked with him on the enemy's impudent attempt to resist our calling evidence: at his suggestion went to Fox and saw him; also called on Burke, who kept me an hour and a half talking about W. Hastings. Felt much when I saw poor Burke.'

April 23. ' At evidence all morning, then to town—and House. Our opponents, blessed be God, fairly beat. A throng at home at night.—27th. Committee as usual—came over and dined, and afterwards Slave business. All this time examining and preparing my evidences and extremely occupied, and seven or eight people living constantly in my house. —28th. Committee as usual. Crowther dined with us, and gave us an account of the shipwreck and Riou's fortitude.'

' April 29. Committee morning—dined at Pitt's before the House.—30th. Morning, committee as usual—and again evening busy on Norris's examination, and so on daily.— May 8. Committee, morning—dined at the Bishop of Salisbury's. Large party—Pitt, Grenville, Montagu, Ryder, Speaker, &c.—20th. Committee, and so indeed every day. All this time perpetual company.'

' Every day,' he writes, May 22, to W. Hey, ' we sit in committee the whole morning; after it we repair to the House, and I have besides to go through the attorney's task of talking with witnesses, and making out what they can say.' ' I am almost worn out, and I pant for a little country air, and quiet: the former I hope soon to enjoy, the latter is more uncertain. If I don't take care mine will be *"a case"* shortly.'

These employments were soon afterwards exchanged for a hasty three weeks' canvass, preparatory to the general election of June, 1790. ' June 7. Prepared a paper on Sir W. Dolben's bill for the Lords. To town to the committee—up soon for Fox's summing up on Hastings' trial. Westminster Hall—all bored and tired. Fox's speech very dull.—9th. Committee—calls on grandees—home, and by exertion got

off and travelled to Stevenage. Muncaster's affection at parting, and Will. Smith's.—10th. Travelled on all day—calling
at Bishop of Lincoln's—talked about Milner.' During this
hasty visit, he received a cordial welcome from his constituents, and was re-elected at its close by general acclamation.

CHAPTER VII.

JULY 1790 TO DECEMBER 1791.

*Summer excursions—Diligent study of Slave Trade question—John
Thornton—New Parliament—Pitt's speech on Hastings' impeachment—
Abridgment of evidence on Slave Trade—Increased strength of West
Indian party—Wesley's 'last words'—Abolition again negatived—
Bath—Sierra Leone Company—Visits to Rothley Temple and Yoxall
Lodge.*

THE material benefit which Mr. Wilberforce had received
from the Buxton waters led him, on Mr. Hey's advice, to
return there this summer. He reached it early in July, but
his further stay was soon interrupted by a call to town.

'July 19. Felt very low on arriving in London. Saw
Pitt that night and discussed.—20th. Dined at Pitt's with
Grenville only. Talked on French Revolution, &c.'

'My dear Cookson,' he writes from Palace Yard, 'how
are you? How is Mrs. C.? How is the bantling? Are you
alive? Are you asleep? Are you disabled in your hands?
Learn to write with your feet, ere you again let me be so
long without hearing from you. I am not stationary here,
but come up to put my Slave business in train. My summer
destination is unfixed.'

'23rd. Off for Teston.—26th. Breakfast till late. Then
with Sir Charles to Langley, to eat cold dinner, see woods,
fish-ponds, &c. Home in the evening. Days are wasted in
these parties.' From Teston he returned to Buxton, and
soon describes himself as 'busily employed.' Aug. 14th.
Rode with P. Ardén, and had some serious talk.—Sept. 6th.
Notification of election to stewardship of York races.' To

pass even a tacit censure upon this particular amusement, required no small measure of faith in the member for the county of York.   There had been a time when he had re- corded in his diary, ' My horse won at the Harrowgate races,' but he was now convinced of their evil tendency.   His line therefore was clear, nor did he ever perceive that he had alienated one supporter by refusing to fill the office, or by exchanging the accustomed contribution to the races for a donation to the county hospital.

His affectionate heart was now full of the marriage of his only surviving sister to the Rev. T. Clarke, vicar of the Trinity church at Hull, at Buxton, upon the 11th of Sep- tember.   After a time, he set out with Mr. Babington for a short tour through Wales, whither Mr. Clarke and his sister had repaired; and joined their party at Caernarvon. 'Sept. 27.   Hard at work—on Ferguson's Civil Society.—29th. With Babington and Miss Sykes to Beddgellert and Pont Aberglasslyn—returned evening—a grand scene.   Welch Bibles and other serious books in a cottage.—Oct. 1.   Off from   Caernarvon — breakfasted   Bangor — called   on   the bishop—he busy in his building, ornamenting the cathedral. Lamented the state of the Welch clergy, arising from mono- poly—Bangor school may produce competition.   Dined at Conway — evening Llanrwst. — Sunday, 3rd, Llangollen — sorry to find no English service.   Read prayers and sermon to servants at home, and the landlord came in.' ' Our society,' wrote Miss Sykes to her mother on the following day,[1] 'has received a sad blow in the departure yesterday of·Mr. Wil- berforce and Mr. Babington.   The former you have long known and admired, and to me he appears truly angelic; had I a spark of enthusiasm about me, I should doubt whether he were not a superior being.'

He was now upon his road to Yoxall Lodge, the seat of the Rev. T. Gisborne.   Their college acquaintance had been interrupted when they left the University; but was after- wards renewed.   He had become well acquainted at Mr. Gisborne's house with his near connection, Mr. Babington. Intercourse between them soon grew into friendship; and

[1] October 2, 1790.

for many years he made Yoxall Lodge, or Rothley Temple, his ordinary summer residence.   Here he enjoyed uninterrupted privacy, combined with the society of his friend's family.   In these visits he fulfilled those intentions which constant company had defeated in his own residence at Rayrigg, and devoted ten or twelve hours every day to study. 'Never,' he has said, 'was I in better spirits than when I thus passed my time in quiet study.'   He sallied forth always for a walk a short time before dinner, amongst the holly groves of the then unenclosed Needwood Forest, where—

His grateful voice
Sang its own joy, and made the woods rejoice.

'Often have I heard its melodious tones,' says his host, 'at such times, amongst the trees, from the distance of full half-a-mile.'

His object in his present visit to Yoxall Lodge was to make himself completely master of the vast mass of evidence which had now been collected upon the subject of the Slave Trade. 'Monday, October 4. Off early from Llangollen— dined at Shrewsbury—begun to work at Slave evidence with Babington.' And on the following day, after entering his return with his accustomed 'thank God, safely,' he adds, 'November 5. Babington and I determined to work hard at Slave evidence.   6th. Hard at work — breakfast alone, and need not come down to supper.   No kind of restraint. I must for a time defer my tract, because it is advantageous to read the evidence rapidly, to detect inconsistencies : besides a great folio volume from the Privy Council, I have also to scrutinize with much care near 1,400 folio pages of Evidence delivered before the House of Commons—I working like a negro.[2]

The entries of his diary show that in spite of the hindrance of infirm health, he rose to the necessities of the occasion. 'Monday, 11. Slave evidence, and very hard at it with Babington all this week,' is a common entry. '30th. Mrs. G. spoke to me to take care of myself—more exercise—I have been applying too closely—too little air—my health disordered

[2] Letter to W. Hey, Esq., Oct. 3.

—my appetite fails, &c.—5th. Heard from Pitt that peace certain on our own terms.—11th. Staid in house hard at work. This is indeed a capital house for doing business. I am but moderate in health.' ' I never sustain the loss of the nourishment and refreshment of sleep without feeling like a hunted hare all the next day, and being very unfit for any strenuous occupation.'[3]

' Mr. Wilberforce and Mr. Babington,' writes a friend from Yoxall Lodge, 'have never appeared downstairs since we came, except to take a hasty dinner, and for half-an-hour after we have supped : the Slave Trade now occupies them nine hours daily. They talk of sitting up one night in each week. The two friends begin to look very ill, but they are in excellent spirits, and at this moment I hear them laughing at some absurd questions in the examination. You would think Mr. W. much altered since we were at Rayrigg. He is now never riotous or noisy, but very cheerful, sometimes lively, but talks a good deal more on serious subjects than he used to do. Food, beyond what is absolutely necessary for his existence, seems quite given up. He has a very slight breakfast, a plain and sparing dinner, and no more that day except some bread about ten o'clock. I have given you this history, as you say everything about him must be interesting to you, and this is all I at present see of him.'

Such were his occupations until his return to London. Throughout this time, with the exception of two days, each of which yielded him eight hours of labour, he devoted daily nine hours and a half to his main employment. His was not the easy service of popular declamation on premises supplied by others, but the real conduct of affairs with all the toil and drudgery of careful preparation.

Upon the 9th he enters in his journal, ' Heard this evening that on Sunday morning, at Bath, died what was mortal of John Thornton.' ' He was allied to me by relationship and family connection. It was by living with great simplicity of intention and conduct in the practice of a Christian life, more than by any superiority of understanding or of knowledge, that he rendered his name illustrious in the view

[3] Letter to W. Hey, Esq.

of all the more respectable part of his contemporaries. He died without a groan. Oh may my last end be like his!'[4]

November 18, he left Yoxall Lodge, and next day reached London, 'plunging,' he writes, 'at once into a dinner circle of cabinet ministers.—Monday, 22nd. Went to Wimbledon —Dundas, Lord Chatham, Pitt, Grenville, Ryder. Much talk about Burke's book.[5] Lord Chatham, Pitt, and I seemed to agree, contra Grenville and Ryder. — 23rd. To town. Obliged to dine with Pitt—Robinson, Montagu, Rose, Addington. Pitt told me of Grenville's peerage and the true reasons (distrust of Lord Thurlow). Saw Thurlow's letter in answer to the news. Kept up till late. Oh how I regret Yoxall Lodge! Gave Pitt a serious word or two.—25th. Morning, archbishop about a chaplain for Botany Bay.—26th. Read Burke's book for three hours—then to the House to be sworn. Had people to dine with me—then made calls. —27th. Called Beaufoy's. Breakfasted with Pitt, and lost time afterwards. Dined at home with Dickson. Slave work at night.

'December 1. Dined R. Smith's — Pitt, Long, Bayham, Dundas, Bankes.—11th. Read and considered on the Convention business. Dined Lord Grenville's with a large mixed House of Commons party—13th, Sunday. Lock—Scott— "God forbid that I should glory," &c. Thought much on it, and I hope with benefit. To Pitt's, where a great circle of House of Commons, chiefly on taxes, &c. Oh how foolish do they seem so to neglect heavenly things!—13th. Debate on Papers—spoke —kept late.—16th. Debate on taxes, and my Slave business put off till after Christmas by Cawthorne and Pitt. I very angry.—17th. Hastings' impeachment question.—22nd. House till past two—Pitt's astonishing speech.[6] ' This was almost the finest speech Pitt ever delivered; it was one which you would say at once he never could have made if he had not been a mathematician. He put things by as he proceeded, and then returned to the very point from which he had started with the most astonishing clearness.

---

[4] Journal. [5] Considerations on the French Revolution.
[6] Maintaining that a pending impeachment is not terminated by a dissolution.

He had all the lawyers against him, but carried a majority of the House mainly by the force of this speech. It pleased Burke prodigiously: "Sir," he said, "the right hon. gent. and I have often been opposed to one another, but his speech to-night has neutralised my opposition; nay, sir, he has dulcified me."' [7]

' 25th. Christmas Day. I have just been receiving the sacrament. At the Lock this evening—much disliked De Coetlegan.'

Ever since his return to London, he had been employed in examining and arranging the evidence on behalf of Abolition. In the preceding summer he had compiled a table of questions with which Mr. Clarkson had set forth to collect, with his wonted energy, all the evidence which could be procured in the northern counties. Several witnesses had been discovered in this journey. Mr. Wilberforce had himself obtained some others. He had now selected the best witnesses, and closely attended their examinations.

' February 2. House met after the recess. — 4th. The renewal of the Slave Committee.—5th. Dined at Lambeth, with Speaker and Eliot — public day. Drove about with Speaker, then home to Story and Clarkson.—7th. Began committee.—10th. Slave friends' day—Granville Sharpe and various evidences dined. — 13th. Blessed be God for the Sunday. Scott—an excellent sermon—very serious thoughts. Held forth to my family as now usual on Sunday night.—15th. Slave Committee, &c., dined with me. W. Smith and Clarkson—Slave business—then I went over to House.—16th. I went to Sumner's to dine, and see Captain Hall, and prevail on him to give evidence, which succeeded.—18th. Pitt and a party dined with me.'—' 24th. Breakfasted with Grant. Went to Holwood, where also Grenville and Ryder.—25th. Dundas added to the others. At Holwood all day.—26th. Rose and Steele vice Grenville. Finance committee—Ryder. —27th. To town. Never was I more busy; besides the daily examinations of the Slave Trade witnesses, there are public and private letters, county matters, &c. Pray for me that I may preserve a sober mind and a single eye amidst all

---

[7] Con. Mem.

my distractions.'[8]   'March 18. Appointed grand motion for April 2.'

And now that the day approached, upon the event of which hung the welfare of his many clients on the shores of Africa, and the success of his own toil and privations for four years of incessant labour, the prospect before him was by no means encouraging.   In the year 1787, when he had undertaken the cause, its advocates looked confidently forward to the speedy suppression of the trade.   In the beginning of 1788, 'more difficulties' met the instructed eyes of Mr. Pitt and Mr. Wilberforce, yet still they deemed the cause prospering.   It is the nature of a defence of established enormities to yield at first to the generous assault, until gathering strength from the slow but certain succour of selfish apprehension, it retracts all its concessions and regains its former ground.   The first burst of generous indignation had promised nothing less than the instant abolition of the trade; but mercantile jealousy had now taken the alarm, and the defenders of the West Indian system soon found themselves strengthened by the independent alliance of commercial men. Thus encouraged, they boldly assailed the public ear with the depositions of their witnesses, who could paint as 'promoted dances'[9] the enforced convulsions of the fettered negro; the hold of a slave ship,[1] 'redolent with frankincense,' as the scene of his happiest hours; whilst his landing in the colonies was an affecting meeting with long parted friends.[2]   Seen through their peculiar medium, the Guinea trade[3] was a nursery for British seamen, whilst it delivered the grateful African from the refinement of native barbarity.

These accounts were confirmed by the votes and speeches of British officers, who were duped by that most fallacious guide, inadequate personal observation.   Their report of exaggerated charges seemed to justify the cautious doubts of men of business; whilst the general bias of the bar in favour of an established trade was confirmed by the defence which burst from the boisterous and unprincipled Thurlow, and for

[8] Letters to W. Hey and Rev. W. Mason.
[9] Evidence of Mr. Norris.   [1] Ib.
[2] Apology for Negro Slavery.   [3] West Indian Evidence, *passim.*

a moment trembled upon the lips of Erskine.[4] Such opposition could not fail of producing great effects. Though Mr. Pitt was a zealous abolitionist, the chancellor was not without support even in the Cabinet, where Lord Hawkesbury was thought ready to support stronger measures than he avowed in Parliament. 'Lord Hawkesbury's carriage,' writes Lord Muncaster, 'was a considerable time waiting at Lord Penrhyn's upon Saturday. Whether he was giving or receiving information you will be better able to decide than I.'[5]

Mr. Fox, giant as he was, fought only with the strength of a single arm; while against him were arrayed, both in the House and in the provinces, his own political adherents, from Lord John Russell in the House of Commons to the Welch county member of whom Mr. Gisborne reports[6]— 'He is a desperate Foxite; he would not open on the Slave Trade; but I fear he is too old, I believe I must add too covetous, to approve of abolition.' 'These Utopian schemes of liberty in the Slave Trade,' wrote Dr. Parr,[7] 'alarm serious men.' So far had such opinions prevailed, that in the months of April and May, 1789, the most unfavourable reports were forwarded to his country retreat, by Mr. Wilberforce's London correspondents.

The debate of the 12th of May gave some promise of more successful progress. But delay was the secret of West Indian policy. They trusted to the strength with which caution, selfishness, and misrepresentation would recruit their ranks; and they were not disappointed. The evil was distant and disputed; the sacrifice immediate and apparent. Self-interest was ever watchful, whilst the advocates of humanity sometimes slumbered on their post. 'The affair goes on slowly in parliament, and with a more pertinacious and assiduous attendance of our adversaries in the committee than of our friends, except indeed Mr. Wilberforce, Mr. Smith, Sir W. Dolben, and a few others; so that we cannot yet guess at the result.'[8] The long protracted examinations of 1788, 1789, 1790, and 1791, though essential

---

[4] 'The bar were all against us. Fox could scarcely prevent Erskine from making a set speech in favour of the trade.'—*Con. Mem.*
[5] April, 1789.   [6] June 26.   [7] Works, i. 346.
[8] Letter from Granville Sharpe, March 17, 1790.

to final success, multiplied for a while the cold and cautious defenders of the trade. The temper, moreover, of events was most favourable to their endeavours. In the repose of peaceful times it is difficult to estimate aright the extreme agitation produced in our own political atmosphere by that hurricane of terror which desolated France. Revolution, which had begun with making fair promises of reasonable liberty, had before this time thrown off the comely mask which concealed her hated features, and openly revelled in infidelity and blood. A small, though soon afterwards a noisy, party watched eagerly the convulsions of the neighbouring kingdom, and dreamed of renovating by French principles the English constitution; but the great bulk of the nation, exhausted by the war with America, and wearied by the strife of parties, viewed with horror the excesses of France, and recoiled with disgust from the abused names of humanity and freedom. Even the ordinary excitement of a general election could not rouse the nation from the political repose of 1790. Nor was it merely this general tendency to quiet which repressed the efforts of the Abolition party. The seed of French principles, which had been widely scattered throughout her foreign settlements, was already ripening into a harvest of colonial insurrection. The strife of Paris, renewed amongst the free inhabitants of St. Domingo, was soon transmitted thence to Dominica; and to the efforts of the true friends of peace were instantly attributed the intestine discords of an English colony.

Amidst such various elements of opposition Mr. Wilberforce approached the contest of April, 1791. Though none could be sanguine of immediate success, yet he was not without many cheering assurances of sympathy. 'You, sir,' writes Dr. Peckard, 'will stand in the British parliament as did Episcopius in the infamous synod of Dort, with the whole force of truth, with every rational argument, and with all the powers of moving eloquence upon your side, and all to no purpose.' Still nearer to the actual conflict, he received an animating charge traced upon the bed of death by the faltering hand of the venerable Wesley.[9]

[9] It seems probable that this was amongst the very last efforts of his

'Unless the Divine power has raised you up to be as · Athanasius contra mundum, I see not how you can go through your glorious enterprise, in opposing that execrable villany which is the scandal of religion, of England, and of human nature.   Unless God has raised you up for this very thing, you will be worn out by the opposition of men and devils; but if God be for you who can be against you.   Are all of them together stronger than God?   Oh be not weary of well-doing.   Go on in the name of God, and in the power of His might, till even American slavery, the vilest that ever saw the sun, shall vanish away before it.   That He who has guided you from your youth up may continue to strengthen you in this and all things, is the prayer of your affectionate servant, JOHN WESLEY.' [1]

Such sympathy no doubt often cheered his spirit in the weary hours of labour and preparation.   But it was by a greater might that he was strengthened.   'May God,' he writes in his private memoranda a few days before the con- test, 'bless me in this great work I have now in hand.   May I look to Him for wisdom and strength and the power of persuasion, and may I surrender myself to Him as to the event with perfect submission, and ascribe to Him all the praise if I succeed, and if I fail say from the heart, Thy will be done.'   'Motion put off,' he adds a few days later, 'from Tuesday, April 12th, to Monday, 18th.   By God's blessing got through pretty well to others' satisfaction, but very little to my own—I knowing how much omitted.—19th. Resumed debate and sadly beat.'   The speech with which he opened the debate reviewed the voluminous, and in some respects conflicting evidence, and, with a careful suppression of irritating topics, proved the trade to be both cruel and impolitic.   He ended with an animated appeal to the higher principles which he sought to establish in the House.

In the course of the debate he was earnestly supported by Mr. W. Smith and Mr. Fox; and Mr. Pitt, in establishing the needless injustice of the traffic, equalled any of those

pen.   On February 25, he sunk into that lethargy in which he lay until his death, upon March 2.   It is docketed by Mr. Wilberforce, 'Wesley's last words.'

[1] February 24, 1791.

great efforts by which he confounded opposition. Two
members had the courage to avow openly their altered [2] or
established [3] sentiments. The Opposition, headed by Lord
John Russell and Colonel Tarleton, and well described in a
speech of one of their own body [4] as the war of the pigmies
against the giants of the House, consisted of little else than
trite imputations of misrepresentation, or unsupported as-
sertions of injury. Their cause was more effectually maintained by a multitude of silent votes, and the character,
talents, and humanity of the House were left in a minority
of 88 to 163. With this adverse decision all attempts to
carry the question further in the House of Commons ended
for this session. It was clear that an appeal must be made
to the justice and humanity of the nation for the redress
which was denied by Parliament.

On May 2, Parliament met after the recess. ' 4th. The
quarrel between Burke and Fox, which I had endeavoured
to prevent.' 'I scarce recollect,' he writes to Mr. Babington,
' being so much struck at anything, and I have been lamenting
ever since that I did not myself interfere—a long-tried and
close worldly connection of five-and-twenty years trampled
to pieces in the conflict of a single night.' ' 7th. Dined Duke
of Montrose—a large party of our peculiar old friends.—11th.
Burke and Fox, further quarrel.—June 6. To town from
Clapham upon business. Wrote the report of our society
for enforcing the King's proclamation.—7th. General meeting
of the society—read the report, which I had been pushed to
get finished—then to the Slave Committee.'

The conclusion of the session released him from London,
and he set out for a house which he had hired at Perry Mead,
in the neighbourhood of Bath. Thence he writes to Lord
Muncaster, [5] 'where, I hear you say, is Perry Mead? It is
situated in a country which, except in the article of water,
comes not far behind Cumberland and Westmoreland themselves; close to Prior Park, and about three-quarters of a
mile from the Pump-room. There old Henry Thornton and

---

[2] Mr. Stanley, member for Lancashire, who came into the House, determined to vote against, and,

[3] The Hon. D. Ryder, who came undetermined to vote for Abolition.

[4] Mr. Drake.   [5] June 16.

I are lodged, and are leading a rational kind of life, and relishing not a little the quiet and retirement it allows us, after the bustle to which we have both been so long condemned. I have heard nothing of the worthy [6] who is the cause of your friendly solicitude.'

Here he spent about a month, and refusing all invitations to dine out, enjoyed at home the society of a few chosen friends, the chief amongst whom were Mr. Henry Thornton, Mr. Grant, and Mr. Eliot. To the house of Mr. Eliot at Burton Pynsent he made an excursion upon June 30.— 'Set off early for Eliot's. Dined with G., his friend. I must beware of this sort of old bachelor's life. G. sadly taking God's name in vain.' [7] To any of his friends who had contracted this irreverent habit, he always wrote some loving remonstrance ; and he has often said that by this custom he never lost, and but once endangered, a friendship. ' I wrote to the late Sir ——, and mentioned to him this bad habit. He sent me in reply an angry letter, returning a book that I had given him; and asking for one he had given me. Instead of it I sent him a second letter of friendly expostulation, which so won him over, that he wrote to me in the kindest tone, and begged me to send him back again the book he had so hastily returned.' [8] 'Got to Pynsent at night—old Lady Chatham a noble antiquity—very like Lady Harriet, and the Pitt voice.—July 1. At Burton all day. Walked and talked with Eliot. Lady Chatham asked about Fox's speaking — is much interested about politics—seventy-five years old, and a very active mind.— 2nd. Off betimes for Cowslip Green—arrived there by the afternoon. Henry Thornton came at night.—3rd, Sunday. Early for Shipham, where church, and one hundred and fifty children. On to Cheddar, where Mrs. Baber's reception — her sudden turning her joy into a right channel, and calling on the children to sing " Praise God from whom all blessings flow," much affected me. Church — catechising — sermon read, and Mrs. Baber's moving address. The Miss Mores are indeed excellent women, and it seems as if God would prosper their benevolent intentions.—4th. D. consulted me

[6] Captain Kimber.   [7] Journal.   [8] Con. Mem.

about a vow—I advised strongly against it. Oh, how ashamed
am I made to feel by finding what is thought of me, and how
little I really correspond with it !—5th. Off betimes to breakfast with *friend* Wright at Bristol, where Mr. Harford met us.
He says that the Slave Trade is growing disgraceful. Saw old
Dr. Stonehouse, who applauded G. Whitefield. Lord Ches-
terfield charmed with him. Home to Perry Mead by dinner
time.—23rd. Heard from Henry Thornton, and pressed by
Clarkson to come up to town about Sierra Leone business.'

The Sierra Leone Company had been founded after the
loss of the Abolition question in the course of this spring.
It was a trading company, formed by the advocates of Abolition with no expectation of mercantile advantage, but with
a view to extend lawful commerce with Africa, to commence her civilization, and so confute, in the most positive manner, all those arguments for the Slave Trade which
were drawn from the alleged intellectual peculiarities of the
negro race. With this view Mr. Wilberforce took a forward
part in its establishment, and consented to act as one of its
first directors.

'Monday, July 28. Off betimes on Sierra Leone business
—reached Sandleford (M. Montagu's) in the evening, where
Dr. Beattie was already arrived.   26th. Off after breakfast.
—dined at the Speaker's, and staid all night.   Speaker will
consider of Sunday levee's transfer to Saturday.—27th. Arrived in town. To H. Thornton's—Sierra Leone meeting.
Then to Dundas on business, and to Hampstead with Pitt.
Dined, and all night.—28th. After breakfast explained a
little to the Master of the Rolls and Lady A.—29th. To
Fulham, Bishop of London's—where all night. Much talk
with the Bishop.—30th. To town—Sierra Leone meeting.
Then to Holwood—Pitt and Grenville there.—31st, Sunday.
Pitt and Grenville went to town. To Holwood chapel, and
afternoon Beckenham church. Home to dinner—Pitt and
Grenville.—August 1. Heard from H. Thornton about Sierra
Leone governor and chaplain, and came to town.—2nd.
Meeting on Sierra Leone business, morning and evening, till
eleven o'clock at night. Dined and slept at H. Thornton's
—Riou, Grant, Sir C. Middleton dined.'

In the discussions which he now attended the plans of the future company were matured.   It was carefully fostered by Mr. Wilberforce, and long engrossed the time and energies of Henry Thornton.   These 'longa negotia' accomplished, he returned into the country.

The whole of this autumn, which was spent in visiting different friends, he devoted to diligent study.   The nature of his occupations may be gathered from his list of subjects on his first establishment at Rothley Temple.   ' Bible, English History, Fenelon's Characters, Horace, by heart.'   The notes and references in his own hand, with which the copy he now used abound, especially throughout the Satires and Epistles, testify the care and diligence with which he studied. ' Cicero de Oratore, Addison's Cato, Hume, Hudibras, Pilgrim's Progress, Doddridge's Sermons, Jonathan Edwards, Owen, *Letters.*'   This last head occupied a large portion of his time.   His advice and assistance, both in charity and business, were eagerly sought for by the doubting and the distressed; whilst it was essential to his usefulness that he should keep up intimate communications with those who in various districts could influence society, or report to him the facts which marked its temper.

Sept. 21. An interesting conversation on religion with Dr. Oliver.   I am apt to be too polemic in arguing with him and H. on points of divinity and morals. — 22nd. I find my mind liable to be intoxicated with the comfort and grandeur of this scene.—27th. Went to town with a view to Sierra Leone business, and for advice.—28th. At Henry Thornton's, Clapham, but so unwell that I could not call on Pitt.   Grant dined, and King Naimbana's son.—29th. Better, though still ill.   Sierra Leone meeting all morning. Dined Pitt's with Grenville and Pybus.   He very kind and glad to see me.—30th. Grant an excellent man of business. Returned to H.

' October 13. To London.   Read all the way there—then at Sierra Leone business till four o'clock, and again till past eleven at night.—15th. Read Adam Smith.   Dined Pitt's— Mornington, Eliot, and Grenville.   They talk much of Burke, particularly Grenville—and against La Fayette, who rather

defended by Pitt.   Refused to go to Holwood that I might
have Sunday quiet.' ' Often in my visits to Holwood,' he has
said, ' when I heard one or another speak of this man's place,
or that man's peerage, I felt a rising inclination to pursue
the same objects; but a Sunday in solitude never failed to
restore me to myself.'[9]—'19th. Public meeting of directors
at King's Head—true specimen of a public meeting.   Lush-
ington's loquacity; but a very sensible, clear man.—20th.
Directors at H. Thornton's all morning.   Went to dine with
Grenville—Mornington, &c.   Returned to meeting at Thornton's, where only excellent Granville Sharpe.   All the directors
almost seem earnest, and some very worthy men.—22nd.
To Gisborne's.—25th. Clarkson called — warned him about
French Revolution.—27th. The Dean of Lichfield called—
I gave up an hour or more to conversation, &c. in hopes of
a church at Buxton.'

' November 16. With Gisborne to Wedgwood's—Etruria,
to dinner—a fine, sensible, spirited family, intelligent and
manly in behaviour — situation good — house rather grand,
and all conveniences. Pictures, &c. Discussed all evening.—
20th. I have been reading Sir M. Hale's life.   What a man
was he! and why may not I love God as well and render to
Christ as gratefully?'

From Yoxall Lodge he wrote to Mr. Pitt : — ' I wish you
may be passing your time half as salubriously and comfort-
ably as I am at Gisborne's, where I am breathing good
air, eating good mutton, keeping good hours, and enjoying the company of good friends. You have only two of
the four at command, nor these always in so pure a state
as in Needwood Forest, your town mutton being apt to be
woolly, and your town friends to be interested ; however, I
sincerely believe you are better off in the latter particular
than has been the fate of ninety-nine ministers out of a hundred ; and as for the former, the quantity you lay in may in
some degree atone for the quality; and it is a sign that neither in friends nor mutton you have yet lost your taste.   I
hope you have no more gout, &c.   If you will at any time

[9] Con. Mem.

H

give me a line (though it be but a *mouthful*) I shall be glad of it. You will think me be-Burked like yourself.'

On December 7 he went to the house of his cousin, Mr. Samuel Smith, at Wilford; where he met 'at dinner Gregory the astronomer, a well-informed man, with a high sense of the ludicrous.' On the 13th he again returned to Yoxall Lodge, and contrasting his own homeless state with the welcome which awaited the return of his host, he describes himself as 'glad to see my friends again, and felt sadly the want of wife and children to hail my return; yet looked up to heaven as the true object of desire. Received a most affecting letter from Milner about his brother. — 14th. At night Henry Thornton and Grant came in suddenly.—16th. Worked at Sierra Leone business preparing the Report.'

CHAPTER VIII.

DECEMBER 1791 TO DECEMBER 1792.

Return to London—Death of Miss Bird, and letter to Manning—Petitions against Slave Trade—Proposal to abstain from West India produce— Cause of Abolition impeded by events in St. Domingo and in France— Pitt suggests postponement—Motion lost—Dundas's resolutions for gradual Abolition—Violence of slave traders—Kimber—Stay at Bath— Letters from Dundas and Pitt—Walmer Castle—Residence at Battersea Rise—Society.

MR. WILBERFORCE'S quiet stay at Yoxall Lodge was suddenly disturbed by a summons from his friend Henry Thornton, on the evening of Dec. 16. Next morning he set off for town. 'All this week,' he says, 'at Sierra Leone business, and therefore staid in the city with H. Thornton. Went one day to dine with Pitt—met V., who seems rather more worldly. Grant with us always at Thornton's—chosen director on Tuesday.'

The hurry and interruptions of his London life were now begun. 'Jan. 7. Out in the morning—employed all day. W. Smith called in the afternoon. I talked to him on religion, but too much as a matter of criticism.—10th. City—

Sierra Leone ; and afternoon Slave business. Then Henry Thornton's, where discussed, and home late; Grant our associate.—11th. Dined R. Smith's—Pitt, Dundas, &c. I staid late.—12th. Pitt, Montrose, Grenville, Attorney-General, &c., dined with me.—18th. Queen's birthday—at St. James's. Dined at Pitt's.—21st. Went tête-a-tête with Pitt to Wimbledon—finance lecture on the way. A long discussion with Dundas after dinner—a most excellent man of business.'

'To you,' he wrote to Mr. Mason,[1] 'who know Yoxall Lodge, and can by the utmost stretch of your imagination form to yourself some idea of *my* London, I need hardly say how I feel the change; yet I am at my post. I endeavour, as much as I can, to preserve my Needwood Forest mind in my Palace Yard habitation.'

He records himself this spring as 'dining from home less than in former years, and giving fewer dinners, either ordinary or formal, upon Milner's persuasion.'

'January 22. Saw the astonishing letter from Miss More, containing an account, written inter moriendum, of Harriet Bird's death, at six o'clock on Wednesday morning. Oh may my latter end be like hers ! Strongly affected; may it be deeply.' 'I have been extremely affected by Miss More's account of Harriet's death-bed scene—how can I but be so —particularly her illumination, and the following agony just before she was taken to glory. She prayed for me on her death-bed. How does her progress shame me ! I am behind, far behind, all of them. But my eyes will not allow me to write ; many tears to-day from mental struggles have injured them. May God, for Christ's sake, cause them not to flow in vain.'

A letter detailing the events which had occurred at Bath, called forth a reply,[2] in which he says : — 'I cannot help almost envying you the scene you have been witnessing. O my dear friend, never forget it ; let it still be present to your mind, and let it force all those concerns which are so apt to engross our imaginations, and interest our hearts, to retire to their proper distance, or rather to shrink to their true point of insignificance. Never let me forget it. When

---

[1] Jan. 2. [2] To W. Manning, Esq., January 20, 1792.

I seem to you at any time to be intoxicated, as it were, by the hurry, the business, or the dissipation of life, spare not the best offices of friendship; recall me to that sobriety and seriousness of mind which become those who know not when they may be called away; place before me the solemn triumphs of which you have been a spectator, and animate me to press forward in emulation of so glorious an example.'

To his other occupations was soon added constant attendance on the parliamentary business of an important session, in which, though other questions received a full share of his attention, the Abolition struggle mainly occupied his thoughts. 'I have considered,' he says, 'with several friends, our plan of operations, and we are agreed, that the best course will be to excite the flame as much as possible, but not to allow it more than to smother until after I shall have given notice of my intention of bringing the subject forward. This must be the signal for the fire's bursting forth. We hope ere that time to have laid all our trains, and that by proper efforts the blaze will then be universal.'[3]

The conduct of this 'appeal to the people' was now his first care. Rendered necessary 'by that vote of the House of Commons on the Slave Trade question, which proved above all things the extremely low ebb of real principle there,'[4] it was addressed to the moral sympathies of the educated and religious classes. County meetings to petition Parliament were what he deemed best. 'I am very desirous,' he writes to Mr. Mason, 'that our great county should deem this, as I am sure it is, a worthy occasion for its interference. Were Yorkshire but to open the path, other counties, I am persuaded, would crowd in after it, and gladly follow in its train. Pray turn this matter over in your mind, and remember only there is little room for delay.'[5] 'Such a meeting might be of great use in stimulating other *countylings* to follow the example.'[6]

'The matter should be pushed forward by those who are not my political friends.'[7] 'Finding myself obliged,' replies

[3] To Rev. C. Wyvill, Dec. 19.　　　[4] To Mr. Gisborne, March 5.
[5] To Mr. Wyvill, Jan. 18.　　　[6] To the Rev. W. Mason, Jan. 15.
　　　　　[7] To W. Hey, Esq., Jan. 9.

Mr. Mason, 'to appear in the pulpit yesterday for the Dean, I contrived (by a sort of lyrical transition in my sermon) not only to applaud the plan of the new colony of Sierra Leone, but also to exhort my audience to renew their petitions for the Abolition.' In many of these he had to settle all the details of the meeting. 'Give us precise directions,' writes Mr. Gisborne; 'I am aware that taking up your time by questions respecting minutiæ which you may reasonably think shifted to me, is as if the Christians in a petty village of Asia Minor were to pester the Pope with voluminous letters respecting the election of a door-keeper to their chapel.'

Many of the friends of Abolition had at this time determined to abstain from the consumption of West Indian produce until the measure should be carried. 'We use East Indian sugar entirely,' writes Mr. Babington, 'and so do full two-thirds of the friends of Abolition in Leicester.' Upon this point the opinion of Mr. Wilberforce was called for from many quarters. 'When you have leisure to favour me with a line,' wrote the venerable Newton, 'I shall be glad of your judgment respecting the associations now rapidly forming to stop the consumption of West Indian produce. If you were to recommend such a measure I should readily adopt it.' Mr. Wilberforce wisely decided 'that such a course should be suspended until, if necessary, it might be adopted with effect by general concurrence.' It was not without a struggle that the more violent of his followers obeyed his temperate counsels.

Whilst he was thus rallying and drilling his country forces, accounts arrived of the recent outrages in St. Domingo. They afforded a pretext for warmer opposition to the enemies of Abolition, and shook the faith of some of its adherents. Many too of those who continued zealous supporters of the cause were for deferring a fresh appeal to Parliament till a more convenient season. 'People here are all panicstruck with the transactions in St. Domingo, and the apprehension, or pretended apprehension, of the like in Jamaica and other of our islands. I am pressed on all hands to defer my motion till next year.'

It was not the natural timidity of irresolute minds alone

which suggested this temporising policy; pressing arguments to the same effect from a very different quarter tried but could not shake his resolution.   The struggle was, for the moment, great; but whilst his tender heart was touched to the quick by the mere apprehension of so sore a trial, he did not hesitate between the loss of his early and intimate friend, if so it must be, and the great cause he had undertaken. 'Called away after dinner to Slave Committee. Pitt threw out against Slave motion on St. Domingo account. I must repose myself on God.   I could hardly bring myself to resolve to do my duty and please God at the expense (as I suspect it will turn out) of my cordiality with Pitt, or rather his with me.'[8]   But the inward conflict was soon over.   'Do not be afraid,' he tells Mr. Babington, 'lest I should give ground. This is a matter wherein all personal, much more all ministerial, attachments must be as dust in the balance.'

Nor was this the only difficulty peculiar to that troubled season.   It was at this time that the fraternising spirit of revolutionary France established affiliated societies in foreign nations, and threatened our own population with infection from her leprous touch. From the contagion of her principles the sounder part of the nation shrunk back with horror, and viewed with the utmost suspicion whatever bore the least resemblance to them.   The supporters of the Slave Trade were not slow in turning to their own advantage this excited state of public feeling. The name of Jacobin, and the charge of holding revolutionary tenets, might be easily affixed to any advocate of liberty; whilst, however wantonly thrown out, such imputations could not in those times of wakeful suspicion be readily removed.   Mr. Wilberforce well understood the danger to his cause which this involved.   'What business had one of your friends,' asked Dundas, 'to attend the Crown and Anchor last Thursday? He could not have done a more mischievous thing to the cause you have taken in hand.'[9]   'On Wednesday last,' says Mr. Wilberforce's diary, shortly after he received this letter, 'to Pitt's at Holwood. Staid till Saturday—with Pitt to town in his phaeton, and

[8] Diary.   [9] To W. Wilberforce, Esq., July 18, 1791.

interesting talk about Abolition.   Some vote against it, not
to encourage Paine's disciples.'

This impression biassed most strongly the mind of the
King, and created henceforth an insuperable obstacle to the
exercise of any ministerial influence in behalf of Abolition.
There had been a time when George III. had whispered at
the levee, ' How go on your black clients, Mr. Wilberforce ? '
but henceforth he was a determined opposer of the cause.
Yet it was clearly right to bring the question forward.   The
sympathy of the country was too much aroused to endure
delay.   Public meetings, and petitions numerously signed,
multiplied both in England and in Scotland.

Upon April 2 Mr. Wilberforce proposed his motion in
a debate, which he describes the following morning to Mr.
Hey :—'After a very long debate (we did not separate till
near seven this morning), my motion for immediate Abolition
was put by; though supported strenuously by Mr. Fox, and
by Mr. Pitt with more energy and ability than were almost
ever exerted in the House of Commons.'   ' Windham, who
has no love for Pitt, tells me that Fox and Grey, with whom
he walked home after the debate, agreed with him in thinking
Pitt's speech one of the most extraordinary displays of eloquence they had ever heard.   For the last twenty minutes he
really seemed to be inspired.'   ' He was dilating upon the
future prospects of civilizing Africa, a topic which I had
suggested to him in the morning.'[1]   ' We carried a motion
however afterwards for gradual Abolition, against the united
forces of Africans and West Indians, by a majority of 238 to
85.   I am congratulated on all hands, yet I cannot but feel
hurt and humiliated.   We must endeavour to force the gradual
Abolitionists in *their* bill (for I will never myself bring forward a parliamentary license to rob and murder) to allow as
short a term as possible, and under as many limitations.'[2]
'On reading the debates,' wrote the Dean of Carlisle,[3] ' I am
satisfied that much ground is gained as far as respects public
opinion; the opposers are plainly overawed and ashamed.'

' On the whole,' he says after the debate,[4] ' I am thankful

[1] Con. Mem.   [2] To Mr. Hey.
[3] April 9.   [4] To Rev. C. Wyvill, April 9.

for what we have obtained.' On the following day he wrote to Mr. Gisborne: 'I have not seen Fox since Dundas gave his notice. Of his plan I have heard no more since we parted. I mean to go to Pitt's to-morrow, and I shall then be able to keep a tolerable look-out.'

On the 23rd Mr. Dundas brought forward his Resolutions for a gradual Abolition. 'After a hard struggle,' writes Mr. Wilberforce,[5] 'we were last night defeated in our attempt to fix the period of the Abolition for January 1, 1795, the numbers being 161 to 121. But we carried January 1, 1796 (Mr. Dundas had proposed 1800), by a majority of 151 against 132. On the whole this is more than I expected two months ago, and I have much cause for thankfulness. We are to contend for the numbers of slaves to be imported ; and *then for the House of Lords.*' 'You have great reason,' writes Dr. Milner, 'to be thankful, for God seems to bless your labours; and I remember I told you long ago, if you carry this point in your whole life, that life will be far better spent than in being prime minister many years.'

Upon May 1, when the question came again before the House, Mr. Dundas declared himself unable to propose his Resolutions as amended by the late division. They were therefore moved by Mr. Pitt, and upon the following day communicated to the Lords. Here the opponents of the measure rallied their broken forces; and, in spite of Lord Grenville, prevailed upon the House to proceed by hearing evidence at their bar ; a resolution equivalent to a direct vote which soon followed, to postpone the business till the ensuing session.

Still much had been gained in these debates. All direct defence of the trade was now abandoned. The charges of its opponents were admitted to be true. Its ultimate necessity to the colonies was no longer maintained. 'No man hereafter,' said Mr. Pitt, 'can pretend to argue that the Abolition of the trade ought not to take place, however he may wish from motives of private interest to defer the day of its suppression.' In conceding so much, and thus changing the ground of conflict, Mr. Dundas showed much of his

[5] April 28. Letter to W. Hey, Esq.

adroit management. A direct defence of the odious traffic was no longer possible. Its existence might be prolonged by the easy expedient of continual delay; whilst the promise of future Abolition gained the irresolute amongst the advocates of humanity, and fully satisfied 'the moderate men,' who hung as doubtful allies upon their skirts. Nor could anyone be fitter than himself for the task he had assumed. A frank and joyous temper was united in Mr. Dundas with great natural sagacity and knowledge of mankind. The apparent honesty and warmth of heart which marked his speeches enabled him to turn aside what he knew well how to represent as a false and sickly humanity. Oppression could not find a kindlier advocate, or abuses a more plausible patron. ' I cannot,' was, thirty years later, Mr. Wilberforce's comment upon a letter which he at the time received, ' at all relish what is here said in favour of gradual abolition. You must remember that it was to the fatal appeal made to that principle, that we chiefly owed the defeat of our first assault, and the twenty years' continuance of the murderous traffic.' [6]

The summer of this year exposed him to a repetition of those threats of personal violence to which ever since he undertook this cause he had been more or less exposed. For the next two years he was thus pursued by a West Indian captain named Kimber. Sir James Stonhouse, to whom Mr. Wilberforce had applied for the particulars of his character, thus describes Kimber :—' He is a very bad man, a great spendthrift; one who would swear to any falsehood, and who is linked with a set of rascals like himself.' This man had been charged by Mr. Wilberforce, in the debate of April 1792, with great cruelty in his conduct of the trade. Several trials in the courts of law followed; in one of which the captain was himself capitally indicted for the murder of a negro girl. Of this charge he was not found guilty; escaping, in the judgment of Mr. Wilberforce, 'through the shameful remissness of the Crown lawyers, and the indecent behaviour of a high personage, who from the bench identified himself with the prisoner's cause.'

[6] Letter to W. Wallace Currie, Esq.

As soon as he was discharged from prison he applied to Mr. Wilberforce for what he termed remuneration for his wrongs. — 'July 11. Morning received Kimber's letter.— Friday, by Pitt's advice, wrote answer to Kimber.' Upon receiving a brief refusal, Kimber had recourse to violence. 'Kimber lying in wait for me—first civil, then abusive.'[7] 'Kimber called between seven and eight, and again about ten. "Very savage-looking," Amos said, "he went away, muttering and shaking his head."'[8]   The interference of Lord Sheffield (an honourable opponent) at last terminated this annoyance, but not before one of his friends (the late Lord Rokeby) had thought it needful to become his armed companion in a journey into Yorkshire, to defend him from anticipated violence.

Being still detained in the neighbourhood of London by Sierra Leone business, he was 'taken in,'[9] he says, 'to dine at W. Smith's, with a vast company—Dr. Aikin, Gillies, Mr. and Mrs. Barbauld, Helen Maria Williams, Mackintosh, Mr. Belsham, Mr. Sabbatière, Mr. and Mrs. Towgood. I was not sufficiently guarded in talking about religion after dinner. Mackintosh talked away — he spoke most highly of Pitt's Slave Trade speech. Came home, as if hunted, to Thornton's quiet family party, and much struck with the difference. I threw out some things which may perhaps be of use.'

On the 31st he set off for Bath, and 'on the road it occurring to me[1] that it might be useful for me to be early in seeing Sir W. Young, who is just come from the West Indies, and that he was not a quarter of a mile out of the road, I drove to his house, Huntercombe, and staid all night. Boswell there, a great enemy of the Abolition—said that he was at Kimber's trial, and gloried in it. Sir William read a letter from G. to his father — some wit, but affected, and full of levity and evil; written in 1773, when he was near sixty, alas! Bozzy talked of Johnson, &c. Wednesday. Had some serious talk with Bozzy, who admitted the depravity of human nature. Last night he expressed his disbelief of eternal punishment. He asked Sir W. to take his boy home, and walked off into the West of England with the

[7] Diary.   [8] Ib.   [9] July 24.   [1] Diary.

"Spirit of Athens" under his arm, and two shirts and a night-cap in his pocket, sans servant.'

'My dear Muncaster,' he writes[2] in answer to a friendly remonstrance upon the postponement of a long-promised visit, 'notwithstanding your admonition behold me entering upon a course of Bath waters, prudently however and moderately like Muncaster the citizen; not rashly and violently like Pennington the soldier. It would be a high gratification to me to be cooling my feet upon the mossy brow of Muncaster Park, instead of burning and parching them on the rest-refusing pavement of Bath.'

'Aug. 17th. This is the day on which Pitt, Dundas, P. Arden, and Steele are at Hamels.'[3]

' I have given directions,' writes Dundas, 'for the appointment of the clergyman[4] you recommend. As to the schoolmasters, I have no difficulty in trusting to your discretion, and the purity of your intentions, in providing and recommending proper persons to me. It will give you pleasure to hear that the King, in the most handsome and gentleman-like manner, has *compelled* Mr. Pitt to accept the appointment of Warden. of the Cinque Ports, vacant by the death of poor Lord Guildford.'—' Mr. Dundas,' the King wrote, ' is to accompany my letter with a few lines expressing that I will not admit of this favour being declined. I desire Lord Chatham may also write.' Mr. Pitt had not left him to gather this appointment from a third person; but with a readiness which showed something of Cæsar's anxiety for the applause of Cato, had written to him on the very day the offer reached him.

' I should like of all things to accept your invitation, but I must be at Windsor on Sunday, and I want to stay here till the last minute for the chance of seeing Eliot and my little niece, who may perhaps arrive from Cornwall before I set out. Since I received your letter, a circumstance has happened, which I believe upon the whole you will not be sorry to learn. Immediately upon Lord Guildford's death the King has written to me in the most gracious terms, to

---

[2] June 6.   [3] Mr. Robert Smith's.
[4] An additional chaplain at Botany Bay.

say that he cannot let the Wardenship of the Cinque Ports go to anyone except myself. Under all the present circumstances, and in the manner in which the offer came, I have no hesitation in accepting it; and I believe you will think I have done right.'[5]

' I told him,' says Mr. Wilberforce, 'that I agreed with him in thinking that upon the whole he had acted right.'

Sunday the 26th. Found him at Cowslip Green, whence he ' accompanied the Miss Mores to Shipham, Hounswick, Axbridge, and Cheddar. God seems indeed to prosper their work; both amongst young and old are those who are turning to Him. Near a thousand children in all. One mere child had brought all his father's household to family prayers. On the 27th, returned to Bath.

'Tuesday, September 4. Set off early for London; and on the 5th went on to Hamels—Smith, Pitt, and Dundas expecting me; found also Pepper and Lady Arden.' Upon the 15th, 'at Mr. Grant's persuasion,' he 'returned to Clapham for the purpose of seeing Shore,[6] (who is just fixed on for governor-general,) and instituting a connection with him for the sake of Indian objects.'—'19th. Dined with Pitt, where Dundas and Shore.'

' The Convention' had bestowed upon Mr. Wilberforce in the course of this summer the doubtful honour of French citizenship. ' I was provoked lately,' writes Mr. Mason,[7] 'to see your name registered among the list of citizens by the French savages.' ' I am considering,' he writes to Mr. Babington, ' how to prevent the ill effect which this vote might have upon our Abolition cause.' He found the opportunity in an attempt to raise subscriptions for the emigrant clergy.

' Friday, 20th. To town to the French clergy public meeting, and consented to be on the committee at Burke's request, partly to do away French citizenship.—26th. Shore and Mrs. S. to dine and sleep—he very pleasing.' This acquaintance with Sir J. Shore, which he sought at first with a view to future exertions for the good of India, grew into an intimate friendship, which outlived the interruptions of middle

[5] Burton Pynsent, Aug. 8, 1792.
[6] Sir John Shore, afterwards Lord Teignmouth.   [7] Sept. 11.

life, and lasted into the peaceful evening of their days.—
'October 1. To town; breakfasted with Shore, and much
pleased with him—dined to meet him at Grenville's. French
clergy's committee in the morning, where Burke flew off on
the French Revolution.—3rd. To Walmer. Pitt received me
with great warmth of affection.—4th. At night alone with
Pitt, but talked politics only—did not find myself equal
to better talk. I came here hoping that I might really find
an opportunity of talking seriously with Pitt. What am I,
to do so with any one? O Christ, help me.—5th. Morning
had some serious talk with Pitt—interrupted or should
have had more. Walked with him. I admire his integrity,
public spirit, and magnanimity in despising unpopularity.
Told me his finance plans. An incident showed the nature
of the King's mind, (Charterhouse governorship,) and Dundas's generous and high spirit. Eliot arrived at a late
dinner. Affection glistened in his countenance, when he
came in to Pitt. I stole off to bed at 11, and got off
early on Saturday morning, thinking no further object of
sufficient magnitude would be attained by my staying, to
balance a quiet instead of an unsabbatical Sunday, feeling
for my servants,' &c.

Upon the 13th he received a letter from Sir C. Middleton,
containing the account of the sudden death of Lady Middleton, and of Edwards' child. 'I resolved,' he says, 'to go to
them, hoping that I might comfort them, and perhaps be of
use to Edwards. Drove to Teston.—15th. Spent most of
the day in talking with Sir C. Middleton. Much affected at
night, and prayed earnestly. Struck solemnly with the thought
of poor Lady M.'s dead body in the house.—16th. Morning
spent in talking; prayed with some earnestness I hope.
The Bishop of London and Mrs. Porteus called, and had
some talk. But how much easier is it to talk of these things
than to be religious.—17th. The funeral this evening. Sir
Charles greatly supported, and Mrs. Edwards still more signally; her ready and powerful help from prayer: prayed to
God if it were His will for strength to bear the funeral of her
child, and she supported it without a wet eye. Sir Charles said
in walking from church that he was really very comfortable,

and that though he felt much in slowly pacing after the coffin, yet on entering the church he found a holy content-ment and composure which was scarce ever disturbed. He went to the grave. I had much talk with Mrs. Bouverie this and the next day.—18th. I had resolved to stay over this day lest they should be at once too solitary. Sir Charles has risen very much in my esteem. Mrs. Bouverie very humble, and though tried with speculative doubts, firmly resolved to do her duty; she talked to me to-day very openly. May God bless them all, and reward and advance them.'

In the course of the next week he went to Yoxall Lodge, where he resumed the diligent employments of the preced-ing summer, giving however more time than formerly to studies of a directly religious character. ' I have been em-ploying,' he says, ' most of this morning[8] in reading St. Paul's Epistles to the Romans and the Galatians.' It was by this careful study, which no press of business ever interrupted, and which continued daily through his life, that he obtained an acquaintance with holy Scripture unusual even in pro-fessed theologians. A marked advance in his character during the course of this year may be traced in the altered tone of his most private entries. They abound in that deep humiliation with which they who have looked closely into the perfect law of liberty must ever contemplate their own fulfilment of its demands; but they bear that calm and peace-ful character which cast so warm a light upon his later days.

This more tranquil tone of feeling was henceforth fostered by a system of greater domestic intercourse with the friends whose principles he valued, and by a consequent freedom from the more turbulent currents of life. ' Henry Thornton,' he says,[9] ' has bought Lubbock's house at Battersea Rise, and I am to share it with him, and pay so much per annum towards expenses. Last night I went over the house and grounds with Grant and Henry Thornton. How thankful I should be, to whom it is the only question, which of many things all comfortable I shall choose!'

Whilst his general influence was silently extending, there grew up around him here a chosen circle of peculiar friends.

[8] November 22.   [9] Diary, Mar . .

Amongst these must especially be noticed the Hon. E. J. Eliot, Mr. Grant, and Mr. Henry Thornton. Mr. Eliot, his early friend, was now settled, for the sake of his society, in the immediate neighbourhood of Battersea Rise. The loss of a wife to whom he was ardently attached (the favourite sister of Mr. Pitt), had given a tone of earnest piety to his whole character, and taught him to cooperate in every useful scheme suggested by his friend; whilst at the same time there had been inflicted on his spirit a wound from which he never rallied. His death, in 1797, was attributed, by those who knew his inmost feelings, to the lingering sorrow of a broken heart. Of Mr. Grant and Mr. Henry Thornton it is needless here to speak. 'Few men,' says the latter, 'have been blest with better friends than have fallen to my lot. Mr. Wilberforce stands at the head of these, for he was the friend of my youth. I owed much to him soon after I came out in life : for his enlarged mind, his affectionate and condescending manners, and his very superior piety, were exactly calculated to supply what was wanting to my improvement and my establishment in a right course. It is chiefly through him that I have been introduced to a variety of other most valuable associates.' 'When I entered life, I saw a great deal of dishonourable conduct among people who made great profession of religion. In my father's house I met with persons of this sort. This so disgusted me that, had it not been for the admirable pattern of consistency and disinterestedness which I saw in Mr. Wilberforce, I should have been in danger of a sort of infidelity.'[1]

Such was at this time his position; high in public estimation, and rich in private friends; engaged in the conduct of a most important cause; with his mind now disciplined by culture, and enriched by study; whilst the inmost life of his spirit, escaping from its early struggles, was strengthening into tranquil vigour, as religion took a firmer hold upon his character, and leavened more thoroughly the whole man. By his early self-discipline he had purchased the calm and peaceful obedience of the remainder of his course. Like the old prophet to whom a severe observer has beautifully

---

[1] Private and conversational memoranda of Mr. Henry Thornton.

compared him, he was prepared by humility and self-denial for the severer trials which now lay before his public life; and like him he supported them with uncorrupted faith. 'From a careful scrutiny,' says Mr. Matthias,[2] 'into the public and private life of Mr. Wilberforce, I am inclined to think that his enemies would be forced into an acknowledgment that they can find no occasion against this man, except they find it against him concerning the law of his God.'

CHAPTER IX.

DECEMBER 1792 TO OCTOBER 1795.

Alarming aspect of the times — Revolutionary principles — Wilberforce anxious to prevent war—Attends East-Riding meeting—His first great difference with Pitt—Motion for Abolition lost in the Commons—Unpromising aspect of the cause—Plan of national religious instruction for India—Defeated—His habits in society—Visits—Return to town —Foreign Slave Bill—Visit to Portsmouth — Composing his Practical Christianity— Visit to Holwood— Returns to town— Opposes the Address — Pitt's temporary alienation — Displeasure of his friends and constituents—Abolition negatived—Allowance to princes—Second motion for peace— Grounds of Pitt's opposition—Personal sentiments— Tour in Yorkshire—Pitt's letter, declaring agreement about peace.

THE autumn of 1792 set in with heavy clouds darkening the political horizon. 'Heard of the militia being called out, and Parliament summoned—talked politics, and of the state of the country, which seems very critical.'[1] 'Dec. 6th arrived in town and alighted at Pitt's.'

None but those who were blinded by party-spirit could contemplate without alarm the aspect of the times. The democratical excitement which the revolutionary fever of France had imparted to some of our own people, had been carefully fostered by the disaffected, and was ready in many places to break out into rebellion. 'Considerable numbers in Bernard Castle,' writes Mr. Wyvill, 'have manifested disaffection to the constitution, and the words, "No King,"

---

[2] Pursuits of Literature.   [1] Diary, Dec. 3.

" Liberty," and " Equality," have been written there upon
the Market Cross. During the late disturbances amongst
the keelmen at Shields and Sunderland, General Lambton
was thus addressed ": Have you read this little work of
Tom Paine's ? " " No." " Then read it—we like it much.
You have a great estate, General ; we shall soon divide it
amongst us." "You will presently spend it in liquor, and what
will you do then ?" "Why then, General, we will divide again."'
' At Carlisle,' writes Dr. Milner, 'we had many reports concerning tumults and sedition, and the affair seemed to be of
considerable magnitude. I am exceedingly sorry to find
that Mr. Paley is as loose in his politics as he is in his religion. He has considerable influence in promoting this sort
of work by his conversation, which has a strong tendency to
destroy all subordination, and bring rulers of every description into contempt. He is naturally very good tempered,
and my stay there was short. These two circumstances
alone prevented our coming to a rupture. Supposing Fox
to oppose, I think it is well at this critical moment that he
has gone so far. There is scarce one of his old friends here
at Cambridge who is not disposed to give him up ; and most
say that he is mad. I think of him much as I always did :
I still doubt whether he has bad principles, but I think it
pretty plain he has none ; and I suppose he is ready for
whatever turns up.'

' Immense pains,' he heard from Leeds,[2] ' are now taken
to make the lower class of people discontented, and to excite
rebellion. Paine's mischievous work on " the Rights of
Man," is compressed into a sixpenny pamphlet, and is sold
and given away in profusion. One merchant in this town
ordered two hundred of them to be given at his expense:
you may see them in the houses of our journeymen cloth-
dressers. The soldiers are everywhere tampered with ; no
pains are spared to render this island a scene of confusion.'

All this was sufficiently alarming ; while the danger was
increased by the probability of a French war, which must
necessarily add to the burdens of the people, and so further
the designs of the revolutionary faction. With his eyes fully

[2] Letter from W. Hey, Esq.

open to these evils, Mr. Wilberforce took a calm and sober view of the amount of danger.

' I see,' he tells Mr. Hey, ' no danger of any speedy commotion. What throws the deepest gloom over my prospects is the prevailing profligacy of the times, and, above all, that self-sufficiency, and proud and ungrateful forgetfulness of God, which is so general in the higher ranks of life.'

The same sober estimate of present appearances led him to check the exultation with which Mr. Hey regarded a temporary burst of loyalty in the town of Leeds. ' " God save the King " was sung, with a chorus of three cheers after each verse, by the whole meeting, the most numerous I ever saw upon any such public occasion ; about 3,000 in number. The populace paraded the streets until night came on, carrying an image of Tom Paine upon a pole, with a rope round his neck, which was held by a man behind, who continually lashed the effigy with a carter's whip. The effigy was at last burned in the market-place, the market-bell tolling slowly. A happy change in this town.'[3] ' I rejoice to hear that so much unanimity prevailed at Leeds,' was his answer, ' but I do not build much on such hasty effusions.'

Parliament met upon December 13, when the Address upon the King's Speech, which Mr. Fox opposed and Mr. Windham defended, expressed a strong desire of maintaining peace. On the following day, in the debate upon Mr. Fox's amendment to the Address, he declared his opinions. ' War,' he said, ' he considered at all times the greatest of human evils, and never more pregnant with injury than at the present moment; but he supported the Address, as the most likely means of preserving peace.'

He was convinced that Mr. Pitt was honestly pursuing a peace policy. ' There is no ground,' is his deliberate judgment, ' for the charge, that some time before the war broke out, Mr. Pitt had been contemplating and wishing to commence hostilities.'

Throughout the warm debates with which this session commenced, he was constantly at his post. ' Dec. 18. Fox's motion about ambassador to France—he very strong.—21st. Gave up the idea of a motion about the French King's fate.

[3] Letter from W. Hey, Esq.

House of Lords in the evening—saw strong French decree, and " Je suis Athée."—26th. A letter came from Mr. Clarke, announcing the intended East Riding meeting for the counteraction of French opinions. Determined to set off immediately to attend it. Got off at three o'clock—overtook Duncombe, Milnes, and Burgh at Biggleswade — got on Friday night to Beverley—occupied all the way in preparing a long speech, which proved all labour thrown away. Saturday. The meeting went off quietly. Gentlemen numerous— they and the people pleased with my appearance. I spoke for about five minutes ; and hardly could more without appearing to *show off.*'

But his hostility to French principles did not alter his view of the need of a reform in Parliament. Some of the reasons which led him, unlike Mr. Pitt, to maintain even in this hour of danger his former views, he opened to Mr. Hey, a strong opponent of reform. 'I think it right to pay great regard to all moderate reformers, who are sincerely attached to our present constitution of King, Lords, and Commons, and to bring them to act cordially for the constitution, and against the republicans. Unless some reforms be made, though we should get well through our present difficulties, they will recur hereafter with aggravated force.'

By January 16 he was again at Clapham ; and on the 21st 'came to Wimbledon (Mr. Dundas's) by Pitt's invitation, to be alone with Pitt, Dundas, and Scott—instead found a strange mixed party.—22nd. Going away because Lord Loughborough coming, but on the whole thought it best to stay, considering that he is about to be made chancellor.' The question of peace or war was now becoming highly critical. 'Dined at Lord Elgin's—Lord St. Helen's, Bishop of Lincoln, Mrs. Carter, &c. Elgin and Lord St. Helen's seem to *think* against war, though averse to oppose the wishes of government.'[4] The war, which broke out almost immediately, led at length to his first decided political separation from Mr. Pitt. Though Mr. Pitt's was not a 'war system,' yet he was in Mr. Wilberforce's judgment too much guided in its commencement by his own sanguine disposi-

[4] Diary, Jan. 28.

tion, hitherto untempered by any disappointment. ' It will be a very short war,' said Mr. Pitt and his friends, 'and certainly ended in one or two campaigns.' ' No, sir,' said Mr. Burke when this language was addressed to him, 'it will be a long war, and a dangerous war, but it must be undertaken.' Mr. Wilberforce was alive to its perils, but not convinced of its necessity. ' Not that,' he thought,[5] ' peace could be a state of as much security as the term " peace " had commonly implied, but he chose it as far the less of two evils. Though at the commencement of the war I could deliberately declare that we were not the assailants, and therefore that it was just and necessary; yet I had but too much reason to know that the ministry had not taken due pains to prevent its breaking out.' In the debate therefore upon the King's message,[6] which intimated the necessity of some military preparations in consequence of the murder of the King of France, he had resolved to declare his persuasion that it was the true policy of this country to continue strictly upon the defensive; that the delirium which now distracted France would probably pass away by degrees, and that she would then see the folly of provoking a war with Great Britain, in addition to the continental storm which was already gathered around her. ' I was actually upon my legs to open my mind fully upon the subject, when Pitt sent Bankes to me, earnestly desiring me not to do so that day, assuring me that my speaking then might do irreparable mischief, and pledging himself that I should have another opportunity before war should be declared.' ' House on King's message—sadly distressed—on my legs to speak against the Address, when stopped by Bankes, and note and assurance from Pitt. Sat very late, and much disturbed afterwards.'[7]—' Feb. 4. Navy voted—embargo laid by France —nothing said.—5th. Pitt's on politics—discussing—Ryder, Steele, and Mornington—till ten at night—they too violent.'

The week passed, and, in spite of Mr. Pitt's assurance, there was no opportunity upon which he could state his sentiments. By an incident to which his whole parliamentary experience could furnish no parallel, the House was com-

[5] Letter to W. Hey, Feb. 14, 1801.   [6] Feb. 1.   [7] Diary.

pelled to adjourn every successive day without entering upon
other business, because there were not a sufficient number
of members present to make a ballot for an election committee. Meanwhile war was declared by the French against
England and the United Provinces, and when hostilities had
actually begun, ' I deemed it,' he says, ' the part of a good
subject not to use language which might tend to prevent the
unanimity which was so desirable at the outset of such a
war.'[8] Yet even now he was not satisfied with the tone
held by the administration. ' Feb. 12. Message on the war
—vexed at Pitt and Dundas for not being explicit enough.'[9]
' Our government,' he wrote long after to Mr. Hey,[1] ' had
been for some months before the breaking out of the war
negotiating with the principal European powers, for the purpose of obtaining a joint representation to France, assuring
her that if she would formally engage to keep within her
limits, and not molest her neighbours, she should be suffered
to settle her own internal government and constitution without interference. I never was so earnest with Mr. Pitt on
any other occasion, as I was in my entreaties before the war
broke out, that he would declare openly in the House of
Commons, that he had been, and then was, negotiating this
treaty. I urged on him that the declaration might possibly
produce an immediate effect in France, where it was manifest
there prevailed an opinion that we were meditating some
interference with their internal affairs, and the restoration of
Louis to his throne; and, at least, must silence all but the
most determined oppositionists in this country. How far
this expectation would have been realised you may estimate
by Mr. Fox's language, when Mr. Pitt, at my instance, did
make the declaration last winter (1799). " If," he said, " the
right hon. gentleman had made the declaration now delivered, to France, as well as to Russia, Austria, and Prussia,
I should have nothing more to say or to desire." '

Yet while he condemned impartially what he deemed the
errors of the minister, he was ready to defend him from all
unmerited censure. Thus, to the author of Jasper Wilson's

[8] MS. Mem.   [9] Diary.
[1] Letter of Feb. 14, 1801, to W. Hey, Esq.

letter (Dr. Currie), a work which he commends, 'as exhibiting originality of thought and force of expression, and solving finely the phenomena of revolutions,' he writes, 'I think that you have spoken very uncandidly of Mr. Pitt's motives and general principles of action. I am convinced, if the flame of pure disinterested patriotism burns in any human bosom, it burns in his. Believe me who am pretty well acquainted with our public men, that he has not his equal for integrity as well as ability in the "primores" of either House of Parliament.'

Now that the war had commenced, he supported the King's government whenever he was able. His mode of life was much what has been described in the preceding year. 'March 12,' he enters, 'Three ballots. So between the first and second gave a dinner to some of my older friends, Apsley, Villiers, F. North, Belgrave, &c.'—'Mason dined with me. Burke's wild speech to Mason about replacing the French clergy.' 'Dined at Pitt's before House —two ballots, and friends came over to my house for dinner between them.' 'Expecting Muncaster, meaning serious discussion; when sent for by Henry Thornton to town, on the state of public credit, &c.—then to Pitt's with and for him. A sadly interrupted day.'

He was now again occupied with the Negro cause. The session of 1792 had closed the period which he has described as the first assault upon the Slave Trade. The effects of the new tactics so skilfully introduced by Mr. Dundas were soon felt. No practical mitigation of the evil had been yet obtained, but the indignation of the country had found a vent, and was rapidly subsiding into comparative indifference.

The circumstances of the times helped forward this reaction. The excitement of the revolutionary war distracted the attention of the volatile; the progress of French principles terrified the thoughtful.

Yet during this darkest period his courage never yielded, nor was his patient diligence relaxed. He was early at his post in the first session of 1793; and sought to hasten the proceedings of the Lords by a new vote of the lower House, which, however, in spite of his eloquence, backed by the seldom united arguments of Mr. Pitt and Mr. Fox, refused by a majority of eight votes to renew its own decision of the preceding year.

This defeat was succeeded by a postponement of the business in the Lords, where the advocates of the trade were reinforced by the avowed and zealous support of a member of the royal family.

He was engaged at this time in another most important effort—the attempt to improve the condition of our Asiatic fellow-subjects. Since the reign of Anne a complete indifference to such attempts had settled upon the mind of the nation: he now attempted to arouse it from this long lethargy. After having 'studied the subject with strenuous and persevering diligence,' and consulted long and earnestly with the Archbishop of Canterbury, the Speaker, and his friend Charles Grant, he brought the question forward in the House of Commons on May 14, in the form of certain Resolutions, which were agreed to in committee, and entered on the Journals. These Resolutions pledged the House in general terms, to the 'peculiar and bounden duty of promoting, by all just and prudent means, the religious improvement' of the native Indians. Two days afterwards he proposed specific resolutions for sending schoolmasters and chaplains throughout India. To these Mr. Dundas had promised his support.— 'May 15th. East Indian Resolutions in hand, and slave business, Lord Carhampton abusing me as a madman.— 17th. Through God's help got the East Indian Resolutions in quietly. The hand of Providence was never more visible than in this East Indian affair. What cause have I for gratitude, and trust, and humiliation!' 'It is of God's unmerited goodness that I am selected as the agent of usefulness.'[2]

But this fair prospect soon clouded over. Upon the 22nd he entered, 'East Indian directors met and strongly reprobated my clauses.' This opposition at once altered the tone of Mr. Dundas. Upon 'the 24th, House on the East India Bill: I argued as strongly as I could.' 'It is not meant,' he said, 'to force our faith upon the natives of India;

[2] Journal.

but gravely, silently, and systematically to prepare the way for the gradual diffusion of religious truth.'

In spite of this appeal he says, ' My clauses thrown out—Dundas most false and double ; but, poor fellow! much to be pitied.' 'The East India directors and proprietors,' he tells Mr. Gisborne, 'have triumphed—all my clauses were last night struck out on the third reading of the Bill, (with Dundas's consent ! ! this is *honour*,) and our territories in Hindostan, twenty millions of people included, are left in the undisturbed and peaceable possession, and committed to the providential protection of—Brama.' 'How mysterious, how humbling, are the dispensations of God's providence !' was his own private meditation.[3] ' I see that I closed with speaking of the East India clauses being carried, of which I have now to record the defeat; thrown out on the third reading by a little tumult in the court of proprietors.'

The general apathy with which his proposals were received, pained him deeply. Yet something had been done. The assertion of the general duty of attempting to evangelise the East, barren as it was for twenty years, remained upon the Journals of the House, and contradicted publicly the profession of infidelity which was made with too much truth this very year, in the person of our nation, at the court of China. ' The English,' declared Lord Macartney, 'never attempt to disturb or dispute the worship or tenets of others, &c. . . they come to China with no such views . . they have no priests or chaplains with them, as have other European nations,' &c.[4]

His Diary continues : ' 27th. Brought in Foreign Slave Bill.—28th. Pitt's birthday, 34.—House till late, then dined Dundas's— Duke of Buccleuch, Grenville, Chatham, Mulgrave, Steele, Ryder, Rose, Bayham, Apsley, Eliot, Pitt.—June 4th. To town—busy about Slave Bill—drawing room —then dined at Pitt's.—5th. Exceedingly hurried—Slave Bill in Committee ; but put off again.—7th. Very busy again all day—then House till eleven. American guarantee of French islands. — 12th. Foreign Slave Bill thrown out. 22nd. To Holwood with Pitt in his phaeton—early dinner and back

---

[3] Journal.   [4] Lord Macartney's Journal, Oct. 21, 1793.

to town.   Discussion about Dowlin—religion—political character, &c.'

On the 20th July he was established at Perry Mead, in the
immediate neighbourhood of Bath, with Mr. Venn.   Such
society, and comparative retirement, he valued highly, and
sought diligently to employ to his own improvement.   ' I
have had,' says his Diary, ' Venn with me near a fortnight;
he is heavenly-minded, and bent on his Master's work, affectionate to all around him.'

During this stay at Bath, he began the execution of his
long-cherished plan of addressing his countrymen on their
estimate and practice of religious duty.   ' Saturday, Aug. 3,'
he says, ' I laid the first timbers of my tract.'   The Diary of
this autumn contains frequent notices of its continuance ;
and it was from this that his ' Practical Christianity' arose.
His first idea was to speak out to his countrymen in one
great utterance, what he was continually endeavouring to dif-
fuse by his use in social life of his fine temper, musical voice,
and winning powers of conversation.   Going at this time on
a passing visit, he writes to Mrs. More for any hints which
might be useful to him as to his conversation there.

After leaving Bath, he lived at Battersea Rise ; and was
'reading Butler, Barrow, Soame Jenyns, and the Scriptures,
and going on with tract, which I discussed with Cecil, who
is now staying with me ; he strongly recommends it.'

His neighbourhood to London enabled him to see more
of Mr. Pitt than had been lately possible ; and earnest were
their discussions upon public business.   ' To town, September
14, to see Pitt—a great map spread out before him.—16th.
To town on Admiralty business of my constituents.   Dined
tête-à-tête with Pitt—he disengaging himself to do so—much
politics.   Home at night.—18th.   To town on business.   Pitt
asked me to dine with Lord G. Conway and grandees ; I
pondered and, approving, went — Dundas, Hawkesbury,
Chatham, Grenville, Mornington, &c.   Slept at Pitt's—he
very kind.—Oct. 11.   To town early.   Pitt's long " discussion
(Elgin) about the war "—dined with him, and home at night.
—14th.   Off for Holwood.   Pitt and I tête-à-téte—he very
open, and we discussed much.'

Upon October 22 he set out for his annual visits at Yoxall Lodge and Rothley Temple ; and during the two months which he spent between them, was principally occupied in preparing the materials for his work on ' Practical Christianity.'

By the end of December he was obliged to lay this work aside for the ordinary business of his London seasons. ' Jan. 18. Long political discussion with Pitt on the King's speech. —20th. To town to dinner with Duncombe to confer with him about politics—then called at Bankes'.—21st. To Grant's to prepare for debate, and be uninterrupted—House till very late.—Feb. 3. House—Pitt uncommonly fine on " armed nation," &c.'

Though he still supported administration, he watched eagerly for any opening for peace ; ' witnessing with deep solicitude, and not without some gloomy anticipations, the progress of the war ; ' [5] often lamenting ' the violent work,' and ' acrimony of debate,' which characterised that stormy period. He was ever ready in his place to maintain the cause of morality and religion ; and took commonly a leading part in all discussions bearing upon these points. Upon February 7 he moved for leave to bring in a Bill to suppress the Foreign Trade. Although this measure left unrestricted the supply of our own islands, and could not therefore impede their cultivation ; yet against it was arrayed almost the whole force of the West Indian interest. With great personal labour he succeeded in carrying the Bill through the House of Commons, after four divisions upon its three readings and recommitment. In the House of Lords on the second reading [6] it was abandoned by the ordinary friends of Abolition (Lord Stanhope alone remaining firm) to the assaults of Lord Abingdon and the Duke of Clarence, even Lord Grenville consenting to defer this first instalment in humanity until the general measure should be adjusted. On this no progress was made by the Lords. Upon March 10 they rejected a proposition made by Bishop Horsley for referring the examination to a select committee ; and it was not until May 6 that they summoned to their bar a single

[5] MS. Mem.   [6] May 2.

witness : two only were examined, and the subject was entirely laid aside.

The session meanwhile advanced with its wonted 'hurry and turmoil ;' 'he never recollected to have had so much business on his hands.' Towards its end he made a hasty excursion with Mr. Grant and Mr. Henry Thornton.

'June 25. To Portsmouth and saw the Gambiers.—26th. Rowed in a revenue boat to the prizes; then to Spithead (firing grand). The Queen and Defence, where pleasing confabulation with Gambier—then valiant Captain Pringle, where ate—then Queen, where dined—sea scene—officers civil—afterwards got off when the ladies did—saw the ship— marine officers and sailors—characteristic manners. Rowed to Haslar hospital, where saw our poor wounded—Gambier well spoken off. Terrible appearance of the men blown up. Home and Gambier's. Portsmouth point—wickedness and blasphemy abounds — shocking scene. —27th. To Forton prison, where much talk with French prisoners ; true democrats ; saw their wounded—and then off to London,' to be present in the House until the conclusion of the session.

In these last debates he observed with pain that Mr. Pitt seemed more averse from peace than in the earlier part of the year. 'July 10. To the House—Sheridan, Grey, &c. Pitt much too strong for war.' On the day following Parliament was prorogued, and his dissatisfaction could therefore for the present lead only to private remonstrance ; but it was an omen of that public opposition into which he was forced at the commencement of the following session.

'July 12. To Holwood—dined tête-à-tête with Pitt, and political discussion—Eliot and his child came in the evening—15th. Pitt went early to town. I staid and discussed with Eliot about my tract. Wednesday. At Holwood all day, and much the same as yesterday. Quiet, comfortable, and I hope useful after my bustle.'

'On Thursday, 17th, after dinner I set off for Betchworth, and reaching it at night, began next morning thinking in earnest about my tract.' ' Here for the first time I have got a little quiet, and have resumed my work diligently; yet I doubt whether I can do anything worth publishing. Henry

Thornton, Venn, and Farish came to me on different days
for discussion about it. I cannot receive their ideas, and
get no benefit from them.—27th, Sunday. Quiet all day, and
a serious Sunday, in which I found solitude useful and comfortable.'

November 8, he says, ' I left off my tract till next year,
and began to apply to politics.' After a short and pleasant
visit to Sandon, 'where he found Ryder not strong about the
war, but yielding to direction,' he returned to town. November 18. 'Discussed politics with H. Thornton and Grant.
—19th. Off at ten to Pitt's—heard that Parliament would be
prorogued until December 30, giving me time to make up my
mind—strongly at present disposed to peace. Talked much
politics with Gisborne, who quite agrees with me. Threw
out some hints of my state of mind, and accepted Pitt's invitation to dine. Party of friends—no general politics. Conversation on the pending trials (of Horne Tooke, &c.) for
high treason.—21st. To dine Ryder's—Grenville, Pitt, Steele,
&c. very friendly.—27th. To town to breakfast with Pitt and
discuss politics.—Dined at Palace Yard tête-à-tête with Jay
—heard openly his opinion in politics—many American war
anecdotes. Then at nine, Pitt's for political discussion till
near one, and not bed till near two. Head and mind full, and
could sleep but very disturbedly.' 'I am making up my mind
cautiously and maturely,[7] and therefore slowly, as to the best
conduct to be observed by Great Britain in the present critical emergency.'

To the early friend[8] whose inflexible independence he most
highly valued, he wrote:—' I have often much comfort and advantage from consulting with you on politics, and we seem to
have agreed in the main, both before the war broke out and
since. If you would be in London a day or two before the
meeting, it might afford us the opportunity of talking the
matter over fully before we should be called to pledge ourselves to the Address. From what I collect on this subject,
Pitt's ideas are as warlike as ever. I allow much to the argument that any peace we could make with a French republic would be insecure, and require an immense peace

[7] Letter to W. Hey, Esq.   [8] Henry Bankes, Esq.

establishment, &c.; but then I see no grounds to hope for a better issue from prosecuting the war. I believe it might be our best plan to declare our willingness to make peace on equitable terms; and I should make no difficulty about giving up all our conquests ; but as to this vile Corsica, I know not how to act. We cannot surrender it to the tender mercies of the French. I am in hopes the Dutch will make peace with France, which will be a fair divorce, and then if ever I consent to a reunion it will be my own fault. Let me know what you think. Remember, all the French know of the intentions of Great Britain is from our declarations, and from Pitt's speeches, and these have been uniformly point-blank against any accommodation with the existing government in France, or in other words, against a republic. Therefore unless we make some new declaration, they can have no idea but that we mean to fight against the republic *usque ad internecionem.* I would gladly get an end put to this war without Pitt's being turned out of office, which will hardly be possible, I fear, if it continue much longer. Much however as this weighs with me, and that not merely on private grounds, the other obvious considerations are far more important. I am quite sick of such a scene of havoc and misery, and unless I am quite clear I shall not dare vote for its continuance.'

'December 26. Much political talk with Grant and H. Thornton, making up my mind.—27th. Much again in political talk.' His course was at length decided. The more settled aspect of affairs in France since the fall of Robespierre gave him some hopes of the possibility of an accommodation, and peace he deemed so inestimable a blessing that no possible opening for restoring it should be neglected. 'Dec. 29. To town. Dined Palace Yard — Duncombe, Muncaster, H. Thornton, Bankes, Montague; talked politics—agreed that I would amend.'

It was not merely the pain of joining in an open opposition to his friend, which made him slow in arriving at this conclusion. It involved his giving some countenance to what he deemed a violent and unprincipled opposition, who in condemning the war acted with all the asperity of party feeling.

He knew, moreover, that he could not hope to carry with him the mass of sober and well-affected people. They still thought the war necessary, and regarded all opposition to it as the effects of some Jacobinical tendency, or party motive. All these objections to his course he had well considered; but having made up his mind, he faced them boldly.

'December 30. Prepared Amendment at Bankes's. Moved it in a very incoherent speech; good arguments, but all in heaps for want of preparation; had no plan whatever when I rose.' The Amendment was seconded by his colleague Mr. Duncombe, who was followed by Mr. Bankes. Though supported by many who had hitherto voted with the minister, it was negatived by a large majority. He moved it indeed under peculiar disadvantages: fearful on the one hand of exciting popular discontent, he was guarded in his own statements; whilst on the other, he was 'forced to adopt an Amendment stronger than he himself liked, by the violent language of the government. We are in a very alarming state, the honest men so obstinate, the others so active and dangerous.'[9]—'31st. Walked with T. Steele, &c., all more candid to me than I could expect.' Upon January 26, on a motion for peace made by Mr. Grey, he again declared his sentiments, and voted with the opposition. 'To town on Grey's motion—spoke well—up in the House till half-past five.'

The painful consequences which he had foreseen, had followed his conscientious action. It would be hard to say whether Pitt or he felt most acutely this temporary separation. Twice only, he used to say, was Pitt's sleep broken by the events of his public life—by the mutiny at the Nore, and by this first opposition of his trusted friend. For himself, he had lived hitherto in habits of such unrestrained intimacy with that great man, he entertained towards him so hearty an affection, and the spring of his life had been so cheered by his friendship, that it was with bitter regret he saw the clouds begin to gather which were, at least for a season, to cast a comparative gloom and chillness over their intercourse.

'February 4. Dined,' he says, 'at Lord Camden's—Pepper and Lady Arden, Steele, &c. I felt queer, and all day out

[9] Letter to W. Hey, Esq.

of spirits—wrong, but hurt by the idea of Pitt's alienation.—
12th. Party of *the old firm* at the Speaker's; I not there.'

Nor was this his only grief. He promoted overtures for
peace, amongst other reasons, because he foresaw that the
war must ultimately become unpopular, and then that Mr.
Pitt's administration ' would be succeeded by a faction, who
knew that they had forced themselves into the Cabinet; and
feeling that they had no footing at St. James's, would seek it
in St. Giles's.' It was not therefore without pain that he
found himself repeatedly dividing with this party, and heard
Mr. Fox say—' You will soon see that you must join us altogether.' For though he loved the frank and kindly temper
of this great man, and though he duly honoured his steady
support of the Abolition of the Slave Trade, he regarded his
public principles with a settled disapprobation, which was
never stronger than at this very moment. The reasons which
made the opposition claim him, rendered him suspected by
the bulk of sober-minded men. ' Your friend Mr. Wilberforce,' said Mr. Windham to Lady Spencer, ' will be very
happy any morning to hand your Ladyship to the guillotine.'
' When I first went to the levee after moving my Amendment, the King cut me.' ' Mr. Wilberforce is a very respectable gentleman,' said Burke to Mr. Pitt, ' but he is not the
people of England.' He was well aware himself, that the
country was not generally with him. Though their strong
personal regard for him kept his constituents silent, he well
knew that even they disliked his course.

He was now exposed to difficulties which no party man
can properly appreciate; for a party man is always immediately surrounded by those who agree with him, and in their
good opinion he can entrench himself. But the independent
politician is assailed with hostile judgments on every side.
Thus whilst on the one hand he offended the partisans of
administration by his Amendment upon the King's Speech,[1]
on the other, by supporting the supply of due resources to
carry on the war vigorously, if it must continue, and by
defending the suspension of the Habeas Corpus Act,[2] he
equally irritated opposition.

[1] January 2.   [2] January 5.

These trials were increased by the expressed disagreement of almost all those personal friends with whom he most freely communicated upon political questions, and by the concurrent accounts they forwarded to him of the disapprobation felt to his conduct. ' I do not perceive,' wrote the Dean of Carlisle before the meeting of Parliament, 'the nature of the opposition to Pitt which you are likely to make. I hope you will not prove a dupe to the dishonest opposition, who will be glad to make use of you in hunting down Pitt, and for no other purpose.' ' You are,' he wrote, 'in a very critical situation, both as to the general good or bad and also in regard to the judgment which will be formed of you personally. I never conceived that you had intended to take so decided a part in this business as to lead the opposition against Pitt.'

' The bulk of people think you are doing a great deal of mischief. It is an intricate and thorny business. The sentiments of your constituents through the West Riding I have had some opportunity of learning, and I am sorry to say, that excepting a few notorious democrats, I have not met with a single person who does not disapprove your conduct. Mr. Sheepshanks, a principal clergyman at Leeds, tells me that you have stood high with the manufacturers, you have managed all their business to their satisfaction ; but that if it had been possible for you to have ruined yourself with your friends at Leeds, you have taken the way to do it.' From Cambridge he writes again, ' I pray God bless you for writing me so affectionate a letter. I wish that you should learn from others, rather than from myself, how vehemently I have defended you from the attacks of Dr. Kipling, Jowett, Turner, &c. ; some of whom hold that you have done the country much more harm than any defeat could do. H.'s conduct is imputed to personal disappointment, and as he wants weight of character, they have no mercy on him. It is now, more than ever before in your life, that the consequence and force of your independence is felt.' So too wrote Dr. Burgh, to whose manly and impartial judgment he deferred greatly.

' My opinion does not concur with yours. On whatever side I look I tremble, but above all evils I most deprecate a peace, in whatever form the present moment could obtain it.

Even our wretched and calamitous war is, comparatively speaking, a state of security and quiet. We must fight till we can fairly lay our arms aside, or compound for a fate similar to that of Holland. The eyes of the country are upon you. Faction begins to claim you; you are quoted, and are growing into the subject of panegyric.'

Yet none of these things moved him. The trial was indeed severe, but it did not shake his constancy; he calmly and steadily adhered to what he saw to be the line of duty, neither deterred by opposition, nor piqued by unmerited reproach into irritation or excess. Upon February 6, whilst he declared his disapprobation of its more violent expressions, he again supported so much of Mr. Grey's motion as tended to promote immediate pacification; and throughout the session he favoured every similar attempt. How carefully he watched against the distractions of such a time, many such entries as the following record : 'This morning I have been much affected—I fasted, and received the sacrament.'

His own cause was not lost sight of amongst these great questions. 'I am,' he says, 'in no degree discouraged. It is my intention to move, next year, for Abolition in January, 1796; and though I dare not hope to carry a Bill for that purpose through both Houses, yet, if I do not deceive myself, this infamous and wicked traffic will not last out this century.'

Accordingly, he gave notice of his motion early in the session. The result is thus recorded : 'Feb. 26. To town— Sierra Leone general meeting, and afterwards Slave business in the House. Said to have spoken well, though less prepared than at any other time. Beat, 78 to 61. Shameful !' 'I cannot help finding,' he writes on the 28th to Mr. Wyvill, 'an argument for reform, in the infamous vote of the House of Commons the night before last. The Slave Trade is a load which hangs heavy on the country.' 'A national support of cruelty and injustice,' he told the House, 'would stamp the fast of the preceding day as a piece of empty pageantry, and a mere mockery of God.'

The motion was opposed, as usual, by the West Indian body, reinforced by new suggestions of the dangers to be

K

apprehended from French intrigue. Mr. Dundas again came
forward to plead for a gradual abolition to take place at
some indefinite period after the termination of the war. He
was powerfully answered by Mr. Pitt, who in rescuing the
cause from the imputation of French principles, showed that
it was in direct opposition to those abstract propositions by
which 'the rights of man' were maintained, and declared
'that he knew not where to find a more determined enemy
of such delusions, than his hon. friend the proposer of the
motion.'

It was worthy of Mr. Pitt, that his zeal suffered no abatement from the political difference which had sprung up
between himself and Mr. Wilberforce. All personal estrange-
ment indeed was soon at an end. ' Dined March 21,' says
the Diary, at ' R. Smith's—(met) Pitt for the first time since
our political difference—I think both meaning to be kind to
each other—both a little embarrassed.' April 15. Called
at Pitt's the first time since before the beginning of the
session—he having the gout, and I going out of town—
talked about Lord Fitzwilliam.'—'25th. To Battersea Rise
—called Eliot's, knowing that Pitt was there, and that Eliot
knew I knew it, and thinking therefore it would seem unkind
not to do it.—26th. Sunday—Venn; morning. I had meant
to be quiet and employ myself in devotional exercises, when
after church Pitt came with Eliot; and considering he did it
out of kindness, I could not but walk back with him. He
talked openly, &c. After my return home, R. Smith came
to see me, and afterwards Rennel came, self-invited, to dinner, and staid—talked all the afternoon—very clever, much
good in him, great courage, scarcely serious enough, but
much respect for good, and zeal against vice—talents to
make him eminently useful.' ' May 2. All Pitt's supporters
believe him disposed to make peace. To Royal Academy
dinner—sat near Lord Spencer, Windham, &c.—catches and
glees—they importunate for Rule Britannia.'

Throughout this period when forced into opposition
upon the war question, his unruffled temper kept political difference from becoming a cause of personal alienation. So mild indeed was his tone, whilst his conduct was
most decided, that there were not wanting some who as-

serted, that 'there was a complete understanding between himself and Mr. Pitt, and that his opposition was only a pre-text.' 'The Duchess of Gordon told me yesterday,' he says on May 13, 'that the Duke of Leeds, Duke of Bedford, and Lord Thurlow dining there the other day, the latter said he would bet (or did bet) five guineas that Pitt and I should vote together on my motion on Thursday for peace. This shows he thinks there is a secret understanding between Pitt and me all this time.'

But though thus temperate in the manner of his resistance, he was firm in its substance. Upon April 21, he gave notice of a specific motion upon the continuance of the war; and even before this debate came on, he was compelled, upon another subject, to oppose the minister. Mr. Pitt proposed to raise the income of the Prince of Wales greatly above all former precedent. 'Bankes,' says his Diary, May 11, 'tells me that Pitt is furious about our meaning to resist the Prince's additional 25,000*l.*' Upon May 14 he opposed this grant in a speech which was warmly commended. He dwelt strongly upon the actual distresses and discontented temper of the times ; ending with acknowledging the nation's 'deep obligation to their Majesties upon the throne for their ad-mirable conduct, by which they have arrested the progress of licentiousness in the higher classes of society, and sus-tained by their example the fainting morals of the age.'

This renewed opposition produced no unkindly feelings. Two days before the debate, he says, 'Eliot called and asked me to dine at Battersea Rise to meet Pitt and Ryder—called and staid two hours with them all ; walking, foining, and laughing, and reading verses, as before.' And the day after the debate, 'called at R. Smith's to see Lady Camden before their departure for Ireland; found Pitt there ; he very cordial.' '20th. I had shown my motion to Pitt on Saturday—he very kind now and good-natured ; he wrung from me to show it others; so I showed it to Grey and Fox. —21st. Thornton told me that owing to Epsom races only twenty-eight members. Called at Pitt's to settle with him when it should come on. Found Grenville, Dundas, Pepper Arden, Ryder, and Pitt—last very kind, first shy, second sour.—27th. To town—debate. Pitt kind. Too proud, and therefore too much hurt by Windham's personalities.' Still he repressed the evident retort which Mr. Windham's recent change of sentiment supplied readily to Mr. Fox's indignation, and contented himself with a powerful assertion of his right to form an independent judgment. 'My high opinion of the minister's integrity (and of no man's political integrity do I think more highly), and my respect for his understanding (and no man's understanding do I more respect), ought certainly to make me give due weight to what I know are his opinions; but when I have allowed them their due influence, and after carefully surveying, and closely scrutinizing, and coolly and gravely and repeatedly weighing the circumstances of the case, have formed at last a deliberate judgment, that judgment, whatever it may be, I am bound to follow. I am sent here by my constituents not to gratify my private feelings, but to discharge a great political trust; and for the faithful administration of the power vested in me, I must answer to my country and my God.' The motion, which was a general overture towards a peace, was still rejected by a large, though a decreased majority; but amongst the minority of 86 who voted with him, were no less than 24 county members.

Within about six months, he had the satisfaction of hearing from Mr. Pitt himself that he too was now convinced of the necessity of peace. That this clear-sighted statesman did not sooner arrive at this conclusion,—that he resisted all arguments when they 'battled the matter together privately' before the commencement of the session, was much to be attributed, says Mr. Wilberforce, 'to the sanguine temperament of his mind, too little chastened by experience. He could not believe that it would be possible for the French government to find resources sufficient for the immense amount of their expenditure both of men and money. How well do I remember his employing in private, with still greater freedom and confidence, the language which in a more moderate tone he used in the House of Commons, that the French were in a gulf of bankruptcy, and that he could almost calculate the time by which their resources would be consumed.' ' I should like to know who was Chancellor of the Exchequer to Attila,' was Monsieur de Lageard's remark, when this argument was maintained at Mr. Wilberforce's table.

But besides this natural leaning of Mr. Pitt's own mind, Mr. Wilberforce ever believed that he had been possessed through the influence of Mr. Dundas with a thirst for colonial conquest. The hope of capturing St. Domingo, an island which in its commerce with France employed more ships and tonnage than our whole West Indian trade, led him to resolve on continuing the war, until he could ' make peace on terms which should afford indemnity for the past, and security for the future.' That Mr. Pitt should have allowed inferior minds to obtain this influence over him, is a striking instance of the inconsistency of human genius. It was not, as has been suggested, from a love of flattery that he yielded to them ; for if there were flatterers in his circle, it was not the general tone of those around him. ' Neither Grenville, nor Ryder, nor many more,' says Mr. Wilberforce, whose own manly independence is the surest guarantee of his accurate observation, ' would ever condescend to flatter Pitt. The truth is, that, great man as he was, he had very little insight into human nature.'[3] This may probably account for the feebleness and ill success of his military expeditions. Genius and vigour which were paralysed in their government at home, rendered the armies of France everywhere victorious; whilst under Mr. Pitt's administration, all was energy in domestic policy, and all weakness in our military operations.

He was now at Battersea Rise. ' Dined and slept at Pepper Arden's. He all kindness and openness.' ' Old Newton breakfasted with me. He talked in the highest terms of Whitefield, as by far the greatest preacher he had ever known.' ' July 6. Off early for the Speaker's. By themselves—exceedingly kind and friendly—discussed long.—7th. Speaker kind in letting me have my own way. I would have gone the next day, but he insisted in so kind a manner on my staying, that I could not bring myself to refuse. Dined

[3] Con. Mem.

with the Speaker at their Berkshire club, at Reading—the second toast most gross—Deans of Hereford, Worcester, and other D.D.'s there—extremely shocked.   They laid it to the chairman's vulgarity.'   '9th. To town about Sheffield corn business.   Privy Council.   Hawkesbury, Portland, &c.' ' Busy all day writing letters about scarcity.   This now much dreaded.'   ' Price of wheat at Nottingham, 12*s.* per bushel. Meeting in St. George's Fields of parliamentary reformers; calling out "War and Want, or Peace and Plenty." '   ' Captain Sharpe on his business — all morning drawing up his case.   Thought it right, though very disagreeable, to go to Rose about him.   Interview—but little done.   Unfairness of both.'   ' Slave Committee meeting at my house.'

He devoted some time this autumn to a tour amongst his Yorkshire constituents, some of whom missed the attentions which were formerly paid to them by Sir George Savile, whilst others had been offended by his opposition to Mr. Pitt.   Upon August 4, accordingly, he began a set of visits through the county.   His private entries abound in searching remarks upon character and manners, and show in the strongest light the care with which he now watched over himself, and sought for opportunities to do good to others. ' G. very light and profane ; I looked grave ; they all laughed ; immediately after this, family prayers, where confessed ourselves miserable sinners.   Much shocked at all this.—August 6. To Grimston, where a letter met me from Sir R. Hildyard that he did see those he could without form. Grimston very kind and friendly; taking an active part in raising volunteers, which do not seem to do well here—people have not been enough alarmed to know their value.   In the evening on to Sir Robert Hildyard's—obliging and hospitable—talked about all things, but neither with Grimston or him much politics. . . . There is much awkwardness in a visitation like mine from having no head-quarters as a centre whence to diverge.   This want gives a canvassing air.   Also another awkwardness, that I go from one house to another which is hostile without intermediate purifying; and when it is known.   Bacon's remark that people more easily forgive ill will to their friends than good will to their enemies.   This

most important when visiting for conciliation.   Dined at
Hornsea, and through Barmston, where the clergyman, Mr.
Good, and Mr. Harland of Burlington, met us and asked us
out.   Went in with them and discussed.   Obtained leave to
send some of Miss More's tracts—accidental good.   Then on to
Creyke's, who very kind and hospitable ; his seven daughters
at home — very pleasing, modest, and rational.   Spent
Sunday at Marton.   Burlington church.   Mr. —— preached
a dry essay on " Woe to those who call evil good," &c.,
which I disliked much—they did too.   Creyke remembered
it to be Dr. Clarke's ; we looked and found it word for
word.—Monday, 10th.   Unwell ; but though otherwise I
should have liked to stay in this family of domestic harmony, diligence, and hospitable kindness, yet fearing that
Mr. Broadley would have asked people to meet me, I
thought it best to come off.   Brought Osborne, and though
tête-à-tête and no reading all the way, yet shamefully
backward in talking with him seriously: felt awkward, no
launchers occurred, alas ! yet it was in my mind the whole
way.   Got to Ferriby to dinner—Mr. and Mrs. B. B. Thompson, Osborne, Robert Broadley, and T. Thompson very civil;
Broadley frank, and kind, and manly in his politeness, a rational companion.'—'17th. To Philip Langdale's—he, Mrs.
Langdale, and priest.   Rational evening — he at prayers
when I arrived.—18th. Much talk with Mr. Langdale and
the priest about their tenets, and pleased to find him much
in earnest, and urging me strongly.   Called at Baskett's, and
he going soon to dinner, could not but stay—pleased to see
old scenes.   On to York.   Saw Burgh, who was all affection.
Called on T—s.   They violently incensed by my political
conduct.   G. would not come down — poor woman, how
foolish !   The coldness of the others seemed to give way by
my being quite unaffected, and apparently undiscerning.'
    There were few who could resist his powers of conversa-
tion.   It possessed indeed a charm which no description can
convey.   As full of natural gaiety as the mirth of childhood,
it abounded in the anecdotes, reflections, and allusions of a
thoughtful mind and retentive memory ; whilst it was continually pointed by humour of a most sparkling quality,

flashes of which played lightly over all he touched upon—
the sports of a fervent imagination sweetened by a temper
naturally kind, and chastened by the continual self-restraint
of a conscience which would not bear the offence of giving
pain to any.   This was a natural endowment, and had been
one great charm of his early years; but it was now carefully
cultivated and conscientiously employed.

' I have been,' says his Diary,[4] ' a few weeks after this time,
' at an assembly at——.   Alas! how little like a company
of Christians!— a sort of hollow cheerfulness on every
countenance.   I grew out of spirits.   I had not been at
pains before I went to fit myself for company, by a store
of conversation topics, *launchers*, &c.'   These were certain
topics carefully arranged before he entered into company,
which might insensibly lead the conversation to useful subjects.   Yet with all this care the perfect naturalism of his
conversation was its especial charm.   He never engrossed
the talk, but let it sway this way and that as it would, without effort or display.   No one ever shone more brightly,
or was more unconscious of his own brilliancy.

From York he passed on into the West Riding, visiting
Leeds, Halifax, and Huddersfield, receiving everywhere a
cordial welcome, and winning back by personal intercourse
those whom political difference had in any degree estranged.
Aug. 22. To Smyth's, who received me most affectionately—
sweet place.   Lady Georgiana a most engaging woman—
kind, unassuming, unaffected.   Clowes there—as positive in
whimsies as in certain and important truths—what a pity!
He is pious, affectionate, humble, self-denying, and I dare
say firm.—24th. A sad birthday—no time for prayer or reflection.   Smyth very kindly made calls with me at Wakefield—came back to dinner, and evening on to Leeds—to
Cookson's, who received me most frankly.—25th. Cookson
a large party to dine.   Morning Cloth Halls—saw the trus-
tees assembled.—26th. Went over Mr. Gott's factory.   A
clever young man.   Dined Mr. Buck's.—28th. To Halifax,
where received with great kindness by the Waterhouses.—
29th. Cloth Hall.—31st. With Mr. Waterhouse to Bradford,

[4] Nov. 15.

where breakfasted.   Returned to Mr. W.'s to dinner, where
large party, who very cordial.

'Sept. 1. Breakfasted Edward's.   Dined at the Talbot
with a large party—toast given, "May the peace of the county
not be disturbed"—people very kind.   Evening the whole
party adjourned to Dr. Coulthurst's. where tea and supper.
Wanted me to explain about my Amendment—they most
decidedly for war.—2nd. Breakfasted Walker's, Crownest.
To Jas. Milnes's to dinner.   Evening walked and talked.—
3rd. To Spencer Stanhope's—he told me that B. had declared he would give 1,000*l.* to turn me out.—Sept. 8. Off
early for Huddersfield.   Mr. Whitacre and T. Atkinson came
—then some Saddleworth friends.   Cloth Hall.   Sheep-
shank's corn idea, and natural eloquence.   Felt I should be
inferior to him.   Saw Mrs. Law Atkinson.   Dined about
twenty-five, very friendly.   Evening Whitacre's.—10th. After
breakfast, and making up books for Stanhope, Burgess, and
Georgiana Smith, off for Flasby Hall.   Preston receives me
very affectionately—sweet poetical lake of his own making
—at night some serious talk, to which Preston led—I told
him my case.—11th. Tried for more serious talk—gave him
some books, and told him of my intended publication, and
its reasons.   Off after dinner for Kendal, where stopped for
the night.—12th. Off early—breakfasted Lowwood—leaves
withered, and scene appears less beautiful than I used to
think it.   On after breakfast to Broughton, where I am
writing.   In the afternoon went on over Stonyhead, a most
steep and toilsome march, to Muncaster.   Muncaster very
glad to see me, and all kind.'   There he staid until September 28, making one excursion to visit the Bishop of Llandaff,
whom he found 'more grandiloquent, and suo genere, than
I ever saw him.   Went on to visit Sir John Legard—he out
—Mrs. Grimston and daughter there.'   'How many scenes,'
was his private reflection on revisiting Muncaster Castle,
'have I gone through, to how many dangers have I been
exposed, since I was last here in 1788 ! I ought to be very
grateful.   What reason have I to devote all my powers to
the service of God, who has preserved me from innumerable
evils !'

He left Muncaster Castle at the end of September; and on his road to Yoxall Lodge passed through a part of Yorkshire, spending 'Oct. 6 with Mr. Mason, to whom I opened a little on religious matters, taking occasion, in particular, from my book to press upon him the duty of talking plainly to our friends. He did not know, he said, whether E. (a man of great moral worth, and with whom he was unusually intimate) believed in revelation or not.'

The London season was now approaching. 'Oh, this vile meeting of Parliament!' he writes to the Speaker, 'when we shall have to discuss again about governments capable of maintaining the relations of peace and amity. Poor fellow —Pitt I mean—I can feel for him from my heart, particularly on a Sunday.'

On reaching Palace Yard, on the 24th, he 'found a letter from Pitt[5] wishing me to come up, hoping we should agree.' ' If it is not very inconvenient to you, it would be a great satisfaction to me if you could come so as to allow time for our having some quiet conversation before we meet in the House. This I am afraid there will not be much chance of, unless you are here a day or two before. I cannot help being more anxious for this, as I think our talking over the present state of things may do a great deal of good, and I am sure at all events it can do no harm. It is hardly possible to form any precise opinion of what is to be done till we see the immediate issue of the crisis just now depending, but I cannot help thinking that it will shortly lead to a state of things in which I hope our opinions cannot materially differ. I need not say how much personal comfort it will give me if my expectation in this respect is realised.'

His own ' personal comfort' was not a little promoted by the tone of this letter; and this was greatly increased by the further intercourse which immediately followed. ' 26th. Kept myself open for Pitt.—27th. Saw Pitt at breakfast this morning, and had a most satisfactory conversation with him. Gave dinner to Duncombe, Samuel and Henry Thornton, and Muncaster—all pleased with my report.—29th. Meant to go to Battersea Rise, but Pitt wished to see me

[5] Downing Street, Saturday, Oct. 24.

on West Indian subject (Address)—another confidential and satisfactory conversation with him.'

On public grounds he rejoiced in the altered sentiments which led the minister to seek for peace, whilst in proportion to the pain of opposing him, was the satisfaction of returning to a renewed career of cordial cooperation with his old friend. All misunderstanding was now gone, and both Mr. Pitt and his adherents recognised the purity of principle from which his former conduct had arisen. 'We might differ at the commencement of last session,' wrote Lord Camden from Dublin Castle,[6] 'as to the line which you then thought it right to pursue. I am candid enough to own that I can conceive it not as inconsistent as I then thought it; and that with the explanation your subsequent conduct has given, I perfectly understand it. Pitt appears to me to have been more able than ever since the meeting of Parliament, and I have little doubt of his making a peace, and of the country supporting him in it.' Never was a thorough union between all real patriots more to be desired.

CHAPTER X.

OCTOBER 1795 TO JULY 1796.

Disordered state of the public mind—Pitt's readiness for peace—Sedition Bills—Popular discontent—Yorkshire meeting, and petitions—Danger of the West Indies—Christmas recess—Abolition Bill reaches a third reading in the Commons—Slave-carrying Bill—Parliament dissolved—Canvass—Re-election.

WITH the autumn of this year began the darkest period of the revolutionary war. Though the arms of France were everywhere triumphant, yet it was not from them that our greatest danger arose. An evil spirit was spreading through Europe, and the enemies of order were but too successful in their attempt to introduce French principles amongst ourselves.

Parliament met October 29, and Mr. Pitt at once avowed

[6] Dec. 24.

his pacific inclination.   'Walked down to Westminster
Hall, and then to the House.   Pitt spoke capitally, and as
distinct as possible on the main point.   Duncombe, and
Muncaster, and Sir Richard Hill appeared to me to be won
by his frank avowal.   Bankes suggested the necessity of a
parliamentary recognition.'[1]   In the course of the debate he
declared that all difference between himself and Mr. Pitt was
at an end.   On the following day, he heard with pleasure the
same sentiments uttered by Lord Grenville in the House of
Peers.—'Heard Lords' debate—Grenville distinct—Lansdowne absurd and clever.   Duke of Bedford heavy and pompous—Robin Hood that can't get on, with newspaper arguments and fustian animation.'

The evil humours which abounded in the state were drawing to a head.   The King was violently mobbed on his way
to open Parliament ; tumultuous meetings were held in the
metropolis ; whilst the most inflammatory publications were
actively disseminated.—'Papers are dispersed against property.   Prints of guillotining the King and others.'[2]   In this
crisis it appeared right to Mr. Wilberforce to arm the executive government with extraordinary powers ; and when upon
November 10, Mr. Pitt proposed to bring in a bill for preventing seditious assemblies, he at once expressed his concurrence.   'Got up after Fox,' but not being called on by the
Speaker, it was late before he addressed the House.   This
speech, which satisfied himself, was highly commended by
the supporters of the measure, though he expressly stipulated
for maintaining unimpaired the full right of petitioning.   'I
do not,' he said, 'willingly support these Bills,[3] but I look
on them as a temporary sacrifice, by which the blessings of
liberty may be transmitted to our children unimpaired.'
They were fiercely attacked by the opposition.   'All my
party,' said a leading man amongst the Yorkshire Whigs,
'opposed the Bills, and an excellent weapon they were to
employ against the ministry ; but I, who had then taken no
part in politics, and was living as a young man in London,
saw enough to convince me that they were necessary.'   Being

---

[1] Diary, Oct. 29.   [2] Ib. Nov. 18.
[3] The 'Treason' and 'Seditious Assembly' Bills.

convinced of their necessity, Mr. Wilberforce laboured to perfect their details. On the 11th, he 'went to Pitt's to look over the Sedition Bill—altered it much for the better by enlarging.' Upon the 12th he again maintained in the House of Commons, in opposition to his colleague Mr. Duncombe, that the Bills did in truth 'raise new bastions to defend the bulwarks of British liberty.' He was still engaged with the details of the measures. 'A meeting at Pitt's about the Sedition Bill, after which supped with him and Mornington— my advice—Pitt's language, "My head would be off in six months, were I to resign." I see that he expects a civil broil. Never was a time when so loudly called on to prepare for the worst.'[4] 'How vain now appears all successful ambition! Poor Pitt! I too am much an object of popular odium. Riot is expected from the Westminster meeting. The people I hear are much exasperated against me. The printers are all angry at the Sedition Bills. How fleeting is public favour!'

'Let me look before me, and solemnly implore the aid of God, to guide, quicken, and preserve me. Let me endeavour to soar above the turmoil of this tempestuous world. Let me remember the peculiar character of a Christian; gravity in the House, cheerfulness, kindness, and placability, with a secret guard and hidden seriousness. God protected me from Norris, Kimber, and innumerable other dangers. He is still able to protect me, and will, if it be for my good.'[5] Popular odium could not shake this confidence, and to the two Bills he gave his full support.

Upon the second reading, (November 17th,) 'House,' he says, 'very late. Will. Smith struck by the extracts read by Mornington. Poor Mornington nervous, and Sheridan brutal. Up to speak, but prevented.' Shortly afterwards he declared his sentiments with singular effect, in the debate upon the Treason Bill, which had now passed the Lords. Mr. Fox had declared, with more than usual violence, that if these Bills became law, submission would be no more a question of duty, but of prudence. This called up Mr. Pitt, who in few, hut weighty words, declared his confidence, that 'there would not be wanting those who would risk all for their country, and enforce the laws against which the people were excited to rebel.' ' The measure,' says an eye-witness, ' had all along been hotly combated ; but after Fox's intemperate assertion, the cheers on each side of the House were positively deafening. At this time Mr. Wilberforce rose ; and after pointing out the strange contrast between the inflammatory language of the opposition, and their pretended zeal for peace ; he exclaimed with an energy, which I remember well, after an interval of forty years, " Peace indeed ! what have they to do with peace ? even now they are unsheathing the sword of civil discord, to plunge it in the bosom of their country." '

The contest was now spreading from the House of Commons to the country. The sentiments of Yorkshire were supposed to be hostile to the Bills. Already were its freeholders multiplied beyond all precedent by the increased numbers of the domestic clothiers : upon their support the opposition calculated confidently ; whilst the friends of peace looked with some alarm to the discontent which a partial scarcity could not but excite amongst them. ' The Bills,' wrote Dr. Burgh,[6] ' are obnoxious in this part of the world to an extreme degree.' ' The dissenters,' adds another correspondent announcing the intended meeting,[7] ' have never forgiven you for opposing the repeal of the Test Act, and I am informed that they are expected to be there in support of opposition.' In these expectations the high sheriff[8] so far coincided that he deemed it inexpedient to hold the meeting. ' The assembling of so large and unwieldy a body,' he replied to the requisition, ' would only tend to raise riot and discontent.' This decision Mr. Wilberforce regretted greatly : and when it was quoted with some triumph in the House of Commons as ' a strong argument against the Bills,' he declared at once that ' he lamented the high sheriff's conduct, because it had prevented a full, fair, and free discussion of the subject.'[9] In spite of the triumphant hopes of his opponents and the gloomy apprehensions of his friends, he trusted

[6] Nov. 19.   [7] Letter from John Naylor, Nov. 12.
[8] Mr. (afterwards Sir) Mark Sykes.
[9] Debate of November 27.

in the good sense of the Yorkshire freeholders. He had not learned in vain the lesson which he had been taught in 1784; and he longed to plead again before the assembled county the cause of liberty and right. ' I regret,' he tells Mr. Hey, 'very much that the high sheriff has refused to call a county meeting, when I had taken steps to secure a full attendance from the East Riding, and have no doubt that by throwing the weight of the county of York into the scale of good order, we should have operated powerfully upon the public mind.'

Such a meeting the opponents of Government had privately resolved to attempt, upon the refusal of the high sheriff to convene the county. To secure the attendance they desired they waited four days, and then issued circulars, requesting ' the freeholders to assemble at the castle-yard of York, if the sheriff will permit it to be used; and if not, at the guild-hall, upon the Tuesday following.' By this manœuvre they deemed themselves secure of the exclusive presence of their partisans. For as no newspaper was then published in the county of York upon Friday, the announcement would reach those only whom they chose to summon. No post left York that afternoon for London, so that they were safe from any unwelcome intrusion from the capital; while the day named for the meeting being that on which the mercantile trans-actions of the six preceding months were settled both at Leeds and Huddersfield, the presence of the merchants and master-manufacturers would be effectually prevented. To-gether with the announcement of the meeting was circulated amongst the lower class of freeholders, a stirring appeal bearing Mr. Wyvill's signature : ' Come forth then from your looms,' was his summons, 'ye honest and industrious clothiers ; quit the labours of your fields for one day, ye stout and inde-pendent yeomen : come forth in the spirit of your ancestors, and show you deserve to be free.'

It was a bold attempt, and would probably have succeeded, if the friends of order had not roused themselves with unusual promptitude. An intimation of what had passed at York was received at Leeds in the course of Friday evening; and a few resolute men instantly met, and resolved that the intelli-

gence should be dispersed throughout the West Riding. On
the Saturday accordingly the freeholders of various districts
were assembled; and it was at once agreed to postpone all
other business, and to respond to Mr. Wyvill's call, though
not in the sense he intended.

Still the meeting promised to be a surprise. 'I knew
nothing of it,' says a leading inhabitant of the East Riding,
'until the afternoon of Monday, and only got in time to
York by riding straight there from the dinner party of a
friend.' In London. of course, all that was passing was
utterly unknown. 'When undressing at twelve o'clock on
Saturday,' says Mr. Wilberforce,[1] 'I received a note from Sir
William Milner, saying that the York meeting was to be held
upon Tuesday next; but I had given up all idea of going.'
It seemed impossible to gather a general meeting on so short
a summons; and to attend a party council of his enemies
would have been mischievous. 'You could not have conceived,' wrote Mr. Hey,[2] after the event, 'that so large a
number of your constituents could have been collected in
the short space of three days.' His suspicions were somewhat aroused by the communication of a friend, 'something
extraordinary is certainly designed in Yorkshire, since ——
was seen to set out on the north road this morning in a
chaise and four.' Enough, however, was not known to show
that his presence was so far necessary as to justify his travelling upon the day which it was his chiefest privilege to
give up to rest and devotion, until he was in his carriage
on his way to church on Sunday morning. Just as he had
got into it, an express arrived from Mr. Hey and Mr. Cookson, informing him of all that been done, and urging him at
all costs to be present at the meeting. 'I sent immediately
to Eliot, and then went there. He and I, on consideration,
determined that it would be right for me to go ; the country's
peace might be much benefited by it.'[3]

Sending back therefore his carriage to be fitted for the
journey, he went himself to the neighbouring church of St.
Margaret's—'Sir George Shuckburgh there—talking—sad
sermon,'[4]—and then called on Mr. Pitt. 'I saw Pitt—he

---

[1] Diary.   [2] Dec. 5.   [3] Diary.   [4] Ib.

clear—much disquieted.'[5]   Whilst they were still together, his servant brought word that his carriage could not be got ready so soon as was required.   ' Mine,' said Mr. Pitt, ' is ready, set off in that.'   ' If they find out whose carriage you have got,' said one amongst the group, ' you will run the risk of being murdered.'   So fierce had been the spirit of the populace in London, that the fear was not entirely ground-less; and an appearance of the same temper in the great cities of the north had led some amongst his friends to write to him, that ' if he ventured down it would be at the hazard of his life.'   But it was not such apprehensions which had ' disquieted' his thoughts; and when once satisfied that duty called him, he cheerfully began the journey.   ' By half-past two,' he says,[6] I was ' off in Pitt's carriage, and travelled to Alconbury Hill, four horses all the way,' two outriders pre-ceding him; a provision then essential to a speedy journey, even on the great north road.   After a few hours' rest, ' I was off early on the Monday morning, and got at night to Ferrybridge.   Employed myself all the way in preparing for the meeting.'[7]   He had been supplied by Mr. Pitt with samples of the various works by which the public mind was poisoned; and of such importance was his mission deemed, that an express was sent after him to Ferrybridge with further specimens.   ' Almost the whole of Monday,' says his secre-tary, ' was spent in dictating; and, between his own manu-scripts and the pamphlets which had followed him, we were almost up to the knees in papers.'   He reached Doncaster by night and thence sent an express across to Leeds, to announce his arrival to Mr. Hey.   ' I have made a forced march, and am going forward.   I am deeply impressed with a sense of the necessity of bold and decided conduct.   *Pray that I may be supported.*   If any of my friends now absenting themselves would go to York, knowing of my intention to be there, send to them betimes.'

The day had not been idly spent by the supporters of the constitution.   The West Riding had been raised; ' The towns of Leeds, Halifax, Wakefield, Huddersfield, and Brad-ford,' writes Dr. Coulthurst,[8] after the event, ' have gained

[5] Diary.   [6] Ib.   [7] Ib.   [8] Dec. 10.

singular credit by their attendance. But the town of Leeds deserves best of the public, for it stood in the front of the battle.' The whole county seemed pouring into York. 'On Monday,' says a private letter of the day,[9] 'there went through Halton turnpike above three thousand horsemen.' These were principally clothiers (Billymen, as they were long called from the event of the next day), riding on the ponies which carried commonly their cloths to the adjoining markets. Many came from Saddleworth, a distance of near sixty miles, spending a great part of the night upon their journey; and stormy as was the next morning (Dec. 1), they still crowded the road from Tadcaster to York. ' It was an alarming moment,' says an eye-witness, ' when these immense numbers began to pour in, while as yet we knew not what part they would take.' But by Monday evening the supporters of the government began to feel their strength. ' When we arrived at York,' says Mr. Atkinson, ' we were told that our adversaries were collected at the great inn in Lendal, and that our friends were to meet at seven, at the George in Coney Street. Thither we repaired without delay, and found a respectable body of gentlemen already assembled. The enemy, through the friendship of the corporation, had previously secured the Guildhall, where they could lay their plans at leisure. We sent a deputation to offer to meet them the next morning in the Castle Yard, according to their first announcement, where both parties could act freely, but they refused. They then proposed to admit our men and theirs into the Guildhall by forties; but this we declined, knowing that the hustings would be filled with the mere dregs of York, hired to drown with noise what they could not overcome by argument; but we offered to meet them on any fair and open ground they chose. In the morning we assembled at the York Tavern, which was about as near to the Guildhall as the tavern at which they met; and at half-past nine we spread our forces even to its gates. They sent out to reconnoitre, and found our strength treble theirs. We were in high spirits, and the enemy were exceedingly discouraged. As soon as the gates of the Guild-

[9] From Rev. Miles Atkinson, of Leeds, to his son at Cambridge.

hall were opened, our men rushed in with theirs; but by entering through the Mansion House they had previously possessed the hustings, and had chaired Sir Thomas Gascoigne. This unfairness stirred up the Leeds' spirit; our men pushed up to the hustings, and lifted several of their number into the midst of their opponents' crowd. These immediately called upon Sir Thomas to quit the chair, and wait till the freeholders had voted in a chairman. He refused to leave it, and they hoisted him out, and voted Mr. Bacon Frank into his place. Our party then proposed and carried by a majority of three to one an adjournment to the Castle Yard, the usual place of meeting, and where numbers had already gathered.'

At this period of the business, the want of any leader of acknowledged power was deeply felt amongst the supporters of the constitution. The plans of the opposite party had been long matured, and their bands were marshalled under their appointed chiefs; but the friends of order had come suddenly together, and there was none to take the lead in their movements, or engage their general love of order in support of these necessary though obnoxious Bills. Just when this want was most acutely felt, Mr. Wilberforce's carriage turned the corner into Coney Street. His approach was not generally known. 'You may conceive our sensations,' says a Leeds gentleman, 'when he dashed by our party in his chariot and four a little before we reached York.' He was received with the same exultation by the assembled concourse. 'He arrived,' says Mr. Atkinson, 'at about a quarter to eleven, amidst the acclamations of thousands. The city resounded with shouts, and hats filled the air.' 'What a row,' he said to his son, when quietly entering the city thirty-two years later by the same road, 'what a row did I make when I turned this corner in 1795; it seemed as if the whole place must come down together.'

Leaving his carriage he pushed through the tumult of the Guildhall, and soon appeared upon the hustings. Here he vainly attempted to prevail on Mr. Wyvill and his friends to concur in the adjournment to the Castle Yard. 'He hoped,' he said, 'to have met his opponents that day face to face, and convince them of the groundlessness of their prejudices, if they were not prepared to shut up all the avenues to the understanding, and all the passages to the heart.'   But they refused to quit the Hall.   He proceeded therefore without them to the Castle Yard. 'And now,' said Mr. Bacon Frank, taking his place upon the great stone steps which supplied the place of a temporary hustings, 'now at least we are upon county ground.' 'It was perhaps the largest assemblage of gentlemen and freeholders which ever met in Yorkshire.'[1] 'Here,' writes Mr. Atkinson, 'we had three good speeches from Colonel Creyke, Mr. Spencer Stanhope, and Mr. Wil berforce.   The last, I think, and so I believe think all that heard him, was never exceeded. A most incomparable speech indeed.   The address and petition against seditious meetings, and in favour of the King and constitution, were carried almost unanimously.'[2]

'Up betimes,' is his own brief entry of this busy day,[3] 'and off to Tadcaster.   There found all the West Riding was in motion. Got to York at eleven. Kindly received. Guildhall— Castle yard—spoke—interview with Wyvill—his sad paper. Thornton giving away his regimentals to the mob.' 'I should have said much more,' he tells Mr. Hey,[4] 'if we had got into debate, for I really had not natural elasticity enough to expand, without opponents, to such a size as I should have swelled to, if I had been as large as I was prepared to be.' Yet his speech, though shorter than he had designed, proved signally effective.   Mr. Wyvill did not hesitate to attribute the decision of the county to his personal efforts and influence. 'It rejoiced my heart,' wrote Dr. Coulthurst, 'to *see* you at York, and much more to *hear* you. Your appearance, but most of all, your very eloquent philippic, was wonderfully beneficial to the cause, the country, and yourself. Many who, to my personal knowledge, came decidedly hostile to the Bills, were induced, on hearing your speech, to sign the addresses and petition. You have gained over almost every man in the five great commercial towns of the West Riding. Our new sheriff, Godfrey Wentworth, declared, after he had heard

---

[1] York Paper of the day.   [2] Letter from Mr. Atkinson.
[3] Diary.   [4] Letter, Dec. 7.

you, that the greatest pleasure he could enjoy in possessing
an extensive influence in Yorkshire, would be in coming forward with a large body of freeholders to support your election.'[5] A letter from an influential merchant[6] in the town of
Leeds fixes in telling language the feeling of the town : —' I
earnestly hope that this will find your body recruited from
its fatigues; and I think your mind will find cause for exultation, now, and so long as the partnership continues, in contemplating your York expedition. The burst of applause
spontaneously flowing from constituents brought here by no
influence whatever, save that of disinterested independence
and purest civic principle—applause from such hearts, and
so uprightly earned—will ever sound in your ears; and you
may rest fully satisfied, that this event has seated you firmly
in the place you have so ably filled. It has confirmed the
staunch, fixed the neutral, and deterred the speculative. The
united West Riding is not easily to be overmatched. You
will have petitions from this division up to-night, though
the shortness of time renders the signatures comparatively
few. The bells were ringing till midnight on Tuesday from
the first moment of intelligence. Twenty King's men to one
Jacobin was the cry, and *the glorious first of December* to be
an era.'

The issue of this effort is well worthy of remark. His success had been complete ; and it was the direct consequence
of an unflinching obedience to the dictates of his conscience
against what at the moment seemed to be his personal interest. When he left London he was entirely ignorant of the
temper of the great towns in the West Riding ; his friends
had warned him to expect their opposition, and this would
certainly have cost him his seat at the approaching election.
But he was determined to discharge his duty; and he returned beyond all expectation at the very highest wave of
popular applause, and safe from all possibility of rivalry. ' I
never saw you but once,' wrote a constituent long afterwards,
' and that day you won my heart, and every honest heart in
the county. It was at the York meeting. I never felt the
power of eloquence until that day. You made my blood

---

[5] Feb. 11, 1796.   [6] F. W. Cookson, Esq., Dec. 3, 1795.

tingle with delight.   The contrast of your address, and the
mellow tone of your voice, of which not one single word was
lost to the hearers, with the bellowing, screaming attempts at
speaking in some others, was most wonderful.   You breathed
energy and vigour into the desponding souls of timid loyal-
ists, and sent us home with joy and delight.'[7] Not less worthy
of remark is the quiet thankfulness which threw a grace over
his triumph.   'With him,' he told Mr. Hey,[8] 'it was matter
of thankfulness to God that the enemies of peace and public
order had been so discomfited.'   He had communicated the
successful issue of the meeting to Mr. Pitt the same evening
by express; and on the following morning he set off himself
for London.   'On Thursday,' he says,[9] 'I travelled on to
Biggleswade, and on Friday got to the House with the petitions.   I told my tale with effect.   I was received with great
gratitude and cordiality.'[1]   He was able to assure the House
that the north approved of the measures of the ministers ;
and every day confirmed his statements in the petitions which
followed him from Yorkshire.   Mr. Pitt felt deeply the importance of his effort.   Other counties followed in the wake
of Yorkshire, 'proving the justice of what Fox often said,
" Yorkshire and Middlesex between them make all England."'[2]

He employed this success to the benefit of his African
clients.   Recent events in the West Indies had revived the
old charge that the friends of the negro race were Jacobins
at heart.   The government of France, finding it impossible
to resist the naval force of England, attempted in despair to
raise against her the whole black population.   For this purpose she enfranchised her own negroes ; and sent the fero-
cious Victor Hugues to proclaim freedom and enforce rebellion amongst the English colonies.   The flame was soon
kindled in Grenada, Dominica, and St. Vincent's ; to them
the opponents of the Abolition pointed with no little triumph;
and quoted, as the fulfilment of their worst prophecies, the
outrages which here walked hand in hand with negro liberation.   It was undoubtedly a fearful sight which was presented

---

[7] From Colonel Cockell, Sept. 10, 1810.   [8] Dec. 7.
[9] Diary.   [1] From Richard Holden, Esq.   [2] Con. Mem.

by these miserable islands; and there were not wanting those amongst the honest friends of Abolition who thought that the question should be let to rest till some more peaceful season. His indisputable attachment to the constitution made at this moment Mr. Wilberforce's advocacy triumphant. 'Your giving notice *at this time,*' writes Dr. Burgh, 'that you intend to bring the Slave Trade again before the House, will snatch the question from that odious connection in which those who contend for the trade have endeavoured to place it before the public eye.'[3]

On December 15, he gave notice that early in the following session he would propose his motion. 'And now,' he added, 'when we are checking the progress of licentiousness, is the very time to show our true principles, by stopping a practice which violates all the real rights of human nature.'

Battersea Rise was his head-quarters during this recess. 'Thursday. Dined at Jeremy Bentham's—Lord St. Helen's, Abbot, and Romilly there. Dined early, and sat late, discussing very pleasantly about Lord St. Helen's travels, &c.'[4] 'Wednesday. Dined with old Newton, where met Henry Thornton and Macaulay. Newton very calm and pleasing —owned that Romaine had made many antinomians. Christmas day. Up early for prayer, and discussed to servants on the Sacrament.' 'Sunday. Battersea Rise all day—Henry and I—up rather early for prayer, which answered through God's grace. I hope a profitable, and I am sure a happy, Sunday. Venn came at night, and told us his grief—that a new chapel talked of because he did not preach the gospel. We discussed, and told Venn his faults; but he acknowledged, and we too, who much agree with him, that he does not agree with any of the gospel preachers. They swell one part to the lessening of another; strain and pervert Scripture.'[5] 'Dr. and Mrs. A. and others dined—this meant for doing two first good; but I doubt if it has at all answered, except that family prayer, &c., may have struck them. Winter evenings not so well as summer (this practical) when one can walk and split into parties.' 'Dined Morton, Pitt's— Pitt, Glasse, Rumford, Bentham, General Bentham, Rose,

---

[3] Letter from Dr. Burgh, Dec. 12.   [4] Diary.   [5] Ib. Dec. 27.

and others.   Poor Bentham! dying of sickness of hope deferred, which forced to stifle.'⁶   'Dined tête-à-tête with Pitt
—long discussion about politics and people—he very open,
and fair, and patriotic—no idea of peace before another
campaign.'

'To town—levee.   King talked to me of "my friend Gisborne's" answer to Paley.' Then 'to Pitt's—he accosted me
very affectionately.'⁷—'9th. To Navestock—found Bishop of
Gloucester there—his opinion about Johnson's irreligious respectable companions.'—'Sunday. Walked long after church
with Lady Waldegrave.⁸   Her deep interest for Lord Cornwallis and Thurlow.⁹   Thurlow's kindness and generosity to
her.   Lord Cornwallis says he is an unhappy, mortified man,
but Lady Waldegrave does not think him so.'

The following Friday he resolved 'to set apart chiefly for
religious exercises ; fasting in my way. My chief reasons are
1st, That the state of public affairs is very critical, and calls
for earnest deprecation of the Divine displeasure.   2ndly,
My station in life is a very difficult one, wherein I am at a
loss to know how to act.   Direction therefore should be
specially sought from time to time.   3rdly, I have been
graciously supported in difficult situations of a public nature.
I have gone out and returned home in safety : my health has
not suffered from fatigue : and favour and a kind reception
have attended me.   I am covered with mercies.   Return
then unto thy rest, O my soul, for the Lord hath dealt bounti-
tifully with thee.¹—16th. Morning felt the fragrant impression
of yesterday.'

Towards the conclusion of the recess he spent 'a day
at Holwood.   Morning walked with Pitt.   Heard part of
Mornington's first number on Seditious Assemblies' and the
other Bill.   Next morning to town—tête-à-tête with Pitt—
he very kind, open and fair about peace, and I think wise
too.'²

Parliament met upon February 2, and on the 18th, he
moved for leave to bring in a Bill to abolish the Slave Trade

⁶ Diary, Dec. 27.   ⁷ Ib. Jan. 6, 1796.   ⁸ Ib. Jan. 10.
⁹ The guardians to her son the late Lord Waldegrave.
¹ Journal.   Friday, Jan. 15.   ² Diary, Jan. 22.

in a time to be limited, fixed afterwards to March 1, 1797. He 'opened the business,' he says, 'coldly and indifferently,' but was roused by the debate, which was unusually animated, and in his reply spoke 'warmly and well.'[3]   The brunt of the contest was borne by the ordinary West Indian opposition ; but some who professed to join in his condemnation of the trade, were in truth its most efficient supporters.   With indefatigable perseverance Mr. Jenkinson declared, 'I anxiously wish that the question were postponed at least till the return of peace.'   'There is something,' he replied, 'not a little provoking in the dry, calm way in which gentlemen are apt to speak of the sufferings of others.   The question suspended!   Is the desolation of wretched Africa suspended ? Are all the complicated miseries of this atrocious trade—is the work of death suspended ?   No, sir, I will not delay this motion, and I call upon the House not to insult the forbearance of Heaven by delaying this tardy act of justice.' 'What !' he said to the boast that the slaves were well fed, clothed, and lodged; 'what ! are these the only claims of a rational being ?   Are the feelings of the heart nothing ? Where are social intercourse and family endearment ? where are willing services and grateful returns ? where, above all, the light of religious truth, and the hope full of immortality ? So far from thanking the honourable gentleman for the feeding, clothing, and lodging, of which he boasts, I protest against the way in which he has mentioned them, as degrading men to the level of brutes, and insulting all the higher qualities of our common nature.'

General Tarleton's motion for an adjournment was negatived by a majority of 26.   'Surprise,' he says,[4] 'and joy in carrying my question.   Speaker asked me and Pitt together to come and sup—thought it would be unkind to Pitt to refuse.   He delighted with having carried it.'

He was now occupied in perfecting his Bill, and frequently enters in his diary, 'Morning at Pitt's about the Slave measure.'   'On Monday, February 22,' says the diary, 'crossed from dinner, and finding the House in a good state brought in Slave Bill without opposition, and recrossed.'   He did not

[3] Diary.   [4] Ib. Feb. 18.

long continue unopposed. The 3rd of March was fixed for the second reading, and after a morning spent upon the Bill at Mr. Pitt's, he was dining in Palace Yard with a party of his House of Commons friends, when early in the evening a supporter of the Slave Trade moved the second reading of his Bill, hoping by this manœuvre to prevent its further progress. His watchfulness defeated the attempt. 'Hurried from dinner at home over to House, to the second reading of the Slave Bill. Spoke against time till many came. Carried it 63 to 31.'[5]

On the 7th the Bill was committed. 'Breakfast,[6] Stephen as before, and Adair. Afterwards, William Smith about Slave Bill. Long busy. A few friends dined before House. Got Bill through committee.'[7] But at the third reading these fresh hopes were again disappointed. 'Dined before House. Slave Bill thrown out by 74 to 70, ten or twelve of those who had supported me absent in the country, or on pleasure. Enough at the Opera[8] to have carried it. Very much vexed and incensed at our opponents.[9]

He had given up everything to the cause. 'The Slave Trade is coming on,' he wrote to a friend,[1] whom he had engaged to visit, 'and everything must give place to the House of Commons,' and his heart sickened at seeing it thus sacrificed to the carelessness of lukewarm friends, and the intrigues of interested enemies. 'I am permanently hurt,' he says, 'about the Slave Trade.'

But though the Slave Trade was his main concern he found time for other useful objects. 'March 5. Received a letter stating the distress of the French emigrant clergy. Kept awake at night. Thought much of them, and formed a plan.'[2] The next day 'after church, saw the Bishop of St. Pol de Leon, and several other persons, on emigrant business. Then with Henry Thornton, by appointment at my desire,

---

[5] Diary, March 3.   [6] Ib.   [7] By a majority of 76 to 31.

[8] 'A new comic opera was brought forward last night, under the name of "I Dui Gobi" (the Two Hunchbacks), the music of which was composed by Portugallo. Vignoni, well known ten years ago, appeared last night, &c. There was a large and splendid audience.'—True Briton, March 16.

[9] Diary, March 15.   [1] Admiral Gambier.   [2] Diary. March 5.

to Lady Buckinghamshire's.   She and Miss Macnamara earnest about the poor emigrants.'[3] On Wednesday, the public
fast day.

But his main business in the House was the Slave-carrying
Bill.   Many of his ordinary opponents declared their appro-
batlon of this measure. . Yet, by the tactics of delay, his bill
was ultimately defeated.   'I find it,' he says May 13, 'too
late to do anything before the dissolution.'[4]   On the day
after the prorogation he went with Mr. Pitt 'tête-à-tête to
Cambridge.   Dined at Chesterford—much talk—he patriotic
—Prince of Wales talked over Thurlow, &c.   Supped at
R.'s—what a bishop in embryo![5]   Pitt's conversation determined me to go off to attend to Beverley and Hull.'

His influence in his native town might, it was hoped, if he
were on the spot, secure the return of two of Mr. Pitt's supporters.   On Saturday the writs were out, and he therefore
'set off for Hull, and having four horses, got at half-past one
to Brigg.   Stanhope at Spittal.'   At Brigg he complains that
there was 'no service on the Sunday morning, and the people
sadly lounging about.   Stanhope filling my head with election
matters.'[6]   'I was in hopes of a day of religious retirement
before my bustle.'

Early on Monday morning he arrived at Hull.   'To the
Bench with S. Thornton.   He sure, and all sure for him.
Canvassing quietly, forbidding show, flags, &c.   Discontent
scarce began to show itself.   Saw Sykes.   Agreed to support
Stanhope.   Dined at home, and after dinner to Sir Samuel
Standridge's—ship people, wrights, &c. there.   T. friendly and
vain.   Blaydes and Bateman had sent off to Pitt to dispatch
a man.   I sent off a messenger to him to stop any one, and
desire all possible support for Stanhope.'   'The next morning
canvassing with Thornton and Stanhope.   The former sure,
the latter successful in canvassing.   Some gathering discontents.   Wednesday.   Doubtful how to act about my own
election, and half inclined to dash into the North Riding.
Wrote many letters.   Great discontent now against S.
Thornton.   Colonel Burton came with pomp to Hull, which

[3] Diary, Sunday, March 6.   [4] Ib. May 13.
[5] Ib. May 20.   [6] Journal.

made his economy more unpopular.   Thursday.   Sir Charles
Turner came to Hull.   I going to Holderness, but put it off
till afternoon.   All the ribbons bought up—people delighted
—a great row, &c.   Dined at home, after writing much, and
into Holderness.   Called on Bethell and Constable; he very
frank about Roman Catholics not enjoying political rights,
and would take no part, &c.   Got back late.   People riotous;
but Thornton having to-night 800 promises, deemed by all
perfectly safe.   Stanhope also.   Friday.[7]   Election day.
Thornton led off the poll, but Sir Charles Turner soon
passed him, and he last.   Thornton's colours torn out, and
not suffered to appear—people abusive—Sir Charles idolised.
At night numbers were, Turner 661, Stanhope 547, Thornton
478.   Sykes extremely distressed at the idea of throwing out
Thornton.   Saturday.   Thornton brought in with difficulty—
Turner 884, Thornton 734, Stanhope 715.'

He now set 'off for York through Beverley—saw Bernard,
found all friendly, and he told me that he had not seen one
single freeholder who was against me.   Got into Philip
Langdale's chaise to Weighton—dined in the carriage, and
on to York.'   'I hold your seat,' Dr. Burgh had written to
him,[8] 'to be as secure as if the county were your own private
borough, yet cross accidents may involve you in expense.'
His colleague had for some months determined to retire.
'After what has passed,' Mr. Duncombe had told him in the
winter,[9] 'having differed from my constituents, and differing
from them still upon a great constitutional question, it will
not be agreeable to them that I should offer myself at the
ensuing election, and certainly it would not be so to myself.'
This conviction and advanced age led Mr. Duncombe to
retire from public life.   Three candidates,[1] all men of wealth
and influence, came forward to contest the seat; and though
none of them opposed Mr. Wilberforce, yet the struggle
must involve him.   He was received at York with the most
hearty greeting; and assurances of universal support poured
in from every quarter.   ' "Are you for Wilberforce?" is the

---

[7] May 27.   [8] May 16.   [9] Jan. 7.
[1] Charles Duncombe, Esq., Walter Fawkes, Esq., and the Hon.
Henry Lascelles.

first question generally asked at Leeds ; and he would have a sorry life of it hereabouts who would undertake to canvass without making you a sine quâ non.'² 'Dined at tavern— Withers the recorder, very kind—Preston—Stanhope—others came dropping in gradually—evening, much talk.'³

On Sunday, May 29, after service in the Minster, he withdrew from the bustling scene around him, to commune with himself and with God. 'This last has been a very hurrying week. To-day I adore that gracious Providence which has led me all my days in ways that I knew not, and has given me so much favour with men. It is His work. His be the glory. May I be enabled to be grateful, and to devote myself first to God's glory, and then diligently to the service of those constituents who are so kind to me.'⁴

Next day was the nomination for the county. 'Day windy and rainy—I spoke but moderately—Milnes very civil—high eulogium—immense majority for me. Most, even of opposition, spoke favourably of me. Meeting over in two hours. Opposition for Fawkes most active. Tavern, and talked with many till dinner. All candidates wishing to bear me harmless, and conference for the purpose, which adjourned till seven o'clock; previous meeting of friends. Evening most distressing—all the West Riding men wishing me to join Lascelles. Inconsistent with my declaration, thought Robert Broadley, T. Williamson, Creyke, Stanhope, Sir Robert Hildyard, and myself. Wharton highly complimentary to me. Much distressed to resist the importunity of friends to join. Lloyd declared that a motion about to be made that they should leave me. I more cool, thank God, than usual. What a mercy I did not yield ! my character would have had a lasting blot. At length at eleven o'clock, when all conference vain, Fawkes sent word by Sir George Armytage that he would spend no more of Lascelles's money than necessary, and declined. Duncombe had resigned before dinner. I told room of friends ; they roared, &c. and still roaring till very late. I called at Lascelles's, and then Fawkes's—he civil and composed. Sat to a cool

² Letter from W. Cookson, Esq., May 27.
³ Diary.   ⁴ Journal.

chat with Williamson, Creyke, &c.   Bacon Frank had anticipated Fawkes's resigning.' 'Next day,' he says, 'people
going away.   Drew up Chas. Duncombe's advertisement,
and told him he must come to election.   Dined Archbishop's—Sir George Armytage told me the anecdote was
true of Brandling's receiving letter promising Duke of Norfolk's, Devonshire's, and Lord Fitzwilliam's support to
Fawkes, and not opening it till next day; it would have
changed their resolution.   Sir George said it was Harewood's
long purse.'[5]

The election was to follow in a week, and he gladly withdrew to the quiet of the country. 'Travelled to Creyke's, who
had been very kind, and pressed me.   Felt excessively comfortable, from calm after fortnight's turbulence and bustle.
Much pleased with Creyke's family peace and rationality.'[6]
Upon June 7, he was 'earlish at York Castle, about half-
past ten.   All, except five or six, West Riding people.   Colonel Lloyd's horse nearly thrown down by the people's tearing off ribands.   Strickland earnest to know if I had joined
Lascelles, and angry at sheriff's putting up names jointly.
Bacon Frank moved, Strickland seconded me.   I spoke
about twenty minutes very well, and people pleased.   Dr.
Tripp's "God bless you, Wilberforce."'[7]   His speech was
followed by the chairing, always a tumultuous scene at York.
'People whilst half down Coney Street tore off the ribbons
from my chair, and almost threw me down — safely out.
Dined tavern—about sixty-five or seventy.   Mr. G.'s coarse,
indecent toast—I would not give it.   Sheriff well behaved.'
The secret of his hidden strength is simply recorded in the
following line:—'Home about seven and prayed.   Much
affected and shed many tears.'

After the election he made a progress through various
parts of Yorkshire; his first visit being to his mother's house
at Hull. 'She seems,' he thought, 'to olden even now, but
better than when at Scarborough last summer.   Thomas
Thompson dined with us.   Too loose and free in morals
about Hedon voters and election management; but people
here by no means shy of election subject, which shows they

---

[5] Diary, May 31.   [6] Ib. June 1.   [7] Ib.

have not done what they think wrong.'[8] 'Milner preached—very practical and good. At night my mother affected at parting, and whispered " Remember me in your prayers. "'

CHAPTER XI.

JULY 1796 TO JUNE 1798.

Buxton—War unpopular—Jeremy Bentham—Plans for the East Indies —Robert Haldane—Sunday drilling—Bath—Bank stops payment— Ellis's motion on Slave Trade—Work on Christianity published—Its great effect—Burke—Sir Charles Middleton—Return to Bath—Mutiny —His marriage—Death of his brother-in-law—Death of Eliot—New session—Support of government—Tripling the assessed taxes—Voluntary contributions for the public service—Self-control—Origin of Church Missionary Society—Feelings towards ministry and opposition — Abolition again defeated—Pitt's duel with Tierney—Letter on church preferment.

THE advice of Mr. Hey had now fixed him for some weeks he says, at Buxton, amidst a crowd of other visitors. 'The weather delightful for Buxton—began the waters yesterday.'[1] He dined commonly at the public table, and mixed much with the miscellaneous group around him; 'leading those he met to talk upon the subjects with which they are best acquainted.'

'Heard Miss Seward repeat and read Cornaro, Translations from Horace. Called upon her several times—once to get serious talk, but in vain. She commended the preacher at the rooms. I said I liked sermons better which made people uneasy.'[2] 'Erskine much with her—his free conversation with Milner about religion.'[3] 'He tells me he has had sixty-six retainers off his circuit at three hundred guineas each.' Though he spent much time in study and resumed his tract, yet his letters from Buxton bear the marks of some increased leisure.

'Whilst I was taking a contemplative walk this morning,' he writes to Mr. Macaulay, 'I rambled in thought to Sierra Leone, and my mind was naturally led to consider the providential dispensations of that Almighty Being, whose infinitely complicated plan embraces all His creatures, and who espe-

---

[8] Diary, June 9. [1] Ib. July 1.
[2] Diary, Aug. 28. [3] Ib. Aug. 22.

cially leads, and directs, and supports all those who in their different walks through this multifarious maze of life, are pursuing in His faith and fear the objects which He has respectively assigned them. " The holy church throughout all the world doth acknowledge Thee." It presents to my mind a most august idea—the praises of God arising from every nation, and kindred, and people, where His name is known, and blending, as they rise, into one note and body of harmony.'

' I rejoice,' he writes to Hannah More, ' to hear of your reforming operations. " Ride on prosperously." It is the contemplation of a scene like this, which refreshes the mind, when wearied by Archduke Charles and General Moreau.'

The war was now becoming unpopular. ' Letters from the West Riding—they begin to be sadly dissatisfied about the war.'[4] ' My good Wilberforce,' wrote ' Honest Henry Duncombe,'[5] ' pray make Pitt conclude a peace, the country is quite tired of fine speeches.' At this very moment ' a letter from Pitt about a direct treaty with Paris, Spanish war, &c.'[6] cut short his stay at Buxton. ' Off early (Sept. 15) for London. Prompted by the possible hope of doing good in pressing Pitt to peace—not to stipulate for islands—perhaps include Slave Trade in treaty. 17th. Hoped to see Pitt to-day. Got to Palace Yard by half-past five—all well. Praise the Lord, O my soul.

' September 19. To Holwood, to have a full political discussion—Joe Smith came there—he, Pitt, and I—full talk of all politics—pleased with my interview on the whole.—20th. Pitt forced to go to town, so I did too. Dined in Downing Street—Rose, Pitt, and I—much politics—tide of success is turned, and Archduke is all. I have been resenting to Pitt the idea of employing Jackson to negotiate with France— every body feels it, but few dare tell Pitt any such thing. People will not so much believe him in earnest in the treaty as if he sent a more important character. The Speaker agrees with me that some important man should go; and even offered to go himself.' These remonstrances at last proved effectual; ' Jackson was quite held a proper man for

---

[4] Diary, August 21.   [5] Oct. 15.   [6] Diary, Sept. o.

this embassy, and Pitt would scarce hear it questioned, but now it is thought ridiculous to hold him fit, and Lord Malmesbury is to go.'[7]

On his road from Buxton, he had been amused by a characteristic letter, in which Jeremy Bentham urged him to volunteer his services as chief negotiator, offering his own assistance in quality of secretary. He was at this time as intimate with Mr. Bentham as the contrariety of their natures rendered possible. 'Bentham,' he says,[8] '(inter alia) professes to have no liking for poetry.' 'Odd enough were the parties I met once or twice every winter at Bentham's house, at which his brother General Bentham, Lord St. Helen's, Abbot, Romilly, old Professor Christian, and myself were the ordinary guests.'[9]

This intimacy had grown out of his attempts to assist Mr. Bentham out of the distress which had followed the failure of his 'panopticon.' The plan of this penitentiary greatly pleased Mr. Dundas, and he obtained Mr. Pitt's sanction for the experiment. Thus encouraged, Mr. Bentham entered into contracts for the building, when Lord Spencer complained loudly, and successfully, of its vicinity to his estate. It proved no easy matter to find another site, whilst the delay seriously involved Mr. Bentham. Mr. Wilberforce took up his cause with zeal; and applied, amongst others, to the Chapter of St. Peter's, Westminster, in furtherance of his design. 'I shall never forget Horsley's[1] keen glance, when in the course of our discussion he asked me, "Mr. Wilberforce, do you think that Mr. Pitt is in earnest in the business?" Never was anyone worse used than Bentham. I have seen the tears run down the cheeks of that strong-minded man through vexation at the pressing importunity of creditors and the insolence of official underlings, when day after day he was begging at the Treasury for what was indeed a mere matter of right. How indignant did I often feel, when I saw him thus treated by men infinitely his inferiors! He was quite soured by it, and I have no doubt that many of his harsh opinions afterwards were the fruit of this ill treat-

[7] Diary, October. [8] Ib. Sept. 6.
[9] Con. Mem. [1] Bishop Horsley, Dean of Westminster.

M

ment.'[2] ' A fit site,' at last wrote the weary man,[3] ' obtainable for my purpose, without a single dissentient voice, is that of the golden tree, and the singing water, and after a three years' consideration I beg to be excused searching for it.'—' Bentham's hard measure '—' Bentham cruelly used '—' Jeremy Bentham, suo more '—are Mr. Wilberforce's docketings upon the letters which at this time passed frequently between them. Some of them are not a little singular.—' Kind sir,' he writes[4] in one, ' the next time you happen on Mr. Attorney-General[5] in the House or elsewhere, be pleased to take a spike, the longer and sharper the better, and apply it to him by way of memento that the Penitentiary Contract Bill has, for I know not what length of time, been sticking in his hands; and you will much oblige your humble servant to command. N.B. A corking-pin was yesterday applied by Mr. Abbot.'

Ever watchful for his great cause, he seized eagerly that autumn upon ' an idea, about which' he tells Lord Muncaster, ' I am very busy, of availing ourselves of the circumstance that all the slave-trading powers (except one of no consideration) will be brought together, for trying at a general convention to abolish. Dundas is favourable to it, and I am very sanguine of its success, if proposed. Less sanguine, however, in my hopes of peace now.'

' Very busy seeing Pitt and Dundas about Abolition convention plan and East India missions—pleased with Dundas's candour.'[6]

Robert Haldane, with the intellectual and moral vigour which so eminently marked his character, had formed, and was ready at the cost of the greatest personal sacrifices, to carry out really grand designs for India. Awakened himself to a true knowledge of Christ's Gospel, he longed to spread it, and India seemed to him a wide and hopeful field for labour. He had obtained the co-operation of Dr. Bogue and other men of eminence and piety, and he was prepared to sacrifice a good estate in his native county to supply the funds for a grand mission, and to settle himself with his co-

[2] Con. Mem.
[4] Feb. 28, 1797.
[6] Diary, Oct. 8.

[3] Aug. 18, to W. Wilberforce, Esq.
[5] Sir John Scott, now Earl of Eldon.

adjutors at Benares, and give himself and all the labours of his associates to the conversion of India. Amongst others whom Mr. Haldane brought to bear on Dundas, whose assent was then essential to his plan, was Mr. Wilberforce. Heartily did he take up the cause. His own keen desire to see some effort made for spreading Christianity in India, his deep respect for the sterling character of Mr. Haldane, and his admiration of the Christian nobleness which prompted him to offer such unusual sacrifices for the cause of God, all stirred up his zeal in seeking to obtain the needful sanction. But Dundas's own prejudices and the fears of the East India Direction were too strong for him, and he enters sadly in his Diary, ' I could not persuade him.' Good was it for Robert Haldane and his fellows that it was in their hearts thus to offer to their God. Why it was permitted that the boon should be withheld from India it may be too much for us to ask. But as it would seem that had it been granted this really great man would have found a premature grave in the massacre at Benares, we may see that he was held in God's hand to do the works which for many following years he so effectively completed both at home and on the continent of Europe. ' But on every ground ' Mr. Wilberforce ' regretted the decision.'

His intercourse with society this autumn may be traced from the Diary. ' Disengaged myself from Lord St. Helen's to dine with Pitt. A note to meet Speaker; but, to my surprise, found a grand dinner—sixteen or seventeen people. Late there.'[7]—' Friday. Lord St. Helen's dined with me tête-à-tête—pleasant day—free conversation—much politics and information.'[8]

' Franklin signed the Peace of Paris in his old spotted velvet coat (it being the time of a court mourning, which rendered it more particular). What, said my friend the negotiator,[9] is the meaning of that harlequin coat? It is that in which he was abused by Wedderburne.' ' He showed much rancour and personal enmity to this country—would

[7] Diary, Sept. 28.   [8] Ib. Sept. 30.
[9] David Hartley, his colleague for Hull, signed the treaty of peace with America, Sept. 3, 1783.

not grant the common passports for trade, which however easily got from Jay or Adams.'

'Johnson, Langton told us, did not get up till some one called to rouse him, whether it was ten, eleven, twelve, or one o'clock. Johnson said, " I am a very well-bred, well-mannered man." '[1]

' On Wednesday, King the American minister, Eliot, Montagu, and Henry Thornton dined with me. Rational day.'[2] Franklin seems, from King, not to be in good estimation in America. Thought a dishonest, tricking, hypocritical character; a free-thinker really, yet pretending to believe in the authority of Scripture. Witherspoon's memory is not held in high respect—thought turbulent, and to have rather left his proper functions.'

Parliament met upon October 6, and was soon the scene of acrimonious controversy. The new overtures for peace met of course with Mr. Fox's approbation, but the Bills for putting the country into a proper state for resisting an expected French invasion were contested hotly. Against the proposed provision that the supplemental corps of militia should be trained on Sunday afternoon, Mr. Wilberforce protested in private with Mr. Pitt. ' Dundas,' Mr. Wilberforce records,[3] ' is now clear that it would shock the general morals of Scotland to exercise their volunteers on Sunday; but I can scarce persuade Pitt, that in England it would excite any disgust.' The Bills themselves he supported strongly, and was more than once called up by the factious temper of the opposition. ' I will not charge them,' he said, November 2, 'with desiring an invasion, but I cannot help thinking that they would rejoice to see just so much mischief befall their country as would bring themselves into office.' ' What you said.' writes Dr. Cookson,[4] ' is what everybody thinks, but what no one else had the courage to speak out.'

It was only by ' seizing short intervals of possible action,' that he accomplished so much. During the hurry of his present London life, he never wholly laid aside the preparation of his work on Christianity. ' Dined at Pitt's to

[1] Diary.   [2] Ib.   [3] Ib.
[4] Letter to W. Wilberforce, Esq., Nov. 7.

talk over finance plan—Steele, Ryder, Mornington, Speaker, &c.—many minds—no determination.'[5]   'Walked two hours with St. Helen's.   Dined Lord Chancellor's—Loughborough, Windham, Pitt, Lord Chatham, Westmoreland, &c.   'Long discussion after breakfast about finance—this useful, but no time for tract, which I wish to get on with.   Eliot presses me much to go to the Bishop of Lincoln's for a few days, think-ing it will answer many good purposes.'   Upon the 17th he set out for Buckden, and spent a week there, engaged chiefly upon his tract, 'hospitably received, and spending a ra-tional life.'[6]   But business soon brought him back to Lon-don.—' 26th. Busy morning about finance and tract.   I hope to finish it for the press by the end of the Christmas recess. —28th. Town—Pitt had asked me on finance.   To Pitt's, evening, where staid late—talked much politics, and found him very fair and honest.—29th. Staid in town for evening meeting at Pitcairne's.[7]   Dined Pitt's to see Ellis from Paris —Lord Chatham, Spencer, Chancellor, Dundas, &c.   Much intelligence from Ellis.—30th.   St. Bartholomew's meeting, morning—then Chancellor's and Battersea Rise.

'Dec. 1. Dined Pitt's—on finance, to consult, but all our consultation anticipated by success of altered plan.   All in spirits, but no thanks to God.   "A great country this," &c. —8th. Dined before House—Eliot and De Lageard.   Sud-den attack on Pitt for Austrian money—spoke on the sudden and did good service—Fox severe.—22nd. Busy this week about Militia and Cavalry Bills.   House—went home with Dundas and Pitt, and staid awhile discussing—Mission busi-ness in hand.—23rd. Breakfasted early with Dundas and Eliot on mission business ; Dundas complying, and appoint-ing us to dinner again, where Grant and David Scott also— sat long.   Then Pitt's, with whom Bishop of Lincoln ;— having just heard of Lord Malmesbury failing, and being ordered back—staid late, talking about it.—24th. Kept in town all morning, expecting House.   Dined Bankes's quietly, then Pitt's, where with Mornington, Speaker, &c. read dis-patches.   Went home heavy.—30th. To town after political preparation.   Dined Bankes's, and talked with him on state

---

[5] Diary.   [6] Ib.   [7] About St. Bartholomew's.

of things—address on Lord Malmesbury's negotiation—
kept late in House.   Pitt very earnest with me not to speak.'

The business of the House of Commons closed with this
debate.   ' Monday, Jan. 2.   Slept ill, and very indifferent—
feared I was about to be as bad as 1788, and suffered much
—sent to Pitcairne.   Had death, as probable, in view, and
felt I hope resigned, but no ardour or warmth.'

By the middle of the following week he was able to move,
at the desire of his physicians, to Bath.   ' Jan. 22.   Sunday.
To Pump-room and church.   Dr. Randolph—sensible sermon and good delivery.   Dined alone.   Jay's, evening.'[8]
Mr. Jay was the well-known Dissenting minister, for whom
Mr. Wilberforce had a strong regard, and whose ministry at
this time he often attended when at Bath, though in later life
he did not think it right to continue the custom.—' Feb. 2.
Dined at Anstey's —large miscellaneous party, and rout afterwards.   Mr. Francillon went from talking of the discipline
of the Calvinist church, to dance a cotillon.—Sunday, 5th.
Randolph's.   Sacrament, which received—afterwards serious
talk with Acklom.   Heard at Pump-room of Austrian defeats.
Poor Burke came down quite emaciated.—9th.   Eliot called,
and a very pleasant day.   Evening, called on Burke, and sat
an hour—no serious talk.'   ' He is very poorly, and Windham
is visiting him.   His faculties are as fresh as ever ; he abstains from talking politics.'

' I find little time here,' he complained, ' for study, not above
two or three hours in a morning hitherto, at tract.'   But he
' managed to be pretty diligent ;' and by the time of his
leaving Bath it was ready for the printer.

On the 14th of February, ' he reached London, and dined
at Pitt's ; but Grenville being there could not get out much,
though I had given up going to Greathed's for suggesting
about Eliot succeeding Lord Cornwallis.'[9]   This he earnestly
desired not only from his warm personal attachment to Mr.
Eliot, but also from his anticipation of benefit to the cause
of Christianity from the appointment.   ' There is considerable probability,' he told Mr. Hey,[1] ' of our being permitted
to send to the East Indies persons, for the purpose of instruct-

ing the natives in the English language, and in the principles of Christianity.   But the plan will need much deliberation. I really dare not plunge into such a depth as is required without previous sounding ; lest instead of pearls and corals, I should come up with my head covered only with sea weed, and become a fair laughing-stock to the listless and unenterprising.   When I return to town we will hold a Cabinet council on the business.   Henry Thornton, Grant, and myself, are the junto.'   When Mr. Eliot's nomination seemed to be secure, both ' Mr. Dundas and Lord Cornwallis preferring him to any other person,'[2] a dangerous attack of illness forced him to resign the appointment.

Parliament reassembled upon February 14 with the gloomiest prospects.   ' I have been trying,' he says on the 26th, ' for several days to see Pitt.   This evening Eliot has been with me to inform me that the Bank is to stop payment by command of Government to-morrow morning.' ' We talked much about it.'   ' I have not been party to this counsel, but have of course suggested what has occurred to me to prevent riots, and secure a supply of provisions for the capital.'[3]   ' Monday, 27th.   Anxious about great event. Went to *General*[4]—found him, Rose, Long, Eliot, Lord Auckland.   Letter from Lord Carrington stating that all going on well and stocks rising.   They seemed cheerful and gay.   When I got back I called upon Bankes and told him so.   He was surprised, because Lord Auckland came in where Mrs. Bankes and Lady Auckland were, and had said this was the beginning of the throat-cutting measures. Samuel Thornton says that the Cabinet very averse to take on themselves the responsibility of the measure.   They were walking about, &c.   " No," said the Chancellor, " this will never do."   At last Pitt said, " My Lords, shall I draw up the minute?"   General really afraid that unless the cash stopped, there would not be enough to pay the army, navy, and ordnance.   General disposed to make large personal sacrifices : not sanguine in ideas that much can be saved in

[2] Letter from Charles Grant, Esq. to W. Wilberforce, Esq. Feb. 4.
[3] Letter to Lord Muncaster.   [4] Mr. Pitt.

public expenditure, or thinking that any material abuses exist. Fearful lest we should so far let down the spirits of men, that they should be ready to patch up any kind of compromise with Jacobin principles.'[5]

Two days afterwards he was chosen one of a Parliamentary Committee which took possession of the Bank, and examined into its solvency. ' Saturday. Committee as usual. Examined Pitt—wanted to sit next day, but I repelled.'[6] After a morning thus occupied, he spent his evenings in the House, where he was frequently called up by the bitterness of party spirit in defence of Mr. Pitt, upon whom he was still urging privately the necessity of making peace. ' Dined at Pitt's quietly—he, R. and I. R. more unmanageable than Pitt. I counsel for peace.'[7] ' Called at Pitt's—a most earnest conversation about peace, and degree in which I may fairly differ from ministry about it. Pitt exceedingly moved.' [8]

To his other business was soon added the Abolition question. His partial success in the preceding session had taught the West Indians the value of Mr. Dundas's policy; and they now met his attempts by illusory concession.

Mr. Ellis moved an address to the Crown praying for the issue of directions to the several island governors, with the professed intention of preparing for the Abolition. This was to leave the matter in the hands of the colonial assemblies, whose hatred to the work was proof against the most earnest representation of their friends at home,[9] ' that they must at least *appear* to act, if they would be safe from the interference of the British Parliament.' Such a measure could not of course satisfy any who heartily opposed the trade. ' Called at the Speaker's,' says the Diary of April 1, 'where Mornington. Discussed about Ellis's motion. Ellis's motion till very late— much hurt—Pitt wanted me to close with it modified, but when I would not, stood stiffly by me.' In this debate the Abolition party found in Mr. Bryan Edwards a new and powerful opponent, while they lost a useful friend in Mr. Windham. The dread of French politics still oppressed the

[5] Diary.   [6] March 4.   [7] Diary, March 28.
[8] Ib. March 31.   [9] Vide Wilberforce on the Slave Trade, p. 226.

House, and the delusive measure was carried by a majority of 30.[1]

He had been engaged about 'his book' ever since his return from Bath. Immediately upon coming to town, he 'had seen Cadell and agreed to begin printing;' and throughout the session its revision occupied his spare time. He corrected the press when business flagged in the committee room;[2] and the index and errata were the work of midnight hours, when the debate was over.

Upon April 12 it was published—'My book out to-day.'[3] Many were those who anxiously watched the issue. Amongst others Dr. Milner had strongly dissuaded his attempt. There was then little demand for religious publications, and his publisher intimated his fear of the speculation. 'He evidently regarded me an amiable enthusiast.'[4] 'You mean to put your name to the work? Then I think we may venture upon 500 copies,' was Mr. Cadell's conclusion. Within a few days it was out of print, and within half a year five editions (7,500 copies) had been called ior. 'I heartily thank you for your book,' wrote Lord Muncaster. 'As a friend I thank you for it; as a man I doubly thank you; but as a member of the Christian world, I render you all gratitude and acknowledgment. I thought I knew you well, but I know you better now, my dearest excellent Wilber.' 'I see no reason,' said his friend James Gordon,[5] 'why you should wish to have given it another year's consideration; the world would only have been so much the worse by one year.' 'I send you herewith,' Mr. Henry Thornton writes to Mr. Macaulay, 'the book on religion lately published by Mr. Wilberforce; it excites even more attention than you would have supposed, amongst all the graver and better disposed people. The bishops in general much approve of it, though some more warmly, some more coolly. Many of his gay and political friends admire and approve of it; though some do but dip into it. Several have recognised the likeness of

---

[1] 93 to 63.
[2] On the Bank Restrictions. An immense mass of notes attests the diligence with which he attended this committee.
[3] Diary.   [4] Con. Mem.
[5] Letter from J. Gordon, Esq.

themselves. The better part of the religious world, and more especially the Church of England, prize it most highly, and consider it as producing an era in the history of the church. The Dissenters, many of them, call it legal,[6] and point at particular parts. Gilbert Wakefield has already scribbled something against it. I myself am amongst those who contemplate it as a most important work.'

' I am truly thankful to Providence,' wrote Bishop Porteus,[7] ' that a work of this nature has made its appearance at this tremendous moment.' ' I deem it,' Mr. Newton told him,[8] ' the most valuable and important publication of the present age, especially as it is yours :' and to Mr. Grant he wrote, ' What a phenomenon has Mr. Wilberforce sent abroad! Such a book by such a man, and at such a time! A book that must and will be read by persons in the higher circles, who are quite inaccessible to us little folk, who will neither hear what we can say, nor read what we may write. I am filled with wonder and with hope. I accept it as a token for good; yea, as the brightest token I can discern in this dark and perilous day. Yes, I trust that the Lord, by raising up such an incontestible witness to the truth and power of the gospel, has a gracious purpose to honour him as an instrument of reviving and strengthening the sense of real religion where it already is, and of communicating it where it is not.'

The aspect of the times, in which, says Mr. Hey,[9] ' hell seems broke loose in the most pestiferous doctrines and abominable practices, which set the Almighty at defiance, and break the bonds of civil society,' led even the less thoughtful to look to its effect with some anxiety. ' I sincerely hope,' wrote the Lord Chancellor (Loughborough),[1] ' that your book will be read by many, with that just and proper temper which the awful circumstances in which we stand ought to produce.' Its tone was well calculated to create these hopes. Its entire reality brought it closely home to the heart and con-

---

[6] In the year 1818, he was assailed in the ' Scotsman ' by an exactly opposite insinuation. ' Mr. Wilberforce is a man of rigid Calvinistic principles,' &c. In the margin of the paper he wrote, ' False.'

[7] To W. Wilberforce, Esq., May 10.   [8] April 21.

[9] To W. Wilberforce, Esq., April 29.

[1] Letter to W. Wilberforce, Esq., May 5.

science. It was not the fine-spun theory of some speculative declaimer, but the heart's utterance of one who had lived and watched those to whom he spoke. 'Let me recommend you to open on the last section of the fourth chapter,' was his advice to Mr. Pitt;[2] 'you will see wherein the religion which I espouse differs practically from the common system. Also the sixth chapter has almost a right to a perusal being the basis of all politics, and particularly addressed to such as you.' 'It is a great relief to my mind,' he writes to Mr. Newton,[3] 'to have published what I may call my manifesto; to have plainly told my worldly acquaintance what I think of their system and conduct, and where it must end. I shall act in my parliamentary situation with more comfort and satisfaction than hitherto, from having openly declared myself as it were on the side of Christ, and having avowed on what my hopes for the well-being of the country bottom.'

He addressed his countrymen from an eminence where he could be heard; as a layman safe from the imputation of professional bias; and as one who lived under the public eye, and was seen to practise what he taught. His rule indeed was strict, but his own example proved that it was practicable. His life had been a puzzle to many. Some had even thought him mad, because they could not comprehend the strange exhibition of his altered habits; but his work supplied the rationale of his conduct, whilst his conduct enforced the precepts of his work. Any one might now examine the staff of the Wizard and learn the secrets of his charmed book. 'How careful ought I to be,' was his own reflection,[4] 'that I may not disgust men by an inconsistency between the picture of a Christian which I draw, and which I exhibit! How else can I expect the blessing of God on my book? May His grace quicken me.' 'That he acted up,' is the judgment of a shrewd observer, 'to his opinions as nearly as is consistent with the inevitable weakness of our nature, is a praise so high that it seems like exaggeration; yet in my conscience I believe it, and I knew him well for at least forty years.'[5]

[2] To the Right Hon. William Pitt, April 16.
[3] To Rev. J. Newton, April 19.   [4] Journal, April 9.
[5] Entry on a blank page of the ' Practical View,' by J. B. S. Morritt, Esq.

The effect of this work can scarcely be overrated. Its circulation was at that time altogether without precedent. In 1826 fifteen editions (and some very large impressions) had issued from the press in England. 'In India,' says Henry Martin in 1807, 'Wilberforce is eagerly read.' In America the work was immediately reprinted, and within the same period twenty-five editions had been sold. It has been translated into the French, Italian, Spanish, Dutch and German languages. Its influence was proportionate to its diffusion. It may be affirmed beyond all question, that it gave the first general impulse to that warmer and more earnest burst of piety which, amongst all its many evils, has happily distinguished the last half century.

'My book,' he says, in his Diary at Bath,[6] 'is universally well received, especially by the Archbishop of Canterbury, and the Bishops of London, Durham, Rochester, and Llandaff, the Duchess of Gloucester, Sir J. Scott. Much pleased by a letter from Lord St. Helen's most highly commending it as adapted to the good of worldly men.' From Mr. Newton he heard again :[7] 'I hope your late publication, which I have now read through with increasing satisfaction a third time, will be useful to me, and of course to those who attend on my ministry. You have not only confirmed but enlarged my views of several important points.' He speaks of it as specially noticeable that 'one harassed with a multiplicity of business and surrounded on all sides with snares, could venture to publish such a book, without fearing a retort either from the many friends or the many enemies amongst whom you have moved so many years. The power of the Lord in your favour seems to be little less remarkable than in the three young men who lived unhurt and unsinged in the midst of the fire, or of Daniel, who sat in peace in the den when surrounded by lions. It plainly shows that His grace is all-sufficient to keep us in any situation which His providence appoints us.'

He received too letters of another class which gave him yet greater satisfaction. Not a year passed, in which he did not receive fresh testimonies to the blessed effects which it

---

[6] Diary, May 28.   [7] Reading, June 7, 1797.

pleased God to produce through its publication.   In acknowledging this goodness of his God, the outpourings of his
heart are warm and frequent; though the particular occasions are for the most part too sacred to be made public.
One such record will suffice.   Heard to-day ' of a clergyman
in the Isle of Wight, the Rev. Legh Richmond, to whom
my book was blessed.   Oh praise, praise !'   Men of the
highest rank and intellect, clergy and laity, traced to it their
first real impressions of personal religion; and tendered
their several acknowledgments in various ways; from the
anonymous correspondent 'who had purchased a small freehold in Yorkshire, that by his vote he might offer him a
slight tribute of respect,' down to the grateful message of the
expiring Burke.   'Have you been told,' Mr. Henry Thornton asks Mrs. Hannah More, 'that Burke spent much of the
two last days of his life reading Wilberforce's book, and
said that he derived much comfort from it, and that if he
lived he should thank Wilberforce for having sent such a
book into the world ?   so says Mrs. Crewe, who was with
Burke at the time.'   Before his death Mr. Burke summoned
Dr. Laurence to his side, and committed specially to him the
expression of these thanks.

Amidst all these circumstances his sobriety of mind was
remarkable.   ' I was much struck,' says a friend who was
with him whilst at Bath, 'with his entire simplicity of manners.   The place was very full; the sensation which his
work produced drew upon him much observation, but he
seemed neither flattered nor embarrassed by the interest he
excited.'   The secret of this humble self-possession may be
read in the entries of his private Journal.   'Bath, April 14,
three o'clock, Good Friday.   I thank God that I *now* do
feel in some degree as I ought this day.   I trust that I feel
true humiliation of soul from a sense of my own extreme
unworthiness ; a humble hope in the favour of God in Christ ;
some emotion from the contemplation of Him who at this
very moment was hanging on the cross ; some desire to devote myself to Him who has so dearly bought me ; some
degree of that universal love and good-will, which the sight
of Christ crucified is calculated to inspire.   Oh if the con-

templation *here* can produce these effects on my hard heart, what will the vision of Christ in glory produce hereafter ! '

April 17, ' Heard,' he says,[8] ' of Portsmouth mutiny—consultation with Burke.'　' The only letter which reached Bath that day by the cross post from Portsmouth was one from Captain Bedford of the Royal Sovereign to Patty More. She brought it me, and I took it at once to Burke. He could not then see me, but at his desire I called again at two o'clock. The whole scene is now before me.　Burke was lying on a sofa much emaciated; and Windham, Laurence, and some other friends were round him.　The attention shown to Burke by all that party was just like the treatment of Ahithophel of old.　" It was as if one went to inquire of the oracle of the Lord."　I reported to them the account I had received, and Burke being satisfied of its authority, we held a consultation on the proper course for Government to follow.　Windham set off for London the same night with the result of our deliberations.　Burke's advice was very much the same as Sir Charles Middleton's had been on a similar occasion, which Pitt often mentioned as an instance of Sir Charles's promptitude and resolution.　Pitt and Lord Chatham, then first Lord of the Admiralty, had sent for Middleton, and met him with the information, "Bad news, Sir Charles, from the fleet—a ship has mutinied ; what are we to do ? "　Sir Charles, who had always been an enemy to pressing, and who resigned his office as Comptroller of the Navy, because he could not carry some reforms, which would have prevented the breaking out of the great mutiny, immediately replied, " You know how ill I think these poor fellows have been used, but now that it has come to a mutiny, there is but one thing to be done—you must show them that you have the superiority ; you must order a ninety-gun ship on each side of her, and sink her on the spot if she does not at once submit."　They were staggered, and said doubtfully, " That is a strong measure, what if they should refuse to obey ? "　" Then indeed all would be over : but they will not refuse to obey, if you give the order resolutely, and it is the only thing which can be done."　He left them still undetermined, and in a few minutes

[8] Diary.

came back with the despatch drawn up; and seeing still some hesitation, said, "Pray sign it instantly, there is much to be done in the office, and we shall scarcely be ready in time to save the post."' [9]

The mutiny which now broke out, and for months kept the nation in alarm, had already gained too much head to be so easily suppressed. The time of its continuance was ever esteemed by Mr. Wilberforce the most critical within his recollection.

Before a fortnight expired his return was earnestly desired by Mr. Pitt. 'I do not,' he wrote,[1] 'easily bring myself to propose to you to exchange any one of the days you would pass at Bath, for such as you will find in the House of Commons. But it seems very important not to delay for a moment more than is necessary the decision on the Austrian loan. The sending the result to Vienna may be of infinite importance. I have therefore been obliged to fix it for Monday, and trust to seeing you in the course of that day.' The summons was peculiarly unwelcome. At Bath he had formed the acquaintance of one whom he judged well fitted to be his companion through life, and for whom he contracted a strong attachment. He was therefore very unwilling to leave Bath at that moment; but it was a call of duty, and he at once 'resolved to obey it.' By Monday evening he was in town. The next morning's post brought news which dispelled Mr. Pitt's hopes as to the loan to Austria. It brought also intelligence of the Emperor's having made a separate peace. Further, as if to crowd together all threatening circumstances, whilst the naval mutiny was yet unappeased, discontents broke out amongst the military in the neighbourhood of London.

Every day was now fully occupied. '23rd. Breakfast at Sir Charles Middleton's. Proclamation committee. Carrington's to read settlements. Dined before House: friends— Muncaster, Carrington, &c. House—Fox on repeal of the two Bills till late.—25th. Morning to city to breakfast on business—very unfit to go—nearly fainted afterwards from the heat. Home and dined—Lord Hawke sitting by me and

[9] Con. Mem.   [1] April 28.

discussing.   Pitt's about turnpike tax.   House—Sir William Pulteney's motion about the Bank—put off, so House up early.   Lock Hospital — about its funds — nearly ruined. —26th.   Lord St. Helen's with me on politics.   Parliamentary Reform day.   Dined before House— Muncaster, Smyth, and Lascelles.   Extremely exhausted by the heat of the House.   Fox, &c. charged all our evils on want of Parliamentary Reform; and thought it would cure them.   Grey moderate—declared as well as Fox a secession — something solemn.   Pitt awaked by Woolwich artillery riot, and went out to Cabinet.'   ' Pitt met us next morning, declaring, " Lord Harrington (a nobleman of the ' vieille cour,' then commanding the forces in London) is, after all, the greatest man in England.   When I saw him in the hurry and alarm last night, he was just as slow, and made as many bows as if he had been loitering at the levee." ' [2]—' May 27.   Off after dinner, calling at Pitt's and strongly urging him to make a liberal offer at first to France ; he convinced at length, that requisite to make immediate effort.   Daily reports of the soldiery rising, and certainly some progress made.   Pitt and the others now convinced that things *in extremis.*'[3]

On the 30th, he was married to Barbara Ann, eldest daughter of Isaac Spooner, Esq., of Elmdon Hall, in the county of Warwick.   ' You will perhaps judge my way of thinking old-fashioned and queer,' was the congratulation of his late colleague Henry Duncombe,[4] ' but I am greatly pleased that you have not chosen your partner from among the titled fair ones of the land.   Do not however tell Lady C. so.'

His first visit with his bride was to Mrs. Hannah More's. ' Received at Cowslip Green with great kindness—delightful day and sweet ride.   Sunday morning, as early as able, tour of the schools — Shipham, Axbridge, and Cheddar.   Delighted with all we saw, Cheddar in particular—a delightful scene, when old people collected together at afternoon reading.   Home at night, after a pleasant drive.'[5]   After a week his head-quarters were in Palace Yard, and for an occasional

---

[2] Con. Mem.   [3] Diary.
[4] To W. Wilberforce, Esq., May 10.   [5] Diary, June 3.

retreat he rented of his friend Mr. Eliot his house on Clapham Common.

Society had now new claims upon him. ' Dined,' he says, ' at N.'s, with all the H.'s—grand dinner, very dull, as grand relations' dinners always are.' 'To the drawing-room with my wife.' He was soon full of work of all sorts. ' Was to meet Pitcairne and Sargent about St. Bartholomew's; but Pitcairne too late. Wanted St. Margaret's and St. John's parishes to associate. Vestry meeting. People would not come in to it. To Pitt's about provisional Cavalry Act. Then House on Ship Owners' Bill.'[6] ' Next morning,[7] by ourselves at Broomfield—happy day. Read Scripture.' ' Pitt told me yesterday about negotiation. My *Skipper* friends saw him, and he with them. Business put off.'[8]

He had carried a Bill through the Commons to enable Romanists to serve in the Militia.[9] In his own county he knew them to be thoroughly loyal men, who ought not to be excluded from joining in the national defence. ' I thank you,' writes Sir John Lawson, ' for obtaining the erasure of the words, " I am a Protestant," from the oath required of every man balloted into the supplemental Militia. I then hoped that every obstacle to my standing forward in the cause of my country was done away, and in that conviction I took the very first occasion to offer my personal services.' This Bill Mr. Pitt sanctioned, but it was supported feebly by his colleagues in the Upper House, where it was contested hotly because, at the motion of another member, Protestant Dissenters had been included in its provisions. ' House of Lords about Roman Catholic Bill. Bishop of Rochester's violent speech. Bishop of Bristol. Bill thrown out. I too much incensed. Grenville and Pitt very like breaking friendship.'[1]

' Thursday. Parliamentary session ended to-day. Speaker's Address to the King, good. Carrington, Pitt, and Speaker came down to us at Broomfield.'

On the 26th he set off, to be 'at York for the assizes.'

[6] Diary, July 7.			[7] July 8.			[8] Diary, July 11.
[9] He had proposed the Bill May 22. It had been read the third time July 4.			[1] Diary, July 12.

My objections to it are much done away by my having published My book, which I consider a sort of explanatory manifesto.' But at Newark he was met by information of the sudden death of Dr. Clarke. This changed his course to Hull, where he joined his mother and his sister. 'I look back,' he writes to Hannah More, 'to the time I spent with Dr. Clarke at Bath with no little pleasure. Being in the same house, I learned more than I could otherwise have done of his habitual frame. He was a Christian of the true breed; quiet, silent, unobtrusive.'

He spent three weeks at Hull, cheering his aged mother and sorrowing sister. 'I am anxious about this negotiation,' he writes to Mr. Pitt ;[2] 'on the whole I augur well from its going on:' 'send me a line or two,' he asks the Speaker, 'in pity to my unenlightened situation; you know how difficult, I may say next to impossible, it is to extort a line from Pitt.'

Meanwhile he was busily engaged in doing what present good he could. The vacant vicarage of the Holy Trinity church was in the gift of the corporation; and Joseph Milner was a candidate for the appointment. 'Went about,' he says, July 31, 'to canvass for Milner—no promises, but hopeful.' 'Milner appointed vicar, August 22. My being here probably got him elected.'

He found little leisure whilst he remained at Hull. 'Late morning hours and early dining, many calls, a vast many letters, and attention to my mother, prevent my getting anything done. Reading the Bible with my wife.'

'It is hardly in human nature, I fear,' wrote Dr. Milner the day after his departure,[3] 'to continue long as happy as you are at present.' 'My cup was before teeming with mercies,' he says himself,[4] 'and it has at length pleased God to add the only ingredient almost which was wanting to its fulness.'

He was soon established at Bath. 'Friday and Saturday quite pleasant days—by ourselves—not unbagged yet—reading, &c., rational.—Sunday. Randolph's, morning—evening,

---

[2] To Right Hon. William Pitt, August 10.
[3] August 30.   [4] September 20.

Jay's — comfortable, happy Sunday. — Monday. Reading, writing, &c., by ourselves.'[5]

But this quiet life was soon interrupted by an unlooked-for sorrow. Thursday.[6] 'Heard of Eliot's death from Pitt; and from Rose saying how much Pitt was affected. Deeply hurt by Eliot's death—kept awake at night by it. Heard yesterday too of Lord Malmesbury's return, re infectâ. Much affected by this too, and regret my plan of open dealing had not been adopted.'

Great as was his grief for the loss of Mr. Eliot, for whom, amongst his many friends he felt almost a distinctive tenderness of affection, he yet looked with Christian thankfulness upon the gathering in to rest of one so ripe for his removal. In him sorrow had accomplished a blessed work—and to the very last letter he had written, Mr. Wilberforce now turned again with deepened interest. 'Your sister's resigned and composed state of mind,' he had written[1] on the death of Dr. Clarke, 'must be a real consolation to you. When a similar calamity befell me, I now think I was little better than an infidel; but it pleased God to sanctify his visitation, and gradually to draw me by it to a better mind. My present infirmity, I am well-nigh convinced, is sent upon the same errand: the necessity for it I sincerely submit to His wisdom, but the effects I certainly feel and willingly acknowledge to have been spiritually beneficial. My thoughts have been much more settled, less disposed to wander and to dwell upon the world or the enjoyments of sense, and my imagination much less uncontrollable than heretofore. For all this I am truly thankful, and though not quite free from the remains of my complaint, I do not pray to God to relieve me from them, if it is to be at the expense of these more substantial blessings. In the meanwhile, by His goodness I am free from any very considerable uneasiness; and if my service be to " stand and wait," it is hitherto without pain, and I trust without impatience: after all, however, I do not mean to state myself as despairing of being restored to more exertion.'

[5] Diary, September 18.   [6] Ib. September 21.
[7] To W. Wilberforce, Esq., August 30.

'Perhaps,' he writes to Lord Muncaster,[8] 'no one but myself knew Eliot thoroughly. He was so modest, retiring, and unassuming, that neither in point of understanding, nor of religious and moral character, did he generally possess his proper estimation. I can truly say, that I scarcely know any one whose loss I have so much cause to regret. The effect produced on Mr. Pitt by the news, which came in a letter from Lord Eliot, by the common post with his others, exceeded conception. Rose says he never saw, and never expects to see, anything like it. To Pitt, the loss of Eliot is a loss indeed—and then his poor little girl.'

'I feel Eliot's loss deeply,' he tells Mrs. H. More, 'and shall continue to feel it; for except Henry Thornton, there is no one living with whom I was so much in the habit of consulting; and whose death so breaks in on all my plans in all directions. We were engaged in a multitude of pursuits together, and he was a bond of connection, which was sure never to fail, between me and Pitt; because a bond not of political, nor merely of a personal quality, but formed by a consciousness of common sentiments, interests, and feelings. Pitt has almost been overwhelmed with it; he suffers more from the very texture of his firm mind. The blow comes just when he has also to bear up against what deeply shocks him, Lord Malmesbury's return, re infectâ. Poor fellow! pray that the grace of God may yet visit him. He is the first of natural men, but "he that is least in the kingdom of heaven is greater than he."'

'Your very touching account,' replies Mrs. Hannah More,[9] 'of Mr. Pitt's sorrow has gone to all our hearts. I had anticipated the strong grief of that strong mind. The boasted *liberality* on which they value themselves in the conduct of the Bristol schools,' as to which he had inquired, 'is that relaxing toleration, which enables them to combine Quakers and Presbyterians, "*the sprinkled and the dipped*," by insisting on no peculiar form of worship or religious instruction; so that I fear in this accommodating and comprehensive plan, Christianity slips through their fingers. The manager is a man who will torment you to death, if you give him the

---

[8] Bath, Sept. 27, 1797.　　　　[9] September 26.

entrée. He is as vain as Erskine in another way; absurd
and injudicious, and as fond of fame as Alexander. With all
this, he is sober, temperate, laborious, and charitable; but
one with whom I never, and you never, could coalesce, with
views and motives so dissimilar.'

A visit to Cowslip Green followed. 'Dr. Fraser dined with
us—he says that Mackintosh is grown antidemocratical.—
Saturday. At dinner had Dr. and Miss Maclaine, and Miss
Bowdler. Rational spirited conversation. B— called, and
talked about schools.'[1]

In such pursuits passed the first recess after his marriage.
Upon the 1st of November he returned to London for the
opening of the session. The conduct of the French government during the negotiation of the summer months, convinced
him that it was his duty as a loyal subject to strengthen the
hands of administration ; and on the first night of the session
being 'moved by Bryan Edwards, and suddenly up,' he made
an effective reply to an extravagant eulogy upon the political
conduct of Mr. Fox.

'The newspapers,' he tells Lord Muncaster, 'mis-stated what
I said ; and I suppose they will as little fairly report a few
words I found it necessary to throw out to-night, in consequence of a very pugnacious speech of Dr. Laurence. I
thought it right to avow my conviction that government have
honestly sought for peace ; and though I have rather hinted
that I might not quite agree with them as to terms, yet I
have laid the blame of the failure of the negotiation on our
enemies, where I really conceive it to be due. It is of extreme importance that the nation should be convinced of
this. Heavy burthens will be necessary, and this only will
make people bear them with any tolerable patience.'

Mr. Pitt's scheme for raising the supplies came before the
House of Commons upon the 24th of November. 'House—
finance—Pitt let off on tripling the assessed taxes. Vexed
that I could not get an opportunity of answering Tierney.
Pitt foolish though, and wrong, to crush him.' The debate
was renewed upon the 4th of December. 'It went off,' he
writes on the following day, 'well upon the whole, except

[1] Diary, October 7.

that Windham made a mischievous speech which I in vain endeavoured to stop, about his retaining all his Burkish opinions, and its being of no consequence whether government had been sincere or not in the negotiations.   Tierney, who was much beyond his usual point in speaking, was truly Jacobinical.   The Speaker did himself great credit, both by the matter and manner of what he uttered.   He intimated that he was willing to contribute to the public necessities, and did it so handsomely as to smooth the way for government to follow ; instead of appearing to shame them into it, and thereby rendering it more difficult.'

On this subject he was now exerting himself greatly. 'Saw very little of Pitt this last week—vexed him by plain dealing.   Talked with others on economy.'[2] 'Fox's language at the Whig Club,' he writes December 6th, 'throws light, if any were wanting, upon their secession, It is my firm opinion, that a conviction of their weakness alone prevents their taking up the sword against government.   Now in such a state of things, it is in the highest degree important that administration should conciliate the good-will, confirm the confidence, and animate the public spirit, of all who are really attached to the constitution.   This can be done only by reforming any manifest abuse, by retrenching needless expenses, and by making personal sacrifices.   I have been urging these considerations in private upon Mr. Pitt, but unless my hands are strengthened, I doubt of my success. He is really one of the most public-spirited and upright, and the most desirous of spending the nation's money economically, and of making sacrifices for the general good, of all the men I ever knew : but I have met only with two or three who have been able to do obnoxious duties, and above all to act in opposition to the feelings of false honour, by resisting the improvidence and restraining the weakness of colleagues.   If the friends of government could make a united representation to them, administration might be compelled, by a kind violence, to consult their own welfare and honour, and the national interest.'[3] 'I have been writing to the Speaker

[2] Diary, Nov. 26.   [3] To William Hey, Esq.

and to Pitt, confirming one and urging the other to a relinquishment of a portion of their income during the war.'[4]

These subjects he continued to urge upon the minister.
'Dec. 2nd. Dined at the Speaker's—large party, talked much
with Pitt. Hatsell speaking of general corruption.—7th.
Dinner at home—Morton, Pitt, Colquhoun, and others—
much talk about police, and assessed taxes—storm louder
and louder. Colquhoun speaks of it as a most unfortunate
plan.—8th. Interview with Pitt—House—much discussion
with Henry Thornton, who sadly worried about assessed
taxes.—9th. Much serious talk with Pitt, stating the necessity of economy, and preventing profusion and jobs.' 'You
may perhaps think,' he wrote afterwards,[5] 'that I was disposed to be liberal at the expense of others in advising
ministers and official men to give up a part of their incomes ;
but in truth, though I originally contended against encouraging the voluntary contributions as a general measure, yet
when they had been set on foot, I subscribed at the Bank
what, with my assessed taxes which are extremely low,
amounted to near an eighth of my clear income, and also
contributed in my parish, 'and for Mrs. Wilberforce in the
ladies' subscription.'

On the night of the 14th, when the question was next discussed, 'Fox and Sheridan returned. Fox speaking well on
assessed taxes:—much shaken. I think Pitt must give them
up. House very late.—18th. Tierney's motion on Dundas's
place—spoke for him.' Whilst the Assessed Tax Bill was
passing through the House he was 'exerting' himself 'to
prevail upon the merchants and bankers in the city to bring
forward in the commercial world a proportionate impost
upon all property.'[6] 'Morning' of December 18, 'off to
city to try to rouse the monied men to exertion—saw several
who are for contribution.—19th. House. Spoke warmly and
plainly for public contribution. Tierney animadverted—
very hot House.—20th. To the city, to stir up some life
amongst citizens for contribution of property.—21st. To the

---

[4] Diary.   [5] To W. Hey, Esq., March 15, 1798.
[6] To W. Hey, Esq.

city again on the same business—got them to agree to meet. House. Assessed Taxes committee.'

At this time he writes, in answer to a question of Lord Muncaster, concerning Lord Duncan:—'It is not only true that after the action he ordered all the crew who could be mustered on deck, and directed his chaplain to read the Thanksgiving, in which they were exhorted by the gallant Admiral to join, as having such reason to be thankful; but (as Dundas told a friend of mine) just before the fleet got into action, having given all the necessary orders he retired into his cabin, and offered up an earnest prayer to God to support him in the approaching trying hour, and to bless his arms with victory; and, added Dundas, "when the brave old veteran told me this the tears ran down his manly cheeks."'

' 22nd. Off to the city, about capital contribution. The meeting held.' 'It was most respectably attended, and they went so far as to propose to Mr. Pitt the measure I desired.' 'Henry Thornton and others to Pitt with it.—23rd. Pitt's about the plan. Found him rational and full of it. Talking with him for half an hour.' Yet, 'after all, nothing came of it.' His support was now of great importance to the ministry; as the judgment of an independent man in favour of the absolute necessity of their bill. 'Nothing,' he declared, 'can make me support it, but the consciousness that we have no alternative. I dread the venomous ranklings which it will produce during the three years of its operation.'[7]

Though so much occupied by public business since his return to London, yet other important matters were not thrust aside. ' Dined and slept at Battersea Rise,' he enters on Nov. 9th, 'for Missionary meeting—Simeon—Charles Grant —Venn. Something, but not much, done—Simeon in earnest.' This was the commencement of what, two years later, issued in the Church Missionary Society for Africa and the East.—'Nov. 23rd. Proclamation Society's meeting. Erskine wanting to waive bringing up Williams[8] for judgment—

---

[7] To William Hey, Esq., Jan. 1, 1798.
[8] Publisher of Paine's Age of Reason.

said he would not compromise his character for any set of men. We firm.' 'Much interested all this week about Hull vicarage.' This was just vacant by the death of Joseph Milner, 'the simple honest fellow you saw in Palace Yard,' he tells Lord Muncaster. 'Your sympathetic kindness had too well anticipated Isaac Milner's feelings. He is the most affectionate of brothers, and the loss has been like tearing off a limb. I hope he will get over it, but it has shaken him sorely.'[9] 'All the time I have been writing, poor Milner has been in my mind.'[1]—'Tuesday. Gave dinner. Mitford, Henry Legge, Thornton, Unwin, &c. St. Helen's snapped up by Stadtholder. They stayed late chatting. Rational day.'— 'Dec. 11th. To Fulham, Bishop of London's, to dinner—by ourselves—much talk, evening with him. Letter about my book, and his answer[2] to a man about his religious state— serious, humble, and very pleasing. Mr. Owen, curate of Fulham, to tea and supper. Next morning the Archbishop came to breakfast, and we discussed long about church matters.'

On the 31st day of December his thoughts review the expiring year. 'An eventful year with me—my book— my marriage—health restored in sickness. Friends died this year—Eliot—Dr. Clarke—Joseph Milner. I still spared. Mutiny terminated—Dutch victory.'

The constant vigilance rendered necessary by the pro- longation of the Abolition struggle may be gathered from a letter[3] during this week to Mr. Pitt: 'My head and heart have both been long full of some thoughts which I wished to state to you, when a little less under extreme pressure than during the sitting of Parliament.

'You may not have happened to see an order in council, allowing an intercourse to subsist between our West Indian colonies and those of Spain, in which negro slaves are the chief articles for us to supply. Let me remind you, that the House of Commons did actually pass the Bill for abolishing the foreign Slave Trade, and that if contracts are made again

---

[9] Dec. 5.   [1] To William Hey, Esq.
[2] Vide the answer in Hodgson's *Life of Porteus*, p. 295.
[3] Jan. 30, 1798.

for supplying Spain for a term of years, it may throw obstacles in the way. It would give me more pleasure than I can express, to find that any further measures were rendered needless, by my hearing the other was revoked.'

In such watchful care he had now an open and most zealous fellow-labourer in Mr. Stephen, who had entered on the Abolition contest as a holy cause, and gave the whole energy of his powerful mind and the great stores of his knowledge, to aid in its conduct. The value of that local knowledge soon showed itself. The removal of the Carib tribes after the insurrection in the island of St. Vincent's, and the conquest of Trinidad in 1797, had opened their virgin lands to British enterprise and capital. In the arrangements to which these events gave rise, Mr. Pitt had almost consented to a plan which, though intended to prevent the importation of Africans for the cultivation of our acquired possessions, would in fact have led to the removal of the Creole slaves from our older islands to the unhealthy work of clearing new lands. Mr. Stephen's local knowledge at once discovered the danger.

'The Carib lands,' he wrote to Mr. W., 'lie heavy at my heart. I learnt on Thursday evening, that Mr. Pitt has come into their secret plans, and has pledged himself that the lands shall be granted on those terms. An. opulent planter of St. Vincent's is raising a large sum by annuities, disadvantageous though the resource is, that he may buy up negroes in the old islands, and be ready to plunge deep into the golden mine. Speculation is opening her rapacious mouth in other directions towards the same object; and Lloyd's Coffee House is in a roar of merriment at the dexterous compromise Mr. Pitt has made between his religious friends and his and Dundas's West India supporters. *The commission is making out, if not already made. The commissioners are named.* Have you stopped, or have you any hopes of stopping, this measure ?'

'Your letter finds me,' replies Mr. Wilberforce, 'not well, with tired eyes and a fatigued head; but it calls forth the little animation of which I am capable. . . . What I can do I will: immediately writing to Mr. Pitt, and bespeaking an

interview with him before he goes any further. . . . Let me
see you on Tuesday. I will if possible see Mr. Pitt previously, and know how the case stands.'

His private remonstrances with the Minister succeeded
after a time in stopping the objectionable plan. 'At last,'
he enters April 1, 'got the proclamation about slaves re-
scinded.' Mr. Stephen's vehement zeal could scarcely rest
contented without a public denunciation of the measure. ' I
still clearly think,' he wrote, 'that you are bound, by the
situation wherein you have placed yourself, to cry aloud
against it. You are even the rather bound to do so, because those high priests of Moloch, Lord Liverpool and Mr.
Dundas, are your political, and Mr. Pitt also your private,
friends.'

He still mixed upon principle as much as he was able in
general society. ' The Bishop of London, Mrs. Kennicott,
Hatsells, Bowdler, and Lady Waldegrave dined with me—
rational talk—the Bishop and Hatsell both opposing me as
to times being gone off in religion. The Bishop preaching
every Friday in Lent. Crowds to hear him—fine people and
gentlemen standing all the time. I affirmed that there is less
thought of God though more refinement.'[4] ' I went to Pitt's
—where I supped tête-à-tête. Much political talk on O'Connor, Favey,[5] &c., arrested: on defence of country, &c. Home
late.'[6] ' To Dundas's in the evening to meet Whitwell on
internal defence—Pitt, Duke of Buccleugh, Bathurst, Samuel
Thornton, Carrington, Chancellor—after discussion went up
stairs till half-past twelve, and supped. Home with Pitt and
Duke.'

Early in the spring he again brought the Abolition question before Parliament. ' April 3. Busy preparing for Slave
motion, which made. Fox, Grey, Sheridan, &c., came.
Thought we had carried it—83 to 87.'

This debate was marked by Mr. Canning giving his first
open support to Abolition; and by the vote as well as the
speech of Mr. Windham, first upholding the continuance of
the Slave Trade. In Mr. Windham this was a part of that

---

[4] Diary, March 3.   [5] James Quigley, otherwise James John Favey.
[6] Diary, March 10.

change which had been wrought by his recoil from French principles. In the debate of 1796, though his vote was with his former friends, his speech was faltering and uncertain. On the motion of Mr. Ellis in 1797, he avowed a preference for *gradual* abolition ; and by April 1798, he had learned to justify his place in the majority, by which the question of immediate Abolition was directly negatived.

Though defeated on the division, 'on the whole,' says Mr. Wilberforce, 'we got ground.'[7]

As the season advanced the 'diary' exhibits his usual occupations, with slight notices of the chief passing events.

'April 5. Busy all morning. Muncaster, Bankes, Henry Thornton, &c., dined with me before House. More and more likelihood of French landing. Schank's discovery much vaunted, of fitting merchant ships' boats with cannon or carronades. Poor E. came to town on Wednesday—age to him setting in gloomily—how kind is Muncaster to him! Great conspiracy detected at Manchester.—21st. Dined Exhibition—annual affair—about 170 present. Great set of democrats taken up, proposing to murder witnesses who are to give evidence at Maidstone. Things begin to look better in Europe.—24th. Out early to Bishop of Durham's—society —on Erskine's refusing' (to retain his brief if Williams was brought up for judgment). ' House on magistrate's Bill.'

' May 5. Dined at Lambeth—public day, with Hatells and Lord Auckland—large party. When there, heard from Pitt about Fox's speech at the Whig club—wrote about it. Talked much with Sir William Scott and Dr. Sturges, who praised my book much.—7th. Pitt gave up any other proceedings against Fox but striking out of the Privy Council which done.—10th. Busy all day on Slave Carrying Bill.— 19th. This last fortnight much Parliamentary business—Land Tax Sale Bill, Shipowners' Bill, Slave Carrying Bill, and African Bill, framing—and House. Took possession of Broomfield for the first time.—21st. With Stephen and Henry Thornton about African limited Abolition.—23rd. Quigley convicted. Democrats speak well of Plumer's behaviour —not so of Attorney-General. Magistrates' Costs Misde-

---

[7] Diary, April 3.

meanour Bill. Beat—argued well, I think.—24th. Much talk about the trials. There appears amongst the democratical gentry much concert and sympathy of knowledge and feeling. I should have acquitted O'Connor on Buller's charge; but doubt on the evidence. Pitt clear about O'Connor's guilt.—27th. Whitsunday. Pleasant day, spent as Sundays should be.—28th. Ashley came in at my dressing time, and brought word of Pitt's and Tierney's duel yesterday. I more shocked than almost ever. I resolved to do something if possible.—30th. To town. Found people much alive about duel, and disposed to take it up. I gave notice [of a motion on the subject in the House of Commons]. Letter from Pitt, evening.'

'I am not the person,' he writes, 'to argue with you on a subject in which I am a good deal concerned. I hope too that I am incapable of doubting your kindness to me (however mistaken I may think it) if you let any sentiment of that sort actuate you on the present occasion. I must suppose that some such feeling has inadvertently operated upon you, because whatever may be your *general* sentiments on subjects of this nature, they can have acquired no new tone or additional argument from anything that has passed in this transaction. You must be supposed to bring this forward in reference to the individual case.

'In doing so, you will be accessary in loading one of the parties with unfair and unmerited obloquy. With respect to the other party, myself, I feel it a real duty to say to you frankly that your motion is one for my removal. If any step on the subject is proposed in Parliament and agreed to, I shall feel from that moment that I can be of more use out of office than in it; for in it, according to the feelings I entertain, I could be of none. I state to you, as I think I ought, distinctly and explicitly what I feel. I hope I need not repeat what I always feel personally to yourself.' [8]

The hope which had led Mr. Wilberforce to give notice of his motion soon faded away. Instead of being able to carry a strong resolution against the principle of duels, through the general feeling which had been excited by an apprehension

[8] Downing Street, Wednesday, May 30th, 1798, 11 P.M.

for the safety of Mr. Pitt, he found that the fear of censuring the Minister would lead many to defend the system in order to screen the man.

'June 1. To town to-day and yesterday, and back in the evening. Much discussion about duel motion. Saw Pitt and others—all pressed me to give it up. Consulted Grant and Henry Thornton, and at length resolved to give it up, as not more than five or six would support me, and not more than one or two speak, and I could only have carried it so far, as for preventing *ministers* fighting duels.—June 2. Being resolved, I wrote to Pitt to give it up.' Here is a portion of his letter:—

'I scarcely need assure you that I have given the most serious and impartial consideration to the question, whether to persist in bringing forward my intended motion or to relinquish it. My own opinion as to the propriety of it in itself, remains unaltered. But being also convinced that it would be productive on the whole of more practical harm than practical good, and that it would probably rather impair than advance the great principle which I wish chiefly to keep in view, I have resolved to give it up; and when thus resolved, I cannot hesitate a moment in·sending you word of my determination. I shall be much obliged to you if you will not mention my resolution generally. The Speaker is the only person of our town friends to whom I shall open myself at present.

'I am sure, my dear P., that I need not tell you that the idea of my being compelled by duty to do anything painful or embarrassing to you has hurt me not a little; but I know you too well not to be sure that you would not wish me to be influenced by this consideration against the dictates of my conscience.'[9]

'Received an answer from Pitt that he was greatly relieved by my relinquishment—he seriously ill.'[1]

'I cannot say to you,' was the answer, 'how much I am relieved by your determination, which I am sincerely convinced is right on your own principles, as much as on those of persons who think differently. Much less can I tell you

[9] Broomfield, Saturday, June 2, 1798.   [1] Diary, June 2.

how sincerely I feel your cordial friendship and kindness on all occasions, as well where we differ as where we agree. Ever affectionately yours.' He adds in a postscript :—

'We have excellent accounts to-day from Ireland, and (what I hope will lead to something still better) an account in the French paper of May 29, that Buonaparte's expedition sailed from Toulon on the 19th, with twelve sail of the line. If we are not unfortunate, Nelson with the same number will meet him in the Mediterranean.'

'Monday, June 4. Staid away from court on account of motion impending. The King asked the Speaker if I persevered. Pitt told me the King approved of his conduct.— 5th. To town. House—declared that I gave up my motion because no support.'

'Friday, June 8. To town. Sad accounts from Ireland. French Toulon fleet out with Buonaparte. I have become an honorary member of St. Margaret's corps, with Bankes, Belgrave, &c.—10th. Taken ill, and for four or five days very threatening. Persuaded not to go to town on St. John's motion about O'Connor.—16th. The Toulon scheme supposed for the West Indies. Buonaparte rivals Alexander the Great. I think he wishes to get off the English invasion. Popery not hinted at as one of the causes of Irish barbarism. Lord Cornwallis is going. Had rather go to India.—22nd. House on Lord G. Cavendish's motion about Ireland—spoke shortly. Sheridan's taunt about my conscience, while he himself convicted of a misstatement. Fox, Grey, &c. there. Fox about Slave Trade. House very late—home near five o'clock.—23rd. Dined Bishop of London's—much talk about Ireland.—28th. Rebel camp at Wexford stormed, all apparently suppressed. Pitt well again. Reported that he insane ; that wounded in the duel; that going into the House of Lords; that disgusted with something that passed in the House of Commons. Letter to Sir Christopher Sykes on his rejoinder to my refusal to ask Pitt for a living for his son —explained to him frankly and fully.'

Some extracts from this letter will show the general principles on which he dealt with such questions :—' I am bound to remember, in the disposal of any living, that the interest

the parishioners have in the nomination is that of as many
persons as the parish consists of, and is of an everlasting,
infinite value.

'It is my fixed opinion, formed on much reading, consideration, and experience, that there has been for many years
among the majority of our clergy a fatal departure from the
true principles of Christianity, and of the Church of England.
In selecting a minister for any living it is not enough to
know that he is diligent and exemplary in his conduct, nor
yet that his talents, knowledge, and manner of officiating are
everything that one could wish, but I must ask, what are his
doctrines?   In the case of those who have been nearest and
dearest to me, I have adhered to these principles.   I will only
instance Dr. Clarke, whose very laborious living produced
him but about 250*l.* per annum.   The place was highly unpleasant to him, and still more so to my sister.   But being
convinced that he was on many accounts better fitted to do
good at Hull than most other men would be, or than he
would be in almost any other place, I made no effort for
fixing him in any situation more eligible as to temporals.'

CHAPTER XII.

JUNE 1798 TO DECEMBER 1810.

Settlement at Broomfield—His mother's death—Letter to Hannah More—
His charities—Christian Observer—Protection of Jersey Methodists—
Parliament meets—Mr. Pitt's designs—Cold Bath Fields' prison—
Debates on the Union—Motion for Abolition again defeated—Slave
Trade Limitation Bill—Lost in Upper House—Broomfield—Buona-
parte's proposals—Scarcity—Defeats an attempt to alter Toleration Act
—Clamours for peace—Bognor—Illness of Mrs. Wilberforce—At-
tempts to remedy the distress of the lower orders.

PARLIAMENT was prorogued upon the 29th of June, and
Mr. Wilberforce went to Broomfield for the summer.   While
he was here engaged with 'books, letters, a little dictating,
and many friends,'[1] he received an account of the illness,

[1] Diary.

and by the next post of the death, of his aged mother. Unwillingly leaving Mrs. Wilberforce, who was on the eve of
her first confinement, he set off immediately for Hull, to
attend his mother's funeral. 'I was in the old house,' he
writes to Mrs. Wilberforce from Stamford,[2] 'by one o'clock
yesterday. This morning, at six o'clock, I set out, with (in
spite of all remonstrances) some little pomp, in the funeral
procession to Beverley, and the last solemn service being
ended, I returned to Hessle, and was again at Barton by
eleven ; and now here I am only eighty-nine miles from London, and hoping to be with you on Monday evening. I shall
of course stay here all to-morrow. I have a pleasure in the
idea of halting, and spending a quiet day in blessing and
praising that gracious Being, who to me has been rich in
mercy, and abundant in loving-kindness. Oh that I were
more warmly thankful and more zealously active !

'My dear mother did not suffer in death, and I trust she
is happy. The change gradually produced in her during the
last eight years was highly gratifying to all who loved her,
and looked forward. It was a solemn and an affecting scene
to me, yesterday evening, to be in my mother's room, and
see the bed where I was born, and where my father and my
mother died, and where she then lay in her coffin. I was
alone, and I need not say to you, I put up my prayers that
the scene might work its due effect.' 'Had a delightful contemplative evening walk in Burleigh Park. I have felt this
day, I hope, in some degree rightly disposed ; but oh let me
not confound occasional feelings with being a true Christian.
This seems a sad careless place, alas ! I talked to several
common people. Found the butchers' shops open. At
church, miserable work. Remnant of Sunday school, only
eight children. I have seldom seen a more apparently irreligious place. A shopkeeper said, none of the clergy active,
or went amongst the poor. One Presbyterian meeting.'[3]

'Monday, up early, and travelled on as fast as I could ;
got to Broomfield by nine o'clock, safely, I thank God, and
found all well.' 'My dear wife,' he notes a few days later,
'is now ill. How dependent does this make me feel upon

---

[2] July 7.   [3] Diary and Journal, July 8.

the power and goodness of God!⁴ 'Oh what abundant cause
have I for gratitude,' he says the following week : 'how well
all has gone on, both with mother and child ! I will take a
musing walk of gratitude and intercession. How full of mercies is God to me !'

At Broomfield he was within reach of his London business,
and was surrounded by his friends. 'July 11. Burgh came
to dinner—Henry Thornton—after it rational conversation.
—12th. Malta taken, and no other news of Buonaparte. La
Fayette talking of assisting the oppressed people of Ireland.
Thornton and Grant to evening council, about Sierra Leone.
—16th. After breakfast to Auckland's, and then on to Pitt
at Holwood. Tête-à-tête with Pitt and much political talk.
He much better—improved in habits also—beautifying his
place with great taste—marks of ingenuousness and integrity.
Resenting and spurning the bigoted fury of Irish Protestants.'⁵ Soon after this visit he wrote to Lord Muncaster:—

'You ask me about Pitt. There is no ground whatever
for the rumour.'⁶ Yet the Opposition papers go on with it.
I spent a day with him lately, tête-à-tête, and, not to say that
the particular story I have been alluding to was disproved,
he appeared better than he has been all the winter, and his
habits much more wholesome.'

'July 18. Montagu came with his family—discussed affairs
with him, he truly pleasing and philosophical. Evening, Carrington, very kindly, about my accounts ; he made me out
richer than I conceived.' This discovery was soon conveyed
in a characteristic mode to Mrs. Hannah More.

'The letter you wrote to Mrs. Henry Thornton, concerning
your Mongewell intercourse, has made a deep impression on
me ; and though no one can prize more highly than myself
your services in Somersetshire, yet I believe it would be
right for you to pay a visit to the Prince Bishop, at Auckland.⁷
Do you remember the idea of a great man, (I think Huy-
gens,) that there might be stars, of which the light, though
always on its journey, had not yet travelled down to us. It

---

⁴ Journal, July 21.   ⁵ Diary.   ⁶ Vide June 28, p. 191.
⁷ Mrs. Hannah More had been invited to assist the Bishop in his
benevolent design of establishing schools in his diocese.

is somewhat like this with the light of the blessed gospel to too many districts in this very country. I wish you to consider this as an opportunity of conveying it into a dark corner of the island. Go then to Auckland, and may the grace of God go with you. I am convinced that, on many accounts, you would be able to do far more than myself, or any other person living, with this primary planet, which is surrounded with satellites. It is more, it is a very sun, the centre of an entire system. I will with all my heart meet you there if possible. The Bishop has often invited me and Mrs. W.

' I have one point more on which I must detain you. I have looked into the state of my finances, and am in good case in what respects this world. I can appropriate as large a sum as may be requisite for your operations. I am clear you ought to purchase ease, which is with you the power of continuing your exertions, though at a dear rate, by allowing yourself the accommodation of a carriage. Surely we know each other well enough to communicate on this or any other subject without embarrassment or reserve. You are the main spring of the machine ; and it is your business to keep that in order, ours to supply subordinate *movements* (I did not mean a pun, but a post-chaise now occurs as one of them). Do not think me tedious in reverting so often to this well-worn remonstrance. When I was with you I saw it was still needed ; and I am like the man who preached for thirty years together against drunkenness, because his parish still continued the vice.[8] You ought to permit the friends of your institutions to assist you with money to any extent which may be requisite for carrying them on. Each partner should supply that in which he most abounds : the moneyed money ; you and your sisters, what is far more valuable, and what no money can procure. Now do *act* if you are convinced.' . . . ' I have talked with Henry Thornton,' he writes again, ' concerning the Somersetshire operations, and we have agreed that 400*l.* per annum should be allotted by us to that service.' ' I love and admire the zeal of your young clergy. Indeed it refreshes and revives me when sickened by the shabby topics and shabby people, great and small, with whom

[8] Dec. 10.

I am of necessity too conversant, to turn my eyes to you and your little Christian communion of saints.' [9]

'Never distress yourself,' he wrote[1] this summer to another correspondent, 'on the ground of my being put to expense on account of yourself, or your near relatives; you give what is far more valuable than money—time, thought, serious, active, affectionate, persevering attention; and as it has pleased God of His good providence to bless me with affluence, and to give me the power, and I hope the heart, to assist those who are less gifted with the good things of this life, how can I employ them more properly than on near relations, and when I strengthen your hands, who are always endeavouring to serve their best interest. You may say to —— that, on your account, I am willing to take the charge of Charles's education for two or three years.'

The sums which, as 'a good steward,' he thus dispensed to those who needed, formed a large portion of his annual income. As a young man, he had been charitable from the natural impulses of a generous spirit. By an account-book, which has escaped destruction, he appears to have expended in the year 1783, between five and six hundred pounds in this way. There are in it many such entries as, 'Sent to the Rev. Mr. Emeson of Keswick, a most excellent man with a large family, and mean to do so annually, a bank note, 20*l*.' But his conduct was no sooner regulated by higher principles than he determined to allot a fixed proportion of his income (obtained often by personal self-denial in small things) to works of charity. Before his marriage, at least one-fourth of it was so employed; and in this year the record still remaining (and it is incomplete) accounts for more than 2000*l*. Some of the particular entries show the hidden channels through which his bounty flowed, cheering many hearts who never knew their benefactor. Besides regular almoners for the distribution of small sums, to one of whom in the course of this year he entrusted above a hundred pounds, he was in the habit of relieving through many others the distress which came under their observation. This he did especially in the case of active clergymen, in whose hands he often placed

[9] Letters of July 11 and 19.   [1] Aug. 24.

an annual sum of considerable amount for parochial distribution. Four of those which occur this year, and are marked annual expenses, are for sums of 25*l.*, 26*l.*, 30*l.*, and 40*l.*, respectively. Great zeal in their vocation constituted of itself a claim on his assistance, even in districts for which he had no local interest ; as, for instance, ' Mr. Charles's schools in Wales, annually, 21*l.*'

Some of these entries are highly characteristic. ' Expenses of Mr. Atkinson's act for Leeds church, 100*l.*' ' Lent Robert Wells 13*l.*, which never expect again : he has a wife and six children to maintain, and ekes out a scanty income by a trade in old clothes.' ' Sent Dr. Chapman 5 guineas for a book which not read, and impertinently sent me ; but Irving says he is a worthy man, and he must be distressed to act in this manner.' ' Sent Captain S. 5 guineas (a gentleman in distress sometimes most of all so).' ' Sent him 10*l.* in addition, which he said would render him completely comfortable.' ' C., only justified by my having advised him originally to enter the law, 50*l.*' ' Captain P. 5*l.* 5*s.* He is but a moderate hand I fear, but in urgent want.' ' Lent M. 100*l.* not very willingly, because, though I sincerely wish to serve him, I think this plan of paying off all his debts will not make him economise. It is Mr. Pitt's plan.' ' In compliance with my rule I' must put it down *given.*' ' Given W. C. 55*l.* on a solemn promise that he will never again issue a bill, and not borrow of any one without previously informing me. He is not economical, but has a claim on me from having lived in my service, and imprudence must be pardoned. He is sure that from his salary he can gradually repay me, but I cannot believe it.' ' Given W. C. 63*l.* to enable him to refund what he has taken of the Board's money. I do it only because it would be ruin to him to withhold it. I doubt if even under these circumstances quite right. I have solemnly assured him it should be the last time of my assisting him, and have given him parting advice. He has treated me ill in applying only 21*l.* of the last 70*l.* I gave him to this purpose. As I have told him plainly, I fear he cannot be saved from ruin. I have had much anxiety and vexation from him, and my only comfort is that I treat him like a Christian, he me as a man of the world. He dislikes me, and feels no gratitude to me, I know, for what I have done. (Private; put down as a record of my judgment and feelings.)' ' For Foulay Expedition, 50*l.*' ' Rev. Mr. Scott, half a year of his son's college allowance, 15*l.*' ' Paid Williams's bill for expenses of Dowlin[2] and Devereux's trial, 200*l.*' ' Remainder of Williams's bill unfairly coming upon me, 500*l.*' ' For St. Anne's School annually, 31*l.* 10*s.*'

Almost every charitable institution of the metropolis, of Yorkshire, and of many other parts (extending in some instances to Edinburgh), is included in his list of annual subscriptions. He had also regular annuitants. Not a few who afterwards acquired independence and wealth were indebted to his support for carrying them through their early struggles. Two who rose to the judicial bench are this year mentioned as receiving from him 300*l.* Besides his contribution to the Elland Society, he supported readily young men of promise in their education for Holy Orders; and through every year of its protracted continuance he drew largely from his own resources for the expenses of the Abolition contest.

It was especially his habit to relieve those who in the higher walks of life were reduced to unexpected indigence. Many letters acknowledging such aid, and tracing to it oftentimes escape from ruin, appear in his correspondence. One such instance has been furnished by his secretary. ' "I have," he once said to me, " an application from an officer of the navy who is imprisoned for debt, will you inquire into the circumstances?" I went, and found an officer in gaol for 80*l.* He had a family dependent on him, with no prospect of paying his debt; and, as a last hope, had made this application, at the suggestion of the governor, who had known Mr. Wilberforce, when of old he used, with the Rev. John Unwin, to visit the London prisons, and relieve the debtors. The officer had referred him to Sir Sidney Smith, to whom he wrote immediately. I was in the room when Sir Sidney called on the following morning. "I know the poor man well," he said; "we were opposed to one another on the

---

[2] The witnesses against Kimber.

Baltic, he in the Russian, I in the Swedish service; he is a brave fellow, and I would do anything I could for him; but you know, Wilberforce, we officers are pinched sometimes, and my charity purse is not very full." "Leave that to me, Sir Sidney," was his answer. Mr. Wilberforce paid his debt, fitted him out, and got him a command.—He met an enemy's ship, captured her, was promoted; and within a year I saw him coming to call in Palace Yard in the uniform of a post captain.'

He continued engaged in his usual pursuits, and surrounded by his friends, until the beginning of September.—'July 29. Venn on "rich and poor meet together"—good. People about to build a new chapel because he "does not preach the gospel." He much disturbed. Much talk with Milner about his preaching, and the growing faults of the young clergy. He conceives them getting into a rational way of preaching.'—'Aug. 21. Our christening in the afternoon. News of Buonaparte's arrival in Alexandria.—Sunday, Sept. 2. How excellent a sermon has Venn been preaching upon Luke xiv. 28—counting the cost if we profess to be Christians. It affected my heart—it humbled me in the dust. My days pass away in hurry, yet I do not think it right to go upon the retired plan. Oh may I wait on God diligently! He will then level hills and fill up plains before me.—Sept. 5. To town, to see Pitt—no news. Saw his Finance plan. They do not believe Buonaparte to be at Alexandria. Emperor of Russia coming forward, and Prussia neutral. Austria must quarrel with France. Bad news from Nelson. Lord Elgin called yesterday.—7th. Report that 30,000 French landed in Ireland.—14th. French landed in Ireland surrendered at discretion.—22nd. Buonaparte's reaching Alexandria confirmed.'

He was much occupied at this time with a plan for setting up a periodical religious publication which should admit 'a moderate degree of political and common intelligence.'[3] 'Mr. Babington and I went this morning to Mr. Henry Thornton's to breakfast, to talk over the matter of the Magazine and its editor. We concur in opinion that a small

[3] Letter to W. Hey, Esq., Nov. 19.

committee, perhaps not more than three, would form the best editor. Mr. Scott is a man of whose strength of understanding, correctness of religious views, integrity, disinterestedness, diligence, and perseverance, I think very highly; he is systematically opposing the vices, both speculative and practical, of the religious world; and they are many and great, and likely to be attended with numerous and important mischiefs. But Mr. Scott is a *rough* diamond, and almost incapable of polish, from his time of life and natural temper; he has not general knowledge, nor taste sufficient for such an office as you would commit to him. We have *anatomized* several other subjects, but I have not time to detail to you the result of our dissection.'[4]

After much consideration and discussion, the first number of the Christian Observer was published in January, 1801. Several of its early articles were from the pens of Mr. Wilberforce, Mr. Henry Thornton, and the Rev. T. Gisborne.

October 3 he reached ' Bath, through beautiful Rodborough vale, where rejoicings for Nelson's glorious victory, news of which first met us in detail there.' 'The very day,' he writes to Lord Muncaster,[5] 'which brought your letter expressing your confidence in the issue of any naval engagement under Nelson's auspices, the intelligence arrived of his most glorious action; the most signal victory[6] with which a gracious Providence ever blessed our arms. The piety and naiveté of his letter would delight you, I am persuaded, as it does us.'

At Bath, finding 'the waters agree well,' he remained above a month, 'much in society,' and engaged in reading 'Locke with my wife and sister, Coxe's Walpole, Montesquieu, Roman History, Wakefield's Life, Bible, and much time in letters.'—'Oct. 18. To-day the news arrived of the defeat of the French fleetling by Sir J. Warren. Sir George Beaumont, Creykes, &c. with us. Jay told his origin and story very simply:—a bricklayer employed on Beckford's house—began to preach at 16—humble and not democratical. Cecil at Bath, and dined with us.—19th. Mayor's dinner— three hundred people—sat between Sir Sidney Smith and

---

[4] Letter to W. Hey, Esq., July 28.   [5] Oct. 5.
[6] The battle of the Nile, Aug. 1.

Fraser. Heard Sir Sidney's story—how got off from confinement, burnt ships at Toulon, and managed in Swedish fleet.—20th. To Cowslip Green—all kind and hospitable. Report of Warren's victory.—22nd. To Bath. Laurelled mail coach brought certain news of Warren's victory over fleet invading Ireland—La Hoche, and eight large frigates.'

He remained at Bath about a fortnight longer. 'Oct. 26. Burgh came to us from Bristol Hot-wells—strongly against the Union—"only to be done by force." Pitt busy about the Irish union.—Nov. 6. Lady St. John and David Hartley dined with us. Rational talk. David quite bitten with the new philosophy at 68 or 69; thinking our times worse than any former, not in science only, but moral conduct. Thinks the last war occasioned by the ambition of kings—" Little men now know their own strength," &c.—7th. Resolved to go to town directly for Methodists' sake.'[7]

He was specially ready, in grateful remembrance for the great spiritual work which they had effected in a time of almost universal apathy, to assist the Wesleyan Methodists as the redresser of their wrongs. The Sunday drilling which had just been introduced into the Channel Islands, violated their religious principles; and their refusal to conform to the appointment of the local government subjected them to fine and imprisonment. They appealed to Mr. Wilberforce, and he had seen Mr. Dundas, and got the promise of his interference in their cause. He now heard from Dr. Coke, that not only were these oppressive measures still maintained, but that on Oct. 18 at the states meeting of the isle of Jersey, it was determined to proceed to banishment against those who refused to perform this military duty. To appeal against this Bill he moved hastily to London; and 'went on the 13th to town on the Methodists' business ;' but found that 'neither Pitt nor Dundas were come.'[8] Within a few days he convinced Mr. Dundas of the injustice of such a needless violation of the rights of conscience, and after some delay succeeded in getting 'the Jersey Methodists' cause decided in their favour—Banishment Bill assent refused.'[9]

On December 14, ' supped,' he says, ' with Pitt tête-à-tête;

<hr />

[7] Journal.   [8] Diary, Nov. 13.   [9] Ib. Dec. 8.

whom and Lord Camden (the first time since Ireland) I saw
for a quarter of an hour in the morning.   Much talk about
Europe, Ireland, income tax, Lord Cornwallis, Union.'[1]   After
the morning's interview he wrote to Mr. Bankes : 'I have
just seen Pitt for a few minutes, and am to have a longer
talk with him perhaps this evening.   He is of course in high
spirits, and, what is better, his health, which had seemed to be
again declining a few weeks ago, is now, I am assured, more
radically improved than one could almost have hoped.   What
I have learned from him as to the state of Europe is, only a
little more in detail, the general opinion we must form of it
from what is known to all the world.   Lord Camden came
in while I was with Pitt with a large party of Hibernians,
who are to dine with him to-day.'

Parliament met November 20.   ' I hear,' he writes the
day preceding, 'that all the Opposition but Mr. Fox mean
to attend to-morrow.   It requires more than common power
of front for all who were at Maidstone, to hold up the
head without blushing.   Mr. Pitt, I may say to you, is extremely favourable to the idea of a union with Ireland.
Though listening myself to the proposal with complacency,
I see many and great difficulties in the way.   Imprimis, let
me ask you, and when you write, answer my question, Would
you admit Papists into the Parliament of the empire ?'

' 26th. Lord Camden called, and sat an hour with me on
Irish matters.   Milner came in the evening.—27th. Milner
and Pearson—long discussion about liberty and necessity.
Pearson conquered completely.   Walked morning, with Pitt
and Grenville—much talk about income tax.   Dec. 6. Milner
off.   Much affected about religious unbelief—"worst and
hardest trial when one has made a bridge, to have it taken
from one."   Pitt's plan of income tax seems well received
upon the whole.'   He took an active part in perfecting the
details of this measure, spending several mornings 'at Pitt's,
with Cookson and Gott from Leeds, about the income tax.
Met Sargent there, and all struck out a plan for commercial
incomes.'[2]   'With Cookson and Gott at Pitt's all morning.

[1] Diary, Dec. 8.   [2] Ib. 13.

We hit off a plan for commercial commission.[3]   Walker says the manufacturers can't and wont pay.'

He held also a conspicuous place in the concluding debates of this year.   'Dec. 20. Complained of misrepresentation of parliamentary speeches, and suggested a remedy.' In opposing the suspension of the Habeas Corpus Act upon the following day, Mr. Courtenay made a violent attack upon the treatment of the state prisoners confined in Cold Bath Fields prison; and in a taunting tone especially invoked in their behalf the sympathies of Mr. Wilberforce.   He was well acquainted with the management of that prison, both from personal inspection (a work of charity to which he had been long accustomed),[4] and constant communication with Dr. Glasse, one of the visiting magistrates.   He entered the House in the course of the debate, and 'found Courtenay speaking.   Got Glasse's minutes, and answered well, but perhaps too lightly.'[5]   His reply was remarkably effective: its accurate acquaintance with the subject completely refuted Mr. Courtenay's graver charges, whilst it abounded in ready humour, and apposite allusions drawn from the most various sources.   'The hon. gentleman tells us the prisoners are starved.   But what says a visiting magistrate who lately sent me the result of his own observation ?   " I saw their dinner; better I would not wish on my own table.   It was roast beef and plum pudding."   Aye, sir, and my friend is a doctor of divinity ! Why this difference of statement reminds me of Parson Adams' bewilderment, when one passenger assured him, as the stage drove by a mansion, that its owner was the best husband and father, and the most generous friend, in the whole world; whilst another woke up at the moment with the exclamation, What a fine estate ! what a pity it belongs to such a rascal !   The simplicity of Parson Adams led him to conclude that they must be speaking of two different persons.   Now, sir, though I do not mean to charge the hon. gentleman with being a Parson Adams in

[3] Diary, Dec. 17.
[4] He had received with no small pleasure from Howard the philanthropist, just before his death, a copy of his last work, with a request that he would 'accept this book from him as a small testimony of his esteem.'   [5] Diary.

simplicity, yet surely when he hears these dissimilar accounts he may well doubt whether they describe the self-same place.' 'How long is it, Wilberforce,' whispered Pitt, leaning over from the treasury bench as he sat down, 'since you read Joseph Andrews?'

Mr. Courtenay, smarting under this unexpected chastisement, attempted a retort, when a few days later the subject was again before the House. After quoting in a tone of ridicule a passage from Mr. Wilberforce's work on 'Practical Christianity,' he complained of the 'Christian rancour and religious facetiousness' with which he had been treated. He was taught in Mr. Wilberforce's answer, that 'a religious man might sometimes be facetious,' as he was reminded that 'the irreligious did not of necessity escape being dull.'

'House, Dec. 22, and found Tierney speaking. Sparred about Lord Auckland. Income tax till late.' 'I am pleading,' he says, 'with Pitt the cause of poor clergymen and other small life-income persons and large families: for the latter I think successfully; for the former I doubt.'[6]

'31st. House—Tierney's complaint of misrepresentation in the *Times*—sad work—went off well providentially. The *Morning Chronicle* falsely charges me with the author[ship], or sending [of the article].'[7] 'We have had warm work in Parliament of late,' he tells Lord Muncaster, 'and I have been taking a more forward part than I like. The most gross and scandalous misrepresentations of my speeches have been lately made in the *Morning Chronicle*, and there seems a general disposition to proceed against the Opposition papers if Tierney compels us to proceed against the *Times*. There never was given in any paper a tolerable account of one of the most masterly pieces of reasoning I ever heard, when Pitt contended at large with a view to prove the impracticability and injustice of taxing capital rather than income.'[8]

'Jan. 1, 1799. I meant to-day to be devoted to religious offices, but the House's meeting prevented more than re-

---

[6] Letter to Mrs. Hannah More, Dec. 15.
[7] Diary.   [8] Dec. 28.

ceiving the sacrament this morning, and a little reading to-night.'[9]

The beginning of this year was almost engrossed by the question of the Irish Union.—'Jan. 7. Supped at Pitt's, about Irish Union—he candid and open, but I do not like it.—11th. I have great doubts about the Union, and Bankes still more. French successes against Neapolitans. No mails arrive. Emperor of Russia behaving well. Pitt thinking things not so bad in Italy, and that the Emperor [of Austria] will be drawn in by the Queen of Naples.—18th. To town to discuss about Union with Bankes and Henry Thornton.— 23rd. Dined Bankes's before House, which on Address for King's message about Union—Sheridan—Canning; what envy of him I saw universally—Grey, Tierney, and others going out when he got up.'—'25th. Pitt sanguine that after Union Roman Catholics would soon acquire political rights: resolved to give up plan rather than exclude them. If Irish House did not pass something violent on Tuesday last he thinks it will go down. Accuses F. of breach of faith in stirring up instead of waiting. Pitt fair and honourable, as always, more than any other political man. Poor Burgh wild. Bankes clear and strong against it. Auckland evidently so secretly. Lord Clare for. Speaker now for, and satisfied. I hear the Roman Catholics more against it than they were. The Bishops all against Pitt's tithe plan. The King said, " I am for it if it is for the good of the church, and against it if contra." '[1]

' 28th. News came yesterday of Irish rejection of the Union. Dundas still talks as if sanguine of carrying it shortly.[2]—Feb. 10. My judgment at length made up for the Union—Lord Cornwallis talks of " Boroughs hawking by those infatuated people, and an apathy about the Union." Bankes's political integrity great.'

He supported the Union, to widen the basis of political power, and so destroy that predominant influence of a few great families, by which Ireland had been long misgoverned. In whatever respects his hopes were frustrated, in this at least he deemed them abundantly fulfilled. 'From this

[9] Journal.　　　[1] Diary.　　　[2] Diary.

time,' he declared, 'never were the true interests of any
country more fairly and liberally consulted.'   Many of the
evils of the old system came out in the discussions which
followed the rebellion.   'When a statement had been made
to the House of the cruel practices, approaching certainly to
torture, by which the discovery of concealed arms had been
enforced, John Claudius Beresford rose to reply, and said
with a force and honesty, the impression of which I never
can forget, "I fear and feel deep shame in making the
avowal—I fear it is too true—I defend it not—but I trust I
may be permitted to refer, as some palliation of these atro-
cities, to the state of my unhappy country, where rebellion
and its attendant horrors had roused on both sides to the
highest pitch all the strongest passions of our nature."   I
was with Pitt in the House of Lords when Lord Clare
replied to a similar charge—"Well, suppose it were so; but
surely," &c.   I shall never forget Pitt's look.   He turned
round to me with that high indignant stare which sometimes
marked his countenance, and stalked out of the House.'[3]

'11th. House. Irish propositions till late. Wanted to
speak, but no opportunity.'—'Feb. 23rd. Gave dinner to
Abbot, H. Legge, Attorney-General,[4] &c. Attorney-General,
Abbot, Legge, all strongly condemning Mackintosh's giving
lectures in Lincoln's Inn Hall. I had thoughts of attending.
Pitt and Speaker prevailed upon the Benchers, and Chan-
cellor approves.'   'Carlyle earnest about editing Bible in
Arabic.'—'Monday. Long discussion with Bishop of London.
He frank, amiable, and pious.—Evening, A.'s, where Hatsel,
alarmed at itineracy. Their low notions about giving livings.'[5]

Upon March 1, he brought forward his motion for immediate Abolition.   The sameness of a contest, which had
lasted for eleven years, was in some degree relieved by
his own and Mr. Pitt's eloquence, and by the wit of Mr.
Canning.   Though defeated by a majority of 84 to 54, he
was convinced that the cause was gaining ground, and set
himself to introduce into the system some immediate mitigation of its horrors.

April 17, he enters: 'Dined at Lord Camden's, first late

---

[3] Con. Mem.   [4] Sir John Scott.   [5] Diary.

dinner for months, to meet Pitt, Lord Chatham, Bishop of Lincoln, Steele, Pepper Arden. Great successes of the Austrians over the French—Pitt less sanguine than formerly, but hoping that six months will see the thing out.—22nd. House till past twelve. Address on the Union—Canning clever indeed—Douglas heavy—Lord Sheffield reading—Pitt pegging Fitzpatrick.'—'May 18. To Holwood by half-past four—Pitt riding out—Lord Camden and I. Villiers came, with whom walked. He said that Mrs. Villiers was reading my book—blamed my not associating. Pitt, Canning, and Pepper Arden came in late to dinner. I attacked Canning on indecency of Anti-Jacobin. Evening he and Pitt reading classics.'[6] 'My heart has been moved,' says his Journal of the following day, 'by the society of my old friends at Pitt's. Alas! alas! how sad to see them thoughtless of their immortal souls; so wise, so acute!'[7]—'May 28. Pitt's birthday—low-spirited—dined Dundas's great entertainment—Duke and Duchess of Gordon and others. I could not assimilate, and all flat and cold.'

Though he mixed less with them in their social meetings, he was careful to avoid all needless separation; and with Mr. Pitt especially, in spite of many political differences, he maintained much of the intimacy of earlier years. 'The Bishop of Lincoln,' he says, 'good-natured; but Pitt having told me of his thinking the great bulk of the more serious clergy great rascals, [he is] not open, I fear. I have stated to Pitt all my ideas about [the] church, its state and evils, and the only mode of providing for its security. He listened earnestly, but no decisive opinion.'[8]

In these familiar interviews, Mr. Pitt laid before him the plans of administration, and often profited by his suggestions. 'Government,' he tells Mr. Hey,[9] 'are about to bring forward some measures for suppressing the societies of "United Englishmen and Britons"; for preventing meetings in private, with engagements or oaths of secresy; for compelling all debating and lecturing societies to furnish the means of notoriety to the magistrate; to secure that no

---

[6] Diary, May 18.   [7] Journal, May 19.
[8] Diary, April 11.   [9] April 8.

printed paper shall be circulated without its bearing the name of some real person ; and in short for giving the means of proceeding against the author or publisher, if really libellous. I see nothing in this contrary to the genuine principles of political and social liberty.   But another thing is under consideration of great delicacy and importance.   Some check is wished to be imposed on the indiscriminate right of preaching, which, as you perhaps know, has lately been exercised to a much greater extent than ever before.   I have not yet thought on this difficult subject.   But the only expedients which have been suggested seem to me on the first view strongly objectionable, *e. g.* making the registration of conventicles not a matter of course, but empowering the magistrates to grant or withhold licences.'

'I saw,' he writes a few months later, 'this storm brewing in the spring, and warned Pitt against any infringement of perfect toleration, telling him that the principles to be adhered to were publicity and responsibility.   To whom can the discretionary power of judging what teachers are duly qualified be justly committed?   I dread these gathering clouds, &c.'[1]

A Bill for confining the trade within certain limits on the coast of Africa had passed the Commons, but was exposed to severe opposition in the Upper House.   He was continually occupied in providing the witnesses who were examined at the bar, and watching daily over the Bill.   'To Grenville's about Slave Limitation Bill.   Drew up petition to the Lords.' 'Pitt exerting himself about our Slave Limitation Bill. (—— never knew so severe a dressing as *Emanuel* received before the whole Cabinet about it.)   Pitt resolves to move to stop new lands' cultivation next year—I wish it this year. French fleet into Toulon.   My spirits low from Pitt's swaggering about finance.   Put down for loan, which refused. I take to Grenville again for his fair Slave Trade conduct. Kenyon prejudiced by Lord Thurlow.'

Nothing could exceed the hearty earnestness with which Lord Grenville defended the Limitation Bill.   Unsupported by the immediate adherents of the government, he was left to withstand the repeated opposition of one member of the

[1] To Thomas Babington, Esq., Nov. 5.

royal family, the commercial sagacity of Lord Liverpool, and the subtle bluntness of Lord Thurlow ; yet he was ready for every encounter, and maintained the conflict to the last.

'We have at length,' he writes to Lord Muncaster, 'the strongest probability of carrying the Slave Limitation Bill. There has been no small ferment on this subject, and both Pitt and Grenville have been conducting themselves with great spirit, and some of our opponents have been humiliated.'

Yet here again he was disappointed. 'July 5. Second reading of Slave Trade Limitation Bill in the House of Lords, when 27 only to 32, and 36 proxies each.' The bishops' proxies all in favour of it. 'Thurlow, profane balderdash. Westmoreland coarse. Bishop of Rochester, ill-judged application of Scripture. Grenville spoke well.'[2] 'Never,' he adds upon the following day, 'so disappointed and grieved by any defeat.'—'8th. To town early, to meet Pitt and Grenville about Slave Trade business—discussion for an hour ; and private with Pitt — he sanguine about carrying it next year. Grenville says we had fourteen more, but for mistakes about proxies, and should have carried it. Pitt clear the King has used no influence against us. Lord A. shabby, staying away and keeping two proxies. Stephen most earnest for our cause, but uncandid about Pitt ; generously returning fees,[3] above 200*l.*, 'in the handsomest way.'

Parliament was prorogued upon the 12th, and Mr. Wilberforce retired to the comparative rest of Broomfield. 'July 29. Pitt sanguine—Buonaparte quite defeated. Pitt hopes a convention signed with King of Prussia and Denmark : Sweden joining also in the measure.—30th. Was going to Holwood, but put off by Pitt, having a large party going to Lord Romney's review.'

'August 12. Lord Romney's great fête to the King— 5,600[4]—volunteer corps—table two miles long—waiting on horseback, &c.—14th. To town about Sierra Leone matters. Saw Pitt, who returned last night. Expedition for Holland

---

[2] Diary.

[3] For examining witnesses, &c., before the House of Lords.

[4] 'The entertainment to which 6,500 persons sat down,' &c. Ann. Reg.

sailed yesterday. Pitt sanguine, but looking forward to other campaigns. King of Prussia worse than ever. Pitt thinks fear—sanguine in hope of co-operation in the country. Littledale, Hope, &c., say no ; they behaved so ill before our soldiery. Our colony[5] in extreme peril ; I pressing Pitt to befriend us.—15th. Town betimes—council of five—Admiralty—then Sierra Leone—House till past four. Dined at Henry Thornton's, King's Arms Yard, with Macaulay.—17th. When intending letters, Venn came in and desired me to go to the Archbishop's about Missionary Society. After deliberation I went and had a long talk with the Archbishop.' The Archbishop, whom he had urged to place himself at the head of the Society, undertook to 'watch its proceedings with candour, but regretted that he could not with propriety at once assume the offered post.'—25th. Milner preached his Buxton Sermon on Christianity's corruptions. All serious persons much struck with it. Disputed with Milner about final perseverance.'

He was soon driven by his health to Bath, whence he returned to the neighbourhood of London January 23 ; and on the 24th 'wrote to Pitt, and he sent for me to town. I saw him. Till then I was strongly disposed to condemn the rejection of Buonaparte's offer to treat; greatly shocked at it. He shook me.—27th. Called at Bankes's and discussed politics. Slowly came over to approve of the rejection of Buonaparte's offer, though not of Lord Grenville's letters.[6]

' I feel,' he writes to Pitt, ' the force of what you urged on Friday; and though I should have rejoiced if you could have seen it safe and proper to consent to negotiate *generally*, yet I yield to the duty of not contradicting those in executive government in whom one has been used to repose confidence, in a case especially of such capital importance, without being at least perfectly sure that they are wrong, and that I am right myself. I hope the address will not go into particulars; indeed, I presume not, as the message does not.'

Having arrived at this conclusion, though with such reluctance, he felt bound, in support of the administration, to avow

---

[5] Sierra Leone.   [6] Diary.

it in the House. ' Pitt,' he says, 'sanguine that Russians and Austrians quite well agreed, and Austrians persuaded by Lord Minto to accept Russian forces; yet, within a week, Russians marching home, quarrelling with Austrians. Some reliance placed upon the Chouans, but nothing heard of them since. Lord St. Helen's quite blaming ministry; so also Lord Teignmouth, Bankes, Henry, and I long doubtful, but on the whole agreeing. I too earnest and strong in speaking, so as to wear the face of being more warlike than I really was.'

In the debate of February 13, upon the suspension of the Habeas Corpus, he again supported Ministers. He was too, he says, ' much occupied about the scarcity; urging Government, which sadly torpid and tardy—Sheffield and Speaker our way. King but middling. Dutch expedition debate. Government made good their point. Canning clever—genius—but too often speaking, and too flippant and ambitious. All things rising in price. What shocking work, Grattan and Corry fighting during debate, and Craddock putting the sheriff into a ditch, who stopping them. All people disapproving of Grenville's uncivil answer, though in general approving of rejection of overture. Pitt too much encouraging Canning; of whom a sad envy prevails. House of Lords' agreement, moved by Archbishop of Canterbury, drawn up by Lord Auckland, who had not told colleagues. Grenville and Chancellor scorning, and saying Parliament had better have let it alone, and that scarcity exaggerated.' ' I am much grieved at Pitt's languor about the scarcity. They will do nothing effectual. Great sufferings of the West Riding people.'

Another matter caused him much anxiety. ' There are ideas,' he tells Mr. Hey, ' of materially abridging the privileges enjoyed under the Toleration Act. I hope that I may be able to prevent any strong measure from being brought forward.'[7] Two days afterwards he writes,[8] ' All remains in statu quo, except that the Methodists have got to the knowledge of some measures being in contemplation, through

---

[7] To W. Hey, Esq., March 29.
[8] To Thomas Babington, Esq., April 2.

Michael Angelo Taylor at Durham. I have kept them quiet. I am more and more clear that, if the measure does go forward, the effects will be most important; it would be the most fatal blow both to church and state, which has been struck since the Restoration.

'I place more dependence on Mr. Pitt's moderation and fairness of mind, than either on the House of Lords or Commons. So utterly ignorant in all religious matters is the gay world, and the busy, and the high, and the political, that any measure government should propose would be easily carried. I find no success in my endeavours to convince my friends on the bench, of the expediency of facilitating the building of new churches with a right of patronage, though more than once I have proposed in private a general law to that effect.'[9]

He lost no time in conferring with Mr. Pitt, 'who,' he says, 'had been strongly biassed in favour of the measure by Bishop Pretyman: on him I urged in vain the serious consequences that must infallibly ensue. I stated to him my firm persuasion, that within a few weeks after the passing of the intended law, several of the dissenting ministers, most distinguished for talents and popularity, would be in prison; and I urged on him, that even supposing them not to be actuated by a sense of duty, for which I myself gave them credit, or to be cheered by the idea of suffering for righteousness' sake, they would be more than compensated for all the evils of imprisonment by their augmented popularity. The Bishop, however, would not assent to my view of the case, and finding Mr. Pitt intended to bring the measure forward, I begged I might have a full confidential discussion of the subject. Accordingly we spent some hours together at a tête-à-tête supper, and I confess I never till then knew how deep a prejudice his mind had conceived against the class of clergy to whom he knew me to be attached.

'It was in vain that I mentioned to him Mr. Robinson of Leicester, Mr. Richardson of York, Mr. Milner of Hull, Mr. Atkinson of Leeds, and others of similar principles; his language was such as to imply that he thought ill of their

[9] To W. Hey, Esq., Sept. 7.

moral character, and it clearly appeared that the prejudice arose out of the confidence he reposed in the Bishop of Lincoln. I proposed to him, to employ any friend whose mind should not already have received a bias on either side, to visit the several places I had mentioned, to inquire into their characters, and to ascertain the principles and conduct of their adherents, adding my confident persuasion that both their moral and political principles would be found favourable to the peace and good order of society; indeed I went further, and alleged that they were in general friendly to his administration, from believing these to be promoted by its continuance. All however was of no avail, and all I could obtain from Mr. Pitt was an assurance that the measure should not be actually introduced without his giving me another opportunity of talking the matter over with him. Happily the attempt never was resumed. I have always been extremely thankful for any share I had in preventing the introduction of this scheme.'[1]

The war meantime proceeded; and men's eyes were fixed with changing hopes upon its various incidents. 'How speedily,' he writes to Lord Muncaster,[2] 'are our prospects clouded! This capture of the Danish frigate is a very awkward business, and we must *succumb* (to borrow the language which you have been lately used to), or we shall be at war, I fear, with the three Northern Powers; and Buonaparte would desire no more. I fear this incident may prompt the Grand Consul to ask higher terms than he would otherwise have required, and thereby prevent a peace. With you I dread that event; strong as France must be for future attack, yet the continuance of the war would be still worse. I hear that the West Riding of Yorkshire is so pacific, that if a meeting should be called, ninety-nine out of a hundred would petition. The wool business and Pitt's demeanour (which last is still rankling) may in part have occasioned this, but it is what must be expected after so long a continuance of war.'

'My Yorkshire friends,' he tells Lord Camden, 'begin to be very impatient for peace. I trust this northern squall will not prevent the settling of the elements into that calm

[1] MS. Mem.   [2] July 1.

which is so desirable. Above all other things, it is to be wished that government should now carry the public along with them.'

'What is most important for your guidance and mine is, that Pitt's language is just what we could wish, firm, but temperate. He is more sanguine than I am in his expectations, or rather in his opinions, that the Austrians *could* still drive Buonaparte out of the field, if they would exert themselves. But there seems a proper sense of the probable necessity of making peace, with a disposition to assume a firm aspect, in order to make it on tolerable terms.'

Summer was now far advanced, but the House was still sitting, and this long continuance of business greatly exhausted his strength. Often through this year he had expressed his longing to exchange his London work for the country scenes in which he delighted.

'A letter from Rossie Castle,' he writes to Mr. Ross, 'finding me stewing in this crowded and dusty city in the middle of a delightful summer day, excites a longing for lakes, and mountains, and shady retreats, and other such luxuries of nature. But we have all our several posts, and, whether in town or country, "the time is short," and we have much to do in it.'[3] To Lord Muncaster he says— 'How I pant for Windermere and Derwent-water! What delight should I feel in carrying my dearest wife to that land of wonders and beauties ! But I think I can turn my time to better account, and give up the idea. The hospitable hall of Muncaster forms a part of the picture, which in my view of the lakes my imagination conjures up.' These pleasures he had not allowed himself But as soon as Parliament rose he set out for the country, feeling that he should 'have but a short time for "pruning my feathers and letting grow my wings." In truth, both body and mind with me, and understanding too, call for a little quiet after the incessant turmoil and drudgery in which they have been engaged for six or seven months.'

'My life,' he tells Lord Muncaster, 'has been one continual worry for some time past, and I quite pant for a little

---

[3] To Hercules Ross, Esq., May 6.

rest. I have been paying and receiving a few visits round the capital, though still a bankrupt in civilities ; and we are now on our way to Bognor Rocks, that my wife and the children may breathe sea air. A box full of unanswered letters accompanies me.' 'Here,' he writes to H. More, 'we are reading and discussing, and, through the mercy and overflowing goodness of God, enjoying ourselves not a little. We seem only too happy. Poor Mrs. Montagu is gone. It is an awful migration !' This rest in the bosom of his family, cheered too by the society of Mr. and Mrs. Henry Thornton, was most refreshing to his spirit. But the repose was not to last long. 'Perhaps,' wrote Dr. Milner (Sept. 19), 'these wonderful smiles are for some future trial: continue to watch.' This very letter found him in the deepest anxiety. 'It has pleased God'[4] he tells Hannah More, 'to visit my dearest Mrs. Wilberforce with a very dangerous fever. I am told the final issue is not likely to be very speedy, but that from the violence of the outset, I have every reason for apprehension, though not for despair. I am sure you will all feel for me, and pray for me, and for my dear sufferer. Mr. and Mrs. Henry Thornton are all kindness and consideration for us.'

'Wilberforce tells me,' wrote Henry Thornton, 'that he has written to you a few lines on Mrs. Wilberforce's illness. Poor fellow ! he cleaves to his old friends, and he finds a relief in employing a little time in writing to them, which we encourage, especially as the sick-room is not the place either for him or for her. He seems more softened and melted than terrified or agonized, and shows the truly Christian character under this very severe and trying dispensation.'

The issue of the fever was long doubtful, and his friends could mark, under new circumstances, the fruits of his religious principles. 'He,' writes Mrs. Henry Thornton, 'has behaved *greatly*.'

'I have heard,' he writes himself to Mr. Hey, when the hand of God was taken off him, 'of all your affectionate sympathy with me in my late heavy trial. God has in His chastisement remembered mercy ; and my beloved wife is

---

[4] Bognor, Sept. 27.

spared to me.   May I improve from the discipline through which I have gone.'

He was called from Bognor to attend a November session of Parliament, summoned, he feared, from the impulses of a 'warlike disposition, and not merely by the scarcity.'   He set to work to mitigate the sufferings which this caused.   He served diligently on the committee of inquiry ; promoted in his own rank of society agreements 'to abridge our luxuries, and comforts, and superfluities;' and speaks of 'the heavy burthen of obtaining relief for our starving manufacturers in the West Riding of Yorkshire.'   He practised what he preached.   'I send you,' he writes to Hannah More, 'half a bank note for 50*l.*   I beg you, besides my ordinary debt, to regard me as your debtor for any sum you may call for, on account of the peculiar distress of the present times.   As to keeping strictly within one's income at such a season as this, it is as unreasonable as it would be for a man to keep determinedly to his ordinary rate of walking, when a hungry lioness was at his heels ; but we feel for our own safety more than for others' sufferings.'

CHAPTER XIII.

JANUARY 1801 TO DECEMBER 1802.

Change of Ministers—Distress of the poor—King's recovery—Peace made—Bath—Guarantee of Turkey prevented—Pitt's support of Addington—His own feelings—Contemplates a general convention for Abolition—Letter to Addington—Opposes settlement of Trinidad lands by newly imported negroes—Abolition motion delayed—Dissolution of Parliament—Unanimously chosen a fourth time member for Yorkshire —Broomfield—Private reflections—Society—Parliament meets—Speech against foreign connections.

THE opening of the nineteenth century was dark and threatening.   'What tempests,' says the Journal of January, 1801, 'rage around.'   Some of the blasts of these tempests are thus echoed (February 7) to Lord Muncaster.[1]

[1] Near London, Feb. 7, 1801.

' I have strange tidings to communicate. The King and his Cabinet have quarrelled concerning the emancipation of the Irish Roman Catholics,—and Pitt, Dundas, Lord Grenville, Windham, and probably Lord Spencer also, and Lord Camden are to go out of office. I think you will guess who· is to succeed—the Speaker, with Pitt's friendly concurrence. Grant is to be Attorney-General [2]—the main pillar, Hawkesbury, Secretary of State—Mitford, Speaker—and of the younger or inferior, as many continue as Mr. Pitt can prevail to stay in. He has acted most magnanimously and patriotically.

' The Speaker, we know, is a man of talents and integrity, and of generous feelings, but not qualified for such rough and rude work as he may have to encounter, but if peace be made the government may last.

' It is strange, and certainly argues great precipitancy and want of foresight, that this was not settled one way or other last year when the Union took place, or at least agreed on so far as to preclude all difference at St. James's. The King and Pitt part on affectionate terms; the King saying, that it is a struggle between duty and affection, in which duty carries it. I am vexed that some of the Cabinet whom I least *affect* are to continue.'

More pacific counsels were to be expected from the new administration, and many of his friends hoped therefore that he would join its ranks. He himself just felt the influence of the eddy which was sweeping by him. ' I had,' he records, ' risings of ambition. Blessed be God for this day of rest and religious occupation, wherein earthly things assume their true size and comparative insignificance ; ambition is stunted, and I hope my affections in some degree rise to things above.' [3] His views upon the Slave Trade differed too decidedly from those of the new Cabinet to allow him to take office with them, and he continued his independent labours. His great present object was to relieve that distress, which the failure of the harvest, and the continuance of the war, had produced

---

[2] Sir Edward Law, afterwards Lord Ellenborough, was made Attorney-General ; Sir William Grant continuing to be Solicitor-General.

[3] Journal, Sunday, Feb. 8.

in the manufacturing districts.   His private aid was given so liberally, that he speaks of having 'spent this year almost 3,000*l*. more than his income;'[4] and as 'thinking in consequence of giving up his villa for a few seasons.'[5]   'I should thus save 400*l*. or 500*l*. per annum, which I could give to the poor.   Yet to give up the means of receiving friends there, where by attending family prayers, and in other ways, an impression may be made upon them, seems a great concession; and with Broomfield I can by management give away at least one-fourth of my income.'

For some time· to come he is 'much busied about the manufacturers in the West Riding.   The committee about the poor makes no progress.   People hard-hearted in general.'[6] 'Addington wavering about plan, and not for giving public money.'[7]   'Poor relief put off most shabbily, till after Easter —sad work—whilst we hear of increasing distress, and even tumult and insurrection.   Much hurt by the coldness and dilatoriness of government.'[8]   'At last, got measure through of allowing parishes to borrow on their rates.'

His Diary just notices the flow of events.   'February 23. Heard in the House of the King's being ill in the old way from Thursday; yet next evening so well as to attend council.' The proposed grant of power to the Roman Catholics disturbed his mind.   'At the levee, January 28, the King said to Dundas, "What is this that this young lord has brought over, which they are going to throw at my head?"—Lord C. came over with the plan in September—"I shall reckon any man my personal enemy who proposes any such measure. The most Jacobinical thing I ever heard of."   "You'll find," said Dundas, "among those who are friendly to that measure, some you never supposed your enemies."'[9]   'Colour of tidings from Prussia unpromising.—Feb. 24.   Pitt's— reading the correspondence.—27th.   House suddenly up from Nichols's absurdity and Pitt's extreme eloquence—too much

---

[4] 'Of the above large sum,' is his remark at the close of the year's account book, 'much, not recurring expenses, and charity much increased by the distress of the times.'   The sum of 3173*l*. is accounted for as bestowed during this year as charity.

[5] Diary, Jan. 21, 1802.   [6] Ib. March 19.   [7] Ib. March 10.
[8] Ib. April 1.   [9] Ib.

partaking of stage effect; but Pitt sincerely affected.—28th. To Buckingham House, to inquire after the King, who better. To Addington's for an hour, about the mode of relieving the poor, and the King's state: highly pleasing account.'

'Saturday, March 7. To Speaker's levee—changed to Saturday night. Shows the good of all such attempts—carried only half way at first. Much talk there, and home late. The King gradually getting better—very calm and resigned, on religious grounds. King of Prussia requiring us to resign Danish and Swedish ships, and resolved to assert by force armed neutrality. Lord St. Vincent talks openly that we must have peace.—12th. House—martial law in Ireland. Irish members spoke well — Lee — French — Fitzgerald.— 13th. House—Poor Bill. Addington's, who has been ill of rheumatic fever. Fleet sailed for North Seas yesterday. Alas, the pride of man! how boastful we are!—17th. Dundas well deserves his pension, though at first honestly refused it. The King recommended a nobleman for office—Dundas refused, saying, "none but who fit could be placed in those offices;" and now trying hard to persuade Charles Grant to go to India. Highly disinterested.—20th. Heard from Leeds of intended insurrection, and went to Addington. The King complaining that government not spirited enough. Forced by suspension of Habeas Corpus Act expiring, to let out some dangerous men. Debate on Lord Darnley's motion for a committee on the state of the nation—Lord Westmoreland coarse but able—Auckland ruining himself by over-refinement. How strikingly cunning men defeat themselves! Marquis of Buckingham in opposition. The new government fairly and honestly bent on peace.—22nd. With Addington by his desire for an hour or more—long talk—poor, and other subjects.—25th. Grey's motion on state of nation— Pitt and Fox—former excellent. Addington's first appearance as Minister—took his seat, Monday. A set of dinners for Pitt—declined them all. Heard of swearing-in against the constitution in West Riding—conferred with Yorke and Mulgrave—received a copy of the oath. The clouds blacken around—no thoughts of God.'

'April 15. We hear of the Emperor of Russia's death by

apoplexy—supposed violence ; and of the astonishing success of our attack on the lines of defence off Copenhagen.— 19th. Nelson's generosity and humanity justly praised.—17th. Saw Lord Eldon, and long talk with him on the best mode of study and discipline—for the young Grants—to be law-yers.' The Chancellor's reply was not encouraging—' I know no rule to give them, but that they must make up their minds to live like a hermit and work like a horse.' ' Eldon had just received the great seal, and I expressed my fears that they were bringing the King into public too soon after his late indisposition. " You shall judge for yourself," he answered, " from what passed between us when I kissed hands on my appointment. The King had been conversing with me, and when I was about to retire he said, " Give my remembrances to Lady Eldon." I acknowledged his conde-scension, and intimated that I was ignorant of Lady Eldon's claim to such a notice. "Yes, yes," he answered, "I know how much I owe to Lady Eldon ; I know that you would have made yourself a country curate, and that she has made you my Lord Chancellor." '[1]

' 20th. No public news. Emperor Paul's death does not seem so decisive for us as was hoped.—28th. Heard to-day of our troops bravely landing in Egypt.—May 15. Heard accounts from Egypt, of the action of March 21. Abercrom-bie dead of wounds : 240 killed, 924 wounded. All fought most bravely.'

' June 12. Sad foolish work about the motion concerning clergy sitting in Parliament. More stir at Cambridge than on any former occasion, about clergy's ineligibility to Parlia-ment. First time St. John's and Trinity agreed. The dispute with the northern nations likely to go off well. Friends uneasy about my health—say I am worn and thin.—18th. Pitt not giving so much satisfaction in the House of Com-mons as were to be wished. Awkwardness about Abbot. French official paper speaks with great civility of Addington, as if meaning to gain on him by courtesy, or as meaning to smooth the way to peace.—' July 4. Our Ministers, I fear, trifling about peace. King going to George Rose at Cuff-

[1] Con. Mem.

nell's.   Duke of Portland at last out: Addington forced to
compel him.—13th. Northern affair made up by Lord St.
Helen's, who made a British peer.   Invasion apprehended
by Government—strange folly not to be better prepared
against it.   Grain still very high, though falling much.   Dundas gone to Scotland.   I fear negotiation with France gone
off, though all kept profoundly secret.'   'This persuasion
gives me great pain on many accounts.'

On October 2,[2] he hears, 'from Pitt and Addington, that
Lord Hawkesbury and M. Otto had signed preliminaries of
peace the evening before.   Pitt calls them on the whole
highly honourable and advantageous, though, in one material respect, different from what might have been wished.'
'Windham, I hear, is to lead a troop of opponents to the
Address, and be very strong against the peace.'

'From 10th,' he says,[3] 'to 27th, at Bath. Queen's parade.
Molested with callers and calling.   Lord Camden down to
mayor's dinner—where dined—next to Bob Steele.   Grenville, Lord Spencer, against the peace.   The people *intoxicated* with joy here and everywhere.   Grand illumination.'
'God has, of His mercy to this sinful nation, allowed a suspension of the work of death and desolation.'   'Dined at
Lord Rosslyn's before I left Bath.   He decided against the
terms of peace : could not have agreed to them. If ministry
had not been changed, the peace would never have taken
place ; not one member of the Cabinet would have approved.
The war would have gone on, and God alone knows what
might have happened.   Invasion was certainly intended—
Massena with 40,000 men on the Essex coast.   I must have
been in opposition.'[4]

'We shall have,' he tells Hannah More, Oct. 27, 'a scene
of strange discordance.   Lord Grenville is to oppose in the
House of Lords, and Lord Spencer also ; and Windham still
more warmly in the House of Commons ; but Pitt will support with all his might : his character now appears in its true
light.'

'In town till November 24.   Northern convention question, and much work about the guarantee of Turkey; Bankes

<hr>

[2] Diary.   [3] Ib.   [4] Ib. Oct. 27.

staying in town for it ; a good deal with us. By our interference we have at last, I trust, carried our point quietly ;
Lord Hawkesbury engaging to give way, and all the rest of
ministers, as well as every individual, understanding the fifth
article in the way we wish. Discussion about Trinidada
with Addington and Pitt. I wish that we had not retained
it.'[5] In answering Mr. Windham, when the Address was
moved upon the second of November, he had declared to
the House his apprehensions, lest our keeping Trinidada
should lead to an extension of the Slave Trade, and nothing
prevented his bringing this subject directly forward, but the
certainty of failure in the House of Commons, and the hopes
of meeting with success elsewhere. 'I am promised,' he tells
Mr. Stephen, 'that there shall be a pause as to the appointment of commissioners for the sale of the Trinidada lands.'[6]

As the session advanced, the popularity of the peace gave
firmness to the new administration. 'Opposition is melting
away manifestly. Grey gone out of town. Tierney has declared himself friendly. Erskine and Lord Moira ditto.
Only Fox and Sheridan still where they were ; probably because Addington could not receive them. Pitt supports
most magnanimously, and assists in every way. Addington
goes on well, is honest and respectable, and improves in
speaking. Little or nothing to do in the House.'[7] 'Pitt and
Rose dined with me quietly to-day. Pitt very pleasant, and
we staid chatting politics. What wonderful magnanimity !
wishing to form for Addington the strongest and best possible administration.'[8] 'Opposition,' he tells Lord Muncaster,[9] 'are laying aside their unreasonable prejudices against
Addington. I should not wonder if several of them could
so far conquer their repugnance as to accept office under
him. You know I was always sanguine as to this administration, knowing Pitt might be depended on. He has
really behaved with a magnanimity unparalleled in a politician ; new instances of it are daily occurring.' 'I do not
wonder if it be misunderstood,' is the remark in one of his

[5].Diary.　　　　　　　　　　[6] Letter to J. Stephen, Esq.
[7] Diary, Nov. 20.　　　　　　[8] Ib. Dec. 1.　　　　[9] Dec. 10.

memoranda ; 'this may be owing not merely to prejudice, but to natural incapacity. Little minds cannot receive the idea ; it is too grand for their comprehension. But to any one who fairly considers it in all its bearings, and who estimates its full worth, it will appear one of the noblest instances of true magnanimity that was ever exhibited to the admiration and imitation of mankind.'

The estimate he here forms of Mr. Pitt may be transferred not unaptly to himself. It is a rare and most instructive sight which his private Journals of this date exhibit. There have been many whom the love of ease has shielded from the temptations of ambition ; and not a few in whom waywardness of temper has nourished a fierce and untractable independence ; but it has seldom happened that one who was possessed of every quality of mind and fortune which could most encourage ambition, and secure its reward, has been seen to put away soberly and cheerfully its utmost offers. This he now did. Those who saw only the result, would never have suspected that his easy course was the result of any struggle—yet so it was : his freedom from ambition was no natural immunity, but a victory of Christian principle. 'I have of late,' he says, 'perceived on looking inwards, the workings of ambition, of love of this world, its honours, riches, estimation, and even of worldly desires for my family, of which before I do not recollect that I was conscious. When I see those who were my equals, or inferiors, rising above me into stations of wealth, rank, &c., I find myself tempted to desire their stations, which yet I *know* would not increase my happiness, or even be more truly honourable.' How completely the temptation was subdued, all his after life witnessed ; on what lofty principles and with what earnestness he wrestled with it, his secret diary explains.

He was now at Broomfield, whither he had escaped to spend the holidays out of the bustle of London. 'Mr. Hughes of Battersea dined with us — dissenting minister. He is a sensible, well-informed, pious man ; strongly dissenting in principle, but moderate in manner. He confessed, not one in twenty of Doddridge's pupils but who turned either Socinian, or tending that way (he himself strictly orthodox); and he said that all the old Presbyterian places of worship were become Socinian congregations. Lord Castlereagh called and staid an hour and a half—about the state and prospects of Ireland and policy to be observed. Four or five thousand annually emigrate from Ulster to America. Less alarming to them than going to the south of Ireland, having so many friends and relations in America. Little farmers, 10*l.* to 20*l.* per annum, with large families. Strong Americans in American war—after, strong liberty-men—then strong for French revolution.'

' Were you not amused,' he asks Lord Muncaster, ' with the account of Sheridan's and Lord Eldon's speeches'? I was peculiarly impressed by Sheridan's appearing to think that being to live on 2000*l.* per annum certain, for some years, would be absolute poverty. I mean in about a fortnight to bring forward the Abolition. I have much to tell you on that head, and I wish you had been in London to seeond some attempts I made in Downing Street.'

These ' Downing Street attempts' aimed at a ' grand Abolition plan,' by 'a general convention.'[1] ' If Mr. Pitt,' he told the Duke of Gloucester, 'had been minister when this peace was negotiated, the question would have come into discussion;' but Lord Hawkesbury and Mr. Addington could not be persuaded.

Yet, though unsuccessful, he was not disheartened. Within a fortnight he was again in $_.c^o{}_{rr}e_{sp}{}^{on}{}_{d}en_ce$ with Mr. Addington. Another matter kept him anxious. He heard with alarm that the commission for the sale of land in Trinidad and St. Vincent was making out. He now writes to Addington: ' You may not know that for several years past Pitt has been assailed by sap and by storm, in all directions and from all quarters, to induce him to sell these lands ; but he never would give way.'

He wrote also to Mr. Pitt, and on February 3 'went to him about the Slave Trade. He firm to prevent importation for cultivating new lands.—4th. Pitt has had a long con-

[1] Diary, Nov. 22, 1801.

versation with Addington, and says it was satisfactory.' 'I
am sure,' Mr. Pitt concludes, ' he will settle nothing finally
till I have seen him again.' But constant watchfulness was
still requisite.—' 11th. Long talk with Canning about his
motion against opening new lands by imported Africans—
staunch and warm for Abolition. Babington was strongly
impressed the other day with Addington's not defending Pitt
upon the army extraordinaries, and said a few more such
days would infallibly break up their friendship. It was but
two hours after that Courtenay, in the House, animadverted
on Addington's losing his regard for his old friends, out of
deference to his new allies. I mentioned it to Addington,
who took it properly.' 'There are those who would rejoice
in separating Pitt and Addington. But they have both
generous minds, and I trust all the efforts of the shabby
will be exerted in vain.—18th. Board of Agriculture. Dined
Lord Camden's—Lord Eldon, Redesdale, Pitt, Villiers,
Castlereagh, and others. Pitt very clever. Long talk with
G. How adroit are people of inferior capacities in defending
themselves ! I hear a shocking account of French morals
from Paris. Massena says he stays there to be " prêt à tout
ce qui peut arriver." People shown through fourteen rooms
before they get to Buonaparte, and officers with pass-words,
without which the First Consul not approachable. Bread
14 sous per lb. The people on the Pont Nœuf said we
brought the king in slavery to Paris when bread was 9 sous,
now we are quiet when it is 14. Lord Sheffield gives a most
pleasing account of Toussaint, of his generous, amiable
temper and disposition ; but in the field a rigid disciplin-
arian—he has 60,000 men trained under him—he behaved
with the utmost kindness to his old master.—25th. Sitting in
Civil List Committee. Bankes and I had doubts, but upon
talking with Addington we agreed we might be left on the
list.'—'March 1. Morning, Proclamation Society meeting.
Then Civil List Committee—considering Report. Extremely
uneasy about the advances to the Princes.' 'If a Committee
of the House of Commons suffers such a concession to pass
without animadversion, no minister can ever refuse the

authority, ascendency, and importunity of a king.[2]—13th. Thought much of Civil List Committee. Occupied all this morning by Sir Sidney Smith. The Duke of Bedford suddenly cut off amidst all his prosperity. Alas!—16th. Dined at Wilbraham Bootle's—meeting Lord and Lady Alvanley, Lord and Lady Belgrave, Bishop of London. A good deal of talk about the Duke of Bedford, &c. Fox had that day spoken his funeral oration in moving writ for Tavistock; speaking of him as one of the best of men.'

'April 2. Canning moved for Trinidada papers. Buonaparte's expedition landed in St. Domingo, and claiming victories. I am busy trying to effect legislative lessening of number of oaths.—7th. House. Sir William Scott's speech, moving for leave to bring in Clergy's Non-residence Bill—curiosa felicitas of language. Sir Robert Peel's Bill—motion well received for morals of apprentices, &c., in cotton factories. — 10th. Recovering from an attack of fever — little done all day. Evening, a long and interesting conversation with W. Smith about Unitarianism and orthodoxy. I have hopes Perceval will still prove a public blessing in a high station: he is to be Attorney-General.—29th. To town. Illumination for the peace. Cobbett's windows broke. The mob very good-natured.' 'The poor Porcupine's windows have been smashed for not rejoicing as you and I do,' writes Mr. Bankes;[3] 'people are shocked by a want of sympathy—ridentibus arrident. However he was not bound to rejoice, but he should have illuminated.'—'May 3. House till late. Windham's preparatory speech about definite treaty. Addington declared our interest concerned in the French West Indian expedition to rescue St. Domingo from the blacks, who had usurped it, &c. I was shocked. "Whatever persons might have thought before," he said, "they must think this now."—6th. I find it is too late to get through Sunday Bill, or Oath measure. I cannot get people to act. Windham, Dr. Lawrence, Tom Grenville, Lord Temple, Elliot, move papers and speechify; all to prove articles of peace disgraceful. — 7th. House, on Nicoll's motion, to censure,

---

[2] Letter to Lord Muncaster, March 1.
[3] Letter from Henry Bankes, Esq., to William Wilberforce, Esq.

and Belgrave's amendment, to thank Pitt, till six in the morning. Good debate—Fox excellently pleasant.—15th. Definite treaty discussion. Windham moved Address by long and able speech. Lord Hawkesbury three hours in answering—very able. In the House till four—adjourned the debate. — 14th. House till near four again — Sheridan infinitely witty, having been drinking.—20th. To town, to meet Pitt upon the Slave Trade.—24th. House on Bull-baiting Bill — Windham's speech aimed expressly at me, though I had not spoken—quite prepared. I too little pos-sessed, and having lost my notes, forgot some things I meant to say, but was told I did very well. Bull-baiting Bill lost, 64 against 51. Windham's malignity against what he calls fanaticism. —27th. Canning's motion — House flat — the motion sadly too short. No division on Addington's sad speech; only holding out hope of inquiry next year, when in 1792 he voted for Abolition, in 1796 against Hawkesbury, even when Dundas had thrown up his resolutions. I grieved to the heart.—28th. At Merchant Taylors' Hall — grand celebration of Pitt's birthday—Lord Spencer chairman— 823 tickets and people—near 200 more asked for. I with-drew, after walking about for an hour and seeing everybody, just as dinner going on table. All went off well. Pitt not there.—29th. Talking with Bankes and Lady Auckland — times very dissipated—masquerades the rage. Dined with General Ross, to meet Lord Cornwallis, Lord and Lady Chatham, and others. Lord Cornwallis very civil, and un-affected, and pleasing. Talked about India in pleasing terms, and the happiness we diffused there, and the equity of our government. He spoke with great apparent pleasure: gave great praise to Barlow. Afraid of Sir William Jones ; and always found him much to do, and took him into his council; where otherwise he might have thwarted. Lord Chatham very friendly. Both talked of West Indies, and of slaves' ill treatment, and West Indian character, in strong terms.—31st. Town. Proclamation Society meeting. House —Non-residence Bill, till half-past eleven. Windham, Ad-dington, Sir William Scott, and Grant, earnest for giving to bishops unqualified discretion, and power over their clergy. Attorney-General Perceval contra.'

The session lingered on another fortnight, during which he 'got through Bill for Hull docks,[4] and moved and unanimously carried a grant of 5,000*l.* as a national reward for Dr. C. Smyth's discovery of a disinfectant. This affair has ended well, and I have cause for thankfulness.'

Parliament was prorogued upon June 28, and dissolved upon the 29th. Upon the 30th, he was on his journey to the north. The ' Beverley, Hull, and York elections' were already 'raging;' but 'no opposition' was 'talked of for the county.'[5]

He reached the West Riding upon July 1, and after a hasty canvass, was at York upon ' the election day, July 12. To tavern by ten, and mounted at half-past ten—Pulleyn's horse. People quiet, till at last, when attacked the horse to get at the ribands. Sir R. Hildyard moved my election; Sir M. Sykes seconded me. Bacon Frank moved Lascelles; Morritt seconded. I pleased people in speaking, and did well. Crowded hall, and castle-yard immensely so.'[6] ' It was, indeed,' says a bystander,[7] ' an august and interesting scene; not one hand was lifted up against him, and the surrounding countenances were expressive of the greatest delight and esteem towards him.'

' The event,' writes his cousin, Lord Carrington [8] (in a letter, docketed, 'kind condolence on my re-election'), 'which has given your other friends so much pleasure, has filled me with sentiments of an opposite nature. No constitution can stand such exertions as yours have been in the service of the county of York. It would have been better if, like Windham, but without his struggle and defeat, you had taken refuge in a close borough, the means of which I should have been proud to have afforded you.'

On the following Wednesday, he ' got to Duncombe's to dinner.' ' It is just such a place,' he tells Mrs. Wilberforce,[9] ' as you and I should like to live in; quiet and beautiful, with-

---

[4] Diary, June 24.   [5] Ib.   [6] Ib. July 12.
[7] William Gray, Esq., to Mrs. Wilberforce, July 14.
[8] July 15.   [9] Ib.

out pomp.' 'You have made your old colleague very happy,' he heard a few days afterwards, from Lord Muncaster,[3] 'by going to him at Copgrove. He has written to me quite a letter of satisfaction and delight at seeing you, and has sent me your speech on the election, which I was most glad to read. Nothing, I think, could be more open and judicious.'

On the 15th, he went to Harewood. 'Repton, the layer-out of ground, there. Music in the evening; I reading also at will. All quite easy and obliging, perfect liberty. The next day I drove out Repton in a single-horse chaise, to survey the grounds.'[2] 'This is one not only of the most magnificent, but of the finest places in England. Great natural beauty, vast woods, expanses of water, a river winding through a valley portioned into innumerable inclosures. Within the house, perfect ease and great good-humour without the smallest mixture of pomp and parade, except in the rooms themselves, which are too gaudy for my taste.'[3] 'Strolled out with a book. William Hey dined, and in the evening I went with him to Leeds.'—'21st. Reached Broomfield. I have been received in Yorkshire with the utmost possible kindness, and even zeal.'[4]

He had now a period of leisure, and took a searching estimate of his situation and his faculties, enquiring where they were most capable of employment and improvement. The general conclusion which he reached was, that it was his 'part to give the example of an independent member of parliament, and a man of religion, discharging with activity and fidelity the duties of his trust, and not seeking to render his parliamentary station a ladder by which to rise to a higher eminence. What has passed of late years (the number of country gentlemen made peers, &c.) renders it particularly necessary to give this lesson.'

The recurrence of his birthday (æt. 43) is marked by the following amongst other entries:—

'Who is there that has so many blessings? Let me record some of them:—Affluence, without the highest rank.[5] A

---

[1] To W. Wilberforce, Esq., July 22. [2] Diary, July 16.
[3] To Mrs. Wilberforce, July 16. [4] Diary.
[5] Looking over this passage on his 71st birthday, he added as a note to the last two words, 'This is a great blessing.'

good understanding and a happy temper. Kind friends, and
a greater number than almost any one. Domestic happiness
beyond what could have been conceived possible. A situation in life most honourable; and, above all, a most favourable situation for eternity. Which way soever I turn I see
marks of the goodness and long-suffering of God. Oh that
I may be more filled with gratitude !

'How merciful that I was not early brought into office, in
1782–3–4! This would probably have prevented my going
abroad, with all that through the providence of God followed.
Then my having such kind friends, my book, &c. All has
succeeded with me, and God has by His preventing grace
kept me from publicly disgracing the Christian profession.
O. my soul, praise the Lord, and forget not all His mercies.
God is love, and His promises are sure.'

The whole of this autumn was spent at Broomfield, where
he saw some interesting people, and got through a good deal
of reading, and occasional composition. 'August 25. Abbé
Gregoire and Smith the chemist breakfasted. I do not much
affect the Abbé; "La Religion, Humanité, la Liberté. That
is my object."' 'Montagu called; fresh from France. The
face of all in Paris military, soldiers with naked bayonets in the
gardens, streets, &c. Men of letters patronized; handsomely
lodged, boarded, &c. Montagu saw Buonaparte at the In-
stitute, attending a debate concerning a canal's course; and
he spoke for a quarter of an hour or twenty minutes, re-
capitulating the arguments, &c. talking of the "gouverne-
ment," what it would do, &c. He seemed nervous at first
—care-worn also. Was dressed plainly; no honours or distinction in his dress, seat, &c. He went away in a carriage,
with one footman. He had been four hours at a council,
and came to this meeting and stayed two hours. The philosophers, even the greatest in mathematics, &c. appeared
extremely ignorant in politics. Several churches converted
into stables, public store-houses, &c. Many noblemen's
houses razed to the ground; Chantilly entirely, yet the buyer
got nothing by it.' 'Writing a paper for the Christian Observer, and letters many.'

'Venn called; kept him to dinner. Most interesting

conversation; telling us many most affecting incidents about his father, displaying especially his zeal and success in God's cause, his powers of conciliating people who were prejudiced against him. Mr. Kershaw and another going over from Halifax to laugh, Kershaw completely conquered, and to his dying day devoted to Mr. Venn.'[6]

' Mr. Hardcastle with me—going to France to enquire, &c. with a view to the diffusion of the Bible. Assured by Fouché that he would assist them gladly. He quite arbitrary at Paris—sent for a loose gambling fellow, and threatened him with imprisonment; and when he resented it, told him that he would imprison him for six weeks unless he was submissive, to show him that he had the power. The splendour very great in Paris in some things, but very unequal. Perhaps a room which has cost 20,000*l*., and an immensely fine dinner, and only two or three servants to wait, valets de place, shabby fellows, being brought by every man. Buonaparte goes to the play every night, but cannot be seen in his box. Land well cultivated, and sells high. Much private society now, and universal extravagance continued from Revolution, when profuseness natural. No talk about politics, except in perfectly confidential parties. Espionage universal, and men of all ranks employed in it. Fox said to be favourably received in Paris by the First Consul.'[7] ' They have dined together in great friendship. One cannot well conceive two people with fewer points of accordance.' ' I am instigating Fox to urge Buonaparte on the Abolition, of which probably he knows nothing, and confounds it with Emancipation.'[8]

He was at this time ' strongly impressed with a persuasion that a good Abolition pamphlet is wanted, and as I do not know any body who will write it, I fear I must try my hand at it.[9] There are very few, indeed, who know at all the grounds on which the subject rests. They adhere to the party,—not all of them, alas!—be it what it may, which they originally joined, and give a languid support, as if by prescription.'[1]

[6] Diary.   [7] Diary, Sept. 17.   [8] Ib. Sept. 11.
[9] Ib. Sept. 19.   [1] To Rev. Thomas Gisborne, Sept. 20.

'Public events. Pitt still kindly helping Addington. Came
to London and visited him at Richmond Park, just after Holwood sold. Pitt spent a day and a quarter at Sir Charles Middleton's, going there to study farming. Sir Charles astonished
at his wonderful sagacity, and power of combining and reasoning out. Says he is the best gentleman farmer he, Sir Charles,
knows, and may be the best farmer in England. Bernard
and I busy together about education plan for children of
lower orders.'[2]

Parliament met on November 16. 'We re-elected Abbot
to-day without opposition, after a most characteristic speech
from Sir William Scott, who moved his being replaced in the
chair. Nothing could be more appropriate than his language.
As I was coming out of the House, Canning accosted me,
telling me that he had a violent quarrel against me; and
when I stared, "Nay," says he, on public grounds; and then
explained that it was on account of my speech at York on
my re-election, against continental connections. I told him
that certainly it was a question in which much must depend
on circumstances and degrees, but that generally I was less
friendly to them than many men; and that having been so
ten years ago, I had not of course become less diffident of
my doctrines from the treatment we had received from our
allies. From Canning's warmth you will guess a good deal,
remembering that partly from constitutional temperament,
partly from opposition feelings, he may carry his principles
further than some others of our great political men. But
I own I dread getting into a war.'[3]

Accordingly, on the moving of the Address upon Nov. 24,
he 'opened debate. Spoke strongly against engaging in continental alliances as principals.'[4] And again, 'Spoke, having
been much urged by Canning and Ryder, on continental
alliances.'[5] 'We hear a great deal of a famous speech of
yours and Sheridan's,' writes Mrs. Hannah More. 'Dec. 11.
Bankes and I called on St. Helen's, and had much talk with
him. He agreed with us on continental alliances, and war
and peace. The Windhamites make a great storm about

[2] Diary.   [3] To Thomas Babington, Esq. Nov. 16.
[4] Diary.   [5] Ib. Dec. 9.

has played deep in our funds. Fox came up to me on the Ministerial side to-day in the House, but Attorney-General Perceval there, so he could say nothing, but I suspect he meant to begin on the war.'[9]

The next day he 'read the papers concerning the rupture with France,' and found himself reluctantly compelled to oppose the Government. April 23. 'House till half-past twelve. Spoke late, and House very impatient, being against their opinions.'[1] The debate was renewed the following day. 'House till four in the morning. Divided in minority of 67 against 398. Henry Thornton, Bankes, and I agreed. Fox spoke three hours with wonderful ability, as Pitt last night, in quite different style, for an hour or more, appealing to national pride, honour, &c.'[2]

On June 2, Mr. Canning communicated to him the resolutions of censure upon Ministers for having so long submitted to the overbearing conduct of France, which were moved by Colonel Patten on the following day. He describes the debate. 'Small speakers for a long time, till at length Tom Grenville ; then Addington and Pitt. Previous question, for which I voted, 56 against 333 ; then Pitt and his friends went away ; I stayed and voted against the motion.'[3] 'Last night discovered more of the influence of the Crown than most incidents of late days ; also more right principle, for people don't like to vote against Pitt, yet only 56 with him. He indicated that only restrained by decency towards Crown, and present state of the King, from moving for dismission.[4] —6th. Pitt strongly urged a decisive measure of military preparation to-day. Windham showed himself a most dangerous adviser. 8th. I heard it rumoured that Government meant to tax the funds. This said to be Tierney's plan. Pitt decidedly against it. It would surely ruin public credit. Tierney made treasurer of the navy.—13th. House. Budget. I had heard of great objections to taxing the funds. This is done by the present plan to 5 per cent., yet no objection was urged.'

The palmy days of Addington's Ministry were past, and

[9] Diary.
[1] Ib. April 23.
[2] Ib. May 24.
[3] Ib.
[4] Ib. June 4.

the difficulties of the war soon brought to light its inherent feebleness. 'July 4. People already begin to sicken of the war. I see secret discontents and fears, but no one speaks openly. The citizens outrageous against Addington's incapacity, as they call it. Against taxing the funds.'[5] This plan was speedily abandoned. On the 13th he says, 'Addington gave up his inequality as to land and funds, on which we had divided with Pitt, 50 to 150.'[6] '16th. Lord St. Helen's, Teignmouth, Henry Thornton, dined. Much talk about invasion. All people seem to think our sea-guard not to be depended on. Many say that now, in the calms of summer, the enemy will row over before we are prepared. I cannot myself expect it at present. Yet we are strangely unprepared, and the confusion might be extreme if the French should come.'[7]

'House. Defence Bill till late. Alas, Sunday drilling introduced contrary to Yorke's declaration. I spoke. Pitt answered me (spoke of it as not contrary to English Church principles). We got the Bill mended though not cured about Sunday exercising.' 'Sir Charles Middleton sent me a plan for defence; getting immediately one hundred large coppered ships, East Indians, West Indians, colliers, &c. with large carronades, and employing them to run down the flotilla. I showed it to Pitt, and gave it to Addington. Both approved. Saw it afterwards at Lord Hobart's, where Sullivan said that he had hit upon the same. All agree we are not ready for the French yet. All the regiments are marched from Hull towards London. If we are not attacked for three months, people seem to think we shall be impregnable. Alas! too haughty and self-sufficient, and Pitt rampant about setting Europe to rights, &c., after vindicating our own safety. Pitt does more in some ways than he would in power, from the deference to colleagues he would then feel. Supported Crawford, and discovered great military genius. His speech capital—urging precautions, yet animating.[8] Buonaparte said to have attacked Hanover personally to vex the King. Addington says he bears it well. Said his

---

[5] Diary, July 4. [6] Ib. July 13.
[7] Ib. [8] Ib. July 26.

determination was taken, and hinted he'd take the field if it came to that. Sir William Scott told me that the farmers in Oxfordshire said that they were so heavily taxed that if Buonaparte did come they could not be worse.'

No one saw with more regret the strange inertness of the Government. His long and tried friendship for Mr. Addington made it the more painful to him, and he did all he could by personal remonstrance to stir him up to greater energy of conduct.

'Government,' he writes to Lord Muncaster, 'would draw on them your vehement indignation if you were near head-quarters, and were to see how shamefully dilatory they are even where the very life and substance of the State is in question. Addington really stands on a precipice.

'Pitt is about to take the command of 3,000 volunteers, as Lord Warden ; I am uneasy at it. He does not engage on equal or common terms, and his spirit will lead him to be foremost in the batttle. Yet as it is his proper post, one can say nothing against it.'

. ˇ 'We got through the Income Tax Bill,' he writes to Mr. Bankes, ' much in the same way as through many of a similar sort, and the same rapid manufacture of clauses which had done such honour to the industry of our friend Rose, was seen to proceed with equal celerity in the hands of his successor Vansittart. When one sees how Acts of Parliament are made, one only wonders they are half as correct, or rather incorrect, as they are. The Army of Reserve Bill passed. Pitt attended constantly ; in the main behaving well, but once I understand, when I not present, saying something towards Addington which indicated ill nature and contempt. It was when Addington declared against taxing the future foreign purchasers of funded property, because it would abridge the market, and thereby depreciate the commodity to the old stockholders, when Pitt congratulated him, or the House, on the supererogatory tenderness for the public faith, which he so suddenly displayed. Pitt had been, however, before so far reconciled, that though I think he never called Addington, individually, his honourable friend, he did the Ministers in general, and Addington called him so frequently.

Pitt communicated freely with Yorke, and showed him his plan for the levy en masse, pressing forward strongly the introduction of the scheme, and secretly grumbling at the dilatoriness of Ministry.　At length he declared to me, and others, that if Government would not move it, he himself would.　Yorke then gave notice of it, and it has gone through, as you see.

'I have been much among the Ministers ; and I am grieved to say that their weakness is lamentable.　The country is now, on this 11th of August, utterly unprepared for the enemy, if he should be more timely in his preparations.　The spirit of the people is roused, and they are in general well disposed to act, but I really fear all may be ruined by the inefficiency of their governors.　Pitt is doing great things as Lord Warden.　Sheridan fights lustily for Addington.　He proposed a sufficiently absurd vote of thanks last night to the volunteers who had so gallantly offered their services ; but you see clearly that the affectionate regard of Government to him knows no bounds in this honey-moon of their union.　By the way, Lord St. Vincent lately offered Tom Sheridan a most lucrative place, which Sheridan refused ; very wisely I think.　The city are out of all patience with Addington.'

Upon the 17th he was in London, and 'at Pitt's house in York Place by four o'clock—talked with him near an hour. —18th. Addington seems convinced, as do all others, that a council of war a wise measure, yet dare not press it against Duke of York.　All are most distrustful of Duke's military talents.　Pitt very ill used by Government, Admiralty chiefly.　Even the river Thames' safety not provided for ; and when the Trinity House proposed the means, the Admiralty foolishly economical.　Lord Romney, Lord-Lieutenant of Kent, with Lords Camden and Darnley, on receiving Lord Hobart's letter about twenty-five muskets for 100 men, &c., would not deliver the contents to the county, and obtained an exemption for Kent.　Pitt's exertions great, and his ascendency striking—on excellent terms with Duke of York.

'It is really shocking how low our establishments reduced. We could not have resisted 40,000 men getting to London.

Pitt says they have been talking lately of preparing against next spring, which makes him half suspect something is intended just now.[9]—28th. My letters out of Yorkshire and elsewhere are now very strong about the discontents occasioned by the Volunteers' limitation. A most pernicious measure, against which I have been remonstrating both in and out of Parliament with all my might.'

Late in August, after spending a week with his family at the house of Matthew Montagu at Sandleford Priory, he arrived on September 3 at the village of Bath Easton, where he took up his quarters for the remainder of the vacation. 'Delighted with the beauty of our new villa. Weather delicious. Afternoon and evening read and heard, out of doors, in a lovely arbour by the river. This is a beautiful country.'[1] On the first Sunday after his arrival,[2] he says, 'A prospect of my living in more quiet than I have long enjoyed. Oh may I improve it for the best purposes.' The record of days of devotion and intercession which follows this entry, shows how diligently his resolutions were carried into act.

Here, whilst enjoying one of those many solitary walks of which he says, ' I never find my mind more lifted up to God than when thus meditating sub Dio,' he records a remarkable escape from danger. His favourite haunt was a retired meadow, which bordered on the Avon. A steep bank shaded by some fine trees, one of which by its projection formed a promontory in a deep part of the stream, was his common seat. On October 25 he says, 'Walked with pencil and book, and wrote. A charming day. I was sitting by the river-side, with my back to the water, on a portable seat, when suddenly it struck me that it was not quite safe. Writing, I might be absent, and suddenly slip off, &c. I moved therefore a few yards, and placed my stool on the grass, when in four or five minutes it suddenly broke, and I fell flat on my back, as if shot. Had it happened five minutes sooner, as I cannot swim, I must, a thousand to one, have been drowned, for I sat so that I must have fallen back-

---

[9] Diary, Aug. 19.   [1] Ib.   [2] Journal, Sept. 4.

R

wards into the river. I had not the smallest fear or idea of
the seat's breaking with me ; and it is very remarkable, that
I had rather moved about while by the river, which would
have been more likely to break it, whereas I sat quite still
when on the grass. A most providential escape. Let me
praise God for it.'

The state of his health had of late alarmed his nearest
friends. The quiet of the vacation, early hours, and the
Bath waters restored him to his average state; though he
' was reminded by' his ' sensations that' his ' frame was not
susceptible of that thorough repair which it used to receive
at Bath in earlier days.'[3]   How he would bear the renewed
fatigues of London seemed a doubtful question, and one
friend wrote repeatedly and urgently to press upon him the
duty of withdrawing altogether from public life. But he was
not of a temper to retire and leave his task half done; and
though he was constitutionally inclined to defer too much
to the opinion of those whose moral qualities he valued
highly, in this instance happily his own view of duty was
unshaken.

He returned on the meeting of Parliament, and entered
the House while the King's speech was reading. ' How I
love to be quiet with my family,' he says at the close of the
recess; ' how long a period of retirement did it appear on
looking forward, and now it is gone like a dream, and I am
about to plunge into the bustle of life again.'[4]

There had been throughout the autumn occasional ' rumours of the return of peace,'[5] but they had now all passed
away. Invasion indeed had been so long expected that men
were becoming hardened to the threat. ' A general sense of
security has taken the place of alarm. Several members of the
government, who were all alive to call up the country, are now
made cooler from the mere effect of having become familiar
with the idea of danger. Men of no great strength of mind act
more from their feelings than their judgment. London now
thought safe—that the French cannot from a flotilla land an
army of many together. Two days ago a good account of

[3] Letter to Rev. T. Gisborne, Oct. 18.
[4] Diary, Nov. 22.   [5] Diary.

Russia's army.'[6]   Yet it was clear that we were entering on
a dangerous struggle, and few looked with any confidence to
the vigour of the present government. 'They seem everywhere,' he complains, 'in low estimation.'[7]   One meets in
the Pump-room people from different parts of England, and
I think, without exception, that in every quarter they are accused of gross remissness and incapacity.'[8] 'The Ministry,'
writes 'the Dean,'[9] from Cambridge,[1] 'are everywhere, but
particularly here, thought weak on the whole, but exceedingly well-intentioned.   I do not hear a mouth opened
against their principles.   I am sure nothing would give so
much general satisfaction as a junction between Pitt and
Addington; Pitt's vigour, and Addington's discretion, would
please exceedingly.' This was exactly his own view. 'I shall
be very glad,' he tells Mr. Babington,[2] 'if it be practicable,
to bring Pitt and Addington together again.'

On December 13th, he was from breakfast till dinner
with Mr. Pitt, in private consultation.   The wishes of all
who were free from party bias pointed in the same direction.
Though 'the government journals talked of immediate invasion,' and 'Mr. Addington showed' him 'a letter from
Lord St. Vincent, in which he said the attempt at invasion
would be made this week,' there was still an evident
languor in all the preparations for defence.

'The general opinion' he records, December 17, 'of government is, that it is sadly blundering and inefficient.   Yet
people are afraid of the old set entire.   Windham and Co.
strong in opposition.   Fox manifestly drawing towards them.
Provoked by cursory remarks.   'Tis said Sheridan trying to
pique him by saying, "You will get Pitt in again if you oppose."
He peevishly says, "I can't bear fools, anything but fools."'

The new session opened upon February 1, and the breach
was evidently widening between Mr. Pitt and Mr. Addington.
'I have endeavoured to keep them in amity, but each has
been surrounded with enemies to the other.   I fear that
"never can true reconcilement grow, where wounds of deadly

---

[6] Diary.   [7] Ib.
[8] Letter to Rev. Thomas Gisborne, Oct. 18.   [9] Milner.
[1] Nov. 2.   [2] Nov. 4.

hate have pierced so deep."' He had talked over the subject with Mr. Pitt before the commencement of the session.
'After breakfast to see Pitt—much political talk—found him
resolved not to hamper himself with engagements, or go into
systematic opposition.'[3] This now combined the most discordant elements. 'Lord Camden tells me that it is certain
that Fox and the Grenvilles have coalesced.'[4] But with
neither of these leaders, whose adherents were called respectively, the old and new opposition, did Mr. Pitt ally himself.
On the 'Volunteers' Bill, Pitt explained his ideas, and
government seemed to approve of them.'[5] Next day, on the
same measure, ' Pitt was excellent and useful,[6] and he did
not even take part in Sir John Wrottesley's motion for an inquiry into the conduct of government in the Irish insurrection.'

In this debate he notices a 'sad opposition between outward speech and inward sentiments:'[7]—' I know well what
would be the variations of your expressive countenance if
you were a witness of the scenes which have lately passed in
St. Stephen's. Of all the achievements of the human face,
however, Tierney's on Wednesday night was the greatest I
ever saw exhibited. You would have had much food for
moralizing, had you been in the House. If, luckily for him,
Fox had not *got* spoken (to use one of Lord Melville's
elegant tournures), he would not have got off so easily.
Windham also could only explain, not reply; and Grey,
of whom hoaxing is not the forte, preserves also an old
liking to Tierney, which, though it did not prevent his striking,
prevented his hitting as hard as Fox would have laid on.
The latter, by the way, seems disposed to have no mercy on
Addington. I really feel for Addington, who is a better man
than most of them, though not well fitted for the warfare of
St. Stephen's. He has exhibited marks of soreness, by losing
his temper readily, once, indeed, without the smallest reason.
Pitt on that occasion behaved nobly. Instead of retorting
angrily, or even showing any contemptuous coolness, he
scarcely seemed conscious of Addington's having exposed

[3] Diary, Jan. 10.   [4] Ib. Feb. 14.
[5] Ib. Feb. 27.   [6] Ib. Feb. 28.
[7] Letter to Lord Muncaster, March 10, 1804.

himself, and answered with perfect good humour.   Yⁱⁱ would have been struck with the difference between Pitt'ⁱⁱ demeanour and that of his friends, many of whom, you know, bear no good-will to Addington. You know the high opinion I entertain of Sir Charles Middleton. He believes our administration to have been strangely negligent ; his opinion weighs with me beyond that of any other naval man, because, besides his providence, his experience, his integrity, he is less of a party man by far than any other I have been able to consult. . Nearly all the naval officers whom I have heard speak their minds, declare that the force by which we are opposing the enemy is insufficient for its purpose. One naval lord of professional celebrity said lately, "We shall soon probably be at war with the navies of France, Spain, Holland, and even Portugal" (he might have added Genoa, which furnishes, as Lord St. Helens assures me, multitudes of excellent sailors), "and we shall have no adequate force to oppose to them."   Our ships are wearing away with unprecedented rapidity, from various circumstances, and no efforts have been made to bring forward new ships as our old ones are expended.'

This was the ground of Mr. Pitt's first act of direct opposition to the government (March 15). 'Pitt's motion on navy state. I, moved by Tierney's low attack, and quite unpremeditatedly, answered him, and, as was told, extremely well. I felt my legs more than I ever remember in argument. Never was a more wretched defence made. Slept five hours, and awoke with the train of my ideas running round like a mill. Though the motion was lost, yet he soon after expresses his conviction that it 'had done good. The Admiralty are exerting themselves with tenfold activity.'   Yet this step exposed Mr. Pitt to unusual reproach. 'Everybody blames him as factious for his motion about the state of the navy. He is conceived to have had little ground for it, and rather to have lost himself, as they phrase it.'[8]   An entry of March 20 shows the freshness of affection which he retained amidst all the roughnesses of his public life :—
' Yesterday, on entering the House, Tom Stanley told me of

[8] Diary, March 24.

~or Lord Alvanley's death after a short illness. Overcome ~ith the event to tears, and retired. In the evening Pitt showed me a few lines he had written to take leave of him the night before, recommending his son, Pitt's godson, to Pitt's protection. "God bless the King, and country in general, in these perilous times."'

The holidays postponed for a season the rising strife of parties, but when Parliament met it wore an angry aspect, and the fall of the government was plainly all but inevitable. Even with all the light since thrown upon its expiring struggles, the observations of one who stood so near the chiefs, and noted so freely the impressions of each day, will be read with interest. Few such passages of history have been more keenly scrutinized, and seldom have the actors in them been subjected to severer judgments. But upon the whole they show, in the clearest manner, Mr. Pitt's high-minded integrity and Lord Eldon's fairness. 'Pitt,' he says, 'disposed to go more decidedly into opposition. He is surrounded by men of party spirit without his integrity, and of strong passions.' Immediately on his return Mr. Pitt desired an interview. 'I was unluckily detained here yesterday,' he writes from York Place on Wednesday, 'till after the hour I had mentioned. If you can find time to come so far, I should be very glad to see you to-day; if not, I will call on you at any hour you please to-morrow.' In the course of Wednesday Mr. Wilberforce 'went up to Pitt, whom missed yesterday. Talked with him; and set him down at dinner. How changed from a few weeks ago!—ready now to vote out Addington, though he has not bound himself to Fox. I fear he has been urged forward by people of less wisdom than himself. I am out of spirits, and doubtful about the path of duty in these political battles.'[9]

His journal of April 22 shows his Sunday's thoughts turning in the same direction. 'I am distressed by the state of political parties. O Lord, enlighten my understanding and direct my judgment, and strengthen me to take the path of duty with a firm and composed though feeling mind. Poor Addington! with all his faults, I feel for him.'

[9] Diary, April 18.

'Fox's motion for a Committee concerning the defence of the country' came on the next day. 'Debate lasted till four in the morning. Fox spoke feebly — Pitt ably, but too strong. Perceval's feeling and warm defence of Addington was greatly to his honour.'[1]

He was most anxious, as he tells Mr. Hey, that Pitt should keep himself clear of that 'co-operation (coalition is a word of bad omen) which has been lately announced, and with which you must, I think, have been disgusted. For my part, I still cherish the hope of seeing him acting with Mr. Addington, and shall use all my endeavours to bring the junction about. There have been busy, ill-meaning friends on each side.' His diary and letters show that he at once attempted to effect this reconciliation, and what was the course of events. Having conversed freely with Pitt, he next explained his views in 'a long talk with Addington,' and then sought to bring the influence of the Lord Chancellor to bear in the same direction. Lord Eldon entered gladly into his views and was open, cordial, and generous, saying 'that he had told Pitt how much he wished to see him and Addington united, that he could not conceive any man in such times as these had a right to think of any thing but the country, and my poor old master there, pointing to Buckingham House.'[2] But the difficulties, in great measure depending on personal feeling, were insuperable. 'My wish,' he writes to Lord Muncaster, 'has been that Pitt might consent to unite with several of the present administration, and especially with Addington himself. Grieved indeed am I to say, when I call to my mind their former long and intimate friendship, that a sad degree of hostility has taken possession of both their bosoms, and chiefly, I fear, of that which, belonging to the strongest character of the two, was likely to partake of that strength.'

On April 30 he wrote thus : 'Pitt had received an intimation that he would be sent for by G. R., or negotiated with through the Chancellor. Fox in the evening showed he knew nothing about it.'[3] This communication, it is now clear, was made to Mr. Pitt at the suggestion of Mr. Addington

---

[1] Diary, April 23. [2] Ib. [3] Diary, April 30.

himself. On the following Monday, ' Pitt saw the King for the first time. All looked foul before. Rose most injudiciously intimated that the King had authorized Pitt to give in a plan of government. But surely this should have been a private intimation. Though no contract, direct or indirect, between Pitt and Fox, yet Fox's friends will abuse Pitt grossly if Fox does not come in, and he does.'[4] Two days later he ' called on Pitt, and heard the state of the political negotiation.'[5] ' Pitt, the 25th of April, wrote to the King, telling him of the open and decisive part he felt it his duty to take about his ministry under Addington, declaring he would never commit himself with any man (he had told me that he would never force Mr. Fox upon the King). The 2nd of May, Pitt submitted to the King, through the Chancellor, by letter, a plan of administration, containing heads of the great parties. King's answer. Pitt returned the 6th a very proper answer, and entreating an interview. Had it next day.' The tone of this interview he thus reports[6] :—

' You will be glad to hear, that during an interview of more than three hours which Pitt had with the King, the latter treated him with great cordiality and even affection, and talked with as much rationality and propriety as at any former period of his life. Before Pitt supported Fox's motion, he wrote the King a private letter, intimating that he felt himself under the painful necessity of opposing his Majesty's government, from a firm conviction that his doing so was indispensable to the national safety and honour, &c. He also afterwards, by the King's desire, submitted to him his general ideas of the sort of administration which it would be best to form in the present conjuncture : viz. an administration composed of the heads of all the several great political parties ; grounding this opinion on the probability of a long war, and the advantages of a strong government at home, abroad, and in Ireland. A few days afterwards he saw the King, and again explained and enforced, as far as he properly could, the same ideas. The King objected a good deal at first to the

[4] Diary, May 7.   [5] Ib. May 9.
[6] Letter to Lord Muncaster, May 1.

Grenvilles, but at length gave way very handsomely, but indicated such a decided determination against Fox, that it
would have been wrong to press it further.

' The Grenvilles, as you hear, say they cannot accept office
without Fox and Co.; and so Pitt is to come in with his own
personal friends, Lord Harrowby, &c., and with some of the
present men. The country in general, I am persuaded, will
like this best, though the old opposition partisans will be
enraged. And though Pitt had most clearly explained
from the first that Fox and Co. were not to consider him
bound in any degree, directly or indirectly, to press their ad-
mission into office, and that they were therefore not to shape
their conduct on any such supposition, yet I see clearly Pitt
will be abused. You cannot think how violent S. is. He is
loud too that the government cannot *stand at all.* Surely
he might have formed some estimate of Pitt's powers. The
Carlton House politics, I hear, are all in favour of Fox. Pitt
of course would have taken any of the Prince's friends.' ' I
am not sure that this arrangement is not the very best possible; the Grenvilles are so wrong-headed and warlike.'

CHAPTER XV.

MAY 1804 TO FEBRUARY 1806.

*Encouraging prospects of Abolition cause—Motion carried in the House
of Commons by a great majority—Delay in the House of Lords—
Pitt's promise of suspending Guiana Slave Trade by proclamation—
Summer at Broomfield—Lyme—Literary employments—Correspondence with Henry Brougham—New Session—Reconciliation between
Pitt and Addington—Abolition Bill defeated—Pitt repeats his promise
of suspending Guiana Slave Trade—Charges against Lord Melville—
Supported by Wilberforce—Trafalgar—Austerlitz—Pitt's death—his
debts, and funeral.*

THE time seemed to Mr. Wilberforce arrived—for again
moving the Abolition of the Slave Trade. It was not
mainly to the change of government that the Abolition

was indebted for these brighter prospects; though the sub-
stitution of a Cabinet, in which it had many warm friends,
for one almost wholly hostile, marked the opportunity as
propitious.   Beside this, as Mr. Pitt declared, Abolition
'had obtained many converts of late years.'[1]   Its failure
in 1792 had been mainly caused by the fear of French principles.   The House of Commons which was returned in
1796, when this fear was at its height, had been unreasonably
prejudiced against change in our Colonial system.   The temper of the times was now altered.   In France, democracy
had assumed the less attractive features of military despot-
ism; while the common danger had kindled a hearty spirit
of loyalty in Great Britain, and Jacobinism was too much discredited either to render to Abolition its destructive aid,
or supply a convenient reproach for its supporters.

Some, moreover, of the West Indian body had moderated
their opposition, and even 'began to talk of Abolition,' and
being 'afraid of the cultivation of Demerara and the Dutch
colonies, offered a three years' suspension.'[2]   'This will probably be moved and carried by Addington, who will be the
sober, practical man, in opposition to the wild enthusiasts
who are for total Abolition.'[3]   Early in the spring he was
'assured that the great West Indian merchants and planters
would be for a five years' suspension.   Five or six names
given me.   They should carry it, it was said, unanimously
at a meeting.'[4]   He therefore 'urged Addington to make
himself the head of a suspending party for five years.'[5]
There would be 'a disinclination in the minds of the West
Indians to accept any proposition I should make . . .
and I could not do more than acquiesce in such a proposal.'[6]

The offer was declined by Mr. Addington 'from a natural
aversion to come forward just at this moment;'[7] and all
hopes of any general support from the West Indian body
soon disappeared, as 'a general meeting of planters and
merchants on May 17 decided "that every legal and
proper step should be taken to oppose the progress of any

---

[1] Speech, May 30.   [2] Diary, Dec. 16, 1803.
[3] Ib. Dec. 24, 1803.   [4] Ib. April 19, 1804.   [5] Ib.
[6] To the Right Hon. H. Addington, May 4.   [7] Diary, May 16.

Bill which may be brought into parliament, either to suspend or abolish the Slave Trade."'

He was left therefore to renew single-handed this great contest, whilst against him was arrayed a body strong for its wealth and numbers, for the character, talents, and station of many of its members; which extended its influence through the aristocracy of the land, which had a Prince of the blood for its avowed advocate in the upper House of Parliament, and which was supported by men who, like George Ellis, ruled the literary world, and plainly told him that they 'differed from him totally on the great subject of Abolition.'

He, nothing daunted, moved on May 30 the first reading of his Bill. 'The anti-Abolitionists,' he says, 'made no stand in speaking.'[8] They failed no less on a division. 'We divided 124 against 49. All the Irish members voted with us. Lee and Lord de Blaquiere spoke and did good. Addington in a speech of one minute opposed us as impracticable, and blindly threw out a Committee. Barham with us. Pitt and Fox a few words. On coming home found Brougham, Stephen, Macaulay, Grant, Henry Thornton, &c. John Villiers came, and he, I, Stephen, Brougham, and William Smith talked over and settled Bill. Stephen and I had more talk afterwards. To bed late.'

Thus was the Abolition of the Slave Trade for a third time voted by the House of Commons, but not, as formerly, through the hesitating concurrence of a bare majority. Its supporters were now as overwhelming in numbers as they had always been in argument. From that night the issue of the question was clear. Accident or artifice might postpone the triumph, but this alteration in the sober judgment of reflecting men showed that the mists which had obscured the plain demands of right were passing away for ever. The venerable Newton doubting whether he, 'within two months of entering upon his eightieth year, should live to see the accomplishment of the work,' cheered the advocates with adding, 'but the prospect will give me daily satisfaction so long as my declining faculties are preserved.'

[8] Diary, May 30.

'It is refreshing to me,' was his answer, 'to turn my eye from the vanities with which it is surrounded, and to fix it on you, who appear in some sort to be already enlightened with the beams of that blessed day which is beginning to rise on you, as you approach to the very boundaries of this world's horizon.   May you soon enjoy it in its meridian lustre.   Pray for us, that we also may be enabled to hold on our way, and at last to join with you in the shout of victory.

'I fear the House of Lords ! But it seems as if He, who has the hearts of all men in his power, was beginning to look with pity on the sufferings of those poor oppressed fellow-creatures whose cause I assert.'

This victory he reports to Muncaster, adding, 'I cannot feel anything of the joys of success.   You will be sufficiently indignant against Addington from reading the account of his speechling (it lasted literally but for about forty seconds), yet you would be ten times more indignant if you knew all. I have the satisfaction of reflecting that I acted towards him, in spite of much provocation, like a true friend.   I had endeavoured to procure for him the credit of effecting a suspension of the Slave Trade for five years.   To all this no answer, no hint of what he thought or intended,   At last he comes with his wretched repetition of our mode being impracticable.   I never felt more indignant.'   The Bill was read a second time on June 7.   'Long discussion.   House sat till two.   Lord Castlereagh's long anti-speech.   Windham against us,   I only shortly spoke at last.   We carried it 102 to 44, or near it.'[9]

Other matters of great interest were in progress.   Mr. Pitt had entered upon office in the face of bitter and powerful parties.   'The old Opposition are extremely angry with Pitt for coming in without Fox.   Pitt himself thinks Grenville will oppose even more warmly than Fox.   They abuse the Chancellor.'[1]   The whole strength of Opposition was mustered against Mr. Pitt's military plans in his Additional Force Bill.   On June 8, 'its second reading came on—only about 40 majority.   Opposition, Foxites especially, in high spirits. It seems probable that more have divided against Pitt on this

[9] Diary, June 7.   [1] Ib.

Bill than (will) on any future measure, because already pledged against it while Addington in; but yet the effect of these bad divisions may cause the rats to run, and so pull him down. It is curious, for several weeks not one word said, or even thought, of invasion. It is next to impossible any one topic can long maintain its place in conversation.'

'June 15. House—Opposition got the better in a first division by surprise. Pitt very angry and his friends—spoke against time. His second division, only about 30 majority. His next will be no better ; but this Bill no test.—18th. House—which very late. Pitt's Bill till half-past four, 265 against 223. Opposition had been very sanguine, and said they would carry the question.—22nd. House—which on Lord Advocate's letter. Whitbread's motion—Pitt's and Perceval's honest, manly, and moderate way of taking it. Lord Advocate's own speech most imprudent. Canning spoke excellently on Monday, talking at the close of Addington's systematic opposition. Though Addington angry, yet the remark may have done good, and prevent his opposing.'

His own Bill meanwhile required his whole attention, as its progress could be maintained only by unwearied vigilance. No claims of local interest secured the attendance of members, while it was resisted by the opposition of a powerful party, and by every practicable parliamentary stratagem. On the 12th it passed the Committee. Next morning he was early ' at the parliamentary offices, and the House. We proceeded to hear counsel on report, when their own friends slipped away, and leaving less than forty, counted us out.' [2] Yet General Gascoigne inveighed against this delay,[3] and threatened to enforce the order of the day ; while Mr. Fuller, who had moved the adjournment, complained of the haste with which Mr. Wilberforce was urging the matter through the House, and quoted as a negro saying, that ' Massa King Wilbee wanted to free them, but that the parliament would not let him.'

The Bill however, through his constant attention, continued to advance through many perils. The Irish members

---

[2] Diary, June 13.   [3] Debate of June 14.

were intending to leave London.   His personal influence
detained them; but, before its two last stages, he 'found
many of his Irish supporters, who, at first all so warm for
Abolition, have since been persuaded by some West Indians
that it is an invasion of private property.'   Nor did the
old opponents relax their hostility.   'Lord Castlereagh
told me, that many years ago he had looked into the
Slave Trade, and adopted his present opinions.   What a
cold-blooded creature!   Somers Cocks (as well as Fox), the
other day, gave Pitt a hard knock about his not being in
earnest about Abolition.   I never was so dissatisfied with
Pitt as this time.'[4]   On the 25th, however, when the case
was again argued before the House, 'Pitt, warming in his
speech, moved against hearing counsel as well as evidence,
and carried it without a division;'[5] and, two days afterwards,
the Bill was read for the third time in the House of Commons—'our majority 99 to 33.   Samuel and John Smith,
&c. most kind in attending, and Attorney General also.
Addington most vexatious.'[6]

He had now triumphed in the House of Commons, but
greater difficulties were behind.   He committed the conduct
of the Bill in the upper House to Lord Grenville, reminding
him 'that it was by advice of you and Pitt that I went down
to the House of Commons, and gave notice of my intention
of bringing forward a proposition on that subject, which in
private had long engaged my attention; and you took a
leading part in drawing up the resolutions, on which we
grounded our measure.   Let me earnestly entreat you, therefore, to undertake this pious charge.'

From Lord Grenville he received 'a most kind and honourable letter.'   Yet 'hope deferred' was still his portion.   He
learned from Bishop Porteus that, 'taking into account the
advanced period of the session, the probable sentiments of
several leading men in administration, and the absence of
by far the greater number of bishops in their respective dio-
ceses,' they 'extremely doubted whether it would be prudent
to risk the Bill this session in the House of Lords.   If, as
we much fear, it were to be rejected, this would injure the

[4] Diary, June 23.   [5] Ib. June 25.   [6] Ib. June 27.

cause, and greatly inpede its success another year.' The same conclusion was pressed on him by others. 'I carried up my Bill. Pitt told me that a meeting had been held of the Cabinet, in which it was agreed that the subject should be hung up till next year, on the ground that the examination of evidence indispensable; that they could make no progress this year, and that therefore it was better not to bring it on.'[7]

Lord Grenville was of the same opinion. He promised ' to be in town to say his say,' on the day of discussion, but pronounced it 'inexpedient to attempt to divide.' 'It quite lowers my spirits,' says Mr. Wilberforce, 'to see all my hopes for this year at once blasted, yet *I can't help myself.*'[8] The debate on the second reading (July 2) was opened by the Chancellor in a very 'threatening speech, full of all moral blunders, yet amiable in some views. He showed himself to labour with feelings, as if he was the legitimate guardian of property. Lord Stanhope's a wild speech. Lord Hawkesbury spoke honourably and handsomely. Westmoreland, like himself, coarse and bullying, but not without talent. Grenville like a man of high and honourable principles, who, like a truly great statesman, regarded right and politic as identical.'[9]

The debate closed with the adjournment of the question. But though Mr. Wilberforce reluctantly agreed to this arrangement, he proposed to prohibit at once, by a resolution of the House of Commons, the supply of the conquered colonies with slaves. This, after ' a conference in Palace Yard—Brougham, Grant, Babington, William Smith, Henry Thornton, and Macaulay,' he gave up on an engagement to stop that branch of the trade by royal proclamation, freely made by Pitt. The delay which intervened before this promise was redeemed, was the one blot on that great man's treatment of this cause. For, in spite of Mr. Wilberforce's repeated entreaties, on one excuse or another, a year elapsed before, under the threat of instant parliamentary proceedings, the Proclamation issued.

All this time the claims of business, of charity, and of hospitable kindness, drew largely upon his time and strength.

[7] Diary, June 28.   [8] To Rev. Thomas Gisborne, Oct. 18.   [9] Diary.

'May 18. Called Pitt's—warned him about East Indian system of aggrandizement, pursued by Lord Wellesley. Settled Apprentice Bill.—13th. Went to hear Hall at meeting—very energetic and simply vehement, on 1 Tim.—" Glorious gospel." He seemed to labour with a sense of the weight and importance of his subject. Truly evangelical also. Excellent indeed—language simple—thoughts just, deep, and often elevated—excelling in experimental applications of Scripture, often with immense effect—begins calmly and simply, warms as proceeds, till vehement, and energetic, and impassioned. All of us struck with him. Simeon with us—his first hearing of Hall.—14th. Breakfast at Henry Thornton's to meet Hall—Hannah More and Patty. Hall very clever, unaffected, and pleasing in conversation. Town —Hatchard's—Suppression of Vice Society—read their report of proceedings—highly useful. Lord Radstock had in a month got them about 153 members, many of them of high rank. Home—letters—House—dined Carrington's to meet Llandaff. Ferguson, Mahon, &c. Mahon seems well disposed and independent in mind and ways of thinking. Summoned to town on Spanish sequestration business. Saw Pitt for some time, and afterwards Harrowby, and talked with him much about West Indian (Dessalines') cruelties. Back to Bloomfield, and dined — Stephen, and Brougham, Teignmouth, &c.'

'July 6. Dined home—Pitt, Lord Camden, Lord Carleton, Rose, Foster, John Villiers, C. Noel, Lord Harrowby— but a dull day. Pitt not in spirits : I very poorly.—9th. To town, having an appointment with Pitt, who had answered my last letter in a very friendly way—really affectionate, as I am sure I felt and acted towards him. Brougham and Grant dined—much talk. Brougham very unassuming, animated, and apparently well inclined to religion.'

' 30th. Morning, breakfast—friends about sending the gospel to the Indians. Mr. Norton's Mohawk's dance— Venn, Dealtry, Cookson, John Thornton—much discussion. We are all extremely struck with Mr. Norton, the Mohawk chief (Teyoninhokarawen); his blended modesty and self-possession; his good sense and apparent simple propriety of demeanour. May it be a providential incident thrown in my way to send the gospel to those ill-used people.'

In the beginning of September, he moved with his family [1] to Lyme, in Dorsetshire, where he 'hoped to enjoy something of to me the greatest of all luxuries, as well as the best of all medicines, quiet.' 'The place,' he tells Mr. Babington,[2] 'suits me mightily: a bold coast, a fine sea view—the clouds often shrouding the tops of the cliffs; a very varied surface of ground; a mild climate, and either fresh air or sheltered walks as you please. I allow myself two or three hours open air daily, and have enjoyed more than one solitary stroll with a Testament, a Cowper, or a Psalter, for my companion. We have not had one call since we came.' 'I never was at any place where I had so much the command of my own time, and the power of living as I please. Only two calls from Justice Tucker.'[3] He delighted to exchange the bustle of his public life for this domestic privacy. He 'read much out of doors, and wrote with a pencil,'[4] and 'had many a delightful walk along the hoarse-resounding shore, meditating on better things than poor blind Homer knew or sung of.'[5]

Yet this was no idle time. 'Much employed,' he says, 'in answering an immense arrear of letters, and continual fresh masses coming in. Wrote an article for the Edinburgh Review,—answer to Defence of the Slave Trade on Grounds of Humanity.' 'Also for Christian Observer—a review of Lord Chatham's Letters; a paper on Baxter; and another, introductory to a Narrative Series.' 'Corresponding with Lord Harrowby; and with Brougham, who had offered to shape his course in a continental tour, so as to make his excursion of use to the great question of Abolition, in Holland, Germany, or the great scenes of bondage (as it is called), Poland, Russia, and Hungary.'[6]

[1] His whole family consisted of four sons and two daughters : William, born 1798; Barbara, born 1799; Elizabeth, born 1801; Robert Isaac, born 1802; Samuel, born 1805; Henry William, born 1807.
[2] Sept. 15.　　　[3] Diary, Dec. 31.　　　[4] Diary.
[5] Letter to Hannah More, Sept. 15. Vide Correspondence, &c.
[6] Letter from Henry Brougham, Esq., July 5.

Three months had passed happily away, and the session of
Parliament was soon to recommence.   Politics had reached
Lyme only as a distant sound.   ' Pitt,' he told Hannah More,
' is indefatigable in attending to the defence of the country.
I have my fears about our continental politics.'   The plans
which excited this misgiving issued during the following
campaign in the disastrous battle of Austerlitz.   ' Our language with foreign courts is, that if they will in good earnest
fall to work, we will help them with all our means, money, &c.;
but that we will not thank them for half measures.'

' I saw Pitt,' he writes to Mr. Bankes,[7] ' not long ago, and
then his language concerning continental connexions was very
much what you and I should wish, except that it indicated
in our court a greater willingness to subsidize than you would
approve.   January 5 he ' heard from Pitt, that an opposition was expected the first day of the session,' and judged ' it
right to come up.'   The summons was brief and earnest :—
' I have hardly time for more than one word, and that
word, I am afraid, must be " *Come*," though I say so with
reluctance under the circumstances you mention.   But, by
my last accounts, Opposition is collecting all its force, and it
is therefore very important that we should secure as full an
attendance as possible.   There are a great many points on
which I shall be very impatient to talk with you, but on
which I have no time to write.   Harrowby is out of all
danger, but his general health, I am sorry to say, will make it
impossible for him to encounter any longer the fatigues of his
office.   The loss of his assistance will be a great misfortune,
but we must do as well as we can.   The person whom, on
the whole, I think best to succeed him is Mulgrave.'[8]

This call he at once obeyed, and on reaching town ' called
on Pitt, who told me of the offer of negotiation from
Buonaparte.   His schemes large and deep.   His hopes sanguine.'[9]   ' Parliament met on Tuesday, but Fox neutralized
by Windham and Grenville, and so said nothing of what he
would otherwise have given us.'[1]   The scene was again
shifting on the busy stage of politics.   ' You will, I know,'
he heard from Mr. Pitt, ' be glad, independent of politics,

[7] Oct. 4, 1804.   [8] Jan. 4, 1805.   [9] Diary, Jan. 14.   [1] Ib. Jan. 15.

that Addington and I have met as friends ; but I hope you will also not be sorry to hear that that event will lead to political re-union.' He was extremely pleased with this reconciliation between 'two friends who had no public ground of difference.' He was gratified too by Mr. Pitt's anxiety to acquaint him with it. 'It showed me that he understood my real feelings.' Upon February 1 he 'called on Pitt, and walked with him round the Park. Pleased with his statements of disposition not to quarrel with Addington.'[2] ' " I am sure," he said, " that you are glad to hear that Addington and I are at one again." And then he .added, with a sweetness of manner which I shall never forget, " I think they are a little hard upon us in finding fault with our making it up again, when we have been friends from our childhood, and our fathers were so before us, while they say nothing to Grenville for uniting with Fox, though they have been fighting all their lives." '

Even with Lord Sidmouth's following Mr. Pitt's majorities were feeble, and he wished to put aside all questions which could divide his friends. On this ground he pressed earnestly for the postponement of the Abolition question ; but Mr. Wilberforce would never 'make that holy cause subservient to the interest of a party ;' and being convinced that, to carry any measure through the House of Lords, he must begin at once, he gave notice of his motion on February 6. ' Pitt, to his honour, called, and was very kind about it.'[3] The Bill was ' read a first time on the 19th, and the second reading fixed for Thursday se'nnight.'[4] No fears were felt as to the House of Commons, but that night brought one of those reverses, by which his constancy was so often tried during the twenty years of this hard struggle, as on a division he was beat by 77 to 70. ' Great canvassing of our enemies, and several of our friends absent through forgetfulness, or accident, or engagements preferred from lukewarmness,'[5] whilst his usual supporters, Mr. Fox alone excepted, were silent.

This failure pained him deeply. ' I could not sleep well,' he says, 'after first waking at night. The poor blacks rushed

[2] Diary, Feb. 1.   [3] Ib. Feb. 7.   [4] Ib. Feb. 19.   [5] Ib. Feb. 28.

into my mind, and the guilt of our wicked land.'[6]   Yet he
had no doubts of his ultimate success.   He entered on the
following Sunday in his diary, 'O Lord, pity these children
of affliction, and terminate their unequalled wrongs ; and O
direct and guide me in this important conjuncture.'

'Alas !' he writes to Lord Muncaster,[7] 'from the fatal moment of our defeat on Thursday evening, I have had a damp
struck into my heart. I have had no spirits to write to you. . . .
I was in the situation of Lord Cornwallis in Virginia, among
lukewarm friends and active enemies.   Many of our friends,
more than enough to have turned the scale in their favour,
were absent.   Still I will do all I can.'

To prevent importation to the conquered colonies was his
immediate business. Much labour it cost him. From the first
Mr. Pitt assented to this measure, and being pressed by a meeting at which parliamentary action on the question was organ-
ized, undertook at once to stop the trade by proclamation.
Still by a habit of procrastination, which Mr. Wilberforce
complains was 'becoming absolutely predominant,' nothing
was done.   But he calmly persevered, and his patience was
at last rewarded. Lord Castlereagh had become Secretary of
State, and 'chiefly through his habits of business, though an
anti-Abolitionist, the cultivation of new lands in Guiana' was
'at length (Sept. 13) stopped. Thus for the time the trade was
greatly checked.   The old islands were the only markets for
our own ships ; whilst the colonies of Holland, France, and
Spain could only be supplied under the neutral colours of
America.'

The rejection of the Abolition Bill was succeeded by one
of the most painful questions of his parliamentary life.   Rumour had for some time impeached Lord Melville's integrity.
In February Mr. Wilberforce 'had much talk with Rose
about him.   Rose is confident Pitt will defend him, though
he tells me some stories (and strong ones) of jobs which
have fallen under his own view.   He says the Bishop of
Lincoln will not mention such matters to Pitt.'[8]

In this uncertainty all looked eagerly for the report of
the commissioners of naval inquiry, who had examined the

[6] Diary, March 1.   [7] London, March 4, 1805.   [8] Diary, Feb. 16.

charge. 'Melville had not mentioned the matter to Pitt, Huskisson, or any human being, till the report was printed.'[9] No one waited for it more anxiously than Mr. Pitt. Mr. Wilberforce was 'at his office about the Guiana Slave Trade' when 'the Tenth Report' came 'out, and Pitt was reading it for the first time.'[1] 'I shall never forget the way in which he seized it, and how eagerly he looked into the leaves without waiting even to cut them open.'[2] The report distinctly charged Mr. Trotter, Lord Melville's deputy paymaster, with misapplication of the public money, and warranted a strong suspicion that he had acted with the connivance of his principal. Public character evidently required that such offences should be dealt with by the strictest rules of justice. But party spirit intruded itself on the seat of judgment. Opposition seized eagerly so fair an opportunity of unseating Government; and Mr. Pitt, in spite of Mr. Wilberforce's remonstrances, was disposed to act rather as an advocate than as a judge. 'Bankes and I saw him on Melville's business—we talked with him above an hour. Bankes very frank, and Pitt very good-humoured. It is melancholy to see Pitt's excellent understanding so befooled by less worthy associates. He evidently thinks that it may shake the Government. Thinks gaining time for men's minds to cool may do much.'[3]

Administration indeed could ill afford to lose the shrewd and practical talents of Lord Melville. But though this motive had its weight, it was not the chief cause of Mr. Pitt's present conduct. Still less was it, as was commonly supposed, the mere effect of personal attachment. 'I had perceived above a year before, that Lord Melville had not the power over Pitt's mind which he had once possessed. Pitt was taking me to Lord Camden's, and in our tête-à-tête he gave me an account of the negotiations which had been on foot to induce him to enter Addington's administration. When they quitted office in 1801, Dundas proposed taking as his motto, "Jam rude donatus." Pitt suggested to him that, having always been an active man, he would probably wish to come again into office, and that then his having taken such a motto would be made a ground for ridicule. Dundas

[9] Diary, March 29. [1] Ib. March 18. [2] Con. Mem. [3] Diary.

assented, and took another motto. Addington had not been long in office, before Pitt's expectation was fulfilled, and Dundas undertook to bring Pitt into the plan, which was to appoint some third person head, and bring in Pitt and Addington on equal terms under him. Dundas accordingly, confiding in his knowledge of all Pitt's ways and feelings, set out for Walmer Castle ; and, after dinner and port wine, began cautiously to open his proposals. But he saw it would not do, and stopped abruptly. " Really," said Pitt, with a sly severity, and it was almost the only sharp thing I ever heard him say of any friend, " I had not the curiosity to ask what I was to be."'[4]

But whatever alienation there had been before, it was now increased to actual coolness. ' While it was generally thought that Pitt defended Melville out of friendship, I knew that they were scarcely upon speaking terms.'[5] Pitt had been wounded by his conduct in the tenderest point ; his own honour had been trifled with, and his confidence abused. ' Some years before Mr. Raikes[6] had hinted to him that the public money was illegally employed. Dundas soon after coming in, Pitt said to him at once, " Dundas, here has been Tom Raikes with a long story of your way of employing the public money ; what does he mean ?" Dundas assured him that it was their mistake, and that no money had been drawn except for public service. When, therefore, the fact came out, Pitt seemed to a degree involved in Melville's fault.'[7] He was, of course, persuaded of Lord Melville's personal integrity. Pitt ' says he is quite sure that there was no real pocketing of public money. All say that he has acted like a fool, though so able at other times.'[8] ' In truth Pitt was chiefly led into supporting Melville by that false principle of honour which was his great fault—he fancied himself bound in honour to defend one who had so long acted with him.'[9]

This was a principle on which Wilberforce could not act. Honour, and still less mere party spirit, fixed for him no standard. ' I have difficult and trying questions before me in

[4] Con. Mem.   [5] Ib.   [6] The Governor of the Bank.
[7] Con. Mem.   [8] Diary, April 3.   [9] Con. Mem.

Parliament,' is the language of his private journal; 'I will pray for wisdom, and pursue the path dictated by conscience, and then peace will follow. Lord, give me wisdom. Do Thou enable me to act, to-morrow, honestly and uprightly, without fear of man, or any other unlawful motive. O Lord, give me Thy wisdom, and set me above this world and all that it contains.' He felt deeply the importance of maintaining, at all costs, a high standard of integrity in public men ; and viewed with peculiar indignation any tendency in Parliament to screen such delinquents for party purposes. Thus in the debate on the debt of Mr. Fordyce,[1] he bitterly complains of 'the most shabby conduct of Opposition, because Lords Rockingham and North concerned—Crevey shied off—Pitt rathèr high.'[2] This led him, in Lord Melville's case, to a strict and judicial scrutiny of all the charges. And when, upon April 8, Mr. Whitbread moved the Resolutions for censuring Lord Melville, he anxiously watched the debate, hoping that some good defence might be established. But, in his judgment, the defence failed; and at last he rose reluctantly to urge the claims of justice. He sat upon the continuation of the Treasury bench, and as he turned towards the chair, looked just across Mr. Pitt, who was watching with intense earnestness to catch the first intimation of the line which he would take. 'It required no little effort to resist the fascination of that penetrating eye, from which Lord Erskine was always thought to shrink.'[3] He stated simply, but forcibly, his impression of Lord Melville's fault, and then impressed upon the House the importance of its deciding on the strictest grounds of justice. 'Let us bear in mind the weighty words of Clarendon in the case of ship-money. The people of England disliked greatly the levying of the money; but they endured it until the judges had wrongfully decided in its favour.' 'A stormy night,' he says on reaching home. 'I spoke late, and from the state of men's minds, with a good deal of effect—216 and 216, and the Speaker decided against Government—adjourned at half-past five. Could not get cool in body or mind.'

His speech was remarkably effective. It appealed boldly

[1] March 19.   [2] Diary.   [3] Con. Mem.

from the cry of party to those high principles of conduct by which, after many doubts, his course had been determined. 'Bankes and I long doubtful what part we should take about Lord Melville, but at length clear, and Abbot, whom he consulted, clear also.'[4] He carried with him the decision of the House. 'The success of the motion seemed doubtful' (wrote Sir John Legard at the next election, as a reason why he could not vote for him), 'or rather, I believe, appearances indicated that it would be thrown out, when you rose, and, supported by a well-earned reputation for integrity and independence, made a speech which at the time was said to influence forty votes. I was told by a member who was present, that Mr. Pitt could not conceal his agitation when he saw the turn your speech was taking; and I believe that the delinquency of Lord Melville, and the desertion of some of his oldest friends, inflicted a wound upon his mind which it never recovered, and contributed to his premature death.'[5]

'I am much abused,' he says at the time, 'by Melville's friends.[6] Sir Charles Middleton told me that I was charged with Melville's removal. I feel hurt at having been thought to wound, yet I have acted rightly, and that is the only stay.' 'Pitt,' he tells Lord Muncaster,[7] 'feels it deeply. I never saw him so *quailed* as on Wednesday night, and part of Monday also; and this in my opinion did him honour, by proving, that though so invincibly firm when all was well within, he could not put a good face on it when his own conscience told him he was defending a bad cause. Sir Charles Middleton told me that Lord Melville had advised Pitt to recommend him to the King for first Lord of the Admiralty. He would be most likely to carry forward Lord Melville's plans, which are in fact Sir Charles's, for the naval force of the kingdom. It is to Lord Melville's honour.'[8]

The House adjourned for one day after this debate, and resumed the subject on the 10th. 'Rafflement whether Whitbread's Bill pressed, for removing Melville from presence and counsels for ever, though Pitt had begun by stating that

[4] Diary.
[5] He has docketed this letter, 'Sir J. Legard—very frank—blaming my conduct about Lord Melville. It did not injure Pitt's health.'
[6] Diary, April 18.   [7] April 13, 1805.   [8] Diary, April 12.

he had resigned. Opposition only determined for it this morning, but now argued as if clearly understood since Monday. Bankes and I deprecated division, and at length it was agreed to lay the Resolutions at the foot of the throne by the whole House.'[9]

His diary just notes the first steps of this most painful case. 'April 29. Spencer Stanhope's motion for civil, Bankes's for criminal, prosecution; Pitt's for a committee of inquiry: I took part.—30th. Debate about committee by ballot and Lord Castlereagh's name; foolish to make it a controversy.—May 2. Thanks to commissioners, which I amended. Opposition very civil.—4th. How foolish of Pitt not to join with Opposition in making proceedings against Melville public; appointing committee by name, not ballot. —6th. Whitbread's motion for striking Melville out of the council. When reached House found Pitt had anticipated wisely.' On the 27th the Committee presented its Report, confirming all the former charges, and stating that, concerning one sum of 10,000*l.*, no account was given by Lord Melville. He now desired to defend himself before the House of Commons; and on June 10, Mr. Wilberforce proceeds, 'I am doubtful how to act in Lord Melville's affair to-morrow.—11th. Duchess of Gordon sending for me to Bankes's. Lord Melville heard. I much affected at first. Excessively absurd speech. Debate till three o'clock. Whitbread able. I moved adjournment.—12th. Criminal prosecution agreed on in preference to impeachment; Opposition's motion. Addington's party supported criminal prosecution. Neither Pitt nor Fox spoke. Melville's declaration, that never had nor would tell any man how the 10,000*l.* or 20,000*l.* went, did him great injury.—25th. The House sat late on changing the criminal proceedings against Melville to impeachment, which carried. A very unwise proceeding, rendering even an acquittal by impeachment scarcely an acquittal.'[1]

Through all these questions he was discharging a most painful duty, for Lord Melville had been for years his intimate acquaintance. But he deemed he had no choice,

[9] Diary, April 10.   [1] Ib.

' as to the necessity of marking strongly our sense of such an instance of misconduct, the rather because in truth it is not religion, but popular opinion, which among us at this day is the general standard of practice.' But once in these proceedings he felt it right to act upon his inclinations ; he would not join the deputation which carried up the Resolutions to St. James's.

These friendly feelings for Lord Melville had been always blended with disapprobation of his principles. ' Pitt's connection with Dundas was his great misfortune. Dundas was a loose man ; yet he was a fine fellow in some things. People have thought him a mean, intriguing creature; but he was in many respects a fine, warm-hearted fellow.'

Wilberforce's treatment by Lord Melville after these public storms, was an instance of this better nature. ' We did not meet for a long time, and all his connections most violently abused me. About a year before he died, we met in the stone passage which leads from the Horse Guards to the Treasury. We came suddenly upon each other, just in the open part where the light struck upon our faces. We saw one another, and at first I thought he was passing on, but he stopped and called out, "Ah, Wilberforce, how do you do?" and gave me a hearty shake by the hand. I would have given a thousand pounds for that shake. I never saw him afterwards.'

' May 13. Fox's motion ' on ' Catholic Emancipation. Grattan amazingly eloquent. Duigenan hard and rough, but forcible and much matter. Adjourned at half-past two. —Tuesday. House till half-past four. Catholic Emancipation, carried against, 336 to 124. Babington and I in majority. H. Thornton, minority—very uncomfortable.'

The session of Parliament closed in the middle of July, but family circumstances detained him in the neighbourhood of London. It was a gloomy period. 'Alas ! alas ! earth is but earth, and its inhabitants earthly. O heaven, heaven, thou seat of perfect love and holiness, where all infirmities will be done away.'[2] ' I have no comfort[3] in public affairs.' ' With the experience of the last war fresh in my recollection,

---

[2] Diary, July 21.   [3] Letter to Mrs. H. More.

how can I participate in those visions of glory, in which I fear a friend[4] of mine is even still ready to indulge.' On these reflections broke suddenly the news of the great victory of Trafalgar, and he did but share the feelings of the nation at the news of Nelson's victory and death, when he was so 'overcome that he could not go on reading for tears.'[5]

The rejoicings for this victory were soon chastened by 'the sad news of the entire defeat of the Austrians and Russians at Austerlitz. God can preserve us—apparently we shall be in the most imminent danger.' But one consequence of this blow he did not anticipate. Throughout this autumn his intercourse with Mr. Pitt had been more than usually frequent and affectionate. He often 'drove into town to see Pitt;' and 'had much talk with him upon political topics, finding him very open and kind.'[6] He was therefore the less prepared for the great loss which was now before him. —'Jan. 21. To London on Parliament's meeting. Heard sad account of Pitt, and Opposition put off intended amendment.' Austerlitz had struck the fatal blow, and a tie was about to be severed to which Mr. Wilberforce had owed much of the influence, and many of the difficulties, of his earlier years.—'22nd. Quite unsettled and uneasy about Pitt, so to town. Heard bad account. Called on Rose, who quite overcome. He had been long at Putney talking to Bishop of Lincoln. Physicians said all was hopeless.—23rd. Heard from Bishop of Lincoln that Pitt had died about half past-four in the morning. Deeply affected by it. Pitt killed by the enemy as much as Nelson. Babington went to dine at Lord Teignmouth's, but I had no mind to go out.'[7]

'There is something,' he writes to Lord Muncaster, 'peculiarly affecting in the time and circumstances of Pitt's death. I have, times without number, hoped that a quiet interval would be afforded him, perhaps in the evening of life, in which he and I might confer freely on the most important of all subjects. But the scene is closed—for ever.'

'I have heard, not without surprise, that his debts are considerable, a sum was named as large as 40,000*l.* or 50,000*l.*

---

[4] Mr. Pitt.   [5] Diary.   [6] Ib.   [7] Ib.

This must have been roguery,[8] for he really has not for many years lived at a rate of more than 5,000*l*. or 6,000*l*. per annum. I do not say this lightly; and he has had an income, since he got the Cinque Ports, of 10,000*l*. per annum. An idea was proposed of the nation's paying them; but, considering the time and circumstances in which he died, and the situation of the country, the burdens which must be laid on, and the sacrifices which must be borne, I should fear that—however, through the mutual connivance of parties (Grenville related to Pitt, Fox, Windham, &c., connected with Grenville), it might be carried in the House of Commons—it might be grudgingly paid by the people at large, and create a feeling very injurious to his memory.

'But again. To whom are the debts due? If to tradesmen they ought to be paid; but might not debts to other sort of people, rich connections, &c., be suspected; and the very idea of the people's paying these is monstrous. . . . Considering the number of affluent men[9] connected with Pitt, some of whom have got great and lucrative places from him, I cannot doubt but that, with perfect privacy and delicacy, a subscription might be made, adequate to the purpose. This late event saddens rather than softens my heart. There is something weighing down to the spirits. I am not in a humour to bear the babble of the day, so I keep quiet here, and therefore know nothing about parties.'

His own generosity made him sanguine as to the success of such an attempt, and on the afternoon of the same day he wrote :[1] 'I will consider how I can best promote the private plan, of the success of which I have no doubt. I am only anxious measures should be taken with delicacy.'

'I have this instant seen the papers, and will certainly attend;[2] but I must say it would have been better in my

---

[8] In the year 1786, Mr. Pitt had requested Mr. Robert Smith to examine his private affairs, which even then were somewhat embarrassed. A letter from Mr. Smith to Mr. Wilberforce fully bears out the opinion expressed in the text.

[9] A list of sixty-three persons, who might be expected to contribute, appears among Mr. Wilberforce's papers.

[1] To the Right Hon. George Rose.

[2] Mr. Lascelles' motion for a public funeral for Mr. Pitt.

Ellenborough. Erskine talking friendly to me, but always absenting himself. Lord Fitzwilliam I am not quite sure, but I think favourable. Windham contra. But the great point would be to get if possible the royal family to give up their opposition.'

Anxious as he was for the support of the Ministry on the subject, he opposed one of their first acts. ' I feel strongly,' he tells Mr. Babington, ' the mischievous effects of making the Chief Justice of England a politician, by giving him for the first time a seat in the Cabinet.' 'So far as regards Lord Ellenborough himself, I should welcome the introduction into the motley Cabinet which has been now formed, of his love of good order, his vigorous understanding, his undaunted firmness; and, so far as I know them, I am disposed to add, his sound constitutional principles. But whether the mischievous consequences of subjecting the decisions of our courts of justice to the influence of party attachments be considered, or the producing in the public mind a general persuasion that this bias exists, it seems to me the most injurious blow our constitution has sustained since the revolution.'[2] These objections he declared in the debate upon the subject on March 3, without causing any alienation between the Lord Chief Justice and himself. Their friendly intercourse had been maintained since their meeting on the continent in the summer of 1785; and he now 'wrote to Lord Ellenborough on the evils of his having a Cabinet office, thinking it most manly and fair to state objections to himself'[3] He 're-turned a very handsome answer;' and, when quitting office thirteen months later, he again alluded in a friendly manner to Mr. Wilberforce's opposition : 'Well, Wilberforce, I hope I have not done much mischief after all.'

The new Government entered heartily into his Abolition views. He describes Fox as 'quite rampant and playful, as he was twenty-two years ago, when not under any awe of his opponents. Consulting about Abolition. Fox and Lord Henry Petty talked as if we might certainly carry our question in the House of Commons, but should certainly

---

[2] Letter to Henry Bankes, Esq.   [3] Diary, Feb. 4.

lose it in the House of Lords.   This looks but ill, as if they wished to please us, and yet not forfeit Prince of Wales's favour, and that of G. R. and other anti-abolitionists.'[4]   The sincerity of Mr. Fox he never questioned ; and he learned afterwards that 'the Prince had given his honour to Fox, not to stir. adversely.'[5]   The prospect was now brightening. 'Our Slave business rather mends.   William Smith saw Lord Moira, who will confer with the Prince of Wales.'[6] After many conferences, in the following week, 'with Lord Grenville, Lord Sidmouth, Fox, Lord Henry Petty, Stephen,'[7] he determined that a Bill for the prohibition of the Foreign Slave Trade should precede his general measure.   This Bill having passed the Commons, was carried triumphantly through the Lords on May 10.   'I saw our strength,' says Lord Grenville, 'and thought the occasion was favourable for launching out a little beyond what the measure itself actually required.   I really think a foundation is laid for doing more and sooner than I have for a long time allowed myself to hope.'[8]   'We have carried the Foreign Slave Bill,' was Mr. Wilberforce's reflection on the following Sunday.   'Meeting Fox at Lord Grenville's, and holding some anxious consultations with them, and also with' his 'own friends about the ex- pediency of proposing the general question this year,' he 'most reluctantly gave up the idea on Lord Grenville's sure opinion, that no chance this session in the House of Lords ; the bishops going out of town, &c.   But we are to have a general resolution for Abolition both in Commons and Lords.   How wonderful are the ways of God, and how are we taught to trust not in man but in Him !   Though intimate with Pitt for all my life since earliest manhood, and he most warm for Abolition, and really honest ; yet now my whole human dependence is placed on Fox, to whom through life opposed, and on Grenville, to whom always rather hostile till of late years, when I heard he was

---

[4] Diary, March 5.
[5] W. Smith, Esq., to W. Wilberforce, Esq., Nov. 17.
[6] Diary, March 13.   [7] Diary.
[8] To W. Wilberforce, Esq., May 17.

me. Then I spoke, and satisfactorily, but forgot much I meant to say. Then Fawkes, able, but rather too florid. All quiet.'[7]

After the election he paid a few visits omitted during his brief canvass, and before the beginning of December was settled at Broomfield, and again at hard work, upon a book upon the Slave Trade, which he finished by 'a great effort about six o'clock on the 27th: it is to be out upon the 31st, by dint of extreme exertion, and sent to the Lords.'[8]

He had expected much from the critical appearance of this book; and he was not disappointed. 'Its beneficial effect,' writes Mr. Roscoe,[9] 'could not escape the observation of anyone, who attended the discussion in the Lords.'

On the progress of his measure in that House his thoughts were now concentrated. The approaching debate called for every exertion. 'Grenville,' he says, 'told me yesterday he could not count more than fifty-six, yet had taken pains, written letters, &c. The Princes canvassing against us, alas.'[1] It seemed clear that he would have no easy triumph. Two Cabinet ministers never withdrew their opposition, and the Dukes of Clarence and of Sussex declared openly against the Bill, speaking, as it was understood, the sentiments of all the reigning family. Yet the ice of prejudice was rapidly dissolving; and when he visited Lord Grenville on the morning of the debate, 'he went over the list of peers, and was sanguine, counting on above seventy in all.'[2] The same evening came the crisis of the struggle. House of Lords, Abolition Bill till five in the morning, when carried, 72 and 28 proxies to 28 and 6 proxies. Grenville's famous speech. Lord Selkirk spoke most sensibly, but with so low a voice that he could scarce be heard. Our old friend Lord Eldon grieved me. Sidmouth fretted and hurt me. Westmoreland bespattered me; but really it was a double pleasure to be praised by Lord Grenville and abused by Lord Westmoreland. The Duke of Clarence was less

---

[7] Diary, Nov. 6.   [8] Diary.   [9] To W. Wilberforce, Esq., Feb. 16.
[1] Diary, Jan. 31.   [2] Ib. Feb. 3.

fluent, at least less able, than formerly. Our success altogether greatly surpassed my expectations.'

'Lord Grenville,' he writes to Lord Muncaster, 'has acted
nobly, and he deserves the more praise, because for many
years I did not behave so well to him, nor even think so
well of him, as I ought to have done. Also his natural
temper is not that of warmth. The high tone of morals
which he took may be essentially beneficial to the country,
as it was truly honourable to himself. The young Duke of
Gloucester did himself very great credit, both for talents
and principles. Lord Moira's speech was also excellent.

The next day he was at the 'House of Lords. Bill in
Committee. Opponents wanting us to strike out from the
preamble, " justice and humanity." Lord Lauderdale very
good.'[3] He had given notice in the Commons, on January
29, that if it was delayed he should there originate a corresponding measure. But it passed rapidly the Upper House;
and, on February 10, 'came from the Lords. A few words
from Gascoigne, Hibbert, &c. and Lord Howick.'[4]

'I receive,' he records February 11, ' congratulations from
all, as if all done. Yet I cannot be sure. May it please
God to give us success. Lord Grenville's speech concluded
with a most handsome compliment to me, and several peers
now speak with quite new civility. How striking to observe
Pitt and Fox both dead before Abolition effected, and now
Lord Grenville, without any particular deference from Court,
carries it so triumphantly! But let us not be too sure.'[5]
Again the next day—'An Abolition Committee. Looking
at the list of the House of Commons. A terrific list of
doubtfuls. Lord Grenville not confident on looking at
Abolition list; yet I think we shall carry it too. Several
West Indians with us. How popular Abolition is just
now! God can turn the hearts of men;'[6] and, two days
latei,[7] 'The decision of the great question approaches.
May it please God, who has the hearts of all in His hands,
to turn them as in the House of Lords; and enable me to
have a single eye, and a simple heart, desiring to please

[3] Diary, Feb. 4.   [4] Diary.   [5] Ib. Feb. 11.
[6] Ib. Feb. 13.   [7] Journal, Sunday, Feb. 15.

God, to do good to my fellow-creatures, and to testify my gratitude to my adorable Redeemer.'

During the following week, counsel was heard against the Bill. But opposition now brought out more clearly the strength of the Abolitionists. 'Lord Howick in earnest and very pleasing. Our prospects brighten.'[8] On the day before the second reading, he says, 'Never surely had I more cause for gratitude than now, when carrying the great object of my life, to which a gracious Providence directed my thoughts twenty-six or twenty-seven years ago, and led my endeavours in 1787 or 1788. O Lord, let me praise Thee with my whole heart: for never surely was there any one so deeply indebted as myself; which way soever I look I am crowded with blessings. Oh may my gratitude be in some degree proportionate.'[9]

It was in this spirit that he entered the House on February 23. 'Busy for Lord Howick in the morning. Friends dined before House. Slave Trade debate. Lord Howick opened—embarrassed and not at ease, but argued ably. Astonishing eagerness of House; six or eight starting up to speak at once, young noblemen, &c., and asserting high principles of rectitude. Lord Milton very well. Fawkes finish, but too much studied, and cut and dried. Solicitor-General excellent; and at length contrasted my feelings, returning to my private roof, and receiving the congratulations of my friends, and laying my head on my pillow, &c., with Buonaparte's, encircled with kings his relatives. It quite overcame me.'[1] The House was little less affected by Sir Samuel Romilly's address. When he entreated the young members of parliament to let this day's event be a lesson to them, how much the rewards of virtue exceeded those of ambition; and then contrasted the feelings of the Emperor of the French in all his greatness with those of that honoured man, who would this day lay his head upon his pillow and remember that the Slave Trade was no more; the whole House, surprised into a forgetfulness of its ordinary habits, burst forth into acclamations of applause. They had seen the unwearied assiduity with which, during

[8] Diary, Feb. 20.   [9] Journal, Sunday, Feb. 22.   [1] Diary, Feb. 23.

twenty years, he seemed to have exhausted in vain all the counsels of wisdom; and when they saw him entering with a prosperous gale the port whence he had been so often driven, they welcomed him with applause 'such as was scarcely ever before given,' says Bishop Porteus, 'to any man sitting in his place in either House of Parliament.'[2] So full was his heart of its own deep thoughts of thankfulness that he scarcely noticed these unusual honours. 'Is it true,' Mr. Hey asked him,[3] 'that the House gave you three cheers upon the conclusion of the Solicitor-General's speech? And if so, was not this an unprecedented effusion of approbation?' 'To the questions you ask me,' he replies,[4] 'I can only say that I was myself so completely overpowered by my feelings when he touched so beautifully on my domestic reception, (which had been precisely realised a few evenings before, on my return from the House of Lords,) that I was insensible to all that was passing around me.'

The debate proceeded with little show of opposition, except from one West Indian planter, who gave him an opportunity of replying in a speech 'distinguished for splendour of eloquence and force of argument;'[5] and then came the cheering issue. 'At length divided, 283 to 16. A good many came over to Palace Yard after House up, and congratulated me. John Thornton and Heber, Sharpe, Macaulay, Grant and Robert Grant, Robert Bird and William Smith, who in the gallery.'[6] It was a triumphant meeting. 'Let us make out the names of these sixteen miscreants; I have four of them,' said William Smith. Mr. Wilberforce, kneeling, as was his wont, upon one knee at the crowded table, looked up hastily from the note which he was writing—'Never mind the miserable 16; let us think of our glorious 283.' This was Reginald Heber's first introduction to Mr. Wilberforce. Heber had entered the room with a strong suspicion of his principles,[7] but he left it saying to his friend

2 Hodgson's Life of Porteus, p. 221.
3 To W. Wilberforce, Esq., Feb. 28.   4 To W. Hey, Esq. March 2.
5 Ann. Reg.   6 Diary, Feb. 23.
7 Heber had resided in the same parish with Sir Richard Hill, and he had imagined that his sentiments, which he deemed disaffected to the Church, were shared by Mr. Wilberforce.

John Thornton, 'How an hour's conversation can dissolve the prejudice of years!' Perhaps his witnessing this night the Christian hero in his triumph after the toil of years, may have helped his gaining afterwards the martyr crown at Trichinopoly.

'How astonishing,' says Mr. Wilberforce, 'is our success, and the eagerness and zeal of the House now, when the members have been so fastidious as scarce to hear a speech about it! Rose and Castlereagh went away without dividing. Roscoe mild, quiet, unaffected, and sensible. Poor Muncaster[8] came up. Brougham useful to Lord Howick about Slave Trade. Everybody taking me by the hand, and several voting with us for the first time.'

The victory was thus gained, but its fruits were to be gathered in with care. Lord Grenville had written, 'suggesting the expediency of taking advantage of their present strength to render the Bill as perfect as possible,'[9] and desiring to see the clauses prepared.

First as this cause stood in his interest, yet he would not advance it by any compromise of principle, and at the risk of losing their aid, he took an active part in opposing the increased grant which Ministers designed for the Roman Catholic College at Maynooth. Popery, he was convinced, was the bane of Ireland, and he deemed it nothing less than infatuation to take any steps for its encouragement. This opinion he fearlessly asserted. ' I am not,' he said,[1] 'one of those men who entertain the large and liberal views on religious subjects, insisted on with so much energy by the honourable gentlemen on the other side; I am not so much like a certain ruler, of whom it has upon a late occasion been so happily said, that he was an honorary member of all religions.' It was much to the credit of the Government that this open opposition in no degree diminished their zeal for Abolition. Upon the 16th came on the third reading. ' 18th. Carried up the Bill to the Lords;' at which time it

---

[8] Lady Muncaster had died Nov. 23.
[9] Lord Howick to W. Wilberforce, Esq., Feb. 25.
[1] Diary, March 4.

was supposed to be 'clear that Government was out, or as good as out.'[2]

But the honour of passing such a measure was not to be reserved for the new Administration. Upon the 23rd of March the Bill was passed. 'Lord Westmoreland's coarse opposition. Lord Grenville's congratulation ;' and two days afterwards it 'received the royal assent . . . the Lord Chancellor, Lord Auckland, and Lord Holland being the Royal Commissioners,' . . . and passed into a law. It was the last act of the expiring Ministry.

And now his labours were indeed completed, and congratulations poured in upon him from every quarter. ' To speak,' wrote Sir James Mackintosh from the other Indies,[3] ' of fame and glory to Mr. Wilberforce, would be to use a language far beneath him ; but he will surely consider the effect of his triumph on the fruitfulness of his example. Who knows whether the greater part of the benefit that he has conferred on the world (the greatest that any individual has had the means of conferring), may not be the encouraging example that the exertions of virtue may be crowned by such splendid success ? We are apt petulantly to express our wonder that so much exertion should be necessary to suppress such flagrant injustice. The more just reflection will be, that a short period of the short life of one man is, well and wisely directed, sufficient to remedy the miseries of millions for ages. Benevolence has hitherto been too often disheartened by frequent failures ; hundreds and thousands will be animated by Mr. Wilberforce's example, by his success, and (let me use the word only in the moral sense of preserving his example) by a renown that can only perish with the world, to attack all the forms of corruption and cruelty that scourge mankind. Oh what twenty years in the life of one man those were which abolished the Slave Trade ! How precious is time ! How valuable and dignified is human life, which in general appears so base and miserable ! How noble and sacred is human nature, made capable of achieving such truly great exploits !'

No selfish exultation disturbed his heartfelt joy. 'God

[2] Diary, March 18.　　　　　[3] Bombay, July 27, 1807.

will bless this country,' was his almost prophetic declaration. 'The first authentic account of the defeat of the French has come to-day.' 'The course of events' hitherto had been 'such as human wisdom and human force' had 'in vain endeavoured to control or resist. The counsels of the wise' had 'been infatuated, the valour of the brave turned to cowardice. Though the storm' had 'been raging for many years, yet instead of having ceased, it' appeared 'to be increasing in fury; the clouds which' had 'long been gathering around' had, 'at length, almost overspread the whole face of the heavens with blackness. In this very moment of unexampled difficulty and danger, those great political characters, to the counsels of the one or the other of whom the nation' had 'been used to look in all private exigencies,' had 'both been taken from us.'[4] But from this time the tide was turned. In the very year which closed this hateful traffic, that series of events began, which ended in the victories of Wellington and the fall of Buonaparte.

For himself, all selfish triumph was lost in unfeigned gratitude to God. 'I have indeed inexpressible reasons for thankfulness on the glorious result of that struggle which, with so many eminent fellow-labourers, I have so long maintained. I cannot account for the fervour which happily has taken the place of that fastidious, well-bred lukewarmness which used to display itself on this subject, except by supposing it to be produced by that Almighty Power who can influence at will the judgment and affections of men.[5]

'Oh what thanks do I owe the Giver of all good, for bringing me in His gracious providence to this great cause, which at length, after almost nineteen years' labour, is successful!'[6]

[4] Letter to the Freeholders of Yorkshire.
[5] To the Rev. Francis Wrangham.   [6] Journal, March 22.

CHAPTER XVII.

MARCH 1807 TO DECEMBER 1808.

*Change of Ministers—Wilberforce's embarrassment—His judgment of the
plan of encouraging Popery—Parliament suddenly dissolved—Hon.
Henry Lascelles and Lord Milton candidates for Yorkshire—Magnitude of the contest — Extraordinary canvass—Immense subscription for
Wilberforce—His speech at Hull—He is lowest on the poll, but soon
heads his competitors—Zeal and liberality of his friends—His review
of his success—Brighton—Attack on Copenhagen—Return to Broomfield—John Bowdler—New session—Roman Catholic question—Spanish
patriots—Eastbourne—Settlement at Kensington Gore.*

MR. WILBERFORCE had anxiously watched the steps which
led to the rupture of the Ministry with the King.

' 20th. Called at Lord Grenville's, who explained to me
all the business, and showed me the King's and the Cabinet's
letters. The Ministry gave up all ; but reserved the right
both of stating their own private opinion, and of proposing
from time to time, such measures as they might deem necessary for the well-being of the country. Peace will
probably be made between France and Russia this winter,
and then Buonaparte will bend the whole force of his
empire against us, and invade Ireland. Then, it is said,
unless we can appease the Roman Catholics, what hope
have we of stemming the torrent? Still I feel no comfort
in grounding our safety on such a bottom. On this the
King thought they would always be teasing him with
some new proposition, and taking any favourable occasion
for pressing their measure ; ergo, better decide at once.
He asked Lord Grenville whether the opinion he had
stated was the final decision of the Cabinet, and on their
saying, Yes ; "Then," said the King, "I must look about
me."'

The change of Government involved him in peculiar difficulties. He was bound by his general principles to support

the new Ministry. He was, moreover, 'impressed with a sense of the importance of not embarking on a Roman Catholic bottom, the interest and well-being of our Protestant empire.' Yet he could not support Mr. Perceval's administration without the appearance of ingratitude towards those who had assisted him so warmly in the Abolition struggle. Even to appear ungrateful gave him no little pain ; but the law of duty was absolute, and he obeyed it strictly, finding only a new proof that 'politics are a most unthankful business.' 'The debt of gratitude,' he told his constituents, 'which is due to the late Ministry from myself, I shall ever be ready to acknowledge, and by all legitimate methods to repay ; but I have no right to recompense their services by my parliamentary support. That is not mine to give or withhold at pleasure.'[1]

To Mr. Hey[2] he cautiously opened this increasing bias of his judgment. 'I am glad that I happened some time ago to state to Lord Grenville my difference of opinion as to the right policy to be observed towards the Roman Catholics in Ireland ; that after all you could grant them, so much would still remain behind as to prevent their being ever cordially attached to a Protestant Government, of which a Protestant church establishment formed a part ; that so long as the bulk of the Irish should be Roman Catholics, the Protestants and friends of Great Britain would be, in truth, a garrison in an enemy's country; and that our great endeavour ought to be to enlighten, and thereby, as I trust, to convert the Roman Catholics.'

'The late Ministers are rushing on, in my judgment, to their own destruction. Their policy as a party, as well as higher considerations, should urge them to moderation now.'

The majority of the new Government in the House of Commons had been so decided, that he was 'astonished by a letter from Perceval announcing a dissolution.' This was most unwelcome intelligence. The angry feelings which had cost Mr. Lascelles his election were by no means allayed

[1] Speech at York.   [2] London, April 2, 1807.

in Yorkshire; and party-spirit had been stirred to an unwonted pitch by late public events. He learned at once
that his former colleague would again take the field; that
Mr. Fawkes, though a man of large fortune, shrunk from
the expenses of a contest; and that Lord Milton came
forward in his place. No one could foresee the result of such
a collision. In their calmer hours, indeed, all moderate
men might think their own victory dearly purchased by the
loss of their independent representative; but such feelings
would be forgotten in the delirium of the conflict, while it
was more than probable that the leaders in the strife would
view, with no great dissatisfaction, a result which would
share again between their families the representation of the
county. Whatever was its issue, the contest must be ruinous
to any man of ordinary fortune. 'Lord Harewood' was
'ready to spend in it his whole Barbadoes property,'[3] and
Wentworth House was not less threatening in its preparations. Mr. Wilberforce's fortune would stand no such demands; 'and the plan of a subscription,' said a leading
politician in an adjoining county, 'may answer very well in
a borough, but it is hopeless where things must be conducted upon such a scale as in the county of York.' Many of
his friends dissuaded him from entering on the contest, but
the moral importance which he attached to it determined
him to stand the contest.

Few things pass more rapidly away than the interest of an
ordinary election contest. But that which engaged all Yorkshire in 1807 deserves a lasting remembrance. Even then it
stood alone; and as, since the legislation of 1833, it can
never be repeated, a more minute account of its events may
interest the future student of English manners in the beginning of the nineteenth century. Mr. Wilberforce left London
upon the 28th, and was immediately engaged in a hasty
canvass of the West Riding, traversing all its populous
parts with his usual rapidity and success. 'Time was,' as
he said the year before, 'when I did not dislike such scenes;'
but he had now reached a calmer age, and 'sickened
at a contest.'[4]

---

[3] Diary. [4] To Lord Muncaster.

The nomination came on at York upon the 13th, and nearly every hand was held up in his favour. 'Morritt's excellent speech. Lord Milton pretty well. I but middling —only in reply, so seemed spirited.' So far all was promising ; but how the expenses of the approaching contest could be safely met, was a most serious question. The nomination was followed by a meeting of his friends, at which this subject was brought forward. He at once 'declared that he never would expose himself to the imputation of endeavouring to make a seat in the House of Commons subservient to the repair of a dilapidated fortune.'[5] He called therefore upon the county to assert its independence. The appeal was replied to nobly. ' It is impossible,' said a gentleman, who rose as soon as he sat down, ' that we can desert Mr. Wilberforce, and therefore I put down my name for 500*l*.' This example spread ; about 18,000*l*. was immediately subscribed ; and it was resolved that his cause was a county object, and that he should not even be permitted to put down his name to the fund.

The next day he set off to canvass the East Riding. On reaching Hull he was met by a great body of freeholders at the hall at Sculcoates ; ' and when standing up to address them, it seemed,' says an eyewitness, 'as if he was struck by the scene before him—the fields and gardens where he had played as a boy, now converted into wharfs, or occupied by buildings ; and pouring forth the thoughts with which the change impressed him—the gradual alteration of external objects, and the still greater alteration which had taken place in themselves—he addressed the people with the most thrilling effect.'

The next day was Sunday. ' I walked with him,' says the Rev. Mr. Dykes, ' for a considerable time, and was much struck to see how totally he had dismissed from his mind all thoughts of the approaching contest. His conversation related entirely to subjects which suited the day. He seemed free from any sort of care about what was coming.'

He returned to York on the day of election, (Wednesday, May 20,) and here things assumed an unexpected aspect.

[5] Annual Register.

The show of hands was against him; and on that day he was second, the next lowest, on the poll. This was owing to want of conveyances, and to the impossibility of giving to volunteer supporters the order and arrangement of professional agents. 'There was among Lord Milton's friends, and in a degree among Mr. Lascelles's, a unity, discipline, and disposition to obey orders and act from a common impulse which belong to a formed party, and are found in proportion to the degree of party-spirit which prevails. We had nothing of this; but the exact opposite—a mixture in our cabinet of a number of heterogeneous particles, and no common impulse either felt or obeyed.'[6] But if the combinations of regular discipline were more prompt, the vast muster of independent freeholders on the third day proved them to be no match for voluntary zeal. 'No carriages are to be procured,' says a letter from Hull, 'but boats are proceeding up the river heavily laden with voters; farmers lend their waggons; even donkeys have the honour of carrying voters for Wilberforce, and hundreds are proceeding on foot. This is just as it should be. No money can convey all the voters; but if their feelings are roused, his election is secure.'

A vast number of freeholders from the North Riding, headed by Sir Robert Hildyard, entered York on the morning of the third day, and would probably have divided their support between Wilberforce and Lascelles, had not the danger of their long-tried representative induced them to give him single votes. Another large body, chiefly of the middle class, from Wensleydale, was met on their road by one of his committee—'For what parties, gentlemen, do you come?' 'Wilberforce, to a man,' was their leader's reply.

The total numbers during the two remaining days of this week were—

W.	L.	M.		
2847	2698	3032	Friday, May 22.	Third day.
4269	3894	4158	Saturday, May 23.	Fourth day.

Raising him to his usual situation at the head of the poll.

[6] Diary.

The poll was kept open for fifteen days. From the third day he continued to head, and the final numbers as declared by the High Sheriff were, for Wilberforce, 11,806, Milton, 11,177, Lascelles, 10,989.

'It is a grand contest,' wrote Mr. Thornton from York, 'and fills one with great ideas.'

Every nerve had been strained by the two great parties which were opposed to him. 'Nothing since the days of the revolution,' says the *York Herald*, 'has ever presented to the world such a scene as this great county for fifteen days and nights. Repose or rest have been unknown in it, except it was seen in a messenger asleep upon his post-horse, or in his carriage. Every day the roads in every direction to and from every remote corner of the county have been covered with vehicles loaded with voters ; and barouches, curricles, gigs, flying waggons, and military cars with eight horses, crowded sometimes with forty voters, have been scouring the country, leaving not the slightest chance for the quiet traveller to urge his humble journey, or find a chair at an inn to sit down upon.'

The mode in which the expenses of his contest were defrayed was no less remarkable than the fact of his success. When it had lasted little more than a week, 64,455*l.* had been subscribed. Contributions poured in unasked from London, Edinburgh, Birmingham, Colchester, Leicester, and many other towns. But the conduct of his own county in this matter was the most gratifying feature in his triumph. So great were the numbers who insisted upon coming at their own charges, that whilst the joint expenses of his two opponents amounted to 200,000*l.* the whole charge of bringing to the poll his great majority was but 28,600*l.* Forty-six per cent. was returned upon the Yorkshire subscriptions. Those of the south consisted of two sums of 10,500*l.*; one provisional, which was returned entire; the other absolute, of which one-half only was employed.

Some instances of devotion are worth recording. A freeholder presented himself to vote, whose appearance seemed to imply that the cost of his journey must be an inconvenient burden to him. The committee therefore proposed to him that they should defray his expenses. This he instantly declined. When however it appeared that he was a clergyman of very small means, who had travelled (and often on foot) from the farthest corner of the county, they renewed the same suggestion; and named a certain sum, which they pressed him to accept. 'Well, gentlemen,' he said at last, 'I will accept your offer, and I request you to add that sum in my name to the subscription for Mr. Wilberforce's expenses.'

'How did you come up?' they asked an honest countryman from the neighbourhood of Rotherham, who had given Mr. Wilberforce a plumper, and denied having spent any thing on his journey. 'Sure enow I cam all'd-way ahint Lord Milton's carriage.'

Three months had witnessed those two great triumphs, the Abolition of the Slave Trade and the Yorkshire election; and unnumbered congratulations poured in upon the chief actor in them. At the close of a letter of this stamp, Hayley subscribes himself 'Tanto homini servus, tantæ virtutis amator;' and adds apologetically, 'Please to remember, that to praise excellence is the privilege of angels and poets.' It is interesting to trace the secret safeguards which kept his simplicity of mind untainted amidst such success. 'Surely,' are his private reflections, 'it calls for deep humiliation, and warm acknowledgment, that God has given me favour with men, that after guiding me by His providence to that great cause, He crowned my efforts with success, and obtained for me so much goodwill and credit. Alas, Thou knowest, Lord, all my failings, errors, infirmities, and negligences in relation to this great cause; but Thou art all goodness and forbearance towards me. I come to the cross with all my sins, negligences, and ignorances, and cast myself on the free mercy of God in Christ as my only hope and refuge. Oh may I bear a part in the bright and glad assemblage ! Who will—who among them all can—have more cause than myself for gratitude and love ? Thou knewest me, and my hardness, and coldness, and unworthy return for all Thy goodness, when Thou calledst me from the giddy throng, and shone into my heart with the light of the glory of God, in the face of Jesus Christ. . . O grant me more and more of humility, and love,

and faith, and hope, and longing for a complete renewal
into Thine image. Lord, help me and hear me. I come to
thee as my only Saviour. O be Thou my help, my strength,
my peace, and joy, and consolation ; my Alpha and Omega ;
my all in all. Amen.'

The new Parliament met upon the 22nd of June, and he
thus shortly reviews the past session. 'Canning has done
most ably, Perceval ill, and below himself; owing, we suppose,
to his wife's illness fagging him, and keeping him up at night.
M. spoke again ; but though very cleverly and bitterly,
according to his own theory, yet I think there is a want of
pathos which will prevent his ever hurrying others along, or
rising to the first, or even to the top of the second rank.'

As soon as the recess began, he joined his family at
Brighton, and found his 'time completely engrossed in
writing letters, being engaged in it for five or six solid hours
daily.'[7]

Here he was 'much amused by London in lustring—yet
a fine pure air, clear sea, and good houses. Awful suspense
whilst doubting what we shall hear from Admiral Gambier.'
On the day following the capitulation the admiral wrote to
him.

'You will be happy to hear that it has pleased God to
bless our endeavours here for the service of the nation, and
that we are in possession of the whole Danish navy at
Copenhagen, consisting of eighteen sail of the line, eleven
frigates, and eleven sloops, with a number of gunboats, &c.'[8]

He was at first disposed to condemn this expedition, but
after full reflection he writes, two months later :—'After
much reflection, I am convinced that under all the circumstances of the case, the Danish expedition was just. It was
absolutely essential to deprive the Danes of a fleet which,
combined with that of Russia, would otherwise have soon
conveyed a French army to Ireland or Scotland, or have
forced us to detach to the north so large a proportion of our
naval strength, as would have left us open to attack in the
south and west of the two islands.'

[7] Diary, Aug. 24.
[8] Prince of Wales, off Copenhagen, Sept. 8, 1807.

'Though,' as he told a friend,[9] 'he scarcely ever in his life had found it so difficult to keep' his 'abstract reasonings on the case from being trampled under foot by the host of feelings which the general view of the whole scene called into action;' yet he was firmly convinced of the soundness of these principles. But while he defended the expedition, he was ready to 'weep with those that weep;' and forthwith proposed 'a subscription for assisting the poorer of the individual sufferers to rebuild their houses.' It is delightful to see the rugged countenance of necessary war thus brightened by acts of Christian charity.

The remainder of this autumn was spent at Broomfield, and, as usual, much with his friends. 'Oct. 26th. Evening, John Bowdler came, a truly amiable and most able young man, and above all, truly pious, and charmingly pleasant. He staid with me till Thursday, and Mr. Henry Thornton met him, and we had much talk.' 'Nov. 12. Dinner home—Grant's two sons, and Bowdler, and C. Noel—very pleasant, rational, conversable evening.' 'To town to see Canning and Perceval—interview with them about Africa and New South Wales, and Lubeck sequestration. Morning, to town —and Canning— about Portugal and America. Bissao Slave Trade, and Mr. Graham about religious instruction of convicts.'

His ordinary occupations were suspended this winter by a dangerous illness, but in March he resumed his attendance at the 'House almost every night,' where he complains of the 'debates' as 'poor compared with former times; yet Perceval improved, and Canning extremely clever.'

Upon the 29th on the 'Maynooth College debate. Opposition contended for completing the college so as to supply all the Roman Catholic priests wanted. Perceval for 250 (vice 400), for which the building already completed.' Upon the 5th of May the 'House' was 'again on Maynooth business, and very hot and violent even to bitterness. I spoke. My own final judgment not made up on the Catholic Question—I strongly incline to their coming into Parliament, though not to their seeing with other men's

---

[9] Letter to — Shore, Esq.

of attaining this advantage. It meets every eye. It costs
far less than the support of splendid equipages and bands
of livery servants, or than grand fêtes and entertainments.
There he is in the eye of the great and fashionable world,
while they drive in Hyde Park, with appearances that proclaim he might live like them if he would—that it is not for
want of fortune Wilberforce has not, like others, sunk his
name in a title ; and that while he abstains from fashionable luxuries, he indulges himself in those congruities to his
station and fortune, which best become the English gentleman and the Christian, in the means of family comfort, and
extensive though simple hospitality.

' In any material degree to exclude guests, would not only
be to impair Wilberforce's usefulness, but to change his nature.
And the witnessing his domestic life is one of the best cures
I know for prepossessions against religion, best human in-
centives to the practice of it, and best guards against those
errors and excesses into which misdirected zeal is apt to
run.

' There is something peculiar in his character and situation,
that seems to point it out as the design of Providence, that
he should serve his Master in this high and special walk ;
and should have, so to speak, a kind of *domestic publicity.*

' But here perhaps, as usual, we may find an unforeseen
coincidence between the dictates of particular and general
duties. If Wilberforce were less hospitable, his children
would see less of what may be most useful to them in his
example. They would have less of that important and difficult lesson, how to live with the world, and yet not be of
the world. Besides, they will thus gain a taste for the pleasures of Christian society, and for that very superior tone of
conversation which distinguishes their father's table and
their father's fireside. I do not think you are sufficiently
aware of this superiority. The trash, the trifles, the insi-
pidities, that make up conversation in general, form a disgusting contrast with even the worst table-talk that one
generally meets at his house. Wilberforce himself does not
see a tenth part so much of this as I have done, because he
knows how to lead conversation wherever he goes ; but rest

assured, his home parties are in this respect useful schools for his children.'

This is a good picture of his household economy. It abounded in cheerful hospitality, and in the highest charms of conversation and social intercourse. But there was nothing luxurious in his style of living,; this was banished on principle, and was missed by none of his guests. 'You can do what you please,' said a friend, who was celebrated for the excellence of his table; 'people go to you to hear you talk, not for a good dinner.' 'I am almost ashamed,' was the thankful simplicity of his own remark when first entering Kensington Gore, 'of the handsomeness of my house, my verandah, &c. I am almost uneasy, lest I am spending too much money upon it.' The very next entry is a good commentary on this characteristic fear. 'E. forced his way in to see me—the poor midshipman who, about eight months ago, wrote to me from Morpeth gaol, at the suit of a tailor for uniform, whom I got released, and sent him a few pounds. He called to thank me, and said he should never forget my kindness—not ashamed of it; and would subscribe five pounds per annum to the Small Debt Society. Eat yesterday a turkey, sent me by the person whom I helped to recover a landed estate of three or four hundred pounds per annum.'

The brief record, a few lines further on, of a visit to an early friend, who had been a keen and a successful suitor for riches and advancement, furnishes a striking contrast to his own happier simplicity of choice. 'To N.'s to dinner, Lord and Lady E. there, and others. The place most complete, and built and fitted up at a vast expense. His son a sweet-looking boy, quite manly; but all, I fear, "honourable" and "dishonourable!" N. has a most anxious face, and she too.' 'Oh, how does that little sentence, "The time is short," laugh to scorn all the left-handed wisdom of these politic contrivers!'

CHAPTER XVIII.

DECEMBER 1808 TO JULY 1810.

Meeting of Parliament—Duke of York—Bible Society—Use and abuse of Government influence—Eastbourne—Walcheren expedition—Cowperizing summer—Duel between Castlereagh and Canning—Parliament meets—Censure on Lord Chatham—Sir Francis Burdett—Windham's death—Parliamentary Reform.

To the session which was now opening, Mr. Wilberforce looked forward as likely to be 'very unpleasant.' It soon surpassed his gloomiest forebodings. 'Wardle's motion on Duke of York—sad work. No apparent sense in the House of the guilt of adultery, only of the political offence—spoke for any other proceedings than bar of the House. Major Cartwright writes about Parliamentary Reform as the only panacea. Alas! 'tis more a moral disease.'[1] 'I have wanted greatly to move the examination of the Duke of York's business from the bar, open gallery, &c., to a committee up-stairs, and some parliamentary inquest on oath. This melancholy business will do irreparable mischief to public morals, by accustoming the public to hear without emotion of shameless violations of decency. House examining Mrs. Clarke for two hours—cross-examining her in the Old Bailey way—she elegantly dressed, consummately impudent, and very clever : clearly got the better in the tussle—a number of particulars let out about life, mother, children, &c. Col. Gordon's evidence would have been sufficient, and I would not have asked one question of Mrs. Clarke.'[2]

'March 8.—Duke of York's business deciding. Perceval's capital speech, which greatly changed my opinion as to his guilt, softening though not quite turning me.'

The debate, which had already occupied two days, was resumed upon the 10th, when Mr. Bankes brought forward

---

[1] Diary, Jan. 26.   [2] Feb. 1.

a second amendment to Colonel Wardle's motion. It had been 'agreed on,' says the Diary, 'between Bankes, Henry Thornton, myself, and others,' and took a middle line between Mr. Perceval and Colonel Wardle, but failed, being 'negatived by about 95 ; near 500 members present.' The next day was a welcome holiday : 'The House having adjourned the Duke of York's business, I staid at Kensington Gore—its peacefulness delightful;' but the contest was renewed the following night.

'Perceval'—Mr. Wilberforce tells Lord Muncaster[3]—'carried last night his vote of purgation, but unless the Duke of York should resign before Monday, I am sanguine in my expectation that we shall either carry the question for his removal, or for some measure which must lead to it, or come so near carrying it as to render it prudent for him to take the hint, and mark such shameful debauchery, thus publicly disclosed, with the stigma of the House of Commons. Alas! what scenes have we been unveiling to the peaceful villagers of Cumberland and Westmoreland.'

His expectations were not disappointed. Before the House met he received a message from the Duke of Cumberland, by Mr. Robert Thornton, that the Duke of York has resigned ; 'wishing to know whether I mean to push any further steps, &c. Thornton says, "the Duke of Cumberland told him the King and all of them extremely angry at me." Yet what could I do as an honest man short of what I have done.'

As soon as the House met on Monday, he 'heard from Perceval the formal statement that the Duke had resigned. Lord Althorpe's motion acceded to, noticing the resignation, and no further proceedings now necessary.'[4]

In the midst of these political contentions, the morning of the 3rd of May presented to him a more grateful sight, in the anniversary of the Bible Society, a 'grand' and pleasing spectacle—'five or six hundred people of all sects and parties, with one heart, and face, and tongue.' But this was only a moment's calm amidst the troubled scenes in which he was compelled to take an active part. 'The times

---

[3] London, March 18, 1809.   [4] May 6.

are highly alarming. The Duke of York's affair, and Parliament's conduct in it, has infused a general jealousy of public men. The House of Commons has lost the public confidence ; there is no man of such talents as to take the ascendency like Pitt or Fox.' In this belief he supported, on the 26th of May, Mr. Curwen's motion for Parliamentary Reform, saying—' I was always a friend to moderate and temperate Reform : in my younger days I espoused it ; though older now, and consequently more cautious, I can see no reason to doubt the propriety of that former opinion.'

The session closed upon June 21, and on July 5, 'cutting the cables, rather than regularly unmooring,' he turned his back on London, and the bustle of politics, and with his whole family took possession of his last summer's quarters at Eastbourne, where, he says, ' I mean to live with my own family, attending closely to their tempers and dispositions.' The outline of his life and thoughts may be traced in a few extracts from these letters.

' What you say,' he writes to Hannah More, ' of good Bishop Porteus, delights me : surely he was one of the most lovely of human beings ; yet even he had his venomous traducers, and even death, as you will have heard, did not silence them all.

' I am glad to see Harrowby in office, he is a very able man. Do you know that far more than half of the nobility both of England and Ireland have been raised to their present elevation since I came into public life ?

' Who should be here but Lady Crewe, whom I doubt if I have seen since 1783. I long to open to her. I find among other obligations I owe you for Coelebs, is that of giving me a text on which to comment, an introduction for opening the way to discussions on the most important topics, which otherwise would be hedged out from access.'

' " What ! did I not know thy old ward, Hal ?" I did not read ten pages before I was reminded of aut Erasmus, &c. And without paying you any compliments, I may say, that it is a piece in my judgment, of which you, even you, with all your well-earned and well-merited credit, need not be ashamed ; on the contrary, I really am delighted with it, and

have been kept up night after night reading it after supper.'
On the appearance of Cœlebs he says :—

' The Henry Thorntons affirm that it cannot be Hannah
More's, and are strong against it, surely without reason.' His
critical discernment was more faithful. 'Reading Cœlebs
in the afternoon, and much pleased with it ; it is Hannah
More's all over.'

From his present resting-place upon the Sussex coast, he
saw the 'gallant trim' of the unhappy Walcheren expedition.

'Whither,' he wrote to Mr. Bankes, 'and for what purpose, is our large army going ? It never can be intended
for a mere coup de main ; though that employment of it in
the first instance, in its way to some ulterior and more important purpose, may be very proper. I am always very
slow to decide on points of great importance, when I know
I have but very inadequate grounds on which to rest my
opinion. But I have seen a sad propensity in men, when
they have got a great army, to set it at work, even where
the prospect is not very encouraging, as being better than
letting it lie idle, and rust for want of exercise. We really
do not enough remember, that our proper arms are not
military, but naval, and that these military enterprises are
dreadfully expensive, at a time when our true policy undoubtedly should be to husband our resources. I hope the
desire of recovering Hanover has had no undue share in
biasing the judgment of government ; but who that remembers how courtly Fox became on that subject, can cast away
all suspicions ? I very well remember old Lord Camden's
telling me, that when the King took him into his closet, and
fairly gave himself to talking him over, he was almost irresistible.'

The offer made him at this moment of a quiet parsonage
near Cowper's haunts fell in exactly with all his inclinations.
' I always observe,' he would often say, 'that the owners of
your grand houses have some snug corner in which they are
glad to shelter themselves from their own magnificence. I
remember dining, when I was a young man, with the Duke
of Queensbury, at his Richmond villa. The party was very
small and select—Pitt, Lord and Lady Chatham, the Duchess

of Gordon, and George Selwyn (who lived for society, and continued in it, till he looked really like the wax-work figure of a corpse) were amongst the guests.   We dined early that some of our party might be ready to attend the opera.   The dinner was sumptuous, the views from the villa quite enchanting, and the Thames in all its glory—but the Duke looked on with indifference.   " What is there," he said, " to make so much of in the Thames—I am quite tired of it— there it goes, flow, flow, flow, always the same."'   ' What a blessing it is,' remarks Mr. Wilberforce, this summer, on meeting an acquaintance who could not be happy out of London, ' to have a taste for simple and virtuous pleasures ! Religion gives this, but some have it naturally.'   He possessed it strongly, and enjoyed, therefore, exceedingly this ' Cowperising summer.'[5]   ' We arrived here,' he tells Mr. Stephen, ' last night, having left Battersea Rise after a prolonged breakfast at H. Thornton's in the same house in which were now contained his own wife and eight; but which he and I once inhabited as chums for several years, when we were solitary bachelors.   We enjoyed the society of many friends ; inter alios, Mr. Knox, of Ireland, of whom you must, I think, have heard me speak, and his friend the Rev. Mr. Jebb.   The former is a man of great piety, uncommon reading, and extraordinary liveliness of imagination and powers of conversation.   He was once, strange to say, Lord Castlereagh's private secretary.   He is the very last man I should have conceived to have gravitated to Lord Castlereagh.'

' I am come inland,' he writes to Lord Muncaster, ' calling first to spend a day with the Speaker, whom I left contrary alike to our own feelings and his kind pressings to stay. From my earliest travelling days, I never passed a parsonage in at all a pretty village, without my mouth watering to reside in it.   The best of this place is, that though the immediate neighbourhood has no other beauties than those of peaceful rural scenery, yet we are near the scene of Cowper's rambles; and, devoted as I am to Cowper, the idea of treading in his track is not a little delightful.   It is quite

[5] See Life of Hannah More.

classic ground to me, and I shall read both his prose and his verse here with a double relish. I have once already carried some cold meat to a venerable old oak, to which he was strongly attached. I have been to see Stowe with my charming young friend Bowdler; a man who will one day, I think, make a figure. How much was I impressed with the idea of grandeur's not being necessary to happiness!'

Here he thoroughly enjoyed himself; his arrear of letters was discharged, and he was commonly safe from interruption. ' A civil invitation from Whitbread civilly declined,' secured his quiet. ' Dined,' he says, ' at Lord Richmond's,' almost his only neighbour. ' It is just twelve years since he became serious from reading my book on Christianity, lent him by a brother divine, who said, " I am no reader," and begged him to run it over, as he did in three days. He showed it me in the original cover.' He attended with delight at a cottage reading, amongst many of ' the people in their common working clothes ;' and he adds that ' Richmond, who is a most affectionate, warm-hearted creature, has made great way in Turvey. Everybody favours him, and God has greatly blessed his preaching.'[6] ' Of Olney I hear but a very melancholy account. It is indeed an awful instance of mercies slighted and privileges abused. I suspect also, from what I have heard, that some of the former ministers of the place, like my excellent friend Mr. Newton, not being quite enough on their guard respecting dissenting and Dissenters, has been not unproductive of evil.'[7]

Here he could walk undisturbed in the solitary fields, sometimes with his favourite Psalter, sometimes reading Pope and Horace, and getting his Odes by heart ' had quite forgotten them, but found them easily regained.' A little more exertion carried him to Cowper's Weston Woods. In this unusual quiet, ' reading much, correcting the Practical View for a new edition, and much with ' his ' family,' the weeks passed happily away. ' Oh what a blessing it is to be living thus in peace ! Surely no one has so much reason to say, that goodness and mercy have followed me all the days of my life. Never was any one so exempted from suffering,

[6] Diary.   [7] To William Hey, Esq.

do I differ from those who speak in disparaging terms of the state of our constitution such as it now exists, that it is from the admiration and love which I feel for it, that I am chiefly decided in wishing for a very moderate and temperate change in the representation. The principle of representation is the vital principle of the House of Commons; and judging both from speculation and experience, I am afraid lest the existence of such boroughs as four or five are, and their manifest inconsistency with the representative principle, if ever the public mind should happen to be heated on this subject, should produce so strong an impression, as to drive men to go lengths and adopt measures, which might have the most dangerous tendency. It is, in fact, these four or five boroughs to which I allude, that give to the violent Reformers the only plausible ground they have to stand on; and this being taken away by a moderate Reform (such, for instance, as that which Mr. Pitt last proposed), all the really well-affected would separate from them. I well remember that great man, not many years before his death, laying down this principle as one of the best and most valuable of all political maxims, that where it was at all practicable, nothing was so wise as to separate the well-intentioned from those who at the bottom had dangerous designs in view.'

These were his fixed opinions on the question of Reform in Parliament. 'All seems quiet now,' he complains this spring, ' but how little are men aware of the real dangers of the country ! How little do they look forward to our probable state fifteen or twenty years hence!' His words seem almost prophetic of that storm of political excitement of 1830, in the midst of which the Reform Bill was at length carried.

CHAPTER XIX.

JULY 1810 TO JANUARY 1812.

*Garden at Kensington Gore—Barham Court—Herstmonceux—Attention
to his children—King's illness—West Indian topics—Conclusion of the
session—Doubts about resigning Yorkshire, or retiring from public life
—West Indian persecutions—Pays visits in the country—Alexander
Knox—Change of ministry expected—Christmas in his family.*

'THE session closed on Thursday,' is the last entry in the
month of June, 'and now a long reach of time is before me,
uninterrupted by parliamentary business.' This he would
fain have spent at Kensington Gore, the garden of which,
with its lilacs, its laburnums, its nightingales, its martins, and
its swallows, was his delight.

During the sitting of Parliament he could 'never get there
sufficiently early, or stay there in the morning long enough,
to witness the progress of the spring;'[1] but now that he had
somewhat more leisure, he sat long whenever the weather
made it possible, both writing and reading, under a spreading walnut tree, which was known in his family as his
'study.' 'Pretty quiet to-day—went out and sat under
walnut-tree, where now writing. I should like much to stay
in this sweet place, with as much admiration of the beauties
of nature as if I were 200 miles from the great city, amidst
my books, if I could be quiet.'[2] Yet he was often reminded
that the 200 miles existed only in imagination.

'In one view,' he tells Mr. Bankes,[3] 'you are better off
at Kingston Hall than I at Kensington Gore. You are out
of invitation distance, whereas I am rather annoyed by cards
to dine with this minister and with that. With one of the
Right Honourables this very day, after fighting off several

---

[1] Diary.   [2] Letter to Lord Muncaster.
[3] Near London, Jan. 12, 1810.

others, I am going to feed; but I shall not hold that eating bread and salt with him forms a compact of political support, as well as of personal goodwill.'

' Dined at Perceval's—mixed party—Pinkney American minister, Attorney-General, M. Montague, and others. Good-natured in Perceval to ask me, considering my differing so much from him. A sweet-tempered man; he commonly bears all ——'s strong speeches, but for Pinkney's sake kindly corrected some to-day.' ' Perceval is really a most generous creature, with many most excellent qualities. Poor Johnson called to-day. Perceval, merely seeing an account of his claims and merits for services in New South Wales, which had been sent [by me] to the Duke of Portland, and left in the office, actually gave him unsolicited a living of above 200*l.* per annum.'

' Whilst at family prayers this morning there appeared in the verandah General Miranda and his two Caraccas deputies, come to settle terms of friendly connexion with this country; they staid till half-past twelve.' ' Marquis Wellesley called and sat with me, and walked in the verandah three-quarters of an hour, talking about Abolition cause in Spain.'

Full of interest as was much of this social intercourse, yet he longed for greater quiet, and soon afterwards withdrew into the country. He moved first to Barham Court, and thus describes his visit to Lord Muncaster.[4]

' Barham Court has none of the grand features of your northern beauties, but for the charms of softness and elegance I never beheld a superior. My good old friend himself is the most extraordinary of all. We suppose he is about eighty-four; he goes on just like any other man of forty or fifty. Have you read the " Lady of the Lake "? Really I did not think that I continued in such a degree subject to the fascination of poetry. I have been absolutely bewitched. There are some parts of the poem that are quite inimitable.'

Early in September he took possession of Herstmonceux, which was lent to him by Mr. Kemp.

[4] July 25, 1810.

'You will scarcely be able,' he writes to Lord Muncaster,[5] 'to make out my lurking-hole.   How much will you be surprised when I go on to tell you, that I am within a very few miles of the tremendous John Fuller.   It must surely be a strange wild region that contains such inhabitants ; some outlandish place beyond the bounds of civilised society, where "sea-monsters whelp and stable."   Indeed, were not Mr. Speaker at a distance but little greater, I should scarcely feel secure within the reach of such a barbarian.   But, as it is said that the fiercest animals feel an unextinguishable dread of the keeper who has once established his ascendancy over them, so I trust to the effect of the recollection of the great wig, and repose in security.   There is a fine old castle here—a mere novus homo, however, compared with yours, having been built in Henry VI.'s time.

'Your kind heart will be sorry to hear that my friend Bowdler is going abroad for a milder climate, but we greatly fear too late.   He is really one of the most extraordinary young men I ever knew.   If it should please God to restore him to health sufficient to enable him to carry on his profession, this will one day appear.   But to those who love him as well as I do, it is an unspeakable comfort to reflect that he is, I believe, perfectly ready to make the great exchange. I often think what a change it is !   What astonishment will seize the minds of those whose thoughts have here been studiously turned away from all such serious subjects !   My dear Muncaster, may we also be ready.   My heart is very heavy.   I know you will sympathise with me.'

'We shall probably,' was Mr. Bowdler's parting address to Mr. Wilberforce, just before his embarkation for the coast of Sicily, 'not meet again for many months ; and it may be the will of God, that in this world we shall meet no more.   Let me assure you that you and yours will be very, very often present to my thoughts, and never without feelings of the warmest gratitude and affection.   The hours which I have passed under your roof have been among the happiest of my life ; and I shall ever esteem the advantages and opportunities of improvement which I have there enjoyed, as among

[5] Herstmonceux, near Battel, Sept. 25, 1810.

the choicest blessings which the mercy of a most merciful
Father has showered on me.	May the same bountiful Lord
repay to you and yours tenfold all your kindness to me.'

One main purpose of his summer retirement was to
watch the tempers and dispositions of his children, and at
its close he says, ' I have had an opportunity of becoming
acquainted with my own children, who, it really is not exaggeration to declare, seldom get a quiet minute with me
during the sitting of Parliament.'

Though this was so through the weeks during the session,
the Sundays were his own, and he spent these in the midst
of his family.	His children, after meeting him at prayers,
went with him to church, repeating to him in the carriage
hymns or verses, or passages from his favourite Cowper.
Then they walked with him in the garden, and each had the
valued privilege of bringing him a Sunday nosegay, for which
the flowers of their gardens had been kept all the week.	Then
all dined together at an early hour, in the midst of cheerful
conversation.	' " Better,' " was one of his Sunday common-
places, ' says the wise man, " is a dinner of herbs where love
is, than a stalled ox and hatred therewith ;" but, my children,
how good is God to us !	He gives us the stalled ox and
love too.'	Never was religion seen in a more engaging
form than in his Sunday intercourse with them.	A festival
air of holy and rational happiness dwelt continually around
him.

But with Sunday ended his domestic life.	'While the
House is sitting I become,' he says, ' almost a bachelor.'[6]
When the session was over, and he had retired into the
country, it was his delight to live amongst his children.
One was selected to read to him while he dressed.
Happy was the one chosen for the office.	The early and
quiet intercourse which his dressing-room afforded drew
forth all a father's tenderness, whilst the reading often
changed into most instructive conversation.	His meals were
taken with them ; he made excursions with them, and joined
in their amusements.	Every day he read aloud with
them, setting apart some time in the afternoon for lighter

[6] Letter to S. Roberts, Esq.

and more entertaining books; one of these this summer was
the 'Arabian Nights,' another Robertson's 'America.' All
his efforts were aimed at opening and strengthening the
mind, and creating a spirit of inquiry; while he was jealous
of such acquirements as yield an immediate return, and so
'flatter vanity and indolence, give the power of shining at
a cheap rate, and of exhibiting a show of knowledge where
there is really none.'

He watched carefully his children's characters, and many
a remaining entry of the long-past incidents of childhood
show how observant was the eye which seemed to take no
note. '—— a heavy-looking child, but showing at times
much thought—used (in fact) in play yesterday Euclid's
axiom, Things that are equal to the same are equal to one
another.' '—— has far more courage and character than all
the other children.'

The practical character of his personal piety was of the
utmost moment in his treatment of his children. He was
always on his guard against forcing or misleading their religious feelings. 'With my family,' he says, 'twice to Basil
Woodd's, because Dr. Hawker preaching at the Lock.'
'How little the modern religionists think of the vices of the
tongue, or even of bad tempers, much less of habits of mind!
Alas, how much easier to make a profession of religion than
to govern the temper!' In the same spirit he says, after
receiving a very promising account of one amongst his
children, 'I am afraid of ——'s making him artificial by
telling him it is God's work on the heart. I fear above all
his being led to affect more than he really feels.' Yet with
all this careful watchfulness, tenderness was the distinctive
feature of his domestic character. Though he never weakly
withheld any necessary punishment, he did not attempt to
dissemble the pain which its infliction cost him.

Above all he constantly referred them to the highest principles of action. He looked with suspicion at all plans for
education which omitted these. 'William Allen,' he says
shortly afterwards, 'and Joseph Fox came about Lancaster's
schools, to tell me all about them, and press me to be
a vice-president. Heard Fox's most interesting account.

It gave me great pain to refuse William Allen; but emulation and vanity are the vital breath of the system.'

On hearing of the death of the Princess Amelia, and of Parliament meeting on the 1st of November, owing to the King's illness, he returned to town, upon the 9th of November, to find all public business stopped by the illness of the King, and the continual hopes which were held forth of his speedy convalescence. ' Our beloved old King, the physicians declare, is recovering, and they have scarcely a doubt of his being even speedily well, if his restoration be not retarded by some of the circumstances which, if he were not a King, he would not experience.'[7] 'Dec. 9th. The King getting better, but with occasional relapses. Perceval said on Thursday, that as well then as when Thurlow declared him well, and sealed the commission in 1789. I believe it. I remember that it was then said in private that the King was not well.' These hopes were continually deferred, and the examination of the royal physicians before a Committee of the House of Commons lasted till before Christmas. He was now occupied with West Indian matters. Above a year before he told his connexion Mr. Manning,[8] 'It has grieved me to hear that the planters in the West Indies are not making such improvements in their system as their new situation requires. . . . Do stir yourself in this good work. There are many West Indian gentlemen in this country, whose private character and disposition encourage the hope of their co-operating in any well-devised plan for this purpose. All the Ellises are of this description ; Barham preeminently so.'

He was, too, just as active in redressing individual wrongs, just as ready to assist the distress, and poverty, and friendlessness which surrounded his own doors, as to labour in the world's eye for the ill-used tribes of Africa. This, while it increased his usefulness, saved him also from that diseased contraction of thought and feeling which is so apt to grow on general philanthropists. Thus, whilst he was ' calling upon Perceval, and discussing with Macaulay, Stephen, Brougham and others, about African and West Indian matters,' he

---

[7] Letter to W. Hey, Esq.	[8] Oct. 18, 1809.

was also ' off early to London to the War Office about the
boy Nowell, unlawfully recruited;' and finding that 'Lord
Palmerston had not yet read the minutes of the second
examination, which decisive,' he went on 'to the Colonial
Office about the case of Marsden and a poor woman,'
getting home at last 'too late for dinner;' and being ' off'
again next morning 'after breakfast to the Horse Guards,
where talked to Lord Palmerston about the poor boy,' and
got the necessary 'orders sent down for his discharge.'[9]

With the new year set in the full tide of public business.
The King's illness seemed hopeless, and the appointment
of a regency inevitable. In these circumstances, the mind
of Mr. Pitt's friend reverted naturally to the debates of 1788,
and to his great fellow-actors in that drama who had left
the stage before himself. His mind was constitutionally free
from that fretfulness of spirit which too often embitters such
recollections, and his estimate of things was therefore eminently just. 'I believe,' he tells Mr. Babington, from whom
he had heard an instance of ' Perceval's sweetness melting
down Whitbread's rough churlishness, and extorting a eulogy
for suavity and kindness,' 'that he is a man of undaunted
spirit, but his modesty prevents his taking that high tone
which, at such a time as the present, rendered Pitt so equal
to the emergency.'

On the 1st of January he was at the ' House till about
twelve. Romilly abusing Pitt. I got up and defended him.'[1]
' In the simple language of the heart,' to quote Sir Samuel
Romilly's account of what he said, ' he defended his friend's
memory.' 'If my honourable and learned friend had enjoyed the opportunities of knowing that great man which
have fallen to my lot, he would have been better enabled to
do justice to his character. I am no worshipper of Mr. Pitt.
I differed from him—with what pain none but myself can
tell; but if I know anything of that great man, I am sure of
this, that every other consideration was absorbed in one
grand ruling passion—the love of his country. Of his
talents there can be, and there is, but one opinion; and with
respect to his other qualities, I can only adopt the words

---

[9] Diary.   [1] Ib.

which those qualities provoked from the admiration of a formidable but generous rival, "amicitia est sempiterna, inamicitia est brevis."' The question was between keeping the whole household irremovable, or agreeing to the moderate opposition principle of a portion. ' Report of Resolutions— I voted for the amendment.' In the next debate there was 'sad quarrelling work. Sheridan's long speech, two-thirds tipsy, dealing about knocks on all sides (after Sir William Grant, who quite capital). He rather attacking me ; and I prepared a very good answer for him, which over-persuaded not to speak. Canning declaring they must not (Foxites) abuse Pitt, or he must watch them closely. Then Sir Samuel Romilly defending himself, &c. Ponsonby reconciling ; though Whitbread could scarce bear it. Heartily wished to lose, but upon constitutional principles voted for amendment, which carried by 217 to 214. Had been carried last night, but moved again by Perceval.

' Jan. 3. Manifest symptoms of Canning's rather making overtures to Opposition. His speeches excellent, but not like Pitt's ; rather exciting admiration than calling forth sympathy. 4th. House till half-past eleven. Opposition made no hand of it. Lords—sharp contest ; Government beat by three. I am quite grieved at their not recovering household resolution, which lost by thirteen. 5th. I am pained by having· voted against the Queen's having the household. I really fear it may hurt our good old King. Yet I acted from sense of duty. How toilsome and unsatisfactory a path is that of politics!'

The notices of his Diary sketch out the conclusion of this business. ' 11th. The answers of the Prince of Wales and the Queen reported to the House. The Prince's highly objectionable. Though the powers committed to him more than in 1788, and the right of making peers almost alone withheld, he says he is willing to use the powers left him for the public benefit ; also talks of his care for the Crown, and in an equal degree for the welfare of the people. Surely it must be his own. 14th. House. Phantom, as the cant phrase is, for the commission to put the great seal.' When the question was further debated—' Sheridan's speech wretched, and Perceval's excellent.'   'All acknowledge the talent, the spirit, integrity, good humour, and various excellences of Perceval through all the conduct of this difficult business.[2] 23rd. Third reading of Regency Bill.   Forced up by Giles, and glad of an opportunity of speaking handsomely of Perceval.'

Through this session his hands were full with his usual variety of public and private business. He 'opposed, upon the Bullion Question, the depreciation of the currency'—'carried an address to the Prince Regent for rewarding Captain Manby—sounded as to making adultery a criminal offence;' and 'took an active part in private business and committees.'[3] Above all he watched diligently over the Abolition cause, urging ' Yorke, First Lord of the Admiralty, to send out ships of war to Africa, and clear the coast by a thorough sweep '— 'acting in the committee for helping the Portuguese, in order to strengthen influence with them for the sake of Abolition'—'supporting Mr. Barham's motion for the introducing free labour into the West Indies,' and ' carrying triumphantly' an 'amendment,' upon the 13th of June,[4] by which the slaves in Trinidad were continued under the milder code of Spain.

A question of great moment to himself occupied much of his thought when the recess gave him time to weigh it closely.   'I am thinking just now whether or not to give up the county of York : it is a most serious question ; may God direct me right in it.   I can truly say that, if I knew which was the right path, I would follow it.'[5]   A little later he says (upon the 24th), ' My birthday again ; born in 1759, so fifty-two complete.'

'I wished to devote to-day specially to the important purpose of seeking God's direction on the question, whether or not I should resign Yorkshire ; and if so, whether to come in for a small borough.'[6]   A few days after this he visited 'the Speaker' and 'talked over the projects with him.   He against both—most of all against quitting the House altogether.'[7]

[2] Diary, Jan. 22.   [3] Ib.   [4] To Mr. Marryatt's motion.
[5] Diary, Aug. 1.   [6] Diary and Journal, Aug. 24.
[7] Diary, Aug. 26.

His great humility disposed him to defer too much to the judgment of his friends; yet perhaps this was more in appearance than in truth; on all important points he acted on his own convictions, though whilst forming his own judgment he was often, as now, 'much embarrassed by the conflicting advice of friends—Babington strong for absolute retiring, Stephen and others for giving up Yorkshire, but Grant and Henry Thornton against my quitting the county.'[8] This fulness of discussion makes his letters an accurate picture of his mind; for to his intimate friends he opened himself with a freedom which corresponded with his warm affections.

'I shrink,' he writes to Mr. Stephen, 'with awe from the idea of at once giving up for life all the efficiency for religious and humane purposes (the former weigh with me ninety-nine parts in a hundred), which would arise from my continuing in the House of Commons. The idea therefore of such a seat in Parliament as that you speak of is a great ease to me; for when I think of sealing up, as it were, my Parliamentary account and having done, as I now am, such a pang of conscience is produced!!! I seem to have been so unprofitable a servant compared with what I might have been. I have always thought that it would be an instance of conduct truly Christian, suited to our times, for a man to retire voluntarily from such a situation as mine without a peerage, &c.'

'I have had it,' he writes to Mr. Hey, 'for some time under consideration whether, at the next election, it would not be advisable for me to take my leave of our great county. I have always thought it right, while in that honourable station, to be a constant attendant—not, as is too common, to make the House of Commons my amusement.'

'There is, however, an alternative[9]—that of coming in for some other place. If I were M.P. for any small place, I should profess to attend only so far as my health and the education of my children would allow. Grant suggests that I could only exercise a general superintendence over them if out of Parliament, and this I may do as *eques calceatus.*

---

[8] Diary, Aug. 24.   [9] Letter to Mr. Babington.

' I see some objections to accepting Lord Calthorpe's offer, yet the opposing opinions of Grant, Henry Thornton, and Bowdler, who are all decided and strong against my resigning the county, make me more disposed than I was to embrace it.'

His black clients could ill spare him. The reluctant conviction that his work for them was incomplete was being forced upon him. The West Indians clung fondly to the vices of the old system, and were, unawares, hurrying on those great attempts to which he 'was led on step by step by the gradual progress of events.

His present object was to stop the 'persecution of the missionaries, or, rather, the forbidding religion to the slaves, in Trinidad and Demerara.'[1] For this purpose he appealed earnestly to Lord Liverpool, pointing out to him that it was ' a cause interesting not merely to the members of the particular sect to which the missionaries belong, though the Methodists are a very numerous and increasing body ; but all religionists will make it theirs too. This puts the finishing hand to the long catalogue of the slaves' wrongs.'

By the 6th of September he was again at Kensington Gore, having spent a day at Kidbrook ('where most kindly received by the Speaker and Mrs. Abbot. Speaker asked me what Commentary on the New Testament I recommended. I answered, " Doddridge's Expositor," mentioning Warburton's eulogium. Yet Doddridge is not satisfactory— Scott will not do—we want such a work'[2]) and felt his 'mind affected by having all around me on my first return home, but somewhat turmoiled from the consciousness of the number of people I had to see and things to do.'[3] Here he spent a busy fortnight, pressing forward by continued personal exertion his West Indian efforts, and consulting with his natural advisers on his own doubtful question. He was coming gradually to his decision. ' It seems best to quit the larger sphere, and yet remain—at least for a while—in Parliament, at the beginning of a new reign, when one knows not what may be intended in favour of Popery, or against morals.' ' I am resolved against Yorkshire, which I

---

[1] Diary, Sept. 6.   [2] Diary, Aug. 29.   [3] Ib.

humbly hope is pleasing to God. I am sure it is not from the love of ease or quiet. I feel exquisitely the giving up all my old ways and habits, and still more, the becoming unable to render any public services such as those in which I am now engaged. Still God can find instruments.'

Meanwhile he was engaged with 'several important matters stored up to meet me. Several missionary concerns. With Lord Liverpool, Lord N. and others. Heard with pleasure from Lord N. that justice would be secured for the Hottentots. He bore strong testimony to the effects of the Moravian missions—less to those of the Methodists; said Vanderkemp and Kichener worthy men, but enthusiasts. Alas! poor Lord N., how little dost thou judge according to the Scripture's estimate! Was not then St. Paul an enthusiast?'

There was no mark of failing vigour in the efforts he was now conducting; and he was followed into Warwickshire, whither, on the 20th, he removed his family, by the glad tidings of their entire success.

The next two months were spent in paying, with his family, some long-promised visits. Signs of thankfulness to God, and love to man, mark every halt along his route. 'Elmdon, Sunday, Sept. 29. Walked a little with Cowper— the beautiful end of the 6th book—"the promised Sabbath." What a prospect! Oh the unspeakable mercies of God! what can I desire which He has not granted me? Oh that I were more grateful! Let me strive more to love God and Christ, to delight in Them, and be grateful to Them in some proportion to what I ought.' 'Oct. 28th. Off for Lord G.'s, where very kindly received. It is a fine place, and improved with great taste. Their kind compulsion kept us over another day. Lord G. very pleasing and friendly, but these fine houses do not suit me. Resolved to take opportunity from a conversation we had at N. to write to Lord G., to press on him the reading of St. Paul's writings. May the effect be blessed! He is of a sweet disposition, and most superior understanding. Alas! how unspeakable are his disadvantages, and how much does he suffer from high life! How thankful should I be for having

a wife who is not of the fashionable sort!   How thankful for
my not having been made a peer in earlier life!   It would,
humanly speaking, have been the ruin of my children, if not
of myself.'   'Mr. S. and E. added to our party.   S. harmless, but dull.   E. a shrewd clever man of the world, mora-
lised down by marriage into a good magistrate and very
decent man, especially when with decent people.'   'Finishing in the evening a letter of Alexander Knox's, of fine imagination, rich in thought and beautiful in language; ingenious
too, and devotional too, but yet fanciful, and full of guesses
and subtleties leading to dangerous practical errors, or,
rather, perhaps arising out of them, and then lending their
filial support.'[4]

By the end of November he was at home.   He found
the political world talking 'of a change of ministers, and
the *Morning Chronicle* pushing hard for the Grenville and
opposition parties, giving the Prince strong hints.'[5]   But
soon afterwards[6] he describes the 'opposition as very angry
and distrustful of the Prince Regent, though they affect to
hold that, bound as he is by the ties of honour, it is impossible for him to retain Perceval.   Prince's health said to be
very bad—he is very nervous.   It is reported that he is
insane, and many well-informed people seem half to suspect
it.   Sir W. Scott looked significantly at Stephen, and said,
" He certainly has done no business for some time."'

The Christmas holidays had now brought his schoolboys
home, and all his six children were gathered round him—
'A true family party.'   He was at this time labouring under
a distressing oppression on the chest, which for some weeks
almost deprived him of his voice.   Yet was he striving to
make his home cheerful to his children.   'It is of great
importance to preserve boys' affections, and prevent their
thinking home a dull place.'[7]

[4] Diary.   [5] Ib. Nov. 29.   [6] Ib. Dec. 12.   [7] Diary.

CHAPTER XX.

JANUARY 1812 TO FEBRUARY 1813.

New-year's day—Trinidad Registration—American War—Christianity in India—Endeavours to keep back Dissenters—Perceval—Ministry— Sessional business—Religious Societies—Archdeacon Pott—Mr. Perceval's assassination—Formation of a ministry—Mr. Sheridan—Mr. Canning—Wilberforce's quietness of character—Summer at Sandgate —Occupations—Approaching dissolution of Parliament—Retires from Yorkshire—County resolution—Returns to London—With his children.

THE new year opened with his usual attendance at the Holy Communion, and with his wonted strain of praise. 'Oh what mercies have I to acknowledge during the past year!'

West Indian matters occupied him first. On the 6th of January he held a consultation with 'Stephen, Sir Samuel Romilly, and Brougham,' and 'settled to proceed with Registry Bill this year.'[1] On this essential safeguard of the Abolition Bill he had long been intent; and did not cease 'to press it upon Perceval,' who assured him of his 'endeavour to put the Privy Council in immediate action upon the Trinidad Registration.'

Other subjects were crowding on. 'I am wanting my voice much, that I may plead the cause of Christianity in India, and soften the asperity of hostile tempers between Great Britain and America.' He declared 'the grief and pain with which the very thought of a war with America filled his heart.' Accordingly, upon the 12th of February, when Mr. Whitbread made his motion, he went, he tells Lord Muncaster, 'to the House for the purpose of dropping a few healing and balsamic expressions which might tend to prevent the rankling of that wound which, however fatal to America if it were actually to break forth into a war, would be in a thousand ways pernicious to this country.'

[1] Diary, Jan. 6.

'Whitbread angry at me for voting and speaking against him, and very rough and rude. He seemed himself to think so next day.'

The other great cause which he 'wanted voice to plead,' and which eighteen years before he had so earnestly advocated, was brought before Parliament at this time by the approaching expiration of the East India Company's charter,[2] from which he hoped 'to obtain some spiritual advantages for Hindostan.'[3] He was most anxious that the Church should assume her proper station in this noble undertaking, and was therefore 'trying to keep back the Dissenters and Methodists, until the Church fairly come forward, from fear that if the sectaries begin the Church will not follow.'

Of this great design he was now full, and his influence in society and his voice in Parliament were alike devoted to it. He saw 'Perceval about introducing Christian light into India,' and 'is sadly disappointed in finding even religious people so cold about it.' March 7th. He 'wrote to the Bishop of St. David's about East India Christianising. Dined at Speaker's—sat next to George Holford. Talked to him about East Indian mission.' 'To Lord Melville, about getting leave for gospel light to pass into India. This is indeed a cause for which it is worth while being a public man.' His labour was ultimately successful.

Public affairs were now full of interest. 'The 18th of February was the day on which the Prince came into possession of his power, and his decision to retain Perceval was what many have anticipated. 27th. House till half-past three on Sir T. Turton's motion on the state of the nation, which, though going off without the great ones coming to combat, at length brought to light its real meaning—who to be minister ; and Canning first time divided with opposition, 136 to 209.'

He was now leading his usual London life ; constantly in the House, full of all plans for public or private charity, and showing no symptoms of decay. One 'day at home writing and correcting a paper about Danish confiscation ;' then 'to Rose at the Council Office with Latrobe about the Moravian

---

[2] Its charter was to expire in May, 1814.　　[3] Diary.

missionaries in Greenland,'[4] or 'all the afternoon busy about setting up a dispensary for our neighbourhood,'[5] and 'waiting on the Duke of York to ask him to be patron of it. He very obliging and civil, and consented.'

Another cause to which he freely gave his time and thoughts was the welfare of the different religious societies. Most of them had arisen since his entry into public life ; for they owed their origin to the increased attention to religion, which was in great measure the fruit of his exertions. When he was most occupied this spring, he still found time to attend the 'general meeting of the Church Missionary Society for Africa and the East.' 'A grand assemblage—I spoke with acceptance. It went off well.'[6] 'To Perceval's, talking with him about the business of Africa and the East, also the East Indies—he very pleasing.' 'May 5th. Bartlett's Buildings, by special summons, on East India Christianising—very full meeting—Archbishop presiding. John Gifford (Anti-Jacobin) properly spirited. Appointed committee to prepare a report and resolutions for Perceval and Lord Buckinghamshire, meaning in Church of England way. African and Asiatic Society's dinner—took the chair. Then House, where sat late. May 6th. British and Foreign Bible Society, annual meeting—all went off admirably. Immense meeting—I spoke with acceptance—several bishops present.'

This meeting of the Society for Promoting Christian Knowledge had important consequences. To the committee then appointed, Mr. Wilberforce transmitted Dr. Buchanan's sketch for an ecclesiastical establishment in India, which they embodied in their resolutions. 'I take the liberty,' wrote Archdeacon Pott, 'of sending you a sort of child that may claim to be laid at your door, for certainly it owes its birth to you, though it would be hard to make you responsible for its manifold defects.' Thus the first steps were taken which led to the appointment of our Indian bishoprics.

In the midst of these peaceful occupations he was startled

---

[4] Diary, March 26.   [5] Ib. March 20.
[6] Ib. April 24.

by a shock which was felt throughout the kingdom. At about a quarter to five Babington came, greatly agitated, stating that Perceval had been shot dead in the lobby. We could scarce believe it. I went, after calling at Perceval's and Arbuthnot's, who quite overwhelmed, to the House, where the poor wretch Bellingham [was, they were] examin-ing him. I carefully perused his face for some time, close to him—a striking face : at times he shed tears, or had shed them ; but strikingly composed and mild, though haggard. Called William Smith's, who close to Perceval when he dropped, and who thought it was myself, till he looked in the face. Smith, with another, carried him into the Secre-tary's room. Poor Lord Arden quite wild with grief—'No, I know he is not here; he is gone to a better world.' The next day he went 'early to town to the Speaker's, by whom summoned about the proposition to be made for the provi-sion for poor Perceval's family.'

'The Speaker stated that he feared he might be blamed for not having asked more persons—Castlereagh and Ryder, Ponsonby and Whitbread, Bathurst and Vansittart, Bankes and myself, Sir William Grant and Scott ; and he added that anyone who wished might bring more. Lord Castlereagh stated that the Prince had ordered a message, desiring the House to enable him, &c., and that Government had thought of 50,000*l.* for the children, and 2,000*l.* per annum for Mrs. Perceval for life—all agreed. House—all went off quite well.' On the 13th the question came before the House; and he, being most anxious that no opposition to it should tarnish the grace and honour of the grant, 'strongly urged the importance of unanimity; for Burdett having laid in a claim to oppose (though he expressed his horror of assassination), I feared a debate, and urged anyone who could not agree to retire, if he could do it consistently with duty. He went away, and [I] succeeded in obtaining for the two'propositions an unanimous vote.'

He took a forward part in the honour rendered to the late minister's memory. 'May 14th. To the Prince of Wales with the whole House to take up the address about poor Perceval.' 'Perceval,' he says in his private Diary, 'had the sweetest of all possible tempers, and was one of the most conscientious men I ever knew ; the most instinctively obedient to the dictates of conscience, the least disposed to give pain to others, the most charitable and truly kind and generous creature I ever knew. He offered me at once a thousand pounds for paying Pitt's debts, though not originally brought forward by Pitt, and going out of office with a large family.'

For a moment, to the honour of all parties, the strife of politics was hushed over the grave of the departed minister; but it was not for long that the busy stream of life could be stayed by such a charm. The eddying gusts of rumour and intrigue leave their mark in Mr. Wilberforce's diary. May 16th. 'I hear that the ministers left are trying to get Wellesley to act without being at the head, and Vansittart as Chancellor of the Exchequer, and of course Canning as one of the Secretaries of State. Nicholas Vansittart made Chancellor of the Exchequer. Lord Liverpool to be First Lord of the Treasury. Wellesley and Canning refused their co-operation, it is said on the ground of not giving up their opinion on the Catholic Question. I do not see how the ministry can stand the battering of the House of Commons.'

Upon the 20th, to stop the formation of this ministry, Mr. Stuart Wortley gave notice of 'An Address to the Regent for a strong and efficient Administration.' 'The opposition,' Mr. Wilberforce tells Mr. Bankes, 'regret it. They all remember the transactions of 1784, and the danger of calling into action the spirit of loyalty in the House of Commons ; yet the Prince of Wales is not beloved as the King was, nor is there a Pitt to stand the brunt of the assailants. I believe that both Wellesley and Canning overrate their weight in the country, though let the latter have the opportunity of exhibiting himself, and he would gain it.'

On the 21st he opposed Mr. Stuart Wortley's motion. When just going to a division Ryder got up, and most unwisely called up Canning, and even forced him, *quod Ithacus velit*, to refer to a theological paper of the Cabinet's. Canning very clever, and Wortley's motion really made for him and Wellesley, though carried by the numbers of the old opposition.[7]   The division lost by ministers, by 172 to 176, but foolish wranglement.   27th.   Wellesley could not make a government, so Earl Moira called to the Prince Regent. 28th. Nothing settled.   The Prince has seen all kinds of people, and is very nervous and distressed; Sheridan told me this afternoon that the several parties were farther off from agreeing than ever.'

Up to the 31st 'no ministry' was 'yet formed.'   On the 1st of June Mr. 'Canning declared that Lord Wellesley was authorised to make a ministry.'[8]   On the 2nd all was 'said to be off because the Prince wishes to preserve a predominance in the Cabinet for the old ministry; but this impossible.'   At length upon the 8th he 'went down with Bankes to the House, and to our astonishment found that Lord Liverpool was first Lord of the Treasury, and empowered to form an administration.   Canning not to join him, but only the old set and the Sidmouths.   How striking is Canning's example !   Had he fairly joined Perceval on the Duke of Portland's death, as Perceval offered, he would now have been the acknowledged head, and supported as such. But his ambitious policy threw him out, and he sunk infinitely in public estimation, and has since with difficulty kept buoyant.   Our House stormy.   I once up to speak, but abstained afterwards, because I remembered Lord Grey and Grenville's good service about Abolition, and would not condemn them now when so pulled down.'   Thus the ministry entered upon office.   'It would have been far the best course,' in Mr. Wilberforce's judgment, 'to have made the Speaker, Premier ; under him Canning might fairly, and would, act.   And so all the independent part of the House and of the country would be combined with known talent and habits of business.'   All however were 'astonished at the first division (June 11th); many thought that ministry would scarce have carried it, whereas 289 to 164.'

The manufacturing districts were still in an alarming state of 'smouldering rebellion,' caused in great measure by extreme distress, but fomented by factious and designing men.   In this state of feeling he saw with deep regret the

---

[7] Diary, May 21.   [8] Diary.

violence which politics engendered even amongst some of
his own friends. ' —— is taking a most violent and factious
part; talking of packed committees; attacking the magis-
tracy : surely as unwise as mischievous.' With such difficulties gathering round them, Government sought strength
by bringing Mr. Canning into office. 'Without the slightest
overture from me, or even my beginning to talk politics with
him, he took me aside and asked my opinion on the negotiation. I told him very frankly, that I wished it to be so
managed as to leave Nicholas Vansittart Chancellor of the
Exchequer, believing that he would be a far better man for
the situation than either Lord Castlereagh or himself. I told
Canning that I would give him an opinion as a juryman on
the case which he submitted to me.' On the 29th he heard
from Mr. Canning. 'The negotiation ended yesterday. It
has failed. The letter which you saw, and which I sent as
you saw it with only a few verbal alterations, did not produce a satisfactory answer. You have seen enough of my
disposition to be sure that I have gone far enough, perhaps
too far, in concession.'[9] This was not far from his own
judgment. 'Canning on negotiation failing,' is his docket
on the letter, when he received it.—'Not wise on either
side, but far more foolish on the other.' This opinion he
gave frankly; and Mr. Canning's answer 'justifying failure
of negotiation,' throws great light upon the actual state of
parties. 'When I found,' he says, 'that the determination
was to keep the substantial management of the House of
Commons in the hands of Lord Castlereagh, I was no
longer anxious to save appearances. I had wished to provide for the public good, not for personal feeling. Many
people say, and you seem inclined to adopt their reasoning,
"The lead after all is merely a feather, what signifies it in
whose hands it is?" Others say, "Why not let Lord C.
have it nominally? It will in effect devolve upon yourself."
Such has been the language of the Regent ; and such that
of many other well-meaning common friends. Now to the
first of these arguments, I answer that it is founded in a

[9] Right Hon. George Canning to William Wilberforce, Esq.,
July 29.

mistake.   To the second, that it is (unintentionally no doubt) a suggestion of dishonesty.

' 1· Is the lead a feather?   What is the definition of it? It is that station in the House of Commons which points out him who holds it as the representative of the government in that House, the possessor of the chief confidence of the Crown and of the minister.   Its prerogative is, that in all doubtful questions, in all questions which have not been previously settled in Cabinet, and which may require instant decision, he is to decide—upon communication with his colleagues sitting by him undoubtedly, if he be courteously inclined—but he is to decide, with or without communication with them, and with or against their consent.

' Now is this a feather?   Or is it substantial authority? But perhaps this is mere theory, and the case never occurs. Look back a few weeks only to the debate on the Orders in Council.   Recollect that it might have happened that I should have been sitting by Lord C.'s side on that night. And I entreat you to figure me to yourself in that situation, while he was giving up to Mr. Brougham's honour and glory (not to peace with America), by three or four successive gradations of concession, a measure which had been for five years the standing policy of the administration.

' He might be right, and I wrong, in the view of the measure itself.   It might be right to give it up.   It could not be right to give it up in such a manner; so spiritless, so profitless, and so senseless.   But right or wrong, the giving up such a measure in such a way, was surely a pretty substantial exercise of a pretty substantial authority.   And it was *that* authority that I should have confirmed to Lord C. if I had agreed to serve under him, as leader or minister of the House of Commons.

' 2. If I had so agreed, it is not a mistake merely—it is a suggestion of dishonesty, to say that the station in which I so bound myself to maintain him would have devolved upon me.   I must not have suffered it to do so.   I must have rejected and repudiated it.   If the troops had wished to salute me Imperator in the field of debate, I must have said, " Nay, my good friends, *there* is your commander.   I have sworn to maintain him such, like him as you may." And yet I will venture to affirm that no effort on my part to reject for myself, and to preserve to Lord C. the station of command, would have prevented him from saying in three weeks that I was studiously labouring to deprive him of it. Pray therefore be not led astray (nor let others where you can help it) by the notion that I have been squabbling about a trifle.

'Nothing indeed is a trifle which by common consent men think otherwise. But exercise of discretion upon great occasions in the House of Commons, is certainly no trifle at any time. Much less in times when great occasions occur daily, and when the government of the country is (too much perhaps, but is) essentially in the House of Commons.

'If I could have placed this power fairly *in medio*, I would have conquered, or endeavoured to conquer, all my other feelings of reluctance. But to place it, and to engage to maintain it, in his hands, in whose it now is, and then to place myself under it, would have been not only a sacrifice of pride, but an extinction of utility.'

'On the whole,' Mr. Wilberforce tells Mr. Bankes, he 'thought government was wrong, because Canning would consent to any terms which should place him and Castlereagh on equal ground; and considering his real superiority I think that was enough to offer.'

'How will all this busy and tumultuous world appear to have been all one great bedlam when we look back on it from a future state!' is his own reflection on the currents which were sweeping past him. Yet in them all, his own inner life was calm, and his natural affections lively. This was the reward of self-discipline and watchfulness; above all of the hours of prayer and secret meditation, which cooled his mind and allayed the rising fever of political excitement. Sunday turned all his feelings into a new channel. His letters were put aside, and all thoughts of business banished. To the closest observer of his private hours he seemed throughout the day as free from all the feelings of a politician, as if he had never mixed in the busy scenes of public life. Thus was his spirit kept unruffled by all the exasperating influences of the life he led; whilst he walked safely, with a cheerful seriousness and disengaged affections, in the heated and infectious air of public life—in the world, but most truly not of the world—ever remembering the end.

'Holding it a duty to stay till the last,'[1] he did not rejoin his family till the 29th of July at Sandgate. 'One,' he writes to a Yorkshire friend, 'of the creations of modern English opulence. A number of very comfortable houses for warm or even moderate weather, with a library, a warm bath, and other appendages. The country by far the most picturesque of any sea coast I have seen in the south of England. The hills so thrown about, and sometimes so fringed with wood, that you are almost reminded of the inferior (but quite the inferior) valleys in Westmoreland.

'Near us, there are also indications of our opulence which are not quite so indicative of our understanding. About a mile from us begins a canal which was formed when the alarm concerning invasion was the most prevalent. It runs parallel with the shore for about twenty-five miles; but I never yet talked with any military man, who conceived that it would oppose any serious obstacle to an enemy, who, besides the ease with which it might be crossed by portable bridges, might *tap* it without difficulty. The number of Martello towers is very great; but unfortunately, instead of being composed of such massy blocks of stone or marble, as defied our attack and returned the fire of our ships with interest in Corsica, for that was our model, they are built of brick; and I am assured the first cannon shot would beat a hole in them, and the centre being broken down or weakened, the twenty-four pounder would fall through with its own weight, and would bury itself in the ruins.'

Here he was exposed to few external interruptions, and was therefore able to devote more time than usual to his children. But one important question pressed for instant decision. Lord Sidmouth informed him privately that an immediate dissolution was at hand; and he must make up his mind to retain or to resign the representation of his county. 'I shrink,' he says, when weighing all the arguments upon

---

[1] Letter to Dr. Coulthurst.

the subject, 'from absolutely deciding to resign my situation as from annihilation. Yet my judgment commends it more and more; and it is not annihilation if I stay in the House, though not for Yorkshire. The urgent claims of my children upon my thoughts, time, and superintendence, strongly enforce my relinquishment, and are the deciding consideration. I ought not to be an occasional attendant on Parliament if an M. P. for Yorkshire. O Lord, give me wisdom to guide me rightly.' His decision was soon made, and was announced two days afterwards in the following letter :[2]

'After much serious consideration, I have resolved to resign that high station with which the kind partiality of my Yorkshire friends has so long honoured me, and in which you have yourself so kindly, and actively, and perseveringly contributed to place me. I must either allot less time and thought to my family than it justly claims, or I must cease to be a constant and assiduous member of Parliament, which I am sure I ought to be if I undertake so serious and weighty a trust as that of the representative of the county of York.

'It is not without difficulty that I have brought myself to this determination ; and having come to a decision, you are the first person to whom I communicate it. I wish it to appear clear that I am not influenced by the fear of an opposition, of which there would be no probability. The higher orders are not liable to sudden changes in cases of this sort, and I should be warmly supported by the great body of the clothiers. If I believed there were in a certain quarter any design to oppose me, that would produce in me so strong a disposition to stand my ground, that I should find it very hard work to force myself to retire, if I could do it at all.

'Several friends on whose judgments I place great reliance, are so earnest with me not to quit Parliament altogether, that I have agreed to accept the very kind offer of a friend, and through marriage a near relation, which will probably place me in a seat in which my occasional attendance in

[2] To C. Duncombe, Esq., the first Lord Feversham, who had been chairman of his committee at the last election.

the House of Commons will not be inconsistent with other claims.'

His intentions did not long remain a secret. On the 21st he sent his 'resigning advertisement.' 'I trust that I have done right; but I cannot say that I do not feel a good deal. Surely it is much to quit such a situation with a high character, and with the wishes of friends that I should retain it.'

This unexpected announcement was very variously received. Many of those who knew the labour which his sense of duty had long imposed upon him, and compared it with the powers of his slight frame and tender health, rejoiced at the step; but his Yorkshire friends, to a man, lamented and would scarcely accept his decision.

But having made up his mind, he abode by it, and listened from his quiet retirement at Sandgate to the din of distant elections. 'Babington's contest still continues. Henry Thornton's election secure. Both the Grants' ditto. Honest Butterworth's success reminds me of "Them that honour me, I will honour;" he was quite the popular candidate, and the crafty, roguish counsel of his opponents was made to recoil on themselves. I feel somewhat like an old retired hunter, who is grazing in a park, and hearing the cry of the hounds pricks up his ears and can scarce keep quiet or refrain from breaking out to join them; but this is mere animal spirits.'

The applause from which he shrank, followed him into his retirement. The county at large on the day of nomination recorded solemnly their judgment of his character by an enthusiastic and unanimous vote of thanks for his services during more than twenty-eight years as their representative in Parliament; for his unremitting and inpartial attention to the private business of the county; and for his independent and honest performance of his trust upon every public occasion. His own town of Hull followed with a similar memorial of affection.

He writes to Lord Muncaster:[3]—'I account myself full ten years older than most men of my own age, and six years was a longer term than I durst venture to engage for.

[3] October 26.

As we grow nearer the great change, it is well to make still ampler preparation for it.'

To the eye of a stranger he appeared at this time full 'ten years older' than he was. Delicacy of health had indeed set on him already some of the external marks of age, and a stoop which he contracted early, and which lessened his apparent stature, added much to this effect. But the agility of his step, the quickness of all his senses, his sparkling eye, and the compass and beauty of his voice, contradicted these first appearances. And those who listened with delight to the freshness and exuberance of thoughts, sometimes deeply serious, sometimes playful and humorous, which enriched his conversation, could hardly believe that he had reached his real age. At the breakfast-table, and again from the setting-in of evening until midnight, were his gayest times; at the last all his faculties were in the fullest exercise, especially when being read to in his family circle, which was his delight, he poured forth all his stores, gathering around him book after book to illustrate, question, or confirm the immediate subject of the evening.

Christmas again brought his family round him, and he joined in all their business and amusements. 'Being read aloud to' by one—'examining' another 'in his history— watching carefully over all their tempers—taking them' one day 'to the British Museum,' and on another 'to see the great fish,' or, a still greater pleasure, reading aloud through the long evenings.

CHAPTER XXI.

FEBRUARY 1813 TO DECEMBER 1814.

Session opens— Catholic Question—East India Company's charter—Efforts for Christianising India—Petitions—Debates—Registry Bill—Foreign Slave Trade—Lord Muncaster's death—Visits—Barley Wood—Successes of the Allies—Madame de Stael—Buonaparte abdicates—Foreign Slave Trade—Lord Castlereagh at Paris—Letter to Emperor Alexander — French Treaty — Interview with Emperor — Amendment to the Address—Bishop Middleton—Letter to Talleyrand—Congress of Vienna—Correspondence with Duke of Wellington—Sismondi—Humboldt—Madame de Staël—Prospects of French Abolition—His private life at Sandgate—Return to London—Slave Trade abolished by Napoleon.

CHRISTMAS soon passed, and a busy session opened. 'I am reading,' he says (Feb. 10th), 'on Catholic Emancipation, and thinking too. I grieve to see so much prejudice. Meetings against Roman Catholics in all parts of England.'[1] 'Talking the question over with friends; one, though a most able man, not knowing that Dissenters may sit in Parliament.' 'I am very doubtful which way right.' This was his only question; popularity and party principle afforded no rule for him to act upon; and though he suffered keenly from shocking the conscientious scruples of many whose principles he valued most, yet this could not bias his decision. 'Lord, direct me,' he prays on this question; 'all the religious people are on the other side, but they are sadly prejudiced.' 'It grieves me to separate from the Dean and all my religious friends; but conscience must be obeyed. God does not direct us to use carnal weapons in His cause.'

'I am,' he tells William Hey, 'decided against granting to the Roman Catholics eligibility to *all* civil offices. My doubts are concerning their admissibility into Parliament; and there is one consideration which I do not see that even

---

[1] Feb. 10.

you have duly borne in mind. It is that whatever the Roman Catholics, if admitted into the House of Commons, could effect for injuring the Protestants in Ireland, they can do just as well (in one important respect better) through the medium of members of Parliament, *called* Protestants, but who, being elected by Roman Catholic voters, are implicitly subservient to their constituents' purposes.

' But while the Roman Catholics thus possess Parlia mentary influence, they do not possess it in such a manner as to render it a personal privilege; and therefore so as to give them an interest in the existing legislature, and to connect them to the Protestant system by the various ties which unite men who act together in Parliament, and which would render it improbable that they would join a foreign enemy in separating Ireland from Great Britain; and where can be the wisdom of retaining the prison dress, when you have set the men at liberty ?'

Under this view the question was entirely one of political expediency. The principle had been long since conceded. Political power the Romanists possessed; all that remained was to provide for its being exercised with least danger to the Constitution. This he believed that emancipation would tend to secure. Upon the 25th came on ' Grattan's motion for a Committee on Catholic Question, according to Canning's motion last year. Bankes spoke early against— Plunket excellently for. House till half-past two. March 2nd. House till four. Question carried, 264 to 224.'[2]

'9th. House till half-past two. Grattan's resolutions in committee carried by a greater majority. Speaker spoke against Roman Catholics, though allowing still greater concessions —the honours of the bar, and army, and something imperfectly explained about the Roman Catholic hierarchy. I spoke. I was well received. I chiefly contended for Roman Catholics' admissibility into Parliament now that the elective franchise is given to them.'

He was still constant in his attendance at the House, and often notes its passing aspects, as on Feb. 11th. 'Long

[2] Diary.

debate on Vice-Chancellor project. Canning inimitable in wit and sarcasm. Bobus Smith spoke first time promisingly.'

His great object this session was the battle of Christianity in India. It was evident that the struggle would be severe. The great mass of Anglo-Indians were convinced that any attempt to Christianise the East would cost us our dominion; and though they gave a reluctant assent to the scanty ecclesiastical establishment[3] for the English residents in India, which government had been persuaded to propose, they abated none of their hostility to missionary efforts. Their policy was to commit the question for the next twenty years to the East India Company, who had shown unequivocally what would be their course. This then was the point of the contest. Upon the 22nd of March, ' Lord Castlereagh opened upon the East India Company's charter—three hours. Sparring about East India religious interests. I, Stephen, and Thomas Thompson. Castlereagh not told by his colleagues what we had pressed, and bad work from it. We foretold petitions.'

The temper of the House of Commons could not be mistaken, and he saw that it was only by bringing the religious feeling of the country forcibly to bear upon it that he could hope for success. He set about the work with an energy and resolution which had never been .exceeded, even when, in the vigour of his early youth, he fought the Abolition battle.

He did not lose a day. To his leading country correspondents he wrote as he now addressed Mrs. H. More. ' You have read Buchanan. You will agree with me that, now the Slave Trade is abolished, this is by far the greatest of our national sins; and it is prodigiously aggravated by its being confirmed confidently by Lord Teignmouth, Mr. Grant, &c., that prudent, and gradual, and successful endeavours to improve and Christianise our East Indian population, would strengthen our hold on that country. All this is to lead you to stir up a petition in Bristol, and any other place. The petitions for abolishing the Slave Trade were very general, and very useful; why not on this occasion also ?'

---

[3] One bishop and three archdeacons.

'It is a shocking idea,' he writes to another friend, 'that we should leave sixty millions of our fellow-subjects, nay of our tenants (for we collect about seventeen millions sterling from the rent of their lands), to remain in a state of barbarism and ignorance, the slaves of the most cruel and degrading superstition.'

He was now 'excessively busy stirring up petitions,' feeling that it was 'the greatest object which men ever pursued.' 'The spirit of petitioning scarcely spreads as one could wish.' Yet the leaven was at work, and he soon adds, that 'already Bristol, Hull, Glasgow (excellent resolutions), and Birmingham have spoken out.' His own personal efforts in committees, in meetings, and in visits were incessant.

On March 30 began the examination of witnesses before the House of Commons. 'Mr. Hastings and Lord Teignmouth. The House exceedingly civil to Mr. Hastings ; sufficiently so to Lord Teignmouth.' This was now his daily business. 'Writing almost all morning about East India Charter—examinations, sharp work—extreme ignorance and bigotry. We examine daily from half-past four till near eight, before other business.' The object of the enemies of missions may be seen from the general tenor of their questions. 'Would not,' they inquired, 'the appearance of bishops encourage a fear amongst the natives that force would ultimately be used to establish Christianity amongst them ?' 'Would it be consistent with the security of the British Empire in India, that missionaries should preach publicly that Mahomet is an impostor, or speak in opprobrious terms of the Brahmins and their religious rites ?' In such a line of examination they had every advantage. Few or no witnesses could be produced to prove the safety of what had so rarely been attempted; whilst almost every Anglo-Indian was ready to come forward and swell by his separate evidence the general cry of danger. The wisest counsels were needed to secure success.

Soon after this he is 'consulting about East India subject in cabinet council with Grant, Babington, and Henry Thornton.' Accordingly the full weight of the religious portion of the nation, it was decided, must be brought effectively to bear on the question, for political assistance as to it he had none. Even Lord Grenville was 'dry and cold upon the matter,' and Mr. Tierney was one of his most obstinate opponents. Government, indeed, were disposed to make some favourable changes in the system, and the Resolutions he had recorded twenty years before were ground gained from which to work ; but no ministry could carry such measures by force, least of all in the face of such an opposition as that of the whole Anglo-Indian body. The ministers, therefore, of the Crown could not be expected to act up to their inclinations, unless supported by some counteracting force. It was the especial charge of Mr. Wilberforce to call up this support from the religious feeling of the country, and then to regulate and guide its action.

This delicate task was one great branch of his exertions. All had access to him, and he could enter everywhere. He was the link between the most dissimilar allies. Bishops and Baptists found in him a common term. 'After breakfast Messrs. Gutteridge, Weymouth, and Shaw, three Baptist committee gentlemen, called on me about East India Baptist missionaries. Called on the Bishop of St. David's, and tried to stir him up. Called Earl ——'s, about East India religion business, found him full of prejudice and ignorance. How sad that so noble a mind as his should be rendered so indifferent to the happiness of our fellow-creatures! Talked to him some time. Got him to say he would read Lord Teignmouth's and Mr. Grant's pieces, and perhaps move for the production of the latter.' 'Dean of Wells breakfasted with me, and met Andrew Fuller and Mr. Ivimey. Much talk of East India missionary affairs. Dined Lambeth—public day—little company—all engaged at grand public dinner for celebrating Sir Joshua Reynolds's fame ; and the whole rooms of British Institution filled with his pictures. Archbishop very civil ; I tried to get him on East India business. As I came back, called for an hour at British Institution rooms. Prince of Wales came up to me and accosted me very handsomely, and spoke a minute or two. Poor Sheridan took me up to his first wife's picture, and stood with me looking at it affectionately some time. All the lovers of the arts there.'[4]

It was left to him to press in person the matter on the government, and he did so with success. May 26th, he says, ' Lord Buckinghamshire acceded to our terms;' and on the following day 'Lord Castlereagh agreed to our arrangement for East India Christianising Resolutions—far surpassing my expectations.'[5] On the following Sunday he records his gratitude. ' I humbly hope that God has great designs in view for the East, and that they will be executed by Great Britain.'[6]

But though the government had yielded, the battle was not won. The House of Commons, in which lay the strength of the enemy, might defeat the Resolutions. Upon the 22nd of June Lord Castlereagh moved the 13th Resolution. ' The appearance of the House at the beginning of the evening was as bad as could be, but Lord Castlereagh opened the subject very discreetly and judiciously.'[7] He referred to the Resolutions which at Mr. Wilberforce's motion had been adopted in 1793, and declared it to be impossible to take a lower tone upon this subject than had then been set. Cautiously proceeding upon this ground, he endeavoured to allay all exaggerated apprehensions. To this Sir Henry Montgomery replied. He was followed by Mr. Douglass, who spoke shortly in favour of the Resolution. Then came Mr. Wilberforce. His mind was full of his subject, and never did he speak with greater power, or produce more impression. Twenty years before he had appeared in the same place, the eloquent advocate of this same cause. He had, beyond all expectation, been spared again to lead the charge.

' It was late,' he says, ' when I got up ; but I thank God I was enabled to speak for two hours, and with great acceptance. I spoke better than of late. Bankes kindly said to me I had got into my old vein, and though the matter was unpopular, yet admirably heard. Only a little afterwards from opponents, and we carried it, about 89 to 36, beyond all hope. I heard afterwards that many good men had been

[4] Diary, May 8.   [5] Diary.   [6] Journal.   [7] Diary.

praying for us all night. Oh what cause for thankfulness !'
His own speech, and that of Lord Castlereagh, had largely
contributed to this result.

On the 12th of July he says : 'The East India Bill passed,
and the Christian cause fought through, without division, to
the last. We were often alarmed. Lord Castlereagh has
managed it admirably—coolly and quietly. The petitions,
of which a greater number than were ever known, have
carried our question instrumentally, the good providence of
God really.'[8]

His own personal influence had been a powerful instrument in gaining this result. Never had he been able to
bring so openly forward in the House his own religious
principles ; never had they been more respectfully received.
'Last session,' says a hostile, adverse, and caustic critic,[9]
'when the House had been tired night after night with discussing the endless questions relating to Indian policy, Mr.
Wilberforce ventured to broach the hackneyed subject of
Hindoo conversion. He spoke three hours, but nobody
seemed fatigued : all indeed were pleased ; some with the
ingenious artifices of his manner, but most with the glowing
language of his heart. Much as I have differed from him
in opinion, it was impossible not to be delighted with his
eloquence.'

Two important objects had, since the Abolition, occupied
the protector of the negroes—the securing in our colonies
its legitimate effects, and the suppression of the trade of
other nations. The first great object must be gained by a
Registry of Slaves, which would prevent illicit importation,
the second by treaty. Our maritime supremacy had for the
time destroyed the Slave Trade of our enemies ; and if we
could secure the concert of our friends, this scourge of
Africa would be extirpated. Every new treaty therefore he
carefully examined, and was ready to compel the government by friendly violence to insert the stipulations which
this cause required. His intervention in the year before had
succeeded in the case of Sweden, and his closing motion this
session was aimed at securing the same point with Portugal.

---

[8] Diary.   [9] Barnes's Political Portraits.

His summer was spent, as usual, amidst his children. The early autumn was marked by the loss of another of the scanty band of his early friends—Lord Muncaster was gone; having left, in words which deeply touched the loving heart of his friend, a bequest to him, 'as a small proof and testimony of the very sincere friendship I felt towards him during the time I walked with him in this vale of tears and sorrowing.'

Amongst the visits which had been the longest promised was one to Barley Wood. He excuses its brief postponement in this characteristic letter:—

'When at Mr. Way's, we shall be within fifteen or eighteen miles of the Sargents. She almost my daughter. Her father my first cousin, who lived thirteen years under my mother's roof throughout the period of my childhood, and who brought her down in his arms at three weeks old, and dying a few weeks afterwards I always regarded her as under my special wing.

'Happily, blessed be God, I have been instrumental in her uniting herself for life to one of the very first Christians I know. These same excellent people thus married, I repeat it, through my aiding and comforting (as the lawyers phrase it,) have been inviting us to their house ever since their union; yet never did we, or I singly, set foot within it. Now if I could come into their neighbourhood and put up at the park and the chateau, and leave the parsonage unvisited, if ever the crime *læsæ amicitiæ* was committed, we should be chargeable with it in an eminent degree. Our arrival will therefore be delayed three or four days.'

It was seven years since he had seen Hannah More, except the single day that she had spent with him in the summer; and it was with no little pleasure that he was again beneath the roof of the sisterhood. Death had visited their dwelling, and taken one of the united band; but she who was gone had died in Christian hope, and they whom she had left lived on in Christian cheerfulness. It was still, as it ever had been, a scene of intellectual and religious sunshine. 'You must have been greatly entertained at Barley Wood,' Mr. Wilberforce wrote a few weeks before to Mrs. Stephen,[1]

[1] Aug. 26.

'but you would miss the eldest sister. There was a place assigned to every one of the sisterhood, and not one of them could be spared without creating a void. I almost envied you the being housed, as I understood you were to be, with Mrs. Siddons.'

Here he spent almost a week, and was charmed with many of their guests. ' 18th. Dean Ryder came from Wells in the evening—truly pleasing and much talk with him. 19th. The Dean and I walked before breakfast. Met Dr. W., the true picture of a sensible, well-informed and educated, polished, old, well-beneficed, nobleman's and gentleman's house-frequenting, literary and chess-playing divine—of the best sort (not adulatory). I hope beginning to be serious. On the 22nd of October we left our kind friends.'

The success of the allied armies was the great event of this autumn. 'The war' had ' begun well after the armistice, Austria having joined the Allies, and Buonaparte being crippled in both flanks, and apparently centre too.'[2] Every step of the Allies was now watched most anxiously. ' We saw last night flashes of cannon on the French coast, which we fear is for some victory. Buonaparte, however, would make the most of a small one. St. Sebastian taken. but by a terrible loss of men—in all to us and our Allies 5,000 killed and wounded.'[3]

The triumphs of this scourge of God were over. The allied armies throughout this campaign steadily advanced upon the retreating Emperor, and upon the 25th of November the guns of the Tower were ' firing at nine and again at four o'clock, for news of Lord Wellington's storming the French lines near the Pyrenees. Also prodigious success of the Allies. Dresden taken, with 16,000 French. The glorious news from Holland better then all the rest.'[4]

The Christmas holidays over and his family broken up, he was in his usual stream of religious, charitable, and House of Commons work. Society, too, asserted its claims. How closely he watched himself in it the following will show. ' When attending,' on the 8th of February, ' a meeting of the African Institution, Sir S. Romilly told me aloud that Madame

---

[2] Diary, Sept. 20.　　　[3] Diary, Sept.　　　[4] Diary.

de Staël assured him she wished more to be acquainted with me than with any other person. The Duke of Gloucester made me by her express desire fix a day for meeting her at dinner, *chez lui*—Saturday sennight. This is mere vanity, and perhaps curiosity; and I feel my vanity a little rising too on the occasion. She told the Duke of Gloucester that I did not think how really religious she was. I must read her *L'Al-lemagne*, in order not to excite her prejudices. It will also enable me better to distinguish between her religion and the true, in conversing with others.'

'19th. Dined Duke of Gloucester's to meet Madame de Staël, at her desire—Madame, her son and daughter, Duke, two aides-de-camp, Vansittart, Lord Erskine, poet Rogers, and others. Madame de Staël quite like her book—complimenting me highly on Abolition—"All Europe," &c.'

'March 18. Dined with Madame de Staël—her son and daughter, and two other foreigners, Lord Harrowby, Lord and Lady Lansdowne, Sir James Mackintosh. Lord and Lady Granville Leveson were to have dined, but Lady Spencer died that morning. She asked me to name the party. A cheerful, pleasant dinner.—She talking of the final cause of creation—not utility but beauty—did not like Paley —wrote about Rousseau at fifteen, and thought differently at fifty. Evening, assembly, but I came away at half-past eleven. A brilliant assembly of rank and talent.' 'The whole scene,' was his next day's reflection, 'was intoxicating even to me. The fever arising from it is not yet gone off (half-past 8, A.M.).'

'I am clear it is right for me to withdraw from the gay and irreligious, though brilliant, society of Madame de Staël and others. I am, I hope, thankful to God that I am not given up to these pleasures.'

Whether he was right or wrong in these scruples, his unsparing judgment of himself is not a little striking to one, whose past labours and long-settled character would have exempted him in the eyes of the most scrupulous from the necessity of such rules of conduct. Nor was it that any touch of age had damped the exuberance of his younger spirits; and that he withdrew morosely from scenes in which

he could not as of old give and experience pleasure. 'Mr.
Wilberforce,' was Madame de Staël's declaration to Sir
James Mackintosh, 'is the best converser I have met with
in this country. I have always heard that he was the most religious, but now I find that he is the wittiest man in England.'
His social qualities are about this very time well described
by Mr. Harford. 'The first time I met Mr. Wilberforce was
at the house of his friend Mr. Henry Thornton. He entered
the room with a smiling, animated countenance, and a lively
vivacity of movement and manner; exchanging as he advanced kind salutations with his friends, whose faces were
lighted up with peculiar pleasure at his presence.

'His frame was extremely spare, but from it proceeded a
voice of uncommon compass and richness, whose varying
and impressive tones, even in common conversation, bespoke
the powers of the orator. His eyes, though small, and singularly set, beamed with the expression of acute intelligence,
and of comprehension quick as lightning, blended with that of
cordial kindness and warmth of heart. A peculiar sweetness
and playfulness marked his whole manner. The mingled
emanations of imagination and intellect, of benevolence and
vivacity, diffused over his countenance a sort of sunny radiance, which irresistibly acted as a powerful magnet on the
hearts of all who approached him.'

Greater projects were suggested by the course of events
to the protectors of the negro race. The progress of the
allied armies promised an early peace to Europe. The
negotiations, indeed, at Chatillon were long protracted, and
after one or two slight successes, 'Buonaparte' was 'swaggering again.' 'Almost all the nation' were 'now against
making peace with Buonaparte.'[5] No peace they thought
could be secure, and complete success seemed within their
reach. The negotiation itself was unpopular. 'Morritt
showed me a letter from Marshal Beresford, having entered
Bordeaux. All Gascony wild against Buonaparte—calling
themselves English—showing the church and castle built by
Edward the Black Prince, and saying, "It was yours, why
do you not retake it?"' 'All deprecating peace except the

[5] Diary, March 6.

opposition, who are silent.'[6]   Four days later 'Lord Erskine told' him 'that' he was 'a strong Bourbonist, and Lord Grenville too.   That Buonaparte is quite the creature of our manufacture, as much as any Birmingham buckle or button.'[7]

All fear of a hollow peace soon vanished.   Buonaparte rejected the proposals made to him, and on the 4th of April 'Vansittart stated that the negotiation was broken off, and that all the Allies are together, and have been and are of one common sentiment.'   The drama was hastening to its close. 'How wonderful,' he says upon the 9th, 'are the events of the last few days !   After hearing that Buonaparte had dashed into the rear of the Allies, it seemed doubtful what would happen ; when suddenly we heard on Tuesday that they were marching on to Paris.   Then we hoped the best; but how little expected that to-day, Saturday, we should hear of Buonaparte's accepting the Emperor of Russia's offer, renouncing the throne and agreeing to retire to Elba!' 'I am delighted that Paris is spared.   Oh for the general Abolition of the Slave Trade!'   On the same day he writes to Mrs. Hannah More—'So the dynasty of Buonaparte has ceased to reign, as friend Talleyrand informs us.   This hath God done.   How can I but wish that my old friend Pitt were still alive to witness this catastrophe of the twenty-five years' drama (since 1789)?   But I recognise the Scriptural prin- ciple of Divine conduct, in selecting for the instruments of its favours not the most admired of human agents, but those I doubt not from whom (Perceval only excepted) the voice of prayer has been most frequently poured forth for the success both of our counsels and arms—" Them that honour me," &c.   The present ministry also has clearly been more favourable than most others to true religion.'

The burst of national joy was proportionate to the length and sufferings of the past struggle, and the completeness of the present success.   London was soon full of the triumphant conquerors, and the whole land rejoiced with them.   Not courts and cities only, but even the ancient rest of the Uni- versities was disturbed by the universal exultations.

Ergo omnis longo solvit se Teucria luctu.

---

[6] March 23.   [7] Diary, March 28.

'Il faut attendre que tout le *bustle* soit passé,' writes Du-
mouriez, with whom he was corresponding on the subject of
the Slave Trade, 'pour voir des hommes sages et parler
raison.' But a deeper tone of feeling filled the mind of the
protector of the negro. On April 11, he says, 'Buonaparte
abdicated, and to have six million livres in Elba. My wife
and children went out to see the illuminations and staid
till late. Harrison [8] came over to me, and I stated to him
my ideas, that I must write a letter to the Emperor Alexander. I wrote to Lords Liverpool and Bathurst, stating
that Alexander's mind was doubtless in full unison with all
grand and humane proposals. I told Liverpool frankly that
we should look to government alone for not restoring any
slave colony without Abolition condition. There they had
no option. Lord Liverpool wrote me a very pleasing answer,
desiring a copy of my Abolition Letter for Castlereagh.'

It was a great crisis for his cause. 'It would be too
shocking,' he says to Mr. Gisborne, 'to restore to Europe
the blessings of peace with professions of our reverence for
the principles of justice and humanity, and at the same moment to be creating, for so it would really be doing wherever
the Slave Trade is extinct, this traffic in the persons of our
fellow-creatures. We are much occupied with the grand
object of prevailing on all the great European powers to
agree to a convention for the general Abolition of the Slave
Trade. Oh may God turn the hearts of these men ! What
a great and blessed close would it be of the twenty-two
years' drama !'

So paramount was this matter that at a 'meeting of the
African Institution at the Duke of Gloucester's—Lords
Grey, and Grenville, and Lansdowne, Macaulay, H. Thornton, W. Smith, James Stephen, Brougham, and Mackintosh '
—it was 'agreed to give up the Register Bill for the present,
and to push for a convention for the general Abolition—to
present an address to the Crown, to negotiate with the
foreign powers, and to forward the measure by all means.'[9]

He undertook to prepare a letter to the Emperor of Russia,
and another to Talleyrand, the anticipated head of the

[8] Secretary to the African Institution.   [9] Diary.

French administration, to whom, he says, ' I was personally known when I was in France thirty years ago with Mr. Pitt.'

His first high hopes were disappointed. It was evident that the French would not willingly abolish. ' Their merchants,' was the report which he received, ' are intent on gain any how. Gregoire and all the old amis-des-noirs men are in exceedingly bad odour. No respectable persons will have anything to do with them.'[1] Although therefore he touched upon the subject in congratulating his early friend, the Archbishop of Rheims, whom he hoped to find open to such an appeal, at the moment when he said 'nous sommes tiré du fond de l'abime, nous rentrons dans notre patrie, dont nous sommes exilés depuis un quart de siècle;'[2] though he began to work through La Fayette, and Baron Humboldt, and every other channel, yet he saw that everything depended on the firmness of the British government. Great Britain held the most important colonies of France, and she might refuse to restore them on any other terms than instant Abolition. Although therefore he was at one time ' doubtful whether he should not go to Paris on the Abolition errand,'[3] yet he thought it better to remain, and move an Address[4] to the Regent. ' My strength lies in the House of Commons ; therefore though more éclat in going over, it would not be politic.'

He urged ' that not a colony should be surrendered but on the condition that no African slaves are to be imported into it;' and was deeply disappointed to find that the treaty of peace restored to France all her colonies upon a vague promise that the Slave Trade should cease in five years.

On the evening, when Lord Castlereagh, on his return from Paris, entered the House of Commons, he was received with enthusiastic cheers. ' The only voice which remained mute amidst the fervent burst of joy, was that of Mr. Wilberforce. No heart beat more highly than his with patriotic emotions, but this feeling was mastered by another which forbad its utterance.'[5] As soon, therefore, as the cheers

[1] Diary, May 15.   [2] To W. Wilberforce, Esq., April 22.
[3] Diary, April 20.   [4] May 2.
[5] Memoranda, by J. S. Harford, Esq.

ceased, amidst which Lord Castlereagh laid on the table a copy of the treaty, he 'opened upon him.'[6]　'I cannot but conceive that in my noble friend's hands I behold the death-warrant of a multitude of innocent victims, whom I had fondly indulged the hope of having myself rescued from destruction.'[7]

His acquiescence in this article of treaty was in vain entreated by ministers on both sides of the water.　On June 13, he had 'a long talk with Lord Liverpool by appointment.'　'He had a letter too from the Prince of Benevento —all flummery.'[8]

Amidst these various disappointments, he was not a little 'thankful to hear that the Emperor Alexander charged himself with the Abolition in a Congress.　He wished to see me.'[9]　'Sunday, 12th. Up by half-past six, that I might pray to God for a blessing on my interview.　Lock—from which, to the Emperor.　In his waiting-room were several of his nobles —Prince Czartoriski, Prince of Oldenburgh, and others.　At length the Emperor, who was absent at Messe (Greek Church), returned, with the Princess of Russia (Oldenburgh).　He took me by the hand very cordially, and assured me that he was much interested for my object, and very glad to see me.　On my stating my fear that the French would not in fact abolish at the time settled, he replied heartily, "We must make them;" and then correcting himself, "we must keep them to it."　He shook hands with me cordially.　When I was expressing my concern about the treaty, he said, "What could be done, when your own ambassador gave way ?" '

It was too plain how far Lord Castlereagh had fallen short of what might have been effected.　Wilberforce felt it deeply; and there were not wanting those who would have gladly fanned this generous indignation into passion.　The day following that on which the treaty had been laid before the House he 'called at Lord Grenville's about Abolition—Lord Grey, Duke of Gloucester, and Ponsonby there.　They showed opposition spirit in their manner of judging, advising, re-

---

[6] Diary.

[7] 'I wrote a sketch of what I had said, the first time for twenty years or more, and sent it to the *Morning Chronicle*.'—Diary.

[8] Diary, June 7.　　　　[9] Ib. June 11.

solving, inquiring, and admitting.'[1] But he was not to be hurried by personal feeling into a hasty opposition. At first, indeed, he was 'much perplexed whether or not to oppose and strongly condemn ministers, and Castlereagh especially, for the Abolition business.' But calmer counsels prevailed, lest the Abolition proceedings should be deemed opposition and party measures.[2]

Further thought confirmed him in this conclusion. His only hope was in the approaching Congress at Vienna, and it must be his care to call forth such a spirit in this country as should compel ministers to take a higher tone.

The spirit for which he looked was awake, but he would have summoned it in vain if he had spoken the language of a party. The nation rejoiced too heartily in the blessings of peace to have any sympathy with opposition. 'I have used my utmost efforts,' he says, 'to keep our cause from becoming a party question, and the opposition have behaved handsomely in giving way to me.' He strove most successfully. On June 17, a great meeting of the Abolitionists was held at Freemasons' Hall, and party spirit was not suffered to intrude. A strong but temperate petition was agreed to; and, the more to mark the absence of an opposition spirit, intrusted for presentation to the Commons to 'William Wilberforce, the father of our great cause.' The same tone was held in Parliament, when, on June 27, the subject was brought forward by Lord Grenville in the Peers, and in the Commons by himself. Lord Grenville urged, as a convincing proof that it was no party measure, that it was in truth 'on these very motives its first promoter originally submitted it to Parliament; he, whose name it will transmit with unfading honour to all posterity; he, whose memory generations yet unborn, and nations yet uncivilised, will learn to bless. With these feelings the two great party leaders of our times fought together, and together conquered under this standard,' establishing within these lists a suspension of all hostilities—a sort of 'Truce of God.'

He brought the matter before the House of Commons, in a speech which produced a great effect, and carried

[1] Diary, June 7.   [2] Ibid.

his Address to the Prince Regent, and two days later an amendment to an Address upon the peace, by the unanimous vote of the Commons.

Though thus successful in Parliament, he was convinced 'that Lord Castlereagh's exertions, and consequently his success at Vienna, and even the disposition of the French government itself to accede to our wishes, will much depend on the degree in which the country appears to feel warmly on the question.' He still therefore called for petitions, and they came in abundance. More than 800, with near a million of signatures, soon covered the table of the House of Commons, and Lord Castlereagh was warned that in the coming Congress the minister of England could not afford to sacrifice the cause of Africa.

The bustle of this triumphant season added its burden to his severer occupations. More than once he was summoned by Alexander to confidential conversations. The Duchess of Oldenburgh, and the King of Prussia, alike desired to see and talk with him ; and from the latter he received a set of Dresden china, 'the only thing,' he playfully declared, 'I ever got by spouting.' But none amongst the band of monarchs and nobles interested him more than the Polish Prince Czartoriski, formerly Secretary to the Emperor. 'Czartoriski came in and talked to me for an hour or two about his country, and especially our institutions, with a view to their adoption. He seems eager for useful information, and whatever could improve the people. He acquiesced when I lamented the Emperor's being only fêted, and not let alone to see useful things, courts of justice, &c.'

The entries of his Journal bear little marks of the social agitation round him. 'The Bishop of Calcutta, Teignmouth, and C. Grant, &c. dined with me. Long and highly interesting talk with Bishop Middleton. He seems very earnest and pondering to do good—hopes for churches in different parts of India—favourable to schools and a public library—a college with discipline. His powers greater than we conceived—though his salary only 5,000*l.* a year—sad work—too little—less by 1,000*l.* a year than a puisne judge.'

At the end of July he left London, to devote the quiet of

the summer to his great design. All his hopes hung on the result of the approaching Congress. It was therefore of the utmost moment to give to the public mind on the continent the same impulse which it had received in England. He had already tried, through Cardinal Gonsalvi, to influence the Romish conclave, and he now opened a correspondence with a number of literati, Alexander Humboldt, Sismondi, Chateaubriand, and Madame de Staël, in the hope that he might act through them upon their countrymen. He was himself preparing a printed letter to Talleyrand, which was to be the manifesto of his supporters.

The Duke of Wellington had now become ambassador at Paris, and Lord Castlereagh had proceeded to his post at Vienna. Whatever was Lord Castlereagh's previous conduct, he now laboured heartily to attain the objects of the Abolitionists. Lord Liverpool declared, 'If I were not anxious for the Abolition of the Slave Trade on principle, I must be from the present state of that question in this country.'[3]

He soon found that France was altogether hostile to Abolition. 'Je vois avec affliction,' writes Humboldt, 'que dans ce pays, où l'on se refroidit sur tout, la question de la traité est consideré avec une coupable indifférence.'[4] 'Elle n'est point ici, comme elle l'étoit en Angleterre, une affaire d'argent; elle est liée uniquement à des passions nationales.'[5] Both as an English and as a revolutionary measure, it was so unpopular that the writers for their stage 'introduced into their old plays sarcasms against it, as *clap-traps*.'[6]

There had been in France no leader, like Mr. Wilberforce, to rescue the cause from the contamination of the Jacobins, and the Royalists looked coldly on a project which had been advocated by the 'amis des noirs.'

The wide circulation of his letter to Talleyrand first turned the tide of opinion. And 'at length,' he says, 'on November 15, I heard from the Duke of Wellington that the

[3] Letter to W. Wilberforce, Esq., Sept. 7.
[4] Letter to W. Wilberforce, Esq., Aug. 30.
[5] M. Sismondi to W. Wilberforce, Esq., March 3, 1815.
[6] J. Stephen, Esq., to W. Wilberforce, Esq., Oct. 14.

French had actually issued an order prohibiting all French subjects from slaving to the north of Cape Formosa.'[7] This news had been preceded a few days by the following letter of congratulation from Madame de Staël :—

'Combien vous devez être heureux de votre triomphe, vous l'emporterez et c'est vous et Lord Wellington qui aurez gagné cette grand bataille pour l'humanité. Soyez sure que votre nom et votre persévérance ont tout fait. D'ordinaire les idées triomphent par elles mêmes et par le tems, mais cette fois c'est vous qui avez devancé les siècles. Vous avez inspiré à votre Héros Wellington autant d'ardeur pour faire du bien qu'il en avoit eu pour remporter des victoires, et son crédit vers la famille royale a servi à vous pauvres noirs. Vous avez écrit une lettre à Sismondi qui est pour lui comme une couronne civique, ma petite fille tient de vous une plume d'or qui sera sa dot dans le ciel.[8] Enfin vous avez donné du mouvement pour la vertu à une génération qui sembloit morte pour elle. Jouissez de votre ouvrage, car jamais gloire plus pure n'a été donnée a un homme.'

At this time he was at Sandgate, living in the midst of his children, studying the Scriptures daily with some of them, 'walking and reading with them all,' and as busy doing good to those around him, as if his sympathies had never wandered from his own immediate circle : entering eagerly into any individual tale of suffering, and labouring, by schools and other institutions, to relieve the want and ignorance he saw. A few hours took him to Deal Castle, where he was 'kindly welcomed.˙ Carrington has made it an excellent house. He and I to Walmer Castle, and went over it. Not there for near thirty years before, in Pitt's time. Next day home again—all delighted to see me, and most kind.'

It is no wonder that causing and enjoying such social happiness, he should have 'felt melancholy at the idea of breaking up and going to town.'[9] But the session was

---

[7] Diary.
[8] The Duchess de Broglie had translated part of Mr. Wilberforce's Letter to his Constituents : an occasion of which Gen. Macaulay had availed himself in order to present to her a gold pen, as from the author.
[9] Diary.

about to open, and duty called him up to London.[1] 'Whitbread strong against government, and overbearing. Opposition seem to mean to practise the game of running down the ministry as drivellers. How impudent this, considering all things! Oh that they had abolished! How cheerily would I then defend them! Much distressed, however, about American war. Yet afraid of talking lest I should do harm rather than good by encouraging Maddison to stick out for terms.'[2] But his main business was still with his own cause. 'We have seen much of Wilberforce,' Mr. Henry Thornton tells Hannah More,[3] 'and heard his letters from many of the renowned of the earth, all seeming to pay homage to him. I almost anticipate more good from these new efforts than even from the Abolition here; and the name of Wilberforce has attained new celebrity, and his character and general opinions a degree of weight, which perhaps no private individual not invested with office ever possessed. My delight has consisted much in observing his Christian simplicity, and the general uniformity in his character and conduct, amidst the multitude of compliments, from the great, made on the part of some with much feeling.'

France was still hostile to Abolition. 'I was in hopes,' writes the Duke of Wellington,[4] 'that the King's measures had in some degree changed the public opinion; but I found yesterday that I was much mistaken. In truth we have nobody for us on the question excepting the King.'

But what Louis XVIII. either would not or could not carry was about to be accomplished by a stronger hand. From his rock of Elba, Buonaparte had been an observant witness of the feelings of this country. Upon his sudden return to power he sought to ingratiate himself with England by proclaiming a total and immediate Abolition of the Slave Trade. Thus was the bloody cup dashed from the hands of France, and the scourge of Europe became the pacificator of Africa. And when Louis was again restored by British arms, he was not suffered to revive the hateful traffic. 'I

---

[1] Nov. 10.   [2] Diary, Nov. 4.   .   [3] Dec. 2.
[4] Duke of Wellington to W. Wilberforce, Esq., Dec. 14.

357 LIFE OF WILBERFORCE. [CH. XXII.

have the gratification of acquainting you,' writes Lord Castle-reagh, ' that the long-desired object is accomplished, and that the present messenger carries to Lord Liverpool the unqualified and total Abolition of the Slave Trade through-out the dominions of France.'[5]

CHAPTER XXII.

JANUARY 1815 TO JULY 1817.

Illness of Henry Thornton—His death—John Bowdler's death—Letters —Abolition matters—Register Bill—Corn Laws—Letter to Lord Liver-pool—Mr. Stephen resolves to resign his seat—Diary—Waterloo— Blucher—Whitbread's death—Brighton Pavilion—West Indian oppo-sition to Registry Bill—Feelings under abuse—Spanish Abolition— Postponement of Registry—Illness—Sister's death—West Indian— Secret Committee—Dr. Chalmers—Habeas Corpus Suspension Act debate—Spanish Abolition.

THE year 1815 opened with a great sorrow. His old and steadfast friend, Henry Thornton, was at this time at Ken-sington Gore, to be nearer medical advice. His strength, never great, had been weakened by illness in the autumn ; but it was hoped that he was rallying from it, and no appre-hensions were expressed of its ultimate result. On January 10th, though ' so busy that he could hardly find time ' to leave the country, thinking ' it would be unkind not to go to town for Henry's sake, if, as they think, I could be any comfort to him,' he went to town, with no idea that his friend was in any danger, and ' was shocked to hear from Halford early the next morning that a sad change had taken place within the last five or six days ; inflammation going towards the heart, and the greatest danger. I had no idea of danger. He is so weak that he could not talk for above a minute or two. His voice broken and feeble. Poor dear Henry !' The next day was devoted to attendance on the

[5] To W. Wilberforce, Esq., July 31, 1815.

sufferer. 'I ordered myself to be refused to all but particular friends. Dealtry and I up praying with Henry and
Mrs. and Miss Thornton.'

'God alone knows,' he writes to H. More, 'what the
event will be. The sudden removal of such a man would
be a most mysterious providence. Poor Mrs. Henry
Thornton—since I have regarded his death as a probable
event, my heart has bled to see her surrounded by all her
nine little ones.'

'Our dear friend,' he tells Mr. Macaulay, 'is continually
before my mind's eye, and his emaciated figure and face are
very affecting.' Sunday brought a more favourable bulletin.
'Dr. Warren had been called in, and saw no reason why
Henry should not recover.'[1] With these rekindled hopes,
he was 'shocked and astonished by a letter from Dealtry,
dated four o'clock on Monday, to say that he was sinking
fast, and could not survive the night. I was off in about an
hour, and posted up to town. Inquired at Palace Yard, and
heard that our dear friend had expired at eight the preceding evening. Went on to Kensington Gore, where I
found his family and sweet Mrs. Grant.'[2] The next day was
spent with the mourners. 'In the morning I saw dear
Henry's body. I should not have known him.'

Another blow soon followed. There was not, amongst
his younger friends, one whom he valued as he did John
Bowdler. 'I loved him so warmly,' he says, when four busy
years with all their obliterating influences had passed by
since his death, 'that it quite delights me to find him esti-
mated at his true value. If poor Kirke White had lived he
might have grown into something of the same kind. But
Bowdler had a dignity—he would have become capable, I
assure you, of thundering and lightening. And then he was
the tenderest, and the humblest, and the most self-forgetting
creature.'[3] Bowdler too had just been mourning with him.
On the sorrowful day which followed Henry Thornton's
death, Mrs. Thornton had 'sent for him. He came in the
evening, and I had much talk with him. I took him to

[1] Diary.   [2] Ib.
[3] To the Rev. Francis Wrangham, July 7, 1819.

town next morning.'[4] It was the last time they met on earth. The very next day 'about one in the morning dear Bowdler burst a blood-vessel, and till seven, when his bed-maker came in, he lay in his chambers, humanly speaking in the most desolate state. Yet he told C. afterwards that his mind was then so filled with the Saviour that he thought of nothing else.' In such peace he was kept for the ten following days, during which he meekly bore the sudden breaking up of the strongest natural affections, and the highest intellectual powers. Upon January 31, he was pronounced 'better, the inflammation of the lungs subdued, and its conquest thought a great point.'[5] Yet on the following evening, 'a note came at seven, telling me of dear Bowdler's death at twelve o'clock this morning. Oh how little did I foresee, when we met lately, that it would be the last time of my intercourse with him on earth! O sit anima mea cum Bowdlero. I went on to Grosvenor Square, and saw his lifeless frame.'[6]

To Hannah More a few days later he opens his heart.

'Scarcely had a week passed away after the death of our dear friend Henry Thornton, before the excellent and elevated Bowdler was called out of this world; and scarcely had we returned from his funeral when tidings arrive of the departure of Dr. Buchanan. We are all involuntarily looking round and asking with an inquiring eye, Who next, Lord? Oh may the warnings have their due effect in rendering us fit for the summons!'

In this spirit he set at once to work. Other important business was pressing for despatch, and above all the general question of the effects of Abolition engrossed his attention. The Abolition party were gradually changing in a most important measure the line of their assault. Their objects had all along been strictly practical; they contended for no abstract rights of man, but they saw a great system of wrong, which called aloud to Heaven for some redressor. The Abolition of the Slave Trade was its first remedy. This would stanch the wounds of Africa; save the present victims of the Trade; and insure, as it was hoped, the kind and

[4] Diary, Jan. 18.   [5] Diary.   [6] Ib.

Christian treatment of the existing stock of labourers. Seven years had passed, and there was no visible improvement in the West. During all this time they had been anxiously waiting for a change of system in the treatment of the negro, and seeking by all private and inoffensive means to help it on.

Some of his more eager partisans could scarcely be held within these prudent limits, but burned, in order to check colonial crimes, to blazon them forth to the English public, and to arm themselves with popular indignation.

Mr. Wilberforce rejected these violent counsels. He sought to promote the ameliorating influence of Abolition, by preventing the illicit introduction of fresh labourers. Thus the Bill for a Register of Negroes was the first act of the new drama; and yet in this mildest and most necessary step, the principle of all his later conduct was in fact involved. For it was in truth carrying the appeal of the negro from the partial island legislatures to the supreme council of the empire; from the corrupted currents of Jamaica and Barbadoes to English sympathy and moral feeling. It led therefore, by legitimate consequences, as lesser remedies failed, step by step to the great principle of Emancipation. But he and others around him saw not as yet whither they should be brought.

The first steps of this transition may be traced in the short entries of Mr. Wilberforce's Diary. It was even at its opening a stormy course; every step in advance had to be fought for. ' 15th. Resolved on pushing Registry Bill immediately.'

' March 1st. An interview with Liverpool, Bathurst, and Vansittart, when they told us they could not support the Register Bill for want of proof of actual smuggling of slaves. 5th. Castlereagh returned yesterday. Public discontent running high, Corn Bill causâ. 6th. House. Corn Bill in committee—sad rioting at night. Both doors of the carriage, which set down members, opened, and member pulled out. None much injured. 8th. Called on Castlereagh by appointment to hear his narrative of Vienna proceedings on Abolition. I believe all done that could be

done.   Much pressed to speak on Corn Bill; and told Huskisson I would, if government would support the Register
Bill.   It would not be right to change my opinion; but one
may fairly take a more or less forward part from considerations of expediency.   House—Report of Corn Bill, and
tendency to riot.   9th. House.   Some mobbing, and people
savage and inveterate.'

' March 10th.   I reflected seriously if it was not my duty
to declare my opinions in favour of the Corn Bill.   I decided
to do it.'

' March 14.   All quite quiet here, but sad accounts from
France; Buonaparte having got to Lyons, and Horner an-
ticipating the worst.   15th.   Stephen decided to give up his
seat in Parliament; government not supporting the Register
Bill.   His integrity is great.'

Mr. Wilberforce's language with the government was
perfectly explicit.

He writes to Lord Liverpool, ' Your decision has not only
grieved me in consequence of the various evils with which I
saw but too plainly that determination was pregnant to Africa
and the black and coloured population of the West Indies,
but also on account of its sowing the seeds of disunion between myself and your government.   For the same consideration would prompt you to decide against a bill to attach
slaves to the soil; indeed against all measures which should
be brought forward for mitigating the sufferings and improving the condition of the slaves and the free coloured
population of the West Indies.

' Hitherto I have abstained from bringing into notice the
miseries of the black population, and I would still abstain,
if without divulging them they might gradually be removed;
but life is wearing away, and I should indeed be sorry if
mine were to terminate before at least a foundation had been
laid of a system of reformation, which I verily believe would
scarcely be more for the comfort of the slaves and free
coloured population than it would be for the ultimate security
of the West India colonies themselves.'[7]

His life was not to close until the very top-stone of this

[7] To the Earl of Liverpool, March 17.

work of reformation had been brought forth with shouting: but its foundations were now laid in heaviness, and for many patient, persevering years its walls and buttresses seemed scarcely to advance.

On the 17th he says, 'All we fear over in France. All the army false—sad work—and the King said to be fled to Belgium. How wonderful are these political changes!'

' 30th. Dined Grant's to meet Mackintosh, who very entertaining—speaking highly of Hall—entertainingly of France, Waverley, &c. How wonderful the change in France; yet what more natural than that an army should pull down and set up sovereigns, and that a vain-glorious nation should admire and be attached to a great warrior, who has extended the bounds and augmented the glory of France, rather than a peaceful king to whom they are long unaccustomed! Mackintosh thinks the French government had many warnings. French society, Mackintosh says, very agreeable. Dine at six—dinner very short—then coffee, and go to various houses. Mr. H. described them from six months' observation as fond of reading; but on pressing it seemed only the gazettes, in the public gardens at Paris.'

' April 1. Ministers are disposed for war; saying the Allies will have 700,000 men, and Buonaparte be unprepared. 7th. House—Lord Castlereagh's address preparatory to discussion about Buonaparte's escape, and the measures to be pursued. Address ambiguous, but Castlereagh's speech tending to war. Liverpool rather pacific. 8th. What an awful interval now: when all Europe collecting troops against Buonaparte. 700,000 mentioned by Lord Liverpool.' ' May 10th. To see Lord Castlereagh and Liverpool about the Abolition and St. Domingo. Castlereagh clear that the Bourbon government will never revive the Trade. I hear everywhere that the Duke of Wellington is in high spirits. Government ought to know both Buonaparte's force and their own. Yet I greatly dread their being deceived, remembering how Pitt was. 13th. All this time a fearful interval, expecting the bursting out of the war. It is amazing how little people seem moved. Generally, I think, for war; especially all who used to be friends of Pitt's government. 24th. Dined Sir T. Acland's, to meet

Walter Scott, Inglis, and others. Scott very unaffected and pleasing; some very clever colloquial hits. 29th. Wordsworth the poet breakfasted with us, and walked garden—staid long—much pleased with him.

'June 1. A report to-day from Brussels that it is still said there will be no fighting; Buonaparte will retire—surely there is no ground for this idea. 9th. Dined Sir G. Beaumont's to meet Wordsworth, who very manly, sensible, and full of knowledge, but independent almost to rudeness.'

Sunday, the 18th, was spent at Taplow, with his family. It is described in his Diary 'as a quiet day.' Above measure did he enjoy its repose. He shook off with delight the dust and bustle of the crowded city; and as he walked up the rising street of the village on his way to the old church of Taplow, he called on all around to rejoice with him in the visible goodness of God. 'Perhaps,' he said to his children, 'at this very moment when we are walking thus in peace together to the house of God, our brave fellows may be fighting hard in Belgium.' Words of almost a prophetic sound, as the battle of Waterloo was even then being fought. '22nd. Dr. Wellesley came and told us of the Duke of Wellington's splendid victory of the 18th.' 'A dreadful battle,' he writes word to Taplow. 'British victorious; but great loss. Duke of Brunswick and Lord Errol's eldest son killed. We are said to have lost 25,000, the French 50,000. My heart sickens at the scene! Yet praise God for this wonderful victory.'

'28th. Yesterday Prince Blucher's aide-de-camp, who had brought the despatches. Desired by Blucher several times over to let me know all that passed.' 'Did Marshal Blucher,' he was asked at his audience by the Regent, 'give you any other charge.' 'Yes, sir, he charged me to acquaint Mr. Wilberforce with all that had passed.' 'Go to him then yourself by all means,' was the Prince's answer, 'you will be delighted with him.' The veteran soldier's lively recollection of the efforts made in the preceding year to succour his afflicted countrymen, is highly to his honour. 'I have fought,' he wrote to the managing committee, 'two pitched battles, five engagements, masked three fortresses, taken two; but I have lost 22,000 men. Will the people of England be satisfied with me now ?   Desire Mr. Wilberforce to bestir himself.'

On the 6th, and more fully on the 7th, he was 'shocked to hear of Whitbread's death—having destroyed himself. It must have been insanity, as the jury immediately found it. Oh how little are we duly thankful for being kept from such catastrophes!' He was glad after their many differences to bear witness on the 11th, when a new writ for Bedford town was moved for, 'in a few words which I found pleased his friends,' to the thoroughly English character of this rugged but manly statesman.

His summer quarters were fixed this year at Brighton, 'a place,' he tells Lord Teignmouth, 'at which you have so often been, that I need scarcely explain why it appears to me so like Piccadilly by the sea-side. And yet so situated, when I can forget that there are at this season of the year woods that wave with all their leafy honours, I can delight in the fresh breeze from the sea, and in the varied forms of the beautiful and sublime, which this single object exhibits.'

Here the presence of the Prince Regent increased the general claims of society upon his straitened time. 'I at the Pavilion once. Lord Sidmouth and Bathurst called on me yesterday. Lord Castlereagh before. The foreign ministers there also. Lord St. Helen's and Carleton here. The Queen here about a week. The Pavilion in Chinese style—beautiful and tasty,'[8] 'though it looks,' he added, 'very much as if St. Paul's had come down to the sea and left behind a litter of cupolas. When there, the Prince and Duke of Clarence too very civil. Prince showed he had read Cobbett. Spoke strongly of the blasphemy of his late papers, and most justly. I was asked again last night, and to-night: but declined, not being well.' Three days afterwards he was again 'at the Pavilion—the Prince came up to me and reminded me of my singing at the Duchess of Devonshire's ball in 1782, of the particular song, and of our then first knowing each other.'[9] 'We are both I trust much altered since, sir,' was his answer. 'Yes, the time which has gone by must have made a great alteration in us.' 'Something better than that too, I trust,

---

[8] Diary.   [9] Ib.

sir.'[1] 'He then asked me to dine with him the next day,
assuring me that I should hear nothing in his house to give
me pain, .. alluding to a rash expression of one of his train,
when I declined the other day—" Mr. Wilberforce will not
dine with you sir."[2] .. that even if there should not be at another time, there should not be when I was there. At dinner
I sat between Lord Ellenborough and Sir James Graham.
The Prince desired I might be brought forward.'[3]

'At night in coming away I opened to Bloomfield, saying
I felt the Prince's kindness, but told him that it was inconvenient to me to come to the Pavilion often—children causâ.
He at once said, " I understand you." When I next saw the
Prince, he gave me a kind and general invitation. I heard
afterwards that Lord Ellenborough was asked to Pavilion
expressly to meet me. I was glad to hear it, as indicating
that I was deemed particular as to my company. What
misrepresentations of facts! Stephen heard that the Prince's
speech to me when inviting me intimated that if I came
hereafter I must take my chance; that commonly the talk
was such as I should dislike to hear. The direct contrary
was the fact. Really had I been covered with titles and
ribands, I could not have been treated with more real, unaffected, unapparently condescending, and therefore more
unostentatious civility.' Several times in the ensuing weeks
he was again a guest at the Pavilion, and met always with
the same treatment. ' The Prince is quite the English
gentleman at the head of his own table.' ' I was consulted
by the Queen's desire, whether proper to keep the Queen's
birth-day which fell on the thanksgiving-day. I replied
that not wrong, but rather doubtful. I went myself, forced
to obey the sergeant and summons, otherwise should have
deemed it for me ineligible, and therefore wrong; but now
went to mark my distinction. The party very large and
splendid. The ladies——sweetly unaffected and kind—
Princess Charlotte still shy—introduced to the bearded Lord
P. and found him under that strange exterior very mild and
pleasing.'

All this society and the late hours it caused, greatly inter-

[1] Con. Mem.   [2] Ib.   [3] Diary.

fered with his regular employments. 'What,' he wrote on the day of his last visit to the Pavilion, 'what with leave-takings and homage-payings and episcopal[4] visitations, and interruptions of the οἱ Πολλοὶ, my poor day has been run away with, so that I shall scarce have any time at my own command. This place is to me far more public than London, or rather than Kensington Gore. Oh how thankful I am that my wife is not one of the Pavilion-monger ladies, about to bring out her daughters!'

With him the expiring year closed with thoughts of soberness and prayer. 'What a change has a single year and less made in the circle of my acquaintance! Henry Thornton and his widow, and their excellent young friend and mine, Bowdler!'

'Sunday, Dec. 31st. Church morning. After church, we and our six children together—I addressed them all collected, and afterwards solemn prayer. How little likely on the 30th May, 1797, when I married, that we and all our six children (we never had another) should all be living and well! Praise the Lord, O my soul!'

The year 1816 opened with a storm of opposition, well fitted to try his firmness. 'The stream runs most strongly against us. Marryatt's violent and rude publication, Matthison's more fair, and Hibbert's well-timed one, all come out to meet us at the first opening of Parliament. But how vast is the influence of government; it is of that only we are afraid! Yet our cause is good, and let us not fear; assuredly God will ultimately vindicate the side of justice and mercy. Marryatt's new pamphlet is extremely bitter against my religious profession, thinking that nail will drive.'

Such attacks were daily repeated throughout his many years of patient perseverance in efforts for the good of others. As often as the old slanders died out, a new set were produced, of such an aggravated kind, that 'if they had been true,' he told the House of Commons,[5] 'nothing but a special Providence could have prevented my being hanged full thirty years ago.' Yet never in his most unguarded hours did he manifest any bitterness of feeling towards his

---

[4] The Archbishop of York.   [5] Debate, May 22.

traducers ; never in public was he led into angry recrimination. Often did he provoke some of his more impetuous
colleagues by taking the part of the West Indian planter —
suggesting excuses for his conduct—alleging that there was
no class of persons from whom it was so much the interest of the actual managers to hide the abuses of the
system—and so extenuating their moral guilt that he drew
upon himself a portion of the storm which lowered over his
West Indian slanderers.

No such opposition stayed him on his course, and he
would at once have pressed forward his Registration Bill, if
he had not been arrested as before by the evident interests of
the cause. Spain and Portugal were now the only European
nations which continued the accursed Trade ; and Portugal
had agreed to present restrictions, and a speedy Abolition.
Spanish co-operation was now therefore of the first importance, and the hope of gaining it held back once more his
hand.

'With unfeigned joy,' he tells Mr. Stephen, ' I have just
heard from Lord Castlereagh that the council of the Indies,
to which the whole question of the Abolition had been referred by the Spanish government, had reported in favour of
total and immediate Abolition. Lord C. says it is of great
importance not to talk of the thing at present.'

To secure the result, he consented, after a consultation with
his principal supporters, Romilly, Brougham, Horner, William
Smith, Macaulay, Stephen, not to bring on the Registry Bill.

But though he consented to this delay, he was at work
to carry the bill. On March 16, he says, ' called on Lord
Wellesley about Register Bill, and talked with him over old
times and persons.'[6] To Lord Liverpool he ' stated the
pain it would cost' him ' to oppose his government systematically on a question which will, I am clear, interest
in our favour the bulk of the religious and moral part of
the community.' The same views he pressed on Lord
Bathurst, ' who assured me that he had told the West Indians frankly, he would next year pass a Registry Bill, if
their colonial assemblies would not do it.'

[6] Diary.

An affection of the lungs kept him much a prisoner during this spring. This only multiplied the private claimants on his time, and this year they abounded, from the tale of ordinary distress, and the throng of 'breakfasters,' to the 'Duke of Kent, who more than once called' on him 'for two hours about his affairs, and why going abroad—hardly used.' Occasionally too he took part in the debates of the House of Commons, and always with effect. In the month of March 'the opposition, of which Ponsonby' was 'the head, but Brougham the most active, incessant, and bitter,' were 'pushing at government about the Property Tax, or, as it is the fashion with opposers to call it, and as it is pretty fairly called, the Income Tax. Many of government's friends are against them on this question. I think that though in itself it were right it would not be expedient.'[7] This view he urged on the House, and had no small effect in causing the defeat of ministry. 'I spoke last of all, after Lord Castlereagh, having been personally alluded to by him. I never remember producing more effect.'

His summer holidays, for which he had gone to Lowestoft, were broken in on by a great grief. Before he could reach her sick bed his only sister died. 'I prayed by my dear sister's dead body, and with the face uncovered. Its fixedness very awful.' 'How affecting it is,' he writes to Lowestoft, 'to leave the person we have known all our lives, on whom we should have been afraid to let the wind blow too roughly, in the cold ground alone! This always strikes my imagination.'

There had been no abatement of the storm which had been raised against the Registration Bill. It was taken up as a colonial question, and one and all clamoured loudly against its proposers. All this tumult of calumny passed over him almost unnoticed. One charge—that he had pledged himself not to interfere with the condition of the slaves, he thought deserved an answer. 'It was,' he tells Mr. Stephen, 'the condition of the West Indian slaves which first drew my attention, and it was in the course of my inquiry that I was led to Africa and the Abolition. As long

[7] Diary, May 10.

ago as in 1781, the very first year of my being in Parliament, and when I was not twenty-two years of age, I wrote a letter to James Gordon, expressing my hopes that some time or other I might become the instrument of breaking, or at least easing, the yoke of these poor creatures.'

The state of public feeling forced him at this time ' to lie upon his oars in the West Indian cause.   When Parliament meets, the whole nation will be looking up for relief from its own burdens, and it would betray an ignorance of all tact to talk to them in such circumstances of the sufferings of the slaves in the West Indies.   We should specially guard against appearing to have a world of our own.'

The opening of Parliament found the political horizon unusually dark.   ' We are here (in the Secret Committee[8])' he writes back to his family at Hastings, 'in the midst of accounts of plots, &c., but a gracious Providence watches over us. Remember to pray in earnest against sedition, privy conspiracy, and rebellion.'[9]   ' The Secret Committee,' he says three days later, ' put off; and the chief conspirators having been taken up the day before, all went off quietly to-day. House.   Lord Milton's business put off for ministers to be at their posts, if there is a riot in Spa Fields.   Hunt's second meeting.'   ' The seizing of the ringleaders prevented bloodshed from the Spa Fields mob.   Hunt seems a foolish, mischief-making fellow, but no conspirator, though the tool of worse and deeper villains.   Cobbett is the most pernicious of all ; but God will bless and keep us, I fear not. The blasphemous songs and papers of the seditious will disgust all who have any religion, or any decency.'

' Battersea Rise (says his Diary of April 26) to dinner, where Southey.   Saw him for the first time, and much struck with him. Acland, Lord Sidmouth, Robert Grant, Governor Raffles, &c.   We dined at seven o'clock, and time flew away so rapidly, that we kept on chatting till two in the morning, and my watch having stopped, I thought it was half-past eleven.'   ' It was at Battersea Rise,' writes Mr. Southey,[1] ' at Sir Robert, then Mr. Inglis's, that I saw Mr. Wilberforce for the first time. A memorable day it was to me.

[8] Appointed Feb. 5.   [9] Feb. 8.   [1] Oct. 31, 1835.

'How it happened I know not, but although no person can be more disinclined to disputation than myself, we got into one upon the question of Catholic Emancipation ; your father and Sir Thomas Acland taking the one side, and I the other. Inglis had not yet been in Parliament, and I did not know what his opinions were upon the subject. Jebb I knew agreed with me ; for with him, as coming from Ireland, the state of that country had been one of the first things on which we had touched when introduced to each other. He took little or no part. It was a subject on which I spoke with no diffidence, because nothing could appear to me more certain, than the perilous consequences which would ensue, if the friends of the Church should be so far deluded by its enemies, as to assist them in throwing down the bulwarks of the Protestant establishment. But if my temper had been likely to hurry me into any unbecoming warmth, your father's manner would effectually have repressed it. His views, when I thought him most mistaken, were so benign, he took the ground of expediency with so religious a feeling, and argued with such manly yet such earnest sincerity, that if it had been possible to have persuaded me out of an opinion so deeply and firmly rooted, he would have done it. Our discussion, for so it may be called, was protracted till two in the morning.'

'9th. Roman Catholic question decided—I would not speak. Canning poor—Peel excellent—Lord Castlereagh very good.'

'16th. Dr. Chalmers breakfasted with me.'

'May 19th. All the world wild about Dr. Chalmers ; he seems truly pious, simple, and unassuming. Sunday, 25th. Off early with Canning, Huskisson, and Lord Binning, to the Scotch Church, London Wall, to hear Dr. Chalmers. Vast crowds—Bobus Smith, Lord Elgin, Harrowby, &c. So pleased with him that I went again ; getting in at a window with Lady D. over iron palisades on a bench. Chalmers most awful on carnal and spiritual man. Home tired, and satisfied that I had better not have gone for edification.' 'I was surprised to see how greatly Canning was affected ; at times he quite melted into tears. I should have thought he had been too much hardened in debate to show such signs of feeling.'

The Secret Committee was still sitting, and he attended constantly at its deliberations, in vain endeavouring, on the 18th, 'to get Ponsonby and Lord Milton to agree to the Report; they decidedly resolved not to do so.' The Report was presented on the 20th, and on the 23rd, the Suspension of the Habeas Corpus Act was proposed by government. Mr. Wilberforce reluctantly supported what he deemed an unavoidable severity. His freedom from all party spirit gave a weight to his decision, which was keenly felt by opposition. Sir Samuel Romilly directed all his powers to destroy the effect of so unimpeachable a judgment; and another member in a different strain attacked him warmly on the third reading with an unworthy sarcasm aimed at his religious work. 'The honourable and religious member,' as he addressed him amidst cries of order from all sides of the House, ' could hardly vote for any measure more thoroughly opposed to vital Christianity.' He was tempted, he said, to retort on his opponent as the honourable and irreligious member, but with a rare forbearance he repressed the impulse to render railing for railing.

His Diary simply states, ' Burdett forced me up in self-defence, and the House sided with me.' 'Never in my parliamentary life,' says a member present, ' did I hear a speech which carried its audience more completely with it, or was listened to with such breathless attention.' 'You know,' says another, ' Burdett's manner when attacked, his head high, his body drawn up. His tall figure as he sat on the upper bench immediately behind was the higher of the two, even when Wilberforce stood up to speak. But when after speaking for a few minutes Wilberforce turned round to address him amidst the cheers of the House, he seemed like a pigmy in the grasp of a giant. I never saw such a display of moral superiority in my life.'

His possession of this ready power of self-defence made his uniform forbearance the nobler. 'If there is anyone,' said Mr. Canning, 'who understands thoroughly the tactics of debate, and knows exactly what will carry the House along with him, it certainly is my honourable friend the member for Bramber.'

His business this Session ended with moving an Address to the Crown to strengthen ministers in their negotiations with Spain for the Abolition of the Slave Trade.

The issue of this he communicates three months later to Macaulay.

'A very friendly letter from Castlereagh informs me, that he has actually received the treaty with Spain (signed) for abolishing the Slave Trade generally and finally in May, 1820, and immediately to the north of the Line. Also, which is scarcely less valuable, that a system of mutual search is agreed to be established for enforcing the Abolition law.'

This was indeed 'glorious intelligence;' a blessed fruit of many years of labour spent in striving calmly and patiently to arouse the slumbering moral sense of a great people. 'Let us,' is his characteristic call to his fellow-worker, Mr. Stephen, 'let us praise God for it.'[2]

CHAPTER XXIII.

JULY 1817 TO OCTOBER 1818.

Recess—Letters — Graffham — Stansted — Haytian correspondence, and Professors—Distressed sailors—West Indian—Mrs. Fry and Newgate —Secret Committee—Employment of Spies—Dissolution of Parliament—Goes into the country—Rokeby—Rydale — Muncaster —Keswick —Southey.

THE vacation gave him time to write to the Emperor of Russia, on the steps to be taken in the approaching Congress for securing the execution of the Abolition compact. Of the reception of this letter he received from its bearer, the Rev. Lewis Way, a characteristic sketch. 'Non erat privati cujusdam cum inperatore, sed Christiani cum Chris-

---

[2] Letter to James Stephen, Esq.

tiano amicissima collatio. Mores humanissimi; vultus ar-
ridens, cor apertum; loquela ardens; amor pœne vel
potius penitus divinus: talia, teste Spiritu, memorabilem
hanc interlocutionem obsignaverunt.'

To the seat of this friend he this year took his family to
spend their summer holidays at Stansted. On the road he
halted a few days at the parsonage of Graffham, of which he
says to Mr. Stephen :—

' I never was at a place where my time was so little at my
own command. Dear Sargent has much to show me in this
beautiful country, and I am therefore forced out in spite of
my remonstrances, and driven in a delightful little open carriage, which to anyone who like me cannot bear much
exercise and feels but languid, is the very acme of luxury.
Then we have some of his good neighbours to dine with us,
so that the evening also is expended. How you would rejoice
in ventilating on the hill under which I am now writing ; and
when at Stansted you are but twelve miles to a horseman
or good footman from this place. You would be delighted
to see the Sargents with seven children, most of them as fair
as the light around them !'

He spent a month at Stansted, 'making an excursion for
twenty-four hours to Huskisson's country-house, where I was
most kindly received.' 'This is an entertaining and healthy
holiday-place for the children.' He delighted in receiving
almost as much as giving such proofs of friendship ; and
with playful philosophy threw aside any of the little troubles
which impeded its exercise. ' Mr. Smith, the steward,' are
his Stansted Park reflections, ' was all that could be desired
—extremely obliging ; in short, just representing his master.
He, dear kind man, had endeavoured in every way to render
me comfortable, had left me wine, and even china, plates,
&c. ; and the key of all his libraries, even of the sanctum
sanctorum. We of course tried to do as little harm as possible.
Though at first I thought we must have gone away on account of the housekeeper's bad temper, which sadly effer-
vesced.' [1] 'You know the Indians have a way of setting
oddly contrasted animals to fight with each other, and I

---

[1] Diary, Oct.

really long to set our old coachman and this fine lady in single combat.'

The affairs of Hayti now occupied much of his time. Christophe, the Emperor of Hayti, was a great man. Born and educated as a slave, he had raised himself to absolute power, which he was most solicitous to use for the good of his countrymen. To educate his people, to substitute the English tongue for that of France, and the Reformed faith for that of Rome, were his leading projects ; and in carrying them into effect he sought for Mr. Wilberforce's aid and counsel. His letters everywhere abound in truly elevated plans. Mr. Wilberforce entered warmly into his views, and laboured, at an unsparing expenditure of time and trouble, to procure for him the professors, clergymen, and schoolmasters he needed—as well as to direct prudently his grand designs for the elevation of his countrymen.

These grander designs never took with him the place of humbler efforts to do good, and while seeking to regenerate Hayti, he was labouring as hard to amend the hardships of the British sailor, as if his eye had never travelled beyond the nearest objects. Thus he had now 'much talk with Lieutenant Gordon about the poor sailors, who are starving with cold and hunger : by his own visitation many of them prove to be not merely sailors of the royal navy, but petty officers ; one a black man, who such in the Shannon when she took the American frigate—wrote letters by him to the city aldermen, Macaulay, &c. Collected a small private meeting— and Stephen going to Croker—a hulk set up by the Admiralty for the poor fellows.'[2] He 'heard' soon after with delight of ' the success of the poor sailors' relieving plan,' from which small beginning sprung all those institutions which are now so frequent at our outports for the reception of these gallant, but often thriftless men.

But though thus zealous in every good work, the year closed upon him with many humiliating thoughts of his own unprofitable service and the goodness of his God. ' I am much affected,' he tells Mr. Stephen, ' with Lord St. John's death, once the inmate of my house for months together.

[2] Diary.

He, his elder brother, and Chaplin (called κατ' εξοχην, "strong Chaplin"), all gone, and I still on earth. Let me work at the eleventh hour. Lord, work in and by me, Amen.'[3] With this sustained humility of tone, his Journal, as years pass on, becomes more and more the record of rejoicing confidence in God. 'Surely He has blessed me in all things, both small and great, in a degree almost unequalled.'

All the natural objects round him had become the symbols of the presence and love of his heavenly Father. ' I was walking with him in his verandah,' says a friend, ' watching for the opening of a night-blowing cereus. As we stood by in eager expectation, it suddenly burst wide open before us. " It reminds me," said he, as we admired its beauty, "of the dispensations of Divine Providence first breaking on the glorified eye, when they shall fully unfold to the view, and appear as beautiful as they are complete."' ' For myself,' says one of his letters, (Aug. 28,) when to his own family he unveiled his heart, ' I can truly say, that scarcely anything has at times given me more pleasure than the consciousness of living as it were in an atmosphere of love; and heaven itself has appeared delightful in that very character of being a place, in which not only everyone would love his brethren, but in which everyone would be assured that his brother loved him, and thus that all was mutual kindness and harmony, without one discordant jarring; all sweetness without the slightest acescency.'

There was no obtrusive display of such emotions. True Christian joy is for the most part a secret as well as a severe thing.[4] The full depth of his feelings was hidden even from his own family. ' I am never affected to tears,' he says more than once, ' except when I am alone.'[5] A stranger might have noticed little else than that he was more uniformly cheerful than most men of his age. Closer observation showed a vein of Christian feeling mingling with and purifying the natural flow of a most happy temper; whilst those who lived most continually with him, could trace distinctly in his tempered sorrows, and sustained and almost child-like gladness of heart, the continual presence of that ' peace

---

[3] Journal.   [4] Res severa est verum gaudium.   [5] Journal.

which the world can neither give nor take away.' The pages
of his later Journal are full of bursts of joy and thankfulness;
and with his children, and his chosen friends, his full heart
welled out ever in the same blessed strains; he seemed too
happy not to express his happiness; his 'song was ever of
the loving-kindness of the Lord.' An occasional meeting at
this time with some who had entered life with him, and were
now drawing wearily to its close with spirits jaded and tempers worn in the service of pleasure or ambition, brought
out strongly the proof of his better 'choice.' 'This session,'
he says, 'I met again Lord ——, whom I had known when
we were both young, but of whom I had lost sight for many
years. He was just again returned to Parliament, and we
were locked up together in a committee-room during a division. I saw that he felt awkward about speaking to me, and
went therefore up to him. "You and I, my Lord, were
pretty well acquainted formerly." "Ah, Mr. Wilberforce,"
he said cordially; and then added with a deep sigh, " you
and I are a great many years older now." "Yes, we are,
and for my part I can truly say that I do not regret it."
"Don't you," he said, with an eager and almost incredulous
voice, and a look of wondering dejection, which I never can
forget.'[6]

These happy fruits were in part the results of a naturally
cheerful temper leavened with religious feeling ; but they
had been perfected by sharp and systematic discipline. He
kept a most strict watch over his heart. He still recorded
by a set of secret marks the results of frequent and close
self-examination under a number of specific heads. He used
every help he could devise for keeping always alive in his
soul a sense of the nearness and goodness of his God. He
'found great benefit in putting down motives for humiliation, motives for thankfulness, and so on, which' he
'carried about with' him, 'and could look at in any time of
leisure.'

The year 1818 was an important era in the West Indian struggle; for in it the friends of Africa were led into
new counsels and a new position. The opposition to the

[6] Con. Mem.

Registration Act forced them to establish its necessity, by showing the actual state of the slave population; and the inquiries which this rendered necessary revealed an amount of crime and cruelty, which showed that there was no cure for the evils of the system, short of its entire overthrow. Now therefore for the first time the word *emancipation* occurs amongst his secret counsels.

The fine shadings of these altering views, and their various colours as they pass into each other, cannot be so well exhibited as by free extracts from the private Diary in which they are recorded at the moment, mingled with the intervening objects which filled up his time. The year opened with his receiving an account, 'Jan. 7th, of the dreadful murder of a poor slave—buried without a coroner's inquest —but dug up, and found all mangled—yet brougnt in by the jury, Died by the visitation of God. My mind becomes so much affected by the sad state of those poor injured wretches that it keeps me awake at night. Oh may God enable us to possess the nation with a due sense of their wrongs, and that we may be the instrument of redressing them!'

'30th. To Stephen's to meet at dinner Sir James Mackintosh, Sir Samuel Romilly, William Smith, Brougham, and Macaulay—an Abolition consultation. 31st. To Castlereagh's after breakfast. He impressed me with a danger of pressing for Emancipation, till Abolition by other powers secured—the French, Dutch, and American right of search. Much struck with his remarks and information.'

'Feb. 4th. With Mrs. Fry at Newgate. The order she has produced is wonderful—a very interesting visit—much talk with the governor and chaplain—Mrs. Fry prayed in recitative—the place from its construction bad.'

'6th. To Freemasons'—meeting for new churches. Archbishop of Canterbury in the chair—many of the bishops. The Duke of Northumberland moved the resolutions. I chosen Vice President with a multitude of high-churchmen, and great men—said a few words.'

'11th. Secret Committee. House—Fazakerley's motion —spoke—avowed openly my abominating the employing of

spies and informers altogether, on the grounds of religion
and morality, and sound policy.' ' I really hope I shall be
able to become an instrument in beating out the system,
and of doing thereby more service to my country than I
almost ever yet effected. Canning very clever, and sometimes quite admirable, but too artificial; Tierney terribly
bitter, and Bennett very coarse, but very strong.'

' March 5th. House on Phillips's motion—spies' and informers' examination. Wished not to speak, and meant ; but
at last forced up. Never did I give a clearer vote ; for never
would there have been a more long, intricate, complicated,
unprofitable inquiry.'

' 26th. Gloucester House to dinner—smaller party than
usual—Lord Limerick, Lord Stuart (I sat next to him, and
talked a little seriously to him, for which the Duke thanked
me afterwards), Baron de Bode, Lord Shaftesbury, who told
me the combined army's going upon Paris was in obedience
to a letter from the Regent written without even advising
with his ministers.'

' June 2nd. Heard Burdett on Parliamentary Reform—
moving for universal suffrage and annual parliaments, and
Cochrane seconding; with tears taking leave of the House.
Then Brougham's excellent reply.

' 10th. The Regent came to the House, and not only
prorogued, but dissolved the Parliament—the first time since
Charles the Second's reign. Tierney resented it. Samuel
Thornton resigns. Dear Babington retires from Leicester—
we are grieved beyond measure. Sad work, my old friends
leaving me.'

He fulfilled this year the second of two intentions of his
earlier life. ' There are two places,' he had said, ' to which,
if I ever marry, I will take my wife—to Barley Wood, and
Westmoreland.' Barley Wood he had often visited, and
this year Mr. Southey enticed him onwards to Westmoreland.
' I am very sorry that you are not in this delightful country
during this delightful weather. We are enjoying a real
honest, old-fashioned summer, such as summers were forty
years ago, when I used to gather grapes from my grand-
mother's chamber window—warm weather for polemical

writing; and yet little as such writing is to my taste, I have been employed in it for the last week. B., with his usual indiscretion, thought fit to attack me from the hustings. It was wholly unprovoked, as I had taken no part whatever in the election, and everything which he said of me was untrue. So I am giving him such a castigation as he never had before, and which it is to be hoped may last him for his life.' Ten days later he writes again. 'The heat of the summer is checked, and we are enjoying sun and showers, with just such a temperature as makes exercise pleasant, and allows one to enjoy a little fire at night. I am as true to the hearth as a cricket or a favourite spaniel, and reckon it a privation when the weather is too hot for enjoying this indulgence.'

A few extracts from the Diary will sketch out this holiday. 'July 18th. Reached Rokeby, and was most kindly received.' '19th. Long home walk—delightful banks of Greta—through stony bed.' From this hospitable house he interrupts a business letter to Mr. Stephen, with 'How I wish you were here, not only that I might see you, but that you might see the sublime and beautiful scenery of this charming place! A highlander long absent from his native land, coming out of the south with a companion, broke out on arriving here, with "Oh this I understand, this river Greta talks Scotch."' '21st. Carriage, and walking by the river Greta—Brignal woods—grand views. Dr. Wollaston was very agreeable—looks forward to greater and greater discoveries, except perhaps in astronomy. Walter Scott came to dinner to stay some time—Scott very entertaining, full of stories, which he tells excellently.' 'Sept. 2nd. R. and S. off to see Keswick.' They went longing to see Southey, but charged not to call upon him, 'lest seeing lads of your age, should too painfully remind him of the son whom he has lost.'

'5th. I took a two hours' walk by Rydale and Grasmere, and a good deal tired.' It was not a little affecting to see him retracing with delight all his haunts of earlier days—another man in many things; his body bent and weakened, but his mind furnished and matured; his soul purer and well established after many struggles; having passed through all the bustling scenes of an unquiet life with the simplicity of early tastes and affections unimpaired, pointing out to his children every well-remembered beauty, and teaching them by golden precepts and a most eloquent example the secret of his own calm and happy temper.

'20th. Fair at church-time, and I went to Grasmere, where —— read a common-place sermon at cantering or rather galloping pace; he preached last Sunday a sad trifling sermon. In the afternoon I walked to two or three cottages, and talked on religion to the people.' His fervent spirit could scarce be contained in the full sight of such a state of things. 'Our population,' Mr. Southey told him, 'is in a deplorable state both as to law and gospel. The magistrates careless to the last degree; whilst the clergyman of —— has the all-comprehensive sin of omission to answer for. The next generation I trust will see fewer of these marrying and christening machines. The manners of the people have dreadfully worsened during his long sleep. Even within my remembrance there has been a great change.'

During his short stay amongst the Lakes Mr. Wilberforce did what he could to check this evil. He strove to rouse the slumbering energies of all whom he could reach or influence, and in all his scenery excursions visited the poor himself. He was now meditating an excursion to Muncaster and Keswick. 'I am almost as much a fixture,' Southey wrote in answer to his inquiries, 'as my great neighbour Skiddaw himself; so that whenever you visit Keswick you will be certain of finding me . . . We have had a longer continuance of fine weather in this country than any person can remember. Saturday was our first wet day . . . The clouds have risen this evening, and we have at this moment some of those beautiful appearances which a stranger would think well purchased by a wet day. I hope this is indicative of another change.'

On September 28th he set off 'by Broughton for Muncaster, over Stoneshead, very near dark. Most kindly received—Morritt there—his nephew Stanley, a gentlemanly young man, Mr. Stow, Lord Muncaster's executor, Lord and Lady Lindsay, and five children. Staid at Muncaster till Friday; strongly pressed to stay longer, but could not.

Morritt very cheerful, unassuming, full of anecdote, and a good deal of knowledge—literary—of the old-fashioned Church of England religion, and high-spirited as to integrity, generosity, gratitude, friendly attachment, &c. Most kind to his family and friends. Never did I see such effects of light on the mountains, except perhaps on the Marine Alps from Nice, as here in the afternoon. I commonly walked with Mr. Stow and Lord Lindsay, and wrote letters.'

On October 2nd he 'exchanged Muncaster for Keswick, reaching it after dark by Ennerdale-head and Loweswater, and got to very comfortable lodgings. I found afterwards that Mrs. L, our hostess, had been a pretty young woman, whom I remember forty-two years ago as Polly Keen of Hawkshead; now she is a toothless, nut-cracker-jawed old woman, but quite upright and active. 3rd. On the lake with poor Thomas Hutton, who now seventy-five or six, but still active.'

'Sunday, 4th. Appearance of the clouds and vapours, half-concealing, half disclosing the mountains, most wonderful from the churchyard. Keswick worse now as to morals than thirty years ago, and still more forty. So says Southey, who has lived there fifteen years; he is always at church. Wordsworth too at Grasmere. Read prayers, &c. to my family in the afternoon. Spent the following week at Keswick—visited Southey, who very pleasing, light as a bird in body, and till the loss of his son, I hear his flow of spirits astonishing. He is a man of extraordinary method and punctuality; hence booksellers love to have to do with him. His library excellent; filled with curious Spanish and Portuguese manuscript volumes. He allots one time (before breakfast) to poetry, another to history, and so on. His History of Brazil is that to which he looks for fame. He is kind, hospitable, generous, virtuous, and, I hope, religious, but too hasty in his judgments, and too rash in politics. Hence he would be a dangerous counsellor though an able defender.'[7]

Four days later, on the eve of his departure from the Lakes, this Keswick visit was returned. 'Southey with us

[7] Diary, Oct. 10.

—much delighted with him.' What Southey thought of him may be told in his own words. 'I saw more of your father during his short residence in this country, than at any or all other times; and certainly I never saw any other man who seemed to enjoy such a perpetual serenity and sunshine of spirits. In conversing with him you felt assured that there was no guile in him; that if ever there was a good and happy man on earth, he was one; and that eminently blessed as he was with a benign and easy disposition, the crown of all his blessings was that inward and undisturbed peace which passeth all understanding.

'I recollect one circumstance during his visit to the Lakes, which shows the perfect reliance his servants had upon his good nature,—forbearance it might have been called in any other person, but in him it was no effort. The coachman came in to say that some provision concerning the horses had been neglected, and your father with a little start of surprise, replied, "that indeed he had not thought of it." "No !" said the coachman, and "since you have been in this country, you have all of you been so lake, and valley, and river, and mountain mad, that you have thought of nothing that you ought to have thought of." '

CHAPTER XXIV.

OCTOBER 1818 TO JANUARY 1822.

Hayti — Aix-la-Chapelle — Christophe, and his professors — Religious anniversaries — Lady Holland — Summer tour — Barham Court — Barley Wood—Blaize Castle—Wells—Malvern—Elmdon—Wood Hall —Disturbed state of the country—Opening of Session — Restrictive Bills— Diary—Opposes education not grounded on religion—Dean of Carlisle's death—Attendance on the sick—Paul's Cray—Arrival of the Queen— His conduct in Parliament——Adjourns the inquiry—Privately addresses the King—Moves and carries an address to the Queen—Her chief law-adviser undertakes that it shall be accepted—Her reception of it—He is exposed to much calumny—Weymouth—Letter from Lord John Russell —Return to London—Bill of Pains and Penalties—its abandonment— Bath —Death of Christophe—Queen's name finally left out of Liturgy —Domestic character—Marden Park and his life there—Illness and death of his eldest daughter.

HIS summer rambles and the expedition to the Lakes had not withdrawn the care of Mr. Wilberforce from his Haytian and West Indian clients. He made great efforts to obtain the recognition of Christophe at the Congress of Aix-la-Chapelle, but in vain. The refusal was most injurious to Hayti. There was nothing to which Mr. Wilberforce more earnestly sought to lead Christophe than to reduce his army, and ' to wean him from his hankering after the conquest of the Haytian republic.'[1] But until his independence was acknowledged, he must maintain his troops to guard against a French invasion ; and this necessity led to his destruction.

The general superintendence of the emigrants to Hayti, which fell on Mr. Wilberforce, was full of disappointment and annoyance. He had to select men from all ranks of life —professors for the royal college, physicians and divines, governesses for the royal daughters, tutors for the King's sons, down to ordinary teachers of a common school, and

[1] To James Stephen, Esq., Sept. 17.

'two ploughmen and their ploughs and families.' They
went into a land where the whole tone of society was utterly
demoralised; and though he inquired most cautiously, scru-
tinised most closely, and chose at last the best who offered,
few could stand the trial. The professors quarrelled with
each other; some, by open vice, disgraced the cause they
were bound to further; some were carried off by dissolute-
ness and disease; whilst those who laboured faithfully found
their hands weakened in their single striving against the multitude of evildoers, and added often, by their desponding letters, to the common burden of this most oppressive correspondence. Still he went on with his labours cheerfully, and never
fainted in them, so long as the opportunity of service lasted.

By December 24 he was again at Kensington, surrounded
by his scattered family; and the new year opens with his
usual tone of deep humility and resolutions of service. 'It
is with a heavy heart that I look forward to the meeting,
so many friends absent.'

As the spring advanced, he took a leading part in the
religious meetings which the first week in May brought
round. Never, perhaps, was his eloquence more winning
than when on these subjects it flowed fresh from his full
heart—and many a stranger to the ordinary excitements of
the town returned, at the week's end, into the country nerved
by it afresh for his path of solitary labour. He delighted,
too, to extend to such visitors his ready hospitality. But
he felt greatly the fatigue these gatherings caused. 'Oh,
how glad I am,' he says, May 15, 'that the tenth meeting is this day over! The consumption of time is really
too great.' 'Would it had been my favoured lot,' writes
Hannah More,[2] 'to hear one of twelve speeches in ten
days!'

'May 17. A very large and miscellaneous party of breakfasters. Afterwards called on —— at Holland House. Shown
up to Lady Holland under the name of its being Lord Holland.' She pressed me to come to breakfast. I see plainly
that —— and —— pay the price of civility to her for their
kind reception at Holland House. But it may be out of

[2] June 26.

good will to Lord Holland, who is truly fascinating, having something of his uncle's good humour.—18th. House, on Tierney's motion,[3] till all over. By far the largest number that ever was known : 354 (amongst whom I myself) against 178, about 24 paired off, 4 tellers, and Speaker. — 24th. House on Secret Committee. Report about the currency. Tierney very bitter. Peel very good—all but at the last, excellent. Adjourned 25th. House. Resumed debate, and at last Opposition persuaded to be quiet.—26th. Canistered,[4] as I went to the House. Sir C. Monck about Parga.' —'27th. Large party. Breakfasters—strange assortment. Lady Holland sends me O'Meara's book.'

'June 10. House. Foreign Enlistment Bill. Sir James Mackintosh made a splendid and beautiful, but not convincing speech. — 11th. Red River business. Sir James Montgomery, Ellice, Scarlett, William Smith, Bennett, and Goulburn, all did well in their several manners—Smith very acute ; Montgomery singularly Attic, simple, and clear. Ellice manly and strong.'

He closed his labours for the session by moving an address to the Regent on the suppression of the Slave Trade, by which he hoped to quicken the exertions of our Government, and produce some effect on France.

He traces pleasantly, in a letter to a friend,[5] the outline of his vacation rambles : ' My summer has been spent almost entirely with various friends—the Noels, at my old haunt of Barham Court, near to which you once endured the labours, if not the dangers of war (on Cox Heath) ;—my valuable old friend, Mrs. Hannah More, whom we the rather visited, because we deemed it but too probable that if we should not see her this summer we might never see her alive in another; and such is the uncertainty of life, that we witnessed the deathbed, and nearly the actual departure, of her younger and stronger sister.' ' Patty sat up with me,' he says in his Diary, 'till near twelve, talking over Hannah's first introduction to a London life, and I, not she, broke off the

---

[3] For a committee on the state of the nation.
[4] *I.e.* Dined from a tin canister.   [5] Ralph Creyke, Esq.

conference; I never saw her more animated. About eight in the morning, when I came out of my bedroom, I found Hannah at the door—" Have you not heard Patty is dying? They called me to her in great alarm," at which, from the ghastliness of her appearance, I could not wonder. About two or three hours after our parting for the night, she had been taken ill.'[6]   She lingered for about a week.

' Then we spent a few days at the romantic and beautiful seat, Blaize Castle, of my friend Mr. Harford; and afterwards a fortnight with the Bishop of Gloucester, who is really what a bishop should be—for humility, industry, zeal with sobriety, hospitality, and, above all, for love in all its kinds and directions, he is really a bright specimen; and the veneration and affection that are felt for him by all who know him, even by those who do not entirely concur with him in religious principles, are seen beaming from every countenance, and sparkling in every eye.   He practically remembers the motto of old Archbishop Usher's seal-ring— Væ mihi si non evangelizavero.   On the week-days he visits different country parishes, whence the income of his deanery is derived, and collects round him as crowded congregations as are usually found in a well-frequented church.   Then we were seduced into spending near a fortnight at Malvern, having visited it with the intention of merely a twenty-four hours' cursory survey.   For the recovery of an invalid, or for the means of enabling an old man to toddle up the mountains (not quite Himalayans) without fatigue or even effort, it is by far the first of all English elysiums.   Then we spent a little time with Mrs. W.'s widowed mother, whence I paid a second short visit to a sweet lady friend to meet, by his and her urgent desire, the Duke of Gloucester for a few days en ami.   Then I was for but four or five days with my dear and most excellent friend Babington, and am here paying a pop visit to my kind friend and relative, Samuel Smith, whose large family now occupies a palace which might be supposed to be graduated high in the scale of edifices as the residence of Rumbold, when it was raised at

[6] Diary, Sept. 9.
C C

least ten degrees higher by becoming the habitation of Paul
Benfield, and now I am crawling like a snail unwillingly to
—— Sutton.

' I believe we think pretty much, perhaps quite, alike as to
the course required by the present state of the country. On
the whole, I cannot but hope well for it, though I dare not
be too confident that we may not witness scenes of something nearer to civil war, than this land has exhibited since
1646.'

In this spirit he entered the House on the first day of the
session ; and then, and on Nov. 26, when he 'spoke with effect
though without premeditation,'[7] and throughout the stormy
session which succeeded, he 'thought it' his 'duty to come
forward in support of the several measures which were proposed for the preservation of the public peace.'[8] His Diary
sketches out the advance of the session, and of his own
employments. ' 30th. House—Lord Althorpe's motion for
referring the papers to a committee—very poor and dull
debate, or rather common sensible talk, shop talk, till Castlereagh at length spurred Tierney, who retaliated very cleverly.
Division 323 to 150. Plunket says that Lord Grenville's
speech in the House of Lords to-night was the finest display
of statesmanlike wisdom and eloquence he ever heard. Wellesley good too. Grey also and Lansdowne good.—Dec. 1.
Called Grenville—found Duke of Montrose calling to thank
him for his speech. No House. Evening, letters.—2nd.
House.—second reading of Seditious Bill. Bed near four.
Brougham's long speech—Peel good—Lyttleton good.—6th.
House on Seditious Meetings Bill. I spoke middlingly well,
though I forgot my chief argument.—9th. Bennett's motion
for a Committee on the National Distresses ruined by
making it a party business. I spoke, and not amiss—Baring
and Ellice very well. Called Canning's this morning.—
10th. House on Courtenay's complaint of Breach of Privilege in Hobhouse's pamphlet. I spoke, and better satisfied
with myself than on any night this session.'[9]

' We are in a state of almost combustion,' he complains,

[7] Diary, Nov. 23.   [8] Letter to Dr. Milner, Dec. 15.
                     [9] Diary.

amidst these nightly contentions,[1] 'which does not suit me
as well as it did thirty years ago—

> . . . . calidus juventâ,
> Consule Planco.
>
> In the hot fit
> Of youth and Pitt.'

Yet his own mind was quiet in the storm. The next day's
diary affords a glimpse of those deep waters which no political tempests could disturb. 'Walked from Hyde Park
Corner, repeating the 119th Psalm, in great comfort.'[2]

'Dec. 14. House—Lord John Russell's motion. He
spoke pleasingly — Lord Normanby seconded with more
talent, though Romeo-like. — 16th. Took my place as for
some little time past, the last seat on the Opposition bench.
Finding that Opposition complained of it, I named it this
evening to Tierney, who behaved very kindly about it.—
17th. Found Owen of Lanark truly placable and good-
humoured; he said Vansittart and I right in voting against
him.' Mr. Owen's plans he never could support, objecting
as he always did simply to 'a system of morals, or instruction
not founded on religion.' 'They would exclude,' he complains of such instructors,[3] 'religion from life, and substitute
knowledge in its stead.'

The spring of 1820 was marked for Mr. Wilberforce by
the fatal illness of his early friend, Dean Milner, of Carlisle,
who came to Kensington Gore, to attend the Board of
Longitude, and after five weeks of suffering illness, breathed
there his last upon April 1. 'Never was there an easier
dismission, which is the more observable because he had
fears of the pain of dying; when he was told he was in
danger, he grew more composed and calm than he had been
before.'[4] Mr. Wilberforce followed his old friend's remains
to their last resting-place at Cambridge, and listened to a
funeral sermon preached on him by 'Daniel Wilson, who
had seized upon the chief constituents of his character—his
ponderous sense, his tenderness and kindness, his solid
and experimental piety.'[5]

---

[1] Letter to Venerable F. Wrangham.   [2] Diary, Dec. 12.
[3] Diary.   [4] Ib.   [5] Diary, April 16.

Many hours he had given to soothing that sick and dying bed. He was no stranger to such scenes ; and never was the genuine tenderness which filled his heart more beautifully shown than in these unwitnessed charities. Here is one instance—' At the close,' says a friend, at this time a frequent inmate in his family, 'of one of his busy days, after the stormy contests of the House of Commons, between twelve and one o'clock he heard that his daughter, who was ill, could get no sleep. Coming into her room, he spoke of the tender Shepherd carrying the weak in his bosom, until He took them from this scene of trial to a world where sorrow and sighing shall flee away—" a beautiful personification, indicating their haste to leave the mansions of the blessed."'

One other instance shall be given. On May 24, he 'went down to Paul's Cray, honest Simons's, where a great party at his school fête. Gerard Noel gave us a beautiful sermon. Lord and Lady Jocelyn, Charles Noel, Lady E. Whitbread, and various friends.'[6] From principle as well as nature, he was all sunshine at such times. 'It is a fault to be silent; everyone is bound to present his contribution to the common stock of conversation and enjoyment;' and wherever the group was the most crowded and attentive, he was its centre. 'From all this,' says the same friend, 'he stole away, and asked me to walk with him down the village. It was to visit a poor woman, of whom he had heard as in a deep decline. He found out the sick room, and sat down by the bed, and began to speak to her of the love of God, which should dwell in his children's hearts. " Now this is the joy I wish for you." And then he knelt down, and asked of God to comfort and support her, and after all her sufferings bring her to a world of joy. " It is delightful to me," he said as we returned, " to visit such a bed of sickness, to be able to take one ray of joy from the full sunshine of the social circle, to gild her sick room. It has been one of the happiest days I ever spent."'

But sterner and more anxious duties were just before him. The death of George the Third and the accession of the new King troubled the just calming waves of political con-

tention.   The first intimation of these new troubles appears
in his diary of April 21.   'The Vice-Chancellor Leach has
been trying to root out Ministry; he has been telling the
King that his present Ministers are not standing by him,
that he ought to have a divorce.   There has been a flirta-
tion between Tierney and the King.   I hear Brougham has
had the sense or patriotism to see that it is better not to
have a public fracas between the King and Queen.'   All
hopes from the St. Omer's conference soon failed.   On June
5, 'the business of the House was stopped by Vansittart's
declaring on the Grampound Disfranchisement Bill, that the
Ministers could not attend, being called to a Cabinet.   It
was said to be on account of the Queen's approaching
return, who had refused the terms brought by Lord Hutchin-
son.   News at night that the Queen had landed, and was to
sleep at Canterbury.'   On the 6th, 'a message was delivered
to the House, announcing the Queen's arrival in England,
and the necessity of disclosures to Parliament.   She arrived
about six in London — crowds greeting her.   She approaches wisely, because boldly.   Fixes at Alderman Wood's.
Brougham in the House.   How deeply interested all are,
indeed I felt it myself, about her!   One can't help admiring
her spirit, though I fear she has been very profligate.   Ber-
gami left her at St. Omer.'

The 7th brought on the 'Green Bag Secret Committee
question.   I moved the adjournment of the debate till Friday, which was approved by a great majority of the House,
in order to give the parties time to effect an amicable accommodation.'[7]   His part was at once taken.   ' I resolved
if possible to prevent the inquiry; an object which could
only be attained by such an amicable adjustment as should
give neither party cause for triumph.   When, therefore, Lord
Castlereagh had made a motion to refer the papers to the
consideration of a secret committee, I endeavoured to inter-
pose a pause, during which the two parties might have an
opportunity of contemplating coolly the prospect before them.
Accordingly I sounded the House; my proposition was immediately adopted, and a pause was made with a declaration

[7] Diary, June 7.

that its purpose was to give opportunity for a private settlement. What followed is before the world—the correspondence, and subsequently the conferences which took place between the King's servants and the Queen's law-officers. The concessions made by the King's servants, as Mr. Brougham afterwards declared in the House of Commons, were various and great. The name and rights of a Queen were granted to her Majesty without reserve, any recognition of which had formerly been carefully avoided. A royal yacht, a frigate, &c. were offered. It was agreed that her name and rank should be notified at the court either of Rome or Milan—the capitals of the countries in which she had expressed her intention to reside; and that an Address should be presented to the Queen no less than another to the King, to thank her Majesty for having acceded to the wish of the House of Commons.'

During the anxious interval which followed, he was far from idle. He sent his son with an earnest letter to the King, entreating him to restore the Queen's name to the Liturgy, 'suggesting the ferment which would be occasioned; that the country would be in a fury, and perhaps the soldiers might take the Queen's part.'[9] The negotiation still proceeded; but all hopes soon vanished. ' 20th. Canning took me to town, and I talked with him about arrangement. Various friends confirmed me that it was right for me to address the Queen, and get her to give up the mention of her name in the Liturgy. So I gave the notice. Tierney pressed to know what my motion was to be. Opposition disposed to take up Queen's cause on party principles. Alas !'[1]

He well knew that by this course he exposed himself to the greatest misconstruction. 'However, I hope I am averting a great evil;'[2] and the grounds for his motion were clear. ' The only material difference which remained between the negotiating parties was that which respected the omission of her Majesty's name from the Liturgy. Her law-officers declared that they pressed the restoration of her name on the

[8] Memorandum among his papers.   [9] Diary, June 9.
[1] Diary.   [2] To Z. Macaulay, Esq.

grounds of the recognition of her rights, and the vindication of her character; but they several times suggested that an equivalent might be devised which might answer the same purpose. An Address of the House of Commons might effect this adjustment. If an Address were carried by a great majority, assuring her Majesty that her giving up the point should be regarded not as arising from any disposition to shrink from inquiry, but from a wish to give up her own opinion to the authority of the House of Commons, this would constitute the equivalent desired. This hope was confirmed by her Majesty's declaration, that she was disposed to yield to the declared sense of the House of Commons;[3] but it was soon shaken. 'Just as I was going up to bed, I heard a knocking at the door announcing a letter from the Queen. Alderman Wood had given her a mistaken account of my notice, and she wrote a warm, expostulatory letter— her own ebullition. Wishing that the Queen should have time to consider my answer, on which I hoped Brougham would comment, I resolved, against the advice of all my friends, to put off my motion till to-morrow. The House all impatience, and I obliged [it] to wait, having had conferences with several persons. Tierney, &c. ill-natured, yet Castlereagh gave way. Several of my friends pressed me strongly to make my motion a defence of Ministry, but I saw all depended on my keeping to my point—no inquiry.'

'June 21. Brougham brought me a second letter from the Queen, more moderate.'[4] 'House—very noisy and impatient; would not hear Acland, or even my own reply quietly. Burdett violent and bitter, but very able. Tierney mischievous. Denman strong and straightforward. Brougham able. Canning clever, but not letting himself out. My reply better than my speech, and would have been more so, but that interrupted. Majority immense—391 to 124. Sad work amongst the soldiers—my first apprehension. Lord Sidmouth very uneasy, &c.'[5]— 'June 29. Went up with the Resolution (Stuart Wortley, Acland, and Bankes also) to the Queen in Portman Street. The populace most violent, and I

---

[3] Mr. Wilberforce's Memoranda.   [4] Diary, June 21.
[5] Diary, June 22.

received a letter (kindly meant) whilst in the House, desiring me to come out postico, but it was not a case for this had I been to be killed (of which in truth there was no danger), we being representatives of the House of Commons.'[6]   'All the four members alighted without any interruption. They were dressed in full Court costume, and showed a proper insensibility to the uncourteous manner in which they were greeted by the multitude.   Mr. Wilberforce read the Resolutions.'[7] 'Alas!' he says, 'the answer most decidedly rejected our mediation.[8]   The Queen's manner was extremely dignified, but very stern and haughty.   I am not surprised by her rejection of our offer, though I deeply regret it.   Whatever ensues, it will always be a consolation to me to reflect that I have done my best to prevent all the evils that may happen.'

'I have never concealed my opinion that it was wrong to leave the Queen's name out of the Liturgy, and consequently I could not but have wished for its re-insertion.   But I had all but an absolute certainty that this motion would be rejected, and then we should have no resource.   All the members of the Cabinet had agreed to resign their offices if the question for restoring the Queen's name to the Liturgy should be carried against them.'

Although deeper thinkers could appreciate his conduct and say, 'Due gratitude cannot be expressed to you for what you have done;'[9] 'the nation feels its obligation to you, or if it does not, historians will record it;'[1] yet the Queen's refusal awoke all the abuse he had expected.   He was accused of trifling with the House of Commons and attempting to deceive the people.   He had in his possession a triumphant answer to the charge in the positive engagement of the Queen's chief law-adviser.   'She will accede to your Address,' he wrote to Mr. Wilberforce (June 22), 'I pledge myself.'   His justly great influence was overborne by a less sagacious counsellor, and with 'a political forbearance which,' says the person whom it spared, 'I never knew equalled,' he never justified himself by making public this unfulfilled pledge, but

[6] Diary   [7] Times, June 26.   [8] Diary.
[9] Lord Kenyon.   [1] Rev. Charles Simeon.

bore quietly the groundless charge of an unreasonable interference.

All negotiation was now at an end. 'June 26. Ministers
resolved to charge the Queen before the House of Lords,
and give up the House of Commons Committee.' 'If the
case,' he said, 'must be inquired into, it will be better done
in the House of Lords, which is a court of justice, than in
this House. Even then, however, it will be long, painful,
and disgusting, and, what in my mind aggravates the evil,
Parliament is not clear in the matter. We marry our kings
and queens contrary to the laws of God and of nature, and
from this source proceed the evils which I am now anxious
to avoid.'

'Your letters,' he writes at this time to Mrs. H. More, 'are
the squeezing a cheering juice, the natural expressed produce of friendly affection, into a turbid, fermenting mixture,
which really at this day teems with as many nauseous ingredients as Macbeth's witches' caldron (the hell-broth, as Shakspeare terms it), while *green bag*, like the roll in the soup,
floats in the midst of the mess, imparting its pungency and
flavour to the whole composition.

'In consequence of a very civil messenger from the Duchess
of Kent, I waited on her this morning. She received me
with her fine animated child on the floor by her with its play-
things, of which I soon became one. She was very civil, but
as she did not sit down, I did not think it right to stay above
a quarter of an hour; and there having been a female attendant and a gentleman present, I could not well get upon
any topic so as to carry on a continued discourse. She
apologised for not speaking English well enough to talk it,
but intimated a hope that she might talk it better and longer
with me at some future time. She spoke of her situation, and
her manner was quite delightful. A friend, between eight and
nine, went last night to Portland Street (22), and found a
most shabby assemblage of quite the lowest of the people,
who every now and then kept calling out Queen, Queen, and
several times, once in about a quarter of an hour, she came
out at one window of a balcony and Alderman Wood at the
other, and she bowed to them; her obeisance of course being

met by augmented acclamations. My friend entered into conversation with a person present who argued for the natural equality of man, and that any other of the people present had as good a right to be King as George the Fourth.'

'July 28. Miss W. came and asked me to be her brother's executor for his West Indian negroes, whom he means, she says, to emancipate. I told her he must prepare them for it. Spent an hour in the pictures of our English worthies. Mulgrave's by Hoffner. Poor Pitt's a vile picture—his face anxious, diseased, reddened with wine, and soured and irritated by disappointments. Poor fellow, how unlike my youthful Pitt!'[2]

He now took his family to Weymouth for summer quarters, halting on the way at Kingston Hall, and as he reached it murmured to himself, not quite inaudibly, 'So here is William Wilberforce going to visit Henry Bankes, and they are the only two of the old set of whom as much can be said.'

His residence at Weymouth was soon interrupted by the threatening aspect of affairs. 'The accounts from London are most alarming.'[3] In this crisis his interference was requested by men of various parties. The first who applied was Lord John Russell, in what Mr. Wilberforce terms his ' curious publication—a letter (in the " Times"), which sadly obstructs the course of proceeding I had before meditated.' 'At least,' says Mr. Bankes,[4] 'he should have sent to you a first impression of his letter, instead of leaving you to pick it up upon the sands of Weymouth, among other jetsam and flotsam that might be cast on the shore.'

' My project,' he tells Mr. Stephen,[5] 'was to urge the King to go to the House of Lords, and declare he gives up his own wishes to the gratifying of his people.'[6] 'But how could he hope that I should prevail on the King to accept my mediation, as that of a neutral man, when publicly called upon to come forward by one of the strongest partisans of the Opposition?'

' I feel with you,' at the same time wrote Mr. Lamb, 'all

[2] Diary, July 28.　　　　　　　　[3] Diary.
[4] Henry Bankes, Esq., to W. Wilberforce, Esq., Aug. 16.
[5] Aug. 8.　　　　　　　　　　[6] D.ary.

the objections you have stated to this publication of Lord John Russell's. Yet you will forgive me for saying that I cannot but think you would do well in returning speedily into the neighbourhood of London. If anything is to be done, your presence and influence will do it.'[7] The day before this letter reached him, he had 'decided that it may be well to be on the spot when the Queen's business is going to begin, that if any opening should present itself it may be embraced. I go up to try if I can prevent the inquiry. Oh the corrupted currents of this world ! Oh for that better world !'[8]

He found all thoughtful men looking forward to the future with alarm—'Lord Castlereagh appears even more impressed with the danger than Liverpool himself.' But matters were too far advanced for any beneficial interference, and he returned after a time to Weymouth, where he was still followed by pressing applications that he should demand an audience of the King, or recommend conciliation to the Queen. One ardent friend, with more zeal than discretion, sent down a messenger 'to fetch me up express, and meet him at Salt Hill to have an audience of the King. I positively refused. He had summoned S. and Lord H. from Hastings, who both came ; he himself went to the cottage and conferred with General Thornton, and sent in to the ·King that he expected me. The King sent a very proper answer.'

Seeing, therefore, no present opening for usefulness, he remained with his family, and watched from a distance the advancing trial. 'The more I think of the whole business,' he writes Sept. 19, 'the worse I like it ;' and as the year advanced, and he began to 'fear this Bill of Pains and Penalties would come down to the Commons,' he added, 'The present inclination of my judgment is strongly against receiving the Bill.'

In this state of feeling he hailed with no small pleasure the actual issue. 'This morning the early coaches from London came in, men and horses covered with white favours, emblematic, I suppose, of her innocence, for the rejection of

---

[7] Hon. William Lamb [Lord Melbourne] to William Wilberforce, Esq., Aug. 10.   [8] Diary, Aug. 11.

the Bill against the Queen, or rather for Lord Liverpool's giving it up when carried only by nine.' [9]

His first hope, that this decision would bring the great scandal to an end, soon passed away. 'The political sky looks very gloomy. I hear from Canning of his resignation because he cannot properly remain neutral.' [1] 'Ministers are resolved to refuse the Queen the restoration of her name to the Liturgy and a palace. She is striving to keep the flame alive and to blow it to fury.' 'She throws out a threat of recriminating, a mode of proceeding which has been wisely reserved for the House of Commons. Even among us, indeed, she will not, I suppose, be admitted to recriminate formally, but she may through her spokesmen, both at the bar and in the House, produce all the effects of recrimination. I myself see Matt. v. 32 precisely in the same light with the Archbishop of Tuam.' [2]

The adjournment of the House of Commons caused a lull in this storm, and Mr. Wilberforce was able to remain quietly at Bath. But a new blow from another quarter pained him deeply. On December 9 he heard of the death of Christophe ; and with Christophe all his plans for Hayti, prepared with such time and labour, must perish.

'Every day something transpires,' wrote a physician from St. Domingo half-a-year afterwards, [3] 'to show the importance of King Henry to the Haytians. His greatest enemies now acknowledge that they never have had a chief whose powers of mind and body were so fitted for command. Had he reigned over a people untutored in the scepticism of modern infidelity, and uncontaminated by the licentiousness of French libertinism, Hayti must centuries hence have regarded his memory with veneration.'

When he returned to the House on the 26th he 'found the question changed by the motion of Lord A. Hamilton, from restoring the Queen's name to the Liturgy, to blaming the leaving it out. Not one man in fifty but thought it wrong, and still more foolish, to leave the name out, yet a large majority voted for the previous question.' Weak

[9] Diary, Nov. 11.　[1] Ib. Nov. 26.　[2] Letter to J. Stephen, Esq.
[3] Dr. Duncan Stewart to W. Wilberforce, Esq., March 6.

health kept him much absent from the House throughout this spring. 'Attendance there,' he writes to a friend, 'is become very distasteful. To those who remember my first years in Parliament, the difference cannot but appear extreme, in point of talent and eloquence.'

'I hope —— will become one of the first stars in our, alas! darkened hemisphere (all our old constellations extinct). To say nothing of the older names, Lord North, Dunning, Wedderburne, Barré, there are no more Fox, Pitt, Burke, Windham; and poor Whitbread, with all his coarseness, had an Anglicism about him, that rendered him a valuable ingredient in a British House of Commons.'

After an Easter spent at Bath Mr. Wilberforce returned to London. 'May 25. Buxton's capital speech on the criminal laws—all information and sense.'—'June 20. I moved my address on the Abolition. Mackintosh spoke capitally.'— '30th. Attended a meeting at the Thatched House Tavern, on the retrospect and prospect quoad Africa, &c.' Little was done during the remainder of the session. 'Interview with Lord Bathurst and Vansittart, about apprenticing captured negroes. A long conversation with Lord Londonderry about French Abolition—he advised newspaper publications. Got Report of American Committee, favourable to the right of search.'[4]

Leaving, not without an 'inward grief,' his house at Kensington, he moved for summer quarters to Marden Park, 'about eighteen miles,' he says, 'from Westminster Bridge, where Hatsell lived for the last twenty summers of his life. It was once a fine place, and is one of the prettiest spots that I ever saw, without water—the form of the ground most beautifully varied, and the wood still fine, though a sad diminution of it was made to supply the demands of a former Lady Clayton, who was very fond of cards. The country also (Surrey) is one of the most beautiful in England, the Lakes and parts of Derbyshire excepted. It is comfortable to me to have a house of my own and my books about me, instead of being in a watering-place, as has been my summer habit for many years.' Here he loved to call his friends around him, and was never

long without having some or other of them as his guests.
'Sir George Grey with us—talked a good deal of the coronation, which all agree to have been the finest raree-show
ever exhibited. But the moral eye seems to have been too
much distracted, and it wanted the solemn effect which the
mind contemplates in a King with his nobles about him,
taking oaths of fidelity to his people, and their emotions of
loyalty towards him.'[5] 'Your brother, the General, just
gleamed in upon us,' he wrote a few days afterwards to Mr.
Macaulay,[6] 'as we have been wishing the sun to do all this
day, to give us a little light and warmth, but with the sun he
rose this morning and pursued his course when we were all
in our beds.' It was a goodly sight to see him here. The
cheerful play of a most happy temper, which more than sixty
years had only mellowed, gladdened all his domestic intercourse. The family meetings were enlivened by his conversation—gay, easy, and natural, yet abounding in manifold
instruction, drawn from books, from life, and from reflection.
Though his step was less elastic than of old, he took his part
in out-of-door occupations ; climbing the neighbouring downs
with the walking parties, pacing in the shade of the tall trees,
or gilding with the old man's smile the innocent cheerfulness
of younger pastimes. 'The sun was very hot to-day, and
the wind south, but under the beech trees on the side of the
hill it was quite cool. Dined by ourselves, and walked with
the boys in the evening.'[7]—19th. 'Gave ale and cricket to the
servants, in honour of the coronation.'

As the summer advanced one heavy cloud darkened his
skies. The health of his eldest daughter was failing, and
on December 30 she died. The trial was lightened by
her manifest preparation for the great change. 'The consciousness,' he says, ' of our dear child's being safe is a cordial
of inestimable efficacy.'

On the day of his daughter's funeral he was kept at home
by the extreme coldness of the weather, and when the band
of mourners had set out he went into his solitary chamber to
commune with his God. In that communing he passed

---

[5] Diary, July 27.   [6] To Zachary Macaulay, Esq., Aug. 8.
[7] Diary, July 18.

the lengthening course of his own life before his eyes, and these are some of his reflections:—'When I look back on my past life, and review it, comparing especially the almost innumerable instances of God's kindness to me with my unworthy returns, I am overwhelmed. The exceeding goodness of God to me, and the almost unequalled advantages I have enjoyed, fill me with humiliation. My days appear few when I look back, but they have been anything but evil. My blessings have been of every kind, and of long continuance; general to me and to other Englishmen, but still more peculiar, from my having a kindly natural temper, a plentiful fortune; all the mercies of my public life; my coming so early into Parliament for Hull, then for Yorkshire, elected six times, and only ceasing to be M.P. for Yorkshire because I resigned. Then my being made the instrument of bringing forward the Abolition; my helping powerfully the cause of Christianity in India; my never having been discredited. There would be no end of the enumeration, were I to put down all the mercies of God. My escape from drowning by a sudden suggestion of Providence. My never having been disgraced for refusing to fight a duel. Then all my domestic blessings. Marrying as late as thirty-six, yet finding one of the most affectionate of wives. Children, all of them attached to me beyond measure. Then my social blessings. No man ever had so many kind friends; they quite overwhelm me with their goodness. Then my having faculties sufficient to make me respectable—a natural faculty of public speaking. Then, almost above all, my having been rendered the instrument of much spiritual good by my work on Christianity. How many have communicated to me that it was the means of their turning to God. Praise the Lord, O my soul!'

CHAPTER XXV.

JANUARY 1822 TO FEBRUARY 1825.

Winter at Marden Park—Address to Alexander—Session—West Indian —Mr. Canning—Motion for Emancipation still postponed—Addresses on Slave Trade—Lord Londonderry's death—Slavery Manifesto—He presents the Quakers' petition against Slavery — Commits the Anti-Slavery motion to Mr. Buxton — West Indian cause — Aspersions thrown upon him—Lord Eldon and Mr. Abercombie—Anti-Slavery debate—Canning and Lord Nugent—Inflammation of the lungs— Return to business—Missionary Smith—Illness at Iver—Retirement at Uxbridge Common—Bath—Company—Christmas at Uxbridge Com-mon—Resolves to retire from Parliament—Effect of the announcement —His place in the House—from eloquence—His feelings at the time— Last frank.

On January 4, Mr. Wilberforce returned with his diminished family to Marden Park, where his recent loss, as well as his decreasing powers of body, tended to detain him. He had been 'strongly advised to attend the House very little, and to dilute his parliamentary campaign as much as possible, by departures to the country;'[1] whilst his wiser friends were anxious 'to form themselves into a cordon of defence to pro-tect him from all manner of intrusion.'[2]

But though his bodily strength was impaired, the fire of his spirit was unquenched, and he longed to be about his Master's work, and make one more effort before the close of his long parliamentary career. Its three last years were spent in giving to the struggle against Slavery that first im-pulse which, before he left the scene, had secured Emancipa-tion throughout all the British colonies.

He at once resumed his address to the Emperor of Russia, which was soon finished, translated into French, and sent to every member of the French Chambers, of the States of Belgium, and of the Cortes of Spain and Portugal. Other

---

[1] Diary.   [2] Letter from Dr. Chalmers to W. Wilberforce, Esq.

exertions for the cause followed. 'The African Institution has got into a strange scrape by asking Canning for twenty guineas as a vice-president, in addition to ten guineas originally given—a proceeding not warranted by the rules, any more than by common decency and common sense. William Smith, Buxton, and I are appointed a small committee for waiting on Canning, and making the amende honorable. I have been preparing him to expect us.'[3] Mr. Canning answers: 'Never surely was so splendid an embassy sent to make atonement for so small an offence since the mission of Ulysses, Ajax, and Phœnix, to apologise for the seizure of Briseis, who in those days was probably worth about 21*l.* I am really very sorry that you should have so much unnecessary trouble: but I shall nevertheless be happy to have the pleasure of receiving all three, on any account whatever, at the time which you mention; and Phœnix at any time, and as often as he will.'

Abolition business was his great charge during the remainder of the session. On July 25 he moved an Address against the introduction of slaves into our new Cape settlements. 'The temper of the House,' he says, 'was clearly favourable to the proposal, and we all came back in high spirits.' 'This was the best speech,' says Mr. Buxton, 'that I ever heard him make. He poured forth his whole mind on the duty of extending civilisation and Christianity to the savage and the heathen.' On this night, too, he introduced his further views for the West Indies. 'Not I only,' he said, 'but all the chief advocates of the Abolition declared from the first that our object was, by ameliorating regulations, to advance towards the period when these unhappy beings might exchange their degraded state of slavery for that of a free and industrious peasantry. To that object I still look forward.'

With the beginning of the holidays he entered upon his usual country residence at Marden Park. His family and friends were gathered round him, and he was reading, conversing, writing letters, and composing with all his usual diligence and vigour. On these domestic occupations broke in the news of Lord Londonderry's death. 'August 19. S. brought a report from Croydon that poor Londonderry had destroyed

[3] Diary, April 2.

himself. I could not believe it, but letters too clearly confirmed it. He was certainly deranged—the effect probably
of continued wear and tear of mind. But the strong impression of my mind is, that it is the effect of the non-observ-
ance of the Sunday, both as abstracting from politics, from
the constant recurrence of the same reflections, and as correcting the false views of worldly things, and bringing them
down to their true diminutiveness.'[4] I cannot tell you how
I feel his loss. Never probably was there anyone called
away on the sudden, by whose extinction such a complica-
tion of threads and lines of human policy were at once cut
short—full of his plans for preserving the peace of Europe,
and maintaining the system of the mutual balancings and de-
pendencies on which he so greatly valued himself. I never
was so shocked by any incident. He really was the last man
in the world who appeared likely to be carried away into the
commission of such an act! So cool, so self-possessed.'

He pressed earnestly, in corresponding with Lord Bath-
hurst and Lord Liverpool, that the plenipotentiary of Great
Britain at the approaching Congress might be 'instructed by
the Cabinet'[5] to make the Abolition a point of leading moment; and, November 23, heard 'of the admirable zeal, perseverance, judgment, and temper, and plain-dealing honesty,
against all the tangled web of the French Machiavellian manufacturers, which the Duke had manifested in conducting what
he calls "our business at the Congress." Dieu défend le droit.
I shall love all generals the better for it as long as I live,
and so I hope will my children after me.'[6]

The plan for the next parliamentary campaign had now to
be settled. As a preliminary measure to other action, he was
urged 'to publish his opinions as to the state of the negro
slaves, the duty of improving it, and of gradually emancipat-
ing them.' He says in reply, 'I am one of those substances,
like sealing-wax and other electric bodies, which require to
be warmed in order to possess the faculty of attracting objects, of covering and clothing itself with them. I cannot
sparkle at all without being rubbed, and this would be effected
by your conversation.' For this end he gathered several

[4] Diary.   [5] To Z. Macaulay, Esq., Sept. 15.   [6] Ib. Dec. 2.

friends of the cause round his Christmas hearth at Marden
Park, and long and deep were their deliberations, how best
to shape those measures which were to change the structure
of society throughout the western world, by rendering the
degraded negro race by degrees a free peasantry.

Thus warmed for the work, he set with all his might about
his address. This appeal was published early in March. It
produced a vast effect. Its kindness and forbearance towards individuals rendered its earnest expostulations irresistible. The fervour of the writer's natural manner was so
happily tempered by Christian candour, and by the wisdom
of age, that no heart could be closed when he spoke, 'sua-
vitate illâ, quâ perfunderet animos, non quâ perfringeret.' Its
perusal, a West Indian proprietor told him, 'has so affected
me, that, should it cost me my whole property, I surrender it
willingly, that my poor negroes may be brought not only to
the liberty of Europeans, but especially to the liberty of
Christians.'

Mr. Wilberforce had learnt too much in his thirty-five
years' apprenticeship in African controversy to expect the
fetters of slavery to fall off at a single blow, and was content
to wait for the end he aimed at. His present measures followed naturally on his former. He had attacked the Slave
Trade as a monstrous evil in itself, while he hoped that its
suppression would lead at once to an improved treatment of
the race of slaves. This he had patiently expected, perfecting the Abolition by international negotiation, and guarding
against smuggled importation by registering the slaves. But he
waited fruitlessly. And now the time was come when he must
demand that from Parliament to which he had hoped that
gradual improvements would have imperceptibly led on the
planters. The nation must be pledged to give the negro freedom, before too many of his masters could be induced to
treat him as a man.

Here opened the second act of the drama. On the 19th of
March he presented to the House of Commons a petition
from the Quakers, who having been the first to protest against
the Slave Trade, now led the way in the attack on Slavery.

May 15, Mr. Buxton, to whom he had committed the lead

in the Emancipation struggle, 'moved a resolution declaring slavery repugnant to Christianity and the constitution. Canning replied, and moved resolutions proclaiming reform of the system, and specifying driving, punishment of females, Sunday work, and market.' With his wonted moderation he prevailed on his followers to accept 'this acknowledgment of the Government, that the grievances of which we complain do exist, and that a remedy ought to be applied.' But no moderation could disarm his opponents. Private calumny, the established weapon of West Indian warfare, awoke in all its strength; and the virulence of Cobbett, who amongst his many changes was constant only in his hatred to the friends of Africa, was reinforced by fresh allies. This lasted throughout the autumn and winter, but never moved him to an angry word.

In February Parliament met, and Mr. Wilberforce was at his post, and active as ever. 'February 3. House met. Brougham clever—first day's speech and address; inculcating on the House to be temperate.—4th. Webster and Hankey with me about the Demerara insurrection.—6th. Calling on Lord Melville about the naval abominations, and conferring with Brougham about circuit question.—14th. Meeting at African Institution. We waited on Canning about twelve. With Canning till two. At lodgings till three. Then Duke of Gloucester's, where Lord Lansdowne, Stephen, and Brougham added to our consultation till five. Then home. Dined at Duke of Gloucester's — Lord and Lady Lansdowne, Lord and Lady Roseberry; Brougham and Mackintosh were to windward of me—most pleasant conversation. Home latish.'[7] ' I drew the highest prize in the lottery; I sat by Sir J. Mackintosh.'[8]—March 1. Went to the House for Martin's Bill on cruelty to animals. Put off by Abercrombie's coming forward with a case of breach of privilege against the Chancellor, for charging him on the bench with falsehood. Brougham spoke admirably, and Abercrombie excellently ; Scarlett also, and all the lawyers, did well. Canning spoke admirably in mitigation, and Peel defended as well as could be, but the case was too strong to be put by without an autho-

---

[7] Diary, March 1.   [8] Con. Mem.

rised apology. So though I longed to go away, I staid and
voted—102 to 150. I seldom recollect, certainly not for
many years, suffering so much pain.' 'I could not forget the
friendly intercourse of former days, when Sir J. Scott used to
be a great deal at my house. I saw much of him then, and
it is no more than his due to say that, when he was Solicitor
and Attorney-General under Pitt, he never fawned and flattered as some did, but always assumed the tone and station
of a man who was conscious that he must show he respected
himself if he wished to be respected by others.'[9]

'16th. Canning opened his plan about West Indies in a very
guarded speech. Buxton strong—above concert pitch. I was
better voiced, and better heard than usual.'[1] ' He was,' he
said, ' determined to wash his hands of the blood which might
be spilled by thus trifling with the hopes of men.'[2] 'I fear that,
despairing of relief from the British Parliament, the negroes
will take the cause into their own hands, and endeavour to
effect their own liberation.' He spoke long and powerfully,
but the effort was too great for his strength. On the 19th he
went to the House, unwell, and not intending to remain,
but was enchained by Mr. Canning's admirable humour.
' Lord John Russell's motion about the French evacuating
Spain. He made no hand of it. Canning invincibly comic.'[3]
He returned home quite full of the exquisite raillery of
the 'light horseman's uniform' and 'heavy Falmouth coach.'
' Canning's drollery of voice and manner were inimitable ;
there is a lighting up of his features, and a comic play about
the mouth, when the full fun of the approaching witticism
strikes his own mind, which prepares you for the burst
which is to follow.'[4] Yet he would not allow himself the
use of these effective weapons, though he had them always
at command. ' Often during a debate,' says Mr. Buxton,
' would he whisper to me hints and witticisms which would
have filled the House with merriment, and overwhelmed
his opponent. But when he rose to speak, though he went
close to the very thoughts he had poured into my ear, he

---

[9] Con. Mem.   [1] Diary.
[2] Mr. Buxton's Con. Mem. of the preceding day.
[3] Diary, March 19.   [4] Con. Mem.

restrained himself from uttering them, nor would he ever give vent to any one allusion which could give another pain.

This night he was seized with inflammation of the lungs. His perfect patience, and the bursts of love and thankfulness which were ever breaking forth throughout this season of restlessness and languor, can never be forgotten by those who watched with the deepest anxiety beside the sick-bed of such a father. None but his own family could fully know the warmth of his heart, or the unequalled sweetness of his temper. With the strictest truth they can affirm, that never in the most unguarded moments of domestic privacy did they see obscured, in word or action, the full sunshine of his kindliest affections:—

> His every deed and word that he did say
> Was like enchantment, which through both the eyes,
> And both the ears, did steal the heart away.

The last entry of his diary, before he was confined wholly to his bed, was, 'Poor Smith, the missionary, died in prison at Demerara! The day of reckoning will come;' and the first public business he attempted, after leaving his sick room, was (June 1) 'Preparing for Smith the missionary's business. I was at the House the first time for eight weeks or more. Brougham made a capital speech, by Mackintosh well termed impregnable. Mackintosh's own was most beautiful, his mind teemed with ideas.'[5] The decision was postponed till the 11th. In the interval he says, 'I very much wish, if my voice should be strong enough, to bear my testimony against the scandalous injustice exercised upon poor Smith.'[6] On June 15 his voice was again raised to record his conviction, that the only real hope of the negro slaves must be from the British Parliament. 'The West Indians,' he said, 'abhor alike the end we have in view, and the means by which we have to reach it. It is with reluctance and pain I come forward, but I esteem it my bounden duty to protest against the policy on which we are now acting. " Liberavi animam meam."'

These prophetic words were the last which he uttered in

---

[5] Diary.   [6] To J. Stephen, Esq., June 4.

the House of Commons. Ten days later he set off, after
attending a meeting held in honour of James Watt, to visit
Lord Gambier at Iver, and on the road was seized with a
new attack. When he reached Lord Gambier's, he was 'but
just able to be helped upstairs to bed,'[7] where he lay in an
alarming state for almost a month. This second attack left
him in so shattered a condition, as to enforce upon him the
necessity of absolute repose, and as soon as he could move
with safety, he took possession of a small house bordering on
Uxbridge Common, where he lived for a time in entire seclu-
sion, though by no means in idleness. What a freshness he
maintained in mind and affection, a letter of about this date to
one of his sons may witness:—'Never omit any opportunity
of getting acquainted with any good or useful man. Acquaintance are the raw material, from which are manufactured
friends, husbands, wives. I wish it may please God that you
may have some good ones to choose from on your first settling at Oxford. T—— seems a very pleasing young man, but
I own I covet a much higher praise for my sons; and oh that
I could have reason to believe they were steadily and stur-
dily setting themselves to act on that beautiful description
of the true Christian's character—"Among whom ye shine as
lights in the world!" O my dearest ——, what would I give
to see you a $\phi\omega\sigma\tau\grave{\eta}\rho$ $\grave{\epsilon}\nu$ $\tau\tilde{\omega}$ $\kappa\acute{o}\sigma\mu\omega$. The idea has brought tears
into my eyes and almost disqualified me from going on with
my letter. My dearest ——, aim high; do not be contented
with being hopeful; strive to be a Christian in the highest
sense of that term. How little do you know to what services Providence may call you! If, when I was your age,
anyone had pointed to me and said, That youth in a few
years will be member for the first county in England, it
would have been deemed the speech of a madman.'

As the year advanced he moved to Bath. The interruptions
of his time here, of which he still complains, were balanced
by meetings with old friends, which no man enjoyed with a
keener relish. 'October 19,' he enters, 'venerable Rowland
Hill dined with me—ætat 80. 22nd. John Smith called yesterday, and talked very pleasingly, full of benevolence, intelligence, and information. Not unfrequently he fell in here

[7] Diary.

with some friend of his early life. 'I talked in the Pump-room with Mr. Neville, whom I had met at Exton near fifty years ago: he 82 ætat—an astonishing man.' It was a striking sight to witness such recognitions, in which general courtesy unfolded itself gradually into a more intimate exchange of early recollections. The sunshine of his own old age was shed for the time at least over his companion; and day after day, as his eye found with pleasure his recovered friend, he would join his side and delight him with his powers of conversation; watching all the time for every opening by which he could lead on their intercourse to higher subjects, and gild, if need was, another's life with the peaceful hope in which he walked himself. His stay at Bath was closed by visits to Blaize Castle and to Barley Wood, where he found Hannah More, 'as animated as ever I knew her, quoting authors, naming people.'

After a few days he returned to Uxbridge, where the new year opened with his wonted thankfulness. 'What cause have I for gratitude, seeing my five children, my son's wife, and two grandchildren all round my table! Praise the Lord, O my soul.'[8] Never did any man live in more perpetual sunshine, or shed its cheerful radiance more constantly around him; yet a deep vein of pathos mingled with his gaiety, discernible to close observers in his great tenderness of spirit. 'I am,' he said of himself, 'much more disposed to melancholy than you would imagine.' These were not his habitual feelings; they were the diapason tones of a mind of infinite compass; but, for the most part, his later years were eminently bright and cheerful.

His strength had been so visibly impaired by the severe attacks of the spring, that he was strongly recommended to retire from public life, but he did not at once acquiesce in this advice. 'The idea of retiring, and not endeavouring to bear' his 'testimony once more in support of truth and righteousness,' he found 'very painful.'[9] 'It is to me almost like a change of nature to quit parliamentary life, all the particulars of which have been formed into habits during almost forty-six years.' But, 'after mature reflection,' he determined to retire. The communication was

---

[8] Diary, Jan. 1, 1825.   [9] Letter to Z. Macaulay, Esq.

received with mingled feelings, which were well expressed by Southey. 'I will not say that I am sorry for it, because I hope you have retired in time, and will therefore live the longer as well as more for yourself; but that House will not look upon your like again.'[1]

He had two years before named Mr. Buxton as the executor of his great West Indian trust, and he now formally committed to him the moving the new writ for Bramber. His not selecting one from the first rank of parliamentary leaders gave some offence. Mr. Canning, Charles Grant, and Henry Brougham were all pressed on him by various friends; but he maintained the 'importance of keeping this great cause in possession of its old honourable distinction of being one in which all party differences were extinguished, Pitt and Fox fighting in the same rank.'[2] His companions in arms lamented bitterly their loss. Mr. Buxton applied to him the inscription which the Carthaginians placed upon the tomb of Hannibal, 'We vehemently desired him in the day of battle;' and Mr. William Smith wrote, 'When our cause loses you, it suffers a calamitous deprivation — the guiding spirit will be missed.' Scarcely less keen was the regret of others, who looked forward to the loss of his authority on moral and religious questions. 'There are,' writes one,[3] 'I hope some young men of promise coming forward; but, alas! there is no one at present who can take your place; would that there were many Elishas on whom your mantle might fall.' This was no exaggerated estimate of the value of his present services. His place as a mere orator was still amongst the very first; and when he lighted on a congenial subject, he broke out into those strains which made Sir Samuel Romilly esteem him 'the most efficient speaker in the House of Commons;' and which had long before led Pitt himself to say repeatedly, 'Of all the men I ever knew, Wilberforce has the greatest natural eloquence.'[4]

Such a man could not bid farewell to public life without much observation from his fellows, and without being followed

---

[1] Robert Southey, Esq., to W. Wilberforce, Esq.
[2] Letter to Z. Macaulay, Esq.
[3] Letter from Joseph Butterworth, Esq., M.P.
[4] Communicated by Lord Harrowby.

into his retirement by the deep regret of multitudes. Nothing can exceed the simple quietness of his own feelings at this abdication. 'I staid quietly at Uxbridge, spending the time very pleasantly;' and the day on which the new writ was to be moved for, he records as 'delightful. The sun full out. The bees seduced to fly about into the crocus cups. The blackbirds singing.'

To two of his sons,[5] who had requested him to send them his last frank, he wrote on the same day. 'When Charles the First was on the very point of exchanging, as I trust, a temporal for an eternal crown, he was forced to be short, so he said but one word—and now I have but a moment in which to use my pen, and, therefore, I also will adopt his language, and add, as he did, REMEMBER.—You can fill up the chasm.'

CHAPTER XXVI.

MARCH 1825 TO OCTOBER 1827.

*Retires from London—Purchase of Highwood—Dropmore—Walmer—
T. Moore—Blaize Castle—Diary—Loss of friends—Wentworth House
and Lord Fitzwilliam—Return to Highwood.*

WHEN Mr. Wilberforce quitted Parliament he bought a freehold residence at Highwood Hill, just 'beyond the disk of the metropolis,' where, he tells Mr. Gisborne,[1] 'I shall be a little zemindar; 140 acres of land, cottages of my own, &c.' His feelings when purchasing this place are expressed in his comments on the habits of a friend. 'How rational is his mode of life! domestic charities sweetening and cheering the defilements of worldly affairs. I partake in his longing for repose; and, oh! may I be enabled more and more to walk during the years which may yet remain for me in the fear of the Lord, and in the comfort of the Holy Ghost.'[2]

---

[5] Robert Isaac and Samuel Wilberforce.
[1] April 6.   [2] Diary, March 4.

'Oh may I only walk with God during my closing years, and then where is of little consequence.'[3]

A few extracts from different pages of his Journal will show the present colour of his life :—'March 24. Inglis and two Thorntons came. Inglis extremely entertaining, and most kind.'—'27th. Macaulay and Tom came to dinner, and night. Tom infinitely overflowing with matter on all subjects, and most good-humoured, fertile and fluent to the last, and with unruffled good nature.'—'To Dropmore, where received very kindly; walked with Grenville for an hour before and after dinner; it grieved me to see him so feeble; said he had profited more from Aristotle's Rhetoric than any other work. Spoke in favour of Reid and Stewart as right against Locke.'—'Went to Walmer to see the Castle, where I had been above thirty years ago, in poor Pitt's time.'—'Introduced to Tom Moore by Sir T. Lethbridge, who walked with us a little. Moore's eye bright, his whole countenance very animated ; but rather joyous than indicating sensibility.' —'Breakfasted with Lord Camden at the York Hotel, and talked over old matters.'—'Spent a few days with Mr. Harford at Blaize Castle;' and here 'he slid,' says his host, 'insensibly into continuous descriptions of parliamentary scenes with which he had been connected :—

' "When Lord Londonderry was in his ordinary mood, he was very tiresome, so slow and heavy, his sentences only half formed, his matter so confined, like what is said of the French army in the Moscow retreat, when horse, foot, and carriages of all sorts were huddled together, helter-skelter ; yet when he was thoroughly warmed and excited, he was often very fine, very statesman-like, and seemed to rise quite into another man."

' "Our general impression of Sheridan was, that he came to the House with his flashes prepared and ready to let off. He avoided encountering Pitt in unforeseen debating, but when forced to it usually came off well."

' " Fox was often truly wonderful. He would begin at full tear, and roll on for hours together without tiring either himself or us."

[3] Diary, July 12.

' " Pitt talked a great deal among his friends. Fox in general society was quiet and unassuming. Sheridan was a jolly companion, and told good stories, but has been over-rated as a wit by Moore."

' " Fox was truly amiable in private life, and great allowance ought to be made for him : his father was a profligate politician, and allowed him as much money to gamble with as ever he wished."

' I asked him if he remembered the miser Elwes in the House of Commons ? " Perfectly ; and that question reminds me of a curious incident which one day befell that strange being. In my younger days we often went to the House in full dress, on nights, for example, when we were any of us going to the opera. Bankes, on an occasion of this kind, was seated next Elwes, who was leaning his head forward just at the moment when Bankes rose hastily to leave his seat, and the hilt of his sword happening to come in contact with the miser's wig, which he had probably picked off some scarecrow, it was unconsciously borne away by Bankes, who walked in his stately way down the House, followed by Elwes full of anxiety to regain his treasure. The House was in a roar of merriment, and for a moment Bankes looked about him, wondering exceedingly what had happened. The explanation was truly amusing, when he became conscious of the sword-hilt which he had acquired." '

His Diary, as the year advanced, will supply, without any formal connection, a sketch of his chief movements, and of the tone of his mind and feelings :—' Lord Liverpool suddenly seized by apoplexy or palsy, so that his political life must be at an end. I fear Canning also is more seriously indisposed than I had hoped. It always affects me deeply, when, either from advancing years, or sudden illness, this world appears to be slipping out of the grasp of an eminent public man. Lord Liverpool, I trust, had serious thoughts. I well remember the former Lady Liverpool's telling me at the Pavilion, many years ago, that she and Lord Liverpool used to contend, each for the favourite of each, Pascal or Fenelon ; and Pascal is an author who has many " pregnant propositions," as Lord Bacon calls them.'—' The companions of my youth, then far stronger and more healthy than I was, are worn out, while I still remain.'—'The two St. Johns and Chaplin—Acklom—George Anderson, died in 1784, Sir Edmund, 1799, ætat forty. It is very affecting to me to inquire after numbers of my contemporaries, and hear, "O he has been long gone"—or, "He died years ago,"—men commonly far younger and stronger than myself.'

This autumn he paid a series of visits in Yorkshire, and was received everywhere with the affectionate respect which ever surrounded him, but which he scarcely admitted to be his due. His account of his visit to Wentworth House may be taken as a specimen of all. 'The cordiality and kindness with which I have been received at this place has deeply affected me. Lord Fitzwilliam might well have been forgiven if he had conceived an unconquerable antipathy to me. When I was first elected county member it was in defiance of his old hereditary interest—I, a mere boy (but twenty-four), without a single acquaintance in the county, and not allowing him the recommendation even of one member, though with Sir George Savile's family connection and name superadded to the Rockingham interest. And then I must have appeared to him to be identified with Mr. Pitt, against whom, not altogether without cause, he had conceived a deadly hostility, even imputing to him (though this was not merely different from the truth, but opposite to it), that Pitt had from the first disliked him. Yet, in spite of all repelling principles, so strongly has worked the general kindliness of his nature, that he, the old gentleman (gentleman I may truly term him, for a finer gentleman cannot be conceived) has behaved to us with an unaffected, unassuming friendliness, that at times has brought tears into my eyes. It has really brought powerfully to my feelings that better state in which all misconstructions will be done away, and all truly good men will love one another.' On October 3 he returned 'to Highwood Hill in safety, and found all there well. What cause for thankfulness, after above six months' absence and thirty-six visits!'[4]

[4] Diary.

CHAPTER XXVII.

OCTOBER 1827 TO AUGUST 1838.

*Mode of spending his day—Love of flowers—Business—Evenings—Con-
versation — Society—Letters descriptive of his life — Reduction of his
income—Anti-Slavery Society—His religious character at this time—
Retirement into Kent and the Isle of Wight—His great happiness there
—Habits of life—Specimen of conversation—Retrospect of life—Thankfulness — Humility — Tenderness—Trust in God—Mr. Richmond's
portrait—Last illness — Death—Funeral.*

His days at Highwood were very regularly spent. He rose
soon after seven, spent the first hour and a-half in his closet ;
then dressed, hearing his reader for three-quarters of an
hour, and by half-past nine met his household for family
worship; always a great matter in his esteem. At this he
read a portion of the Scriptures, generally of the New Testament, in course, and explained and enforced it, often with a
natural and glowing eloquence, always with affectionate earnestness, and an extraordinary knowledge of the word of
God.

After family prayers, which occupied about half-an-hour,
he never failed to sally forth for a few minutes

> To take the air and hear the thrushes sing.

He enjoyed this stroll exceedingly. Thus he records one—
'Oct. 23. A delightful morning. Walked out and saw the
most abundant dewdrops sparkling in the sunbeams on the
gazon. How it calls forth the devotional feelings in the
morning, when the mind is vacant from worldly business, to
see all nature pour forth, as it were, its song of praise to the
great Creator and Preserver of all things ! I love to repeat
Psalms ciii. civ. cxlv. &c. at such a season.'

Breakfast followed, prolonged and animated by his unwearied powers of conversation, and, when congenial friends

were gathered round him, their discussions lasted sometimes till noon. Then he went till post time to his study. If his letters were finished he turned to some other business, never enduring to be idle all the day.

About three o'clock he sallied forth into the garden, humming often to himself, in the gladness of his heart, some favourite tune, alone, or in the company of some few friends, or with his reader. Here he would pace up and down some sheltered sunny walk, rejoicing especially in one which had been formed for him by a son, and was called ever after, with some hint of affection, by his name.

'The picture which the dead leave on the minds of their survivors,' says Mr. Gurney,[1] 'is not always lively or distinct; but no one who has been accustomed to observe Wilberforce will ever find the slightest difficulty in picturing him on the tablet of the mind. Who that knew him can fail to recall the rapid movements of his somewhat diminutive form, the illumination of his expressive countenance, and the nimble finger with which he used to seize on every little object which happened to adorn or diversify his path? Much less can we forget his vivacious wit—so playful, yet so harmless; the glow of his affections; the urbanity of his manners; and the wondrous celerity with which he was ever wont to turn from one bright thought to another. Above all, however, his friends will never cease to remember that peculiar sunshine which he threw over a company by the influence of a mind perpetually tuned to love and praise.'

This was most true of his hour of daily exercise. Who that ever joined him in it cannot see him as he walked round his garden at Highwood? Now in animated and even playful conversation, and then drawing from his copious pockets (to contain Dalrymple's State Papers was their standard measure) some favourite volume or other; a Psalter, a Horace, a Shakespeare, or Cowper, and reading, and reciting, or 'refreshing' passages; and then catching at long-stored flower-leaves as the wind blew them from the pages, or standing before a favourite gum cistus to repair the loss. Then he would point out the harmony of the tints, the

---

[1] Mem.

beauty of the pencilling, the perfection of the colouring, and run up all into those ascriptions of praise to the Almighty which were ever welling forth from his grateful heart. He loved flowers with all the simple delight of childhood. He would hover from bed to bed over his favourites ; and when he came in, even from his shortest walk, deposit a few that he had gathered safely in his room before he joined the breakfast table. Often would he say, as he enjoyed their fragrance, 'How good is God to us! What should we think of a friend who had furnished us with a magnificent house and all we needed, and then coming in to see that all had been provided according to his wishes, should be hurt to find that no scents had been placed in the rooms? Yet so has God dealt with us. Surely flowers are the smiles of His goodness.'

He staid out till near dinner at five, and early in the evening lay down for an hour and a half. He would then rise for a new term of existence, and sparkle through a long evening, to the astonishment of those who expected, at his time of life, to see his mind and spirits flag, even if his strength was not exhausted. The whole evening was seldom spent in conversation, for he had commonly some book in 'family reading' which was a text for multiplied digressions, full of incident and illustration. Never was he happier than in that calm old age, on which he entered with the elasticity of youth, and the simplicity of childhood Gay, busy, social, and affable, tender without softness, and witty without sting, he was still the delight of old and young ; and whether he was joining in the 'animated talk amongst the young hands,' or discoursing with his remaining equals, it was in the busiest and happiest groups that he was always to be found.

In such occupations as these he would go on till very late ; for, from long use in Parliament, 'the midnight hour was his zenith, and, like the beautiful cereus with all her petals expanded, he was then in full bloom.'[2] Thus, as his peaceful life ran on, did he exhibit to another generation what had lately struck Lord Milton as the most instructive feature in his character, 'the close union between the most rigid

[2] Mr. Gurney's Mem.

principles and the most gay and playful disposition.'[3] So deep were the springs of this gaiety that they were as little affected by the ordinary trials of life as by the advance of years. In 1830 he was subjected to heavy losses. At this very time, on a visit to Battersea Rise, he renewed his intercourse with Sir James Mackintosh. 'Mackintosh came in,' he says, 'and sat most kindly chatting with me during my dinner —what a paragon of a companion he is—quite unequalled;[4] his conversation is always rich and sparkling!' Mackintosh's account of this intercourse gives the other side. 'Do you remember Madame de Maintenon's exclamation, "Oh the misery of having to amuse an old King, qui n'est pas amusable!" Now if I were called upon to describe Wilberforce in one word, I should say he was the most "amusable" man I ever met with in my life. Instead of having to think what subjects will interest him, it is perfectly impossible to hit on one that does not. I never saw anyone who touched life at so many points; and this is the more remarkable in a man who is supposed to live absorbed in the contemplation of a future state. When he was in the House of Commons, he seemed to have the freshest mind of any man there. There was all the charm of youth about him. And he is quite as remarkable in this bright evening of his days as when I saw him in his glory many years ago.'

Once more, in the course of this spring, the darkened prospects of the negro cause called him from his retirement. He consented with a weakened voice, and an enfeebled frame, to take the chair, on May 15, at a great meeting of the Anti-Slavery Society. 'All the old friends of the cause gathered round'[5] him; and Freemasons' Hall overflowed with an unusual audience. This was the last time he took any public part in London for this cause.

The fruit of this effort was reaped in the elections which succeeded, when Yorkshire, which had ever led the way in this great cause, chose four representatives pledged to Emancipa-

---

[3] Letter to J. Stephen, Esq., Nov. 12, 1830. The writers feel more deeply than any who may read these pages, that to this great and leading feature of Mr. Wilberforce's character, they have been unable to do any justice in the necessary coldness of description.

[4] Diary, Nov. 25, 1829. [5] Diary.

tion, and amongst them Henry Brougham—though uncon-
nected with the county—because he was its advocate. 'The
election,' Mr. Wilberforce heard from him,[6] 'turned very
much on Slavery; your name was in every mouth, and your
health the most enthusiastically received.' 'Depend upon
it,' was the encouraging augury with which he cheered some
desponding friends, 'we are getting forward. The standard
of public opinion is rising under the influence of an improving body of clergy.' With this effort his long public life
closed, and we have henceforth to view the veteran Christian waiting for his last call.

The great characteristic of these latest years was his closer
walk with God, and the degree to which he was literally kept
in perfect peace through every trial. Those who lived with
him and marked his unmixed cheerfulness could scarcely believe the natural pain which the relinquishing of his house
in 1831 cost him. 'The loss incurred,' he says, 'has been
so heavy as to compel me to descend from my present level,
and greatly to diminish my establishment. But I am bound
to recognise in this dispensation the gracious mitigation of
the severity of the stroke. Mrs. Wilberforce and I are supplied with a delightful asylum under the roofs of two of our
own children. And what better could we desire? A kind
Providence has enabled me with truth to adopt the declaration of David, that goodness and mercy have followed me
all my days. And now, when the cup presented to me has
some bitter ingredients, yet surely no draught can be deemed
distasteful which comes from such a hand, and contains such
grateful infusions as those of social intercourse and the sweet
endearments of filial gratitude and affection. What I shall
most miss will be my books and my garden, though I feel
the not being able to ask my friends under my own roof.
And as even the great Apostle did not think the "having no
certain dwelling-place," associated with his other far greater
sufferings, unworthy of mention, so I may feel this also to
be some, though, I grant, not a great evil.' It should be
mentioned to the credit of our times, that by no less than
six persons, one of them a West Indian, such private offers

---

[6] H. Brougham, Esq., to W. Wilberforce, Esq.

were now made to Mr. Wilberforce as would, if he had consented to accept them, have at once restored his fortune.[7]

His leaving Highwood was soon followed by another trial,
—the death of his surviving daughter. To this, too, he
yielded himself with all a Christian's submission. ' I was
much impressed,' he says, ' yesterday, with the similarity in
some respects of my own situation to that of her dear little
innocent, who was undergoing the operation of vaccination.
The infant gave up its little arm to the operator without
suspicion or fear. But when it felt the puncture, which must
have been sharp, no words can express the astonishment
and grief that followed. I could not have thought the mouth
could have been distended so widely as it continued, till the
nurse's soothing restored her usual calmness. What an illustration is this of the impatient feelings we are often apt to
experience, and sometimes even to express, when suffering
from the dispensations of a Being, whose wisdom we profess
to believe to be unerring, whose kindness we know to be
unfailing, whose truth also is sure, and who has declared to
us, that all things shall work together for good to them that
love Him, and that the object of His inflictions is to make
us partakers of His holiness.'

Now was seen the fruit of the high degree in which he
had learned to ' walk by faith rather than by sight.' ' I have
often heard,' he says, ' that sailors on a voyage will drink
" friends astern " till they are half way over, then " friends
a-head." With me it has been " friends a-head " this long
time.' It was not by the slow process of reasoning that he
learned to regard this as a short separation; he at once felt
that they should not long be parted; and he soon describes
himself ' as enjoying as much peace and social comfort as
any ought to expect in this stormy world.'[8] ' The closing
scene,' he writes to Mr. Babington, ' was such as to call forth
from our dear friend Sargent declarations of satisfaction and

---

[7] One of these offers, made, highly to his honour, by the late Lord
Fitzwilliam, never reached Mr. Wilberforce's ears ; a near connection,
through whom it was made, and who knew his former decision, declining
it without consulting him.

[8] To J. Stephen, Esq., March 30.

thankfulness, which will be sources of comfort and joy to us as long as we live. The Monday after she was taken away we removed to St. Boniface, which we had taken in the hope of its conducing to her recovery. It is certainly one of the most delightful of all possible retirements. The most romantic scenery, sheltered from every cold wind, and abound·ing in the most delightful walks, both sea and inland. There the Sargents; my S. and his wife, and little toddler and prattler; my H. and ourselves, passed a delightful fortnight. Really it was an oasis in the wilderness.'

At East Farleigh vicarage, to which Lord Brougham had presented his second son, and at Brighstone, in the Isle of Wight, to which the Bishop of Winchester had collated his third son, to the great joy of those with whom he was an inmate, his remaining years were spent. A few extracts from his diary and letters will give the outline of this holy and peaceful age. 'We have now been here,' he writes from one of his parsonage houses,[9] 'for about six weeks. How can I but rejoice rather than lament at a loss which brought us to dwell under the roofs of our dear children, and witness their enjoyment of domestic comforts, and their conscientious discharge of the duties of the most important of all professions.' 'I thank God,' he tells another friend,[1] 'my health is in about its ordinary state, though I am becoming yearly more and more stiff and crazy. But what causes have I for gratitude! Surely no one ought more habitually to feel and adopt the psalmist's language, "Goodness and mercy have followed me all my days." And now have not we great cause for thankfulness in being moored in our latter days in the peaceful haven which we enjoy (after all my tossings during my long and stormy voyage in the sea of politics), under the roofs of our sons in Kent and in the Isle of Wight, witnessing the usefulness of those most dear to us.'

Some of his letters fill in other features of the picture. 'It gives me no little pleasure,[2] and calls for a large return of gratitude to the Giver of all good, to witness the delightful scene that is here exhibited of pastoral service and domestic happiness. You are able from experience to judge how a

[9] To James Stephen, Esq. [1] Lady Olivia Sparrow.
[2] To Mr. Babington, Aug. 17.

parent must feel in witnessing the pastoral labours of his own child. —— is not eating the bread of idleness. His lady was not well endowed with pecuniary charms: but they will have enough, I trust, for comfort; and even if it were not a sin, as it certainly is, to marry for money, I should deem it one of the basest actions a gentleman could commit. This house is enlivened by a delightful infant, which twaddles about most captivatingly, and begins to lisp out papa and mamma with more than Cicero's eloquence.' 'That lovely baby! What a manifest benevolence there is in the Almighty's having rendered young children so eminently attractive. How little could I expect to complete my seventy-second year! Yet it is on this day completed.'

His overflowing gratitude to God was the chief feature of his later years. 'What thanks,' he says, 'do I owe to God, that my declining strength appears likely not to be attended with painful diseases, but rather to lessen gradually and by moderate degrees! How good a friend God is to me!' Habits of devotional retirement, which grew with his increasing years, and the Psalms and St. Paul's epistles became more and more dear to him. He notes at this time, in his pocketbook, the importance of 'meditating more on God as the Creator and Governor of the universe. Eighty millions of fixed stars, each as large at least as our sun. Combine the considerations hence arising with the madness and guilt of sin as setting up our will against that of God. Combine with it Christ's unspeakable mercy and love, and that of God in Christ.' 'I find unspeakable pleasure,' he tells a friend, 'in the declarations so often reiterated in the Word of God, of the unvarying truth of the Supreme Being. There is something inexpressibly sublime in the assurance, that throughout the whole immeasurable extent of the all but infinite empire of God truth always extends, and, like a master-key, unlocks and opens all the mysterious wisdom, and goodness, and mercy of the Divine dispensations.'

He still continued his early and afternoon walks, pacing at East Farleigh, during the winter, up and down a 'sheltered, sunny, gravel walk;' and in the summer, climbing with delight at Brighstone to the top of the chalk downs, or of an intermediate terrace, still bearing, in the traditions of the parish, his name, or walking long upon the unfrequented shore. 'April 4. Like the finest summer day. The air singularly mild and balmy, and not a leaf stirring. S. engaged at a cottage reading. R. drove me out in the pony-chaise ; which very pleasant.—5th. Day, if possible, even sweeter than yesterday; as balmy and more air. Walked with my sons up the hill.'

His evenings were as bright as ever, and though his power of retaining new impressions was impaired, the colours of his earlier recollections seemed scarcely to fade. 'How full he is of anecdote !' said a friend, when he had for a moment left the room, to one of the party who was writing at another table. 'It would be quite worth while some evening to put down notes of his conversation.' The suggestion was at once acted on, and some extracts from the notes taken down, as far as the pen could follow him, will give a faint idea of the richness of his usual conversation, though the life and play of mind which dressed up every sentence can never be transferred into the copy.

'One day, while Hastings' trial was proceeding, an important point came on when only Burke and two or three more were present—little Michael Angelo among them, very pompous. Ned Law, who was to argue the case as Hastings' counsel began, "It is a pity, sir, to raise a discussion on this matter. This is no doubtful question of political expedience ; it is a mere point of law, and my honourable friend there," pointing to little Michael, " from his accurate knowledge of the law, which he has practised with so much success, can confirm fully what I say." Michael puffed and swelled, and almost assented. Burke was quite furious, and ran to him and shook him, saying, " You little rogue, what do you mean by assenting to this ? " Michael is talked of for a peer. It is not unlikely; he has no son. He was left a good fortune by his father, who was a builder, and he got on by keeping a good cook and giving excellent dinners. I remember Sheridan playing off on him one of his amusing tricks. He did not know where to go for a dinner, so, sitting down by Michael Angelo, he said, " There is a law question likely to rise presently, on which, from your legal knowledge, you will be wanted to reply to Pitt, so I hope you will not think of leaving the House." Michael sat still with no little pleasure, while Sheridan slipped out, walked over to Michael's house, and ordered up dinner, saying to the servants, "Your master is not coming home this evening." He made an excellent dinner, came back to the House, and seeing Michael looking expectant, went to release him, saying, "I am sorry to have kept you, for, after all, I believe this matter will not now come on to-night." Michael immediately walked home, and heard to his no little consternation, when he rang for dinner, "Mr. Sheridan had it, sir, about two hours ago."

'Poor Boswell! I once had some serious conversation with him; he was evidently low and depressed, and appeared to have many serious feelings. He told me that Dr. Johnson had assured him he was never intimately acquainted with one religious clergyman. I was determined not to let him off; so I replied, "that can only be because he never sought their acquaintance. They knew that he had about him such persons as they would not choose for companions."

'General Smith, Sir Sidney's uncle, put his papers into my hands: amongst them a most extraordinary correspondence between Lord Elgin and Sir Sidney. Sir Sidney was most scandalously used. Others had ribands and peerages, but he never had anything. At the time of the siege of Acre, he got from the old Pacha a ring, or some other emblem of authority, which gave him absolute command over all the gates; and one of his first employments of it was, to go to the Pacha's dungeons and set all the captives free. The Pacha grumbled in vain, exclaiming pathetically, "But, Sir Sidney, they owe me moneys. . . ."

'Whitbread was a rough speaker; he spoke as if he had a pot of porter at his lips and all his words came through it. I remember his drawing tears from me upon the Lottery question. After Canning's speech on Lord Bexley's resolution about a pound note and a shilling being of equal value with a guinea, he said to me, "Well, I do envy him the power of making that speech." This was very curious to me, because I never could have guessed that it was at all the model to which he aspired. Poor Canning! I knew him well, and he knew that I knew him. He felt that I knew him before he became well acquainted with Pitt. He had a mind susceptible of the forms of great ideas; as for these men, they have not minds up to anything of the sort; their minds would burst with the attempt. I have often talked openly with Canning, and I cannot but hope that some good may have come from it. When I was with him once, he was in bed, on a sort of sofa-bed, at Gloucester Lodge, and Southey was mentioned. " I did not know that he was in town." "Yes, he is, and dines with me to-morrow; but I am afraid you will not come because it is Sunday." Canning was not a first-rate speaker! Oh, he was as different as possible from Pitt, and from old Fox too, though he was so rough; he had not that art, " celare artem." If effect is the criterion of good speaking, Canning was nothing to them, for he never drew you to him in spite of yourself. You never lost sight of Canning; even in that admirable speech of his about Sir John C. Hippisley, when your muscles were so exercised by laughing, it was the same thing; yet he was a more finished orator than Pitt. Oh, how little justice was done to Pitt on Warren Hastings' business. People were asking, what could make Pitt support him on this point and on that, as if he was acting from political motives; whereas he was always weighing in every particular whether Hastings had exceeded the discretionary power lodged in him. I well remember, I could swear to it now, Pitt listening most attentively to some facts which were coming out either in the first or second case. He beckoned me over, and went with me behind the chair, and said, " Does not this look very ill to you?" "Very bad indeed." He then returned to his place and made his speech, giving up Hastings' case. He paid as much impartial attention to it as if he were a juryman.

'One of the most remarkable things about Romilly was, that though he had such an immense quantity of business, he always seemed an idle man. If you had not known who and what he was, you would have said—"he is a remarkably gentlemanlike, pleasant man; I suppose, poor fellow, he has no business;" for he would stand at the bar of the House, and chat with you, and talk over the last novel, with which he was as well acquainted as if he had nothing else to think about. Once, indeed, I remember coming to speak to him in court, and seeing him look fagged and with an immense pile of papers by him. This was at a time when Lord Eldon had been reproached for having left business undischarged, and had declared that he would get through all arrears by sitting on until the business was done. As I went up to Romilly, old Eldon saw me, and beckoned to me with as much cheerfulness and gaiety as possible. When I was alone with Romilly, and asked him how he was, he answered, " I am worn to death; here have we been sitting on in the vacation, from nine in the morning until four; and, when we leave this place, I have to read through all my papers, to be ready for to-morrow morning; but the most extraordinary part of all is, that Eldon, who has not only mine, but all the other business to go through, is just as cheerful and untired as ever."'

The conversation turned on a sick person—' Poor soul,' he said, ' how little we know of the afflictions of those in other ranks of life! I am quite abashed to think of them. I have to find sorrows for myself; God has so crowded His mercies upon me. I can fancy how delightful it would be to pour in oil and wine into her wounds.' And soon after, speaking of Herschel's saying, ' These are things which must be for ever hid from man,' he broke out, ' No, that they shall not; I shall know all these things. Oh, how low at the best are your wise men and philosophers? Truly, he that is least in the kingdom of heaven is greater than he.' He then began to speak of the astonishing truths of the gospel. ' Only think of that one declaration, God is perfect truth and perfect love. Why, that one thought worked out is enough to fit a man for heaven.'

That which, on the whole, was most worthy of remark in his review of his past life, was his unfeigned humility. He had always detested flattery. Mr. Gisborne never saw in him so much display of temper as when, being addressed with servility by a person who wished for his favourable influence with Mr. Pitt, he threw the letter on the ground, with the exclamation, ' How much rather would I have the man spit in my face !' This beautiful simplicity survived all the unfavourable influences of his life; and the old man, whose name was a familiar word in every mouth, whose country parsonage was visited almost like a shrine, and who was told by Rammohun Roy that, when ' he left the East, one of his chief wishes was to see Mr. Wilberforce,' was still altogether lowly in his own sight, and could say with natural simplicity when treated in a place of public concourse with some marks of courtesy, ' How very civil they were to me; they made way for me, and treated me as if I were some great man !'

Almost the only growing mark of age was a still increasing love of that rest to which he was drawing nearer. ' The grasshopper had become a burden to him,' and he could not leave the quiet of his country retirement even for the most friendly asylum, without his spirits failing him.[3] His need of its waters still carried him to Bath, and he paid a few short visits to his oldest and most valued friends. One of these was in the autumn of 1832, to his old haunts at Battersea Rise ; and during his stay there Mr. Richmond took his admirable picture. This was begun whilst he was joining in general conversation, but it was found impossible to fix him in the necessary position until an ingenious device succeeded. Mr. Forster,[4] who was staying in the house, undertook to draw him into argument. ' Pray, Mr. Wilberforce,' he began as he sat by him, ' is it true that the last accounts from the West Indies prove that the slaves are, on the whole, so much better off than they were thought to be, that you have much altered your views as to slavery?' ' Mr. Forster,' he replied, with sudden animation, 'I am astonished at you. What ! a sensible man like you believe such reports ? Why, sir, they flog them with a whip as thick as my arm,' grasping it as he spoke. A most animated conversation followed, and Mr. Forster was not convinced until Richmond's beautiful likeness was secured. On this subject he was full of energy to the very last.

But the time was drawing near when his dust was to return to the earth, and his spirit to God who gave it. On April 20 he left East Farleigh, and after a short visit to the Isle of Wight, arrived at Bath on May 17. These waters,

---

[3] Letter to the Rev. R. I. Wilberforce.
[4] The Rev. C. Forster, chaplain to the late Bishop of Limerick.

to which in great measure he owed the prolongation of his life till his 74th year, would help, it was hoped, to throw off the effects of the influenza, from which he had suffered greatly in Kent. Here his strength visibly declined, and it was soon seen that, if his life was spared, it would be but for a season of weakness and suffering. But while all around him were full of thought about himself, his own anxiety was altogether for two of his daughters-in-law; for, a month only before his removal, two grandsons were born to inherit the name of William Wilberforce,

Et quasi cursores vitai lampada tradunt.

He had always judged that the most fitting state for the last hours of life was one in which the mind, while it is conscious of the awful nature of the approaching change, could yet resign itself to its reconciled, all-merciful Father, with the humility as well as the confidence of a child. He often mentioned it as a proof of great wisdom, that while the younger believer is described in the ' Pilgrim's Progress ' as passing easily through the stream of death, a less buoyant hope and a deeper flood is represented as the portion of the aged ' Christian.' ' It is the peculiarity,' he said, ' of the Christian religion, that humility and holiness increase in equal proportions.'

His youngest son, who was with him during these last weeks, recorded at the time various memoranda of his state of mind. ' Saturday, July 6, he was taken suddenly ill. I ran for a medical man, and before I returned he was got to bed. He was suffering much from giddiness and sickness, but his words to me were, " I have been thinking of the great mercy of God in trying me with illness of this kind, which, though very distressing, is scarcely to be called pain, rather than with severe suffering, which my bodily constitution could hardly bear." Soon after he said, " What is that text, ' He hath hid pride from man ? ' I was thinking how God had taught him the folly of pride, because the most beautiful and delicate woman, and the proudest man, of the highest birth and station, who was never approached but with deference and formality, is exposed to exactly the same infirmities of this body of our humiliation that I am." Generally, except in his remark about pride, there was hardly a word he uttered that was not a bursting forth of praise.'

Two days afterwards (July 11), a friend[5] paid him a visit, which he thus describes:—'I was introduced to an apartment upstairs, where I found the veteran Christian reclining on a sofa, and his countenance bespeaking increased age. He received me with the warmest marks of affection. I freely spoke to him of the good and glorious things which, as I believed, assuredly awaited him in the kingdom of rest and peace. The illuminated expression of his furrowed countenance, with his clasped and uplifted hands, were indicative of profound devotion and holy joy. "With regard to myself," he said, " I have nothing whatsoever to urge, but the poor publican's plea, 'God be merciful to me a sinner.'" These words were expressed with peculiar feeling and emphasis, and have since called to my remembrance his own definition of the word mercy—"kindness to those that deserve punishment." '

One or two other notices of his conversation before he left Bath show how thoroughly his mind retained its powers. With Mr. Joseph (who was then taking his bust), the conversation turned upon Pitt. 'Michael Angelo Taylor,' he said, 'was one day going up St. James's Street with M. when they saw Pitt walking down it with immense strides. I do not know whether you ever happened to observe that the fall in St. James's Street makes those who are coming down it seem to overlook those who are going the other way. " I am very sorry," said Michael Angelo, " but Pitt's conduct has been such, that I feel it my duty to cut him, as you will see." Pitt walked by, giving rather a haughty nod to M., and never observing Michael Angelo at all. "You saw I cut him." "I am truly glad you told me. I should have thought he cut you."

'Never was there a man whose character was so much misunderstood. He was thought very proud. Now he was a very little proud and very shy.

'While he still condescended to practise the law, he was pleading in Chancery against the opening the biddings for an estate which had been sold by the court, and he said, "If this is done, no sensible man will ever bid again for an

[5] Joseph John Gurney.

estate sold by Chancery. I am sure I never will," a declaration which of course filled the court with merriment.'

After two months at Bath, he moved to London for advice. Parliament was sitting, and many of his friends flocked around him. 'What cause it is for thankfulness,' he said, 'that God has always disposed people to treat me so kindly.' His manner at this time was more than usually affectionate, and he received with great cheerfulness the visits of many old associates, from whom he had long been separated. It was not a little remarkable that he should have come to London at that time—to die. The Bill for the Abolition of Slavery was read for the second time in the House of Commons on the Friday night, and the last public information he received was its success. 'Thank God,' said he, 'that I should have lived to witness a day in which England is willing to give twenty millions sterling for the Abolition of Slavery.'

Not less remarkable was it that London, which of late he had seldom visited, and where he purposed to remain but a day or two, should be the place of his departure. Had it been otherwise, the funeral, which so fitly closed his course, as that of the man whom his country 'delighted to honour,' would have been impossible.

On the Friday evening, his son thus concludes his notes:—
'There seems to be little anticipation, though he is strongly impressed with a feeling that he is near his end. He speaks very little, as if looking forward to future happiness; but he seems more like a person in the actual enjoyment of heaven within: he hardly speaks, except to express his thankfulness, even of the things which try him most. " What cause for thankfulness have I that I am not lying in pain, and in a suffering posture, as so many are! Certainly it is a great privation to me from my habits not to be able to walk about, and to lie still so much as I do; but, then, how many there are who are lying in severe pain ! "

' The next morning [6] his amendment seemed to continue, and the fervency with which he offered up the family prayer was particularly noticed. This night his weakness greatly increased, and the next day he suffered from a succession

[6] July 27.

of fainting fits, to which he had been for two years subject, which were followed by much distress. During an interval in the evening of Sunday, "I am in a very distressed state," he said. "Yes," it was answered, "but you have your feet on the Rock." "I do not venture," he replied, "to speak so positively; but I hope I have." And after this expression of his humble trust, with but one groan, he entered into that world where pain and doubt are for ever at an end. He died at three o'clock in the morning of Monday, July 29, 1833, aged 73 years and 11 months.'

As soon as his death was known, the following letter was sent to his son:—'We, the undersigned members of both Houses of Parliament, being anxious upon public grounds to show our respect for the memory of the late William Wilberforce, and being also satisfied that public honours can never be more fitly bestowed than upon such benefactors of mankind, earnestly request that he may be buried in Westminster Abbey; and that we, and others who may agree with us in these sentiments, may have permission to attend his funeral.

WILLIAM FREDERICK	W. CANTUAR.
BROUGHAM, C.	WELLINGTON
ELDON	RIPON, P. S.
LANSDOWNE, P. C.	HADDINGTON
VASSALL HOLLAND	PLUNKET
WESTMINSTER	J. LINCOLN
CLARENDON	E. CHICHESTER
ESSEX	BRISTOL
CLIFDEN	GOSFORD
WELLESLEY	HARROWBY
GREY	ALBEMARLE
BEXLEY	C. J. LONDON
SIDMOUTH	GODOLPHIN
GRAFTON	ROSSLYN
CALTHORPE	CLANRICARDE
BUTE	MORLEY
DENBIGH	EDWARD HEREFORD
DUCIE	DACRE.
CALEDON	

In conveying this requisition,[7] the Lord Chancellor declared himself authorised to add, that nearly all the members

[7] July 31.

of both Houses of Parliament would have joined, had the time allowed;' and an application couched in the same terms was signed by almost one hundred members of all parties in the House of Commons.

Mr. Wilberforce had chosen for the place of his interment a vault at Stoke Newington, where his sister and his eldest daughter had been buried.[8] But his family had no hesitation in acceding to this request. All mere external parade was banished from that last scene. It was to owe all its effect to its moral grandeur. It was his characteristic distinction that, without quitting the rank in which he was born, he had cast on it a lustre peculiarly his own. Nothing therefore could be more appropriate, than that the Bishops of the Church, the Princes of the Blood, the great warrior of the age, the King's chief servants, and the highest legal functionaries— whatever England owned most renowned for talent and greatness — should assemble as they did around his un- pretending bier. His name was its noblest decoration.

When his funeral reached Westminster Abbey on Satur- day, August 5, the procession was joined by the members then attending the two Houses of Parliament. Public business was suspended; the Speaker of the House of Commons, the Lord Chancellor, one Prince of the Blood, with others of the highest rank, took their place as pall-bearers beside the bier. It was followed by his sons, his relations, and immediate friends. The Prebendary then in residence, one of his few surviving college friends, met it at the minster gate with the Church's funeral office; and whilst the vaulted roof gave back the anthem, his body was laid in the north transept, close to the tombs of Pitt, Fox, and Canning.

The posthumous honours, not alien from the character of his life, followed fitly on his death. His friends placed his statue in Westminster Abbey, and, as a yet more appropriate memorial, founded at York a county asylum for the blind ; while his townsmen of Hull raised a column to his memory.

A number of those who had been indebted to his kind- ness met after his funeral, 'with feelings almost as discon- solate as those of the bereaved apostles, to lament his loss.'

[8] The second was laid in the churchyard of her brother's parish, Brighstone, Isle of Wight.

'Great part of our coloured population, who form here an important body,' writes a dignified clergyman from the West Indies, 'went into mourning at the news of his death.'[9] The same honour was paid him by this class of persons at New York, where also an eulogium (since printed) was pronounced upon him by a person publicly selected for the task, and their brethren throughout the United States were called upon to pay the marks of external respect to the memory of their benefactor.   For departed kings there are appointed honours, and the wealthy have their gorgeous obsequies: it was his nobler portion to clothe a people with spontaneous mourning, and go down to the grave amid the benedictions of the poor.

It is impossible to conclude this history without noting the truth of the inspired words: 'Godliness has the promise of the life that now is as well as of that which is to come.' If ever any man drew the lot of a happy life, he did so who has been here described.   Yet his Christian faith was from first to last the talisman of his happiness.   Without it the buoyancy of his youthful spirits led to a frivolous and unsatisfying waste of life.   With it came lofty conceptions— an energy which triumphed over sickness and languor, over the coldness of friends and the violence of enemies—a calmness not to be provoked —a perseverance which repulse could not baffle.   To these virtues was owing the happiness of his active days.   Through the power of the same sustaining principle, his affection towards his fellow-creatures was not dulled by the intercourse with the world, nor his sweetness of temper impaired by the irritability of age.   A firm trust in God, an undeviating submission to His will, an overflowing thankfulness—these maintained in him to the last that cheerfulness which this world could neither give nor take away.   They poured even upon his earthly pilgrimage the anticipated radiance of that brighter region, to which the servants of God are admitted.   For 'THE PATH OF THE JUST IS LIKE THE SHINING LIGHT, WHICH SHINETH MORE AND MORE UNTO THE PERFECT DAY.'

[9] July 29.

INDEX.

F F

INDEX.

Boston Public Library
Central Library, Copley Square

Division of
Reference and Research Services

CPSIA information can be obtained
at www.ICGtesting.com
Printed in the USA
BVOW11s1137230617
487684BV00021B/570/P

9 781331 563747